CLARK P. READ, Ph.D., Rice University, is Professor of Biology at that institution. He has also taught at the University of California at Los Angeles and at The Johns Hopkins University. Dr. Read has served as a Visiting Professor at Cambridge University while a Guggenheim Fellow, as a Trustee of the Marine Biological Laboratory at Woods Hole, and as Chairman of the Study Section on Tropical Medicine and Parasitology of the U. S. Public Health Service. He was awarded the first Henry B. Ward Medal of the American Society of Parasitologists.

PARASITISM
AND SYMBIOLOGY

AN INTRODUCTORY TEXT

CLARK P. READ

RICE UNIVERSITY

THE RONALD PRESS COMPANY · NEW YORK

Library of Congress Catalog Card Number: 75-110390
PRINTED IN THE UNITED STATES OF AMERICA

This book is dedicated to Lee,
the love of my life

Preface

Biology tells us that humans are not unique in exhibiting differences at the chemical, physiological, or sociological level. Interaction between organisms is a common feature of the life process. Since this is the case, the study of these interactions is important to the biologist. However, there has been a paucity of attempts to examine, in general terms, the interaction of different species living in intimate physiological association. As a consequence the study of symbiosis as a part of general biology has been sadly neglected. This book was written with the conviction that a broad study of symbiosis in a nontraditional context would be an exciting and rewarding venture.

In reexamining the question of what parasitology is all about, it became apparent that among biologists the field was markedly oriented to animal parasites as special organisms rather than to parasitism as a universal biological phenomenon. Surveys of other disciplines, such as plant pathology and medical bacteriology, revealed a similar specialized emphasis. Fortunately, I was asked several years ago to serve on an ad hoc panel on Parasitism Courses chaired by Dr. Clay G. Huff and sponsored by the Committee on Educational Policies of the National Academy of Sciences—National Research Council. The report of the committee was subsequently published (Huff, et al., "Toward a Course on the Principles of Parasitism," 1958, *J. of Parasitology, 44*:28). From these experiences I undertook to restructure an undergraduate course in parasitology to emphasize symbiosis as a biological phenomenon. The approach used in this book grew out of that experience and has been tested in the classroom for several years.

During the last decade animal parasitology and symbiology have undergone considerable change. The broad implications of biochemistry, the "new" genetics and cell biology have allowed the reframing of many questions posed, but not answered, by preceding researchers. Advances made in other areas of biology concerned with the phenomena of symbiosis have been greatly accelerated. It is my conviction that study and teaching in this field should be restructured around symbiosis with parasitism as an important aspect of it. This book represents such an approach.

The book is aimed at the motivated student of biology who seeks to understand life processes. The subject matter can be comprehended by the advanced undergraduate student. Some knowledge of biochemistry, genetics, and cell biology is required. As will be evident, I have tried to develop the broad outline for a study of functional symbiosis using a limited number of examples.

The focus is on the levels of interaction between organisms living in association rather than on the detailed systematic treatment of the organisms themselves. Examples drawn from animal parasitology, plant pathology, bacteriology, mycology, and virology are used to illustrate the adaptations for reaching hosts, recognizing hosts, and establishment in hosts. Sections on nutrition and metabolism of symbiotes summarize the comparative biochemistry of organisms specialized for symbiotic life. Information concerning genetics and evolution points up the plasticity of these systems in space and time.

In his book *Parasitism and Disease* (published in 1934) Theobald Smith wrote: "It may be said that the half century just closed covered the adventurous and romantic period of searching for living agents of disease. . . . It was the naturalist's period as distinguished from the precise and experimental machine age in which we now find ourselves." Much of the teaching about parasitism in American colleges has followed the format of the romantic period of which Smith spoke, and there has been little effort to include in teaching other types of symbiosis. This book represents a serious effort to treat parasitism within the spectrum of symbiology.

The comprehensive citation bibliography found at the end of the book, plus the suggested readings given after each chapter, will, if properly utilized, greatly aid the reader in expanding his knowledge of the field.

My highest hope is that the book may stimulate thought among students in the broad framework of symbiology, and that its relevance concerns the relationships of men to men as well as other organisms.

CLARK P. READ

Houston, Texas
January, 1970

Contents

PARASITISM
AND SYMBIOLOGY

1

Introduction

This book is concerned with a special aspect of the lives of all living organisms. Although we frequently give it only a passing thought, it is widely recognized by biologists and non-biologists alike that organisms are inhabited and inhabit other kinds of organisms. It may not be so widely appreciated that such relationships are common to all living organisms. Even those laboratory-reared organisms referred to as germ-free cannot be safely assumed to be free of the mysterious and marvelous particles known as viruses.

SYMBIOSIS AND BIOLOGY

The interorganismal relationships with which we are concerned are those involving bodily contact between different species. These relationships can be considered to fall within the province of the field of biological science known as ecology, defined by Odum (1959) as the study of the structure and function of nature. Considered from this broad standpoint, the interspecific relationships of living things in physical contact may be treated in a broader fashion than has been commonly utilized in the past. As a matter of fact, a term was coined in 1879 by De Bary to describe, in a very general sense, such relationships. The term used by De Bary was *symbiosis*, which means nothing more than "living together." It may be defined somewhat more specifically as the sharing of physiological mechanisms by different species, without specifying the relative benefits derived or the outcome of the association.

Although there is value in using the term symbiosis, in the general sense indicated above, many authors have applied it in a restricted sense to mutually advantageous associations. Some authors have further restricted it to cases in which the associated species cannot live apart. Hertig et al. (1937) examined this question of usage and concluded that, contrary to many statements in the literature, De Bary (1879) had presented an unambiguous definition of the term symbiosis. In this book, the term is used in the broad sense, defined above. Although general study of symbiosis has not been dignified by a term to designate it as a field of research, it seems logical to refer to that field as *symbiology*.

During the past few years, revolutionary changes have been occurring in biology. The framework of biology may be visualized as progressing, in order of increasing complexity of subject matter, from submolecular and molecular biology to cell biology to organismal biology to population biology. When we speak of increasing complexity, we are, of course, referring to the

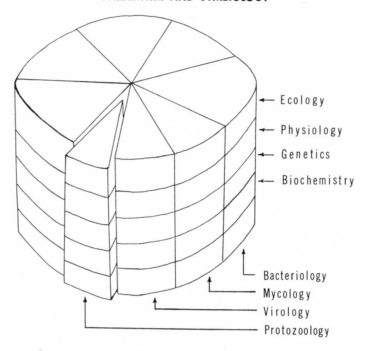

← Ecology

← Physiology

← Genetics

← Biochemistry

└─── Bacteriology

──── Mycology

─── Virology

──── Protozoology

Fig. 1–1 Biological science envisioned as a cake. The layers are made up of those divisions concerned with fundamental characteristics common to all living things. The slices are "taxonomic" divisions dealing wth specific groups of organisms. Some layers and many slices are not shown in this figure. (Adapted from E. Odum, 1959, *Fundamentals of Ecology*, 2nd Edition, with permission of Dr. Odum and W. B. Saunders Company.)

components of each level. In actual fact, the state of organization, and thus the predictive value, is considerably better developed on the ends of this series than in the middle.

Odum has furnished a useful analysis of the relationships among the divisions of biology. Biology may be structured as in Figure 1–1. The basic layers of the structure are concerned with fundamental aspects common to all living things or at least not restricted to particular kinds of living things. Looked at from this standpoint, symbiology is a broad portion of ecology. Where ecology may be defined as the study of the relation of organisms to their environment, symbiology may be defined as the study of intimate interrelations between different species of organisms in the framework of environment. Luria and Darnell have pointed out that the biological sciences can be classified as taxonomic, integrative, or reductionist sciences. In such a classification, symbiology would be an integrative science.

From the standpoint of everyday life, symbiosis has affected mankind in a variety of ways. Men have studied symbioses by separating them into fields or provinces of study based on the taxonomic classification of the hosts (plant or animal) or on the taxonomic classification of the symbiotes— in other words, as a series of taxonomic sciences. As a consequence, we recognize as fields of teaching and study such subjects as bacteriology, plant pathology, insect pathology, medical and veterinary mycology, animal parasitology, virology, and perhaps a few others. It may be argued that these separations make sense from the standpoint of utility, but it should be emphasized that to a considerable extent they are contrived divisions of study, often based on socioeconomic considerations, on specialized techniques, or, in more recent times, on the "craft guilds" which have grown up in these special fields of study. This arrangement has constituted a useful mode for seeking solutions to specific problems, involving diseases of man, his domestic animals, and his crops. There has been the disadvantage that some of the fields have lain outside the mainstream of biology. As at the Tower of Babel, much specialized verbiage associated with the development of each field has also tended to interfere with communication between them. The author has attempted to ignore some of these barriers between disciplines, although this book is written with a strong bias toward animal parasitology. The emphasis followed is a focus on symbiology rather than on diseases or on specific symbiotes. Thus, following Luria and Darnell's classification of sciences, an attempt has been made to move a variety of phenomena from a taxonomic approach to an integrative approach.

The vast quantity of information available on specific symbioses would overwhelm the brief confines of this volume. Whenever possible, references to books or articles dealing in more detailed fashion with specific subjects have been included at the end of each chapter. These references are not exhaustive but may serve the student in gaining an introduction to various specialized aspects of symbiosis. Most of us recognize that we live in an age of the specialist. The day of the natural philosopher such as da Vinci, who could encompass the scientific literature of his time, is gone. However, there is still reason to examine knowledge in a broad sense, if only to attain and maintain perspective. Further, important new discoveries continue to be made in areas of study which may be described as interstitial, that is, not clearly lying in one field or another.

KINDS OF SYMBIOSIS

As already indicated, intimate association of two species of organisms is termed symbiosis. Such associations may be further subdivided. If neither of the associates profits at the expense of the other, the association is termed *commensalism* and the members called *host* and *commensal*. If only one member profits significantly, the association is called *parasitism* and the members are called *host* and *parasite*. When both members benefit, the association is termed *mutualism*, the members being termed *mutuals*. When speaking of symbiosis in general or when the nature of a symbiosis is unclear and not readily referable to one of the above categories, it is convenient to call the larger member of the association the *host* and the smaller member the *symbiote*, although the terms "host" and "symbiote" will apply to any of the cases defined above. The term *symbiote* is used in preference to the term *symbiont* used by some authors. *Symbiote* is philologically correct as a derivation from the Greek.

Table 1–1 presents the foregoing relations on a different—perhaps more meaningful—basis: the reciprocal effects of interaction, in terms of effects on populations. In this scheme, parasitism and predation are considered to involve the same interaction—a conclusion which is not precisely true, as will be discussed in a later chapter. The table also shows that populations of commensals are limited by hosts when not interacting.

From the viewpoint of ecology, the host is the environment during all or part of the life of the symbiote. Since the environment is a living organism, ecological analysis quickly resolves itself in part into biochemical and physiological study. However, it will become apparent that there are great difficulties in the examination of symbiosis in terms of the physiology and biochemistry of interaction in the integrated system. Many symbiotes show gross modifications

Table 1–1

Two-Species Population Interactions [a]

Type of Interaction	When Not Interacting		When Interacting		General Result
	A	B	A	B	
Neutralism (A and B independent)	0	0	0	0	Neither affects the other
Competition (A and B competitors)	0	0	−	−	Population most affected is eliminated
Mutualism (A and B mutuals)	−	−	+	+	Interaction obligatory
Protocooperation (A and B cooperators)	0	0	+	+	Interaction favorable to both but not obligatory
Commensalism (A commensal; B host)	−	0	+	0	Obligatory for A; B not affected
Amensalism (A amensal; B inhibitor)	0	0	−	0	A inhibited; B not affected
Parasitism (A parasite; B host) Predation (A predator; B prey)	−	0	+	−	Obligatory for A; B inhibited

+ = Population growth increased
− = Population growth decreased
0 = Population growth not affected

[a] Modified from Odum, 1959.

of physiology when grown in culture outside a host. The modification of the disease-producing capacity of many parasites effected by growing them in artificial media has been widely recognized for many years. Although our understanding of many of the detailed molecular relationships in symbiosis is quite imperfect, we know a great deal about the biology of organisms living in symbiosis.

Symbiosis, particularly parasitism, is frequently regarded in distasteful terms by the hygiene-conscious citizen. We have a tendency to think of it as a peculiar and abnormal association of some lower organism with a higher one. There is an element of snobbishness in such a view, which must quickly be abandoned when a discerning look is taken at the living world. In nature there is probably no such thing as a symbiote-free metazoan or metaphyte. The phenomenon of symbiosis is quite as common as life itself.

THE STUDY OF SYMBIOSIS

The scientific study of parasitism usually emphasizes parasites as agents which produce disease. However, many, perhaps most, parasites only produce frank "disease" under certain conditions, and many so-called parasites have never been shown to cause overt disease. Although the study of diseases has undoubtedly resulted in a great deal of knowledge concerning symbiosis, from the standpoint of biology this has led to only a limited number of broad unifying ideas useful in understanding symbiosis.

The study of disease, in its broadest sense, has not been the province of any single discipline; rather, its study has been so widely scattered in the scientific community that communication has frequently failed. The study of plant diseases has been carried on by botanists or agricultural scientists. The study of animal parasites and the diseases they cause has been carried on by zoologists, veterinarians, and physicians. Bacteriologists have studied bacterial parasites, and the diseases attributed to bacteria have been investigated by bacteriologists, physicians, and veterinarians.

Much of this research has been concerned with parasites rather than with parasitism. Some of the most dramatic discoveries have been further scattered in the scientific literature of zoology and botany. Because of this distribution of the study of symbiosis among various branches of biological science, the student generally finds that he is exposed to the teaching of specialists in animal parasitology, plant pathology, bacteriology, mycology, or such, and that meager attempts are made to relate the information available in one field to information in another. One group of specialists may even give a term a special meaning, remote from the usage of other fields. For this reason, usage of some terms in this book may not be palatable to certain specialists, but for the sake of consistency some compromise is necessary. Such terms will be defined wherever feasible. However, terms having commonly accepted usage in general biology will not be defined.

In considering the biology of symbiotic relationships it is important to realize that, in some cases, the relationships may be essential for the life of one or both of the associates. This is referred to as an *obligate* relationship. Most often the association is obligatory for the symbiote rather than for the host. When symbiosis is not actually essential for the life and reproduction of one or both of the associates the relationship is called a *facultative* one.

There is a tendency for animal symbiotes, particularly parasites, to have obligate relations with hosts. The viruses, without exception, are obligate symbiotes. On the other hand, the bacteria and fungi frequently seem to be facultative in their symbiotic relationships with other organisms. The fact that an organism is so physiologically constructed that it finds symbiosis to be obligate or facultative will have far-reaching effects in determining its survival, its adaptiveness, and its ultimate role as a precursor in evolution. This will be dealt with more fully in other portions of the text.

One group of research workers in Germany has consistently maintained that there is a sharp and distinctive boundary between what is termed "symbiosis" ("mutualism" in the present work) and parasitism. This view seems to rest on a definition in which parasitism results in disease and death. Through this book, it will be apparent that such a criterion cannot be applied in the real world of nature. Definitions of mutualism, commensalism, and parasitism actually rest on those defined examples in nature which readily fall within one of these man-made categories. Many examples do not readily fit one of these concise definitions. In addition, we will cite certain examples which fit one definition under a particular set of natural circumstances but will be placed in another category under some other set of circumstances. This state of affairs should not be surprising if we consider symbiosis as a biological entity which is composed of two or more species. The species constituting the symbiosis may be expected to show some independence of adaptive response and of evolution; nonetheless, environmental or genetic alterations of either member of a symbiosis would be expected to have consequences for the other member of the pair and thus for the symbiosis itself. Biologists have found it difficult to think in terms of the dependence-independence characteristics of the members of symbiotic relationships. This difficulty may be attributed in large part to lack of information on the operation of the symbiosis ensemble itself.

We have already remarked that symbiosis is extremely common in nature and this may be further emphasized. In their now classical work in ecology Allee et al. (1949) remarked, "Living organisms, as hosts to parasites, form one of the three major habitats on the earth, comparable to the aquatic and terrestrial habitats in which the hosts themselves dwell." No phylum of living organisms lacks representatives living in symbiosis. There are a few such groups in which members are not known to function as symbiotes but do function as hosts. The viruses are the only large group of organisms not known to serve as hosts, although there is some evidence for mutualistic relationship between viruses.

During the past few years, some enthusiastic public health workers have expounded the view that infectious human disease can be eradicated. Couched in such general terms, this is very much like saying that human life can be eradicated, a view with which one cannot quarrel. While it is true that we may look forward to the eradication of specific diseases in specific places, there is little support for the conclusion that man may eradicate his symbiotes. We have been discovering new symbiotes at a higher rate than we can deal with them. Many of them produce little or no disease; but, as will become apparent, the status quo is an illusory concept in symbiosis. The character of any symbiosis changes with time.

INTEGRATION IN SYMBIOSIS

A further word may be said about the levels of study of nature attempted in this book. As will become apparent, symbiosis may be examined at several levels. Molecular interactions between organisms, par-

ticularly viruses and bacteria, have been a favorite subject in recent investigations of biochemical genetics, and a start has been made in elucidating chemical interactions in various other kinds of symbiosis. Such researches have been concerned with interactions between individuals. On the other hand, symbioses may be examined at the level of the population, the community, or the ecosystem. In actual practice, it is essential to examine symbiosis at all levels; yet abrupt transitions in our thinking in moving from one level to another seem to parallel deficiencies in our understanding of nature.

The difficulties involved in the pursuit of understanding symbiosis are implicit in the concept of *integrative levels.* Simply stated, this concept asserts that, with increase in system complexity, new properties may arise which are not predictable from the detectable properties of the separate constituent units. For example, the CO_2 molecule generally has characteristics quite different from those of its component atoms; knowledge of the properties of these atoms does not suffice to anticipate the properties of the molecule. It can of course be argued that if we could adequately understand the properties of carbon and oxygen we could predict the properties of CO_2. The key word in this objection is "if." Further, it rests on the notion that a complete understanding of the atoms could be attained by studying them in isolation. This assumption is not valid: much of our understanding or ideas about the atoms rests on our knowledge of the properties of the compounds which they form. The existence and properties of elementary particles have been in large part inferred from the known properties of the larger units which they compose. As Kluyver and Van Niel (1956) pointed out, the whole structure of natural science is the result of extrapolations.

It is not at all difficult to think of examples of symbiosis in which new properties arise as a result of host-symbiote integration. These properties would frequently be essentially impossible to predict from the known properties of host and parasite in isolation. Some of the most obvious of these properties are seen in disease phenomena. For example, there is nothing in the makeup of a malaria parasite in isolation which would lead us to predict the cyclic events of a malaria paroxysm in the infected host. Similarly, there is nothing in the known makeup of the host which would predict this particular course of events when the two are placed together. It seems extremely doubtful that, however long we continued to study the malaria parasite and the host separately, we would be able to predict the peculiar nature of the interaction of the two organisms. When we put the two together we tacitly recognize that there is a new array of properties, referred to as "malaria." Sometimes the appearance of quite novel characteristics, somewhat more precise than disease, are seen in symbiosis. For example, the appearance of hemoglobin in some clover plant–bacterial symbioses is not predictable from the presently known features of the separated component organisms.

"PRINCIPLES" OF SYMBIOSIS AND PARASITISM

It has been remarked that the study of symbiosis has been to a great extent oriented to the study of symbiotes rather than to the phenomenon of symbiosis. Some parasitologists have been concerned with the lack of generalizations which can be made concerning parasitism (Huff, 1956). It is indeed true that very few generalizations are discernible and practically no "laws" are extant. Some have been led to suggest that the explanation for this failure to discern general rules lies in the simple fact that none are specifically applicable (Noble and Noble, 1964). The present author is not yet willing to accept this verdict. It seems more probable that the failure to produce

generalizing concepts is a failure of our methods of approach to the phenomena of symbiosis as special interaction between species. If, as has been recognized by other authors, the study of symbiosis is a study of ecology, it may be expected that some general principles apply. Some of these will be principles in the broad context of ecology. Others may fall in a narrower context of symbiology. At this stage the problem of developing generalizations invites investigation.

As the author has indicated elsewhere, the problem seems to involve definition of the degree and extent of integration in symbiosis. The ability or failure to make such definitions will indicate in what measure the study of symbiosis is properly a part of (1) natural history, as records of assembled concrete facts, or (2) natural science, as an abstract system of principles which will allow prediction of natural events (Read, 1963).

The Search for Principles

It may be remarked that the possibility of discovering "principles" is not really questionable unless we lay a cloak of mysticism over symbiosis. The failure to discern principles may be attributed to the methods used. Most scientists would recognize the limitations of the Greek method, a postulation of axioms and the application of the rules of inference. Many fewer would recognize the limitations of the second type of science, the Baconian utilization of the experimental method. The latter has been most fruitful and was revolutionary in allowing a questioning of nature so that relevant laws could be constructed. However, until recently the Baconian method has been under a serious limitation: namely, that the scientist must stand outside the experiment and science is thus deterministic and material.

In the past thirty years, an almost unnoticed revolution has occurred in scientific thought. In this third kind of science, very significant limitations of the second type (Baconian) have been removed by the development of a non-deterministic theory of matter and of mathematical theorems of logic which allow an assessment of the creativity of thinking. Glimmerings of this third type of science appeared in Darwin's recognition that living nature operates on a trial-and-error basis. Third science had its first serious applications in the development of what was termed information theory, which deals not with objects or energy but with simple descriptors of organization. Very simple deterministic versions have appeared in what is called "linear programming" for industrial and military operations. However, the expansion and utilization of the new third science in the examination of problems appropriate to biology is quite scanty, and a theory in depth for handling such problems is only in the making. From our standpoint, it is relevant that the emission of symbols is important in applying the methods of third science. An example is seen in the man-machine symbiosis, selected because of the essential simplicity of the second component. The man is able to control the machine with a very low power consumption because he has the capacity for emitting symbols. These symbols resolve some of the indeterminacy residing in the structure of the machine, or in nature. A simple application of third science places this relationship in a very different context than would second science. Thus, the third type of science utilizes a branched logic and a necessary role is played by symbols.

Some attempts have been made by Whitlock (1962) to apply methods of third science to the study of symbiosis, but these have not been widely understood. Goodall (1965) has furnished a concise and thought-provoking discussion of the broad meaning of third science. It will be apparent that the present work is written mainly in terms of second science. This approach has been tempered with the recognition that principles applicable to the relationships of symbiosis will of necessity be derived from the application of third science.

At several points in preceding pages we have pointed up the idea that many of the properties of symbiotic associations do not appear to be predictable when the associated organisms are examined separately. This was a deliberate overstatement of the case, treading dangerously close to the now discredited "philosophy" of holism. During the last century, and in the early part of this one, the antiscientific, mystic view that the whole could not be understood in terms of the parts was used to impede science. The entire history of modern biology, and the purely physical sciences as well, has shown that the examination of the parts of an entity *and* the relationships between these parts can lead to understanding of the entity as a *system*. The critical point to be made is that the system constituted by a symbiosis must be recognized as a system. Analysis of the system requires that study of the components is valuable in understanding the system only if the relations of the components are examined. The emphasis is thus placed on the interactions between the components. In those cases in which the study of component organisms appears to have brought little understanding of symbiotic systems, the research has not been directed to questions concerning the relations of the components. Several years ago Dubos (1954) pointed up the deficiencies of analyses in microorganism-vertebrate systems. Few striking advances have been made since the publication of Dubos' monograph.

CLASSIFICATION OF SYMBIOTES

If we examine the plant and animal kingdoms, we are impressed by the fact that there are very few groups at the phylum level which do not contain forms which live as symbiotes. Some phyla seem to have more such members than others, and there are even a few cases in which all members of a major taxonomic group live as symbiotes. It is not intended to give a detailed classification of the plant and animal kingdoms, as would be necessary if a scheme for classifying *all* symbiotes were to be presented. However, some discussion of classification is necessary; references at the end of this chapter will furnish more detailed exposition of the classification of specific groups.

As already noted, the frameworks of classification are to some extent accountable for the historic failure of communication between scientists working with different kinds of hosts or symbiotes. These frameworks are supposed to represent the natural relationships between the organisms concerned. It is unfortunate that they do not always do so. From earliest times man has recognized two types of larger living organisms, plants and animals, scientifically formulated in the recognition of two kingdoms. This clear separation was very satisfactory until the realization of the existence of a microbial world intruded itself. As more information on microorganisms accumulated, it became plain that some of them were plant-like and some animal-like. The botanists claimed the algae and fungi for the plant kingdom and the zoologists adopted the Protozoa.

However, some groups continue to cause considerable difficulty; for example, the alga-like flagellates, such as *Euglena*, were not clearly plants or animals. In 1866 Haeckel proposed that a third kingdom, the Protista, be recognized to embrace the algae, fungi, Protozoa, and bacteria. Haeckel's concept was not widely adopted and until recent years was almost forgotten. Many recent investigators have been more impressed with the desirability of recognizing Haeckel's concept, and the author believes it to be a more useful one than the rigorous separation of plant-like and animal-like forms, in spite of the inclusion of

procaryotic and eucaryotic cell types in the same group.

It may be asked: What shall be done with those well-publicized "parasites," the viruses? Authorities have been wrestling for some time with the question as to whether they should be considered to be living organisms. One group wishes to call them chemicals and another wishes to grace them with the title of "living." Now, the decision of what is or is not living is a thorny one. When we are dealing with a living horse or the carcass of a horse the distinction is not so difficult. However, the viruses lack many of the characteristics which we recognize as common to the living, whether we are examining horses or bacteria. Most of them seem to be devoid of the enzymatic machinery which we have come to identify with living things. On the other hand, there is no question that they can reproduce, although this is not known to occur outside living cells. They seem to have a great deal in common with cell organelles, such as the mitochondria and various plastids. It would seem that a rigorous decision as to whether viruses are living organisms is not appropriate in the framework of our present definition of what constitutes "living." We shall refer to viruses as though they were organisms, but this does not constitute a rigorous endorsement of such a view. Those who find this an evasion of the question are referred to the book of Luria and Darnell (1967), who attempted to arrive at a definition. Some additional comments on the possible evolution of the viruses will be found in Chapter 10.

A special remark may be made concerning the submicroscopic organisms no longer claimed by the virologists. These include the pleuropneumonia organisms (*Mycoplasma*) and the psittacosis–lymphogranuloma venereum group. Unlike the viruses, they contain two types of nucleic acids (which suggests a cellular organization) and they grow in size, dividing by binary fission. Biochemically, they are more complex than the viruses (Moulder, 1964; Kliene-berger-Nobel, 1964). Both groups have been considered to be "stripped-down" bacteria.

HISTORICAL BACKGROUND

In reviewing the literature on parasitism, it becomes apparent that most information has been obtained on parasitisms involving man or his domestic animals and crops. It is rather startling to find that the fields involved, bacteriology, plant pathology, animal parasitology, and virology, have developed at somewhat different rates and at different points in human history. These contrasts may in part be related to the very different sizes and types of organisms involved; in some instances, it is plain that advances in technique were extremely important determining factors. The development of the microscope was the outstanding of the technical advances leading to investigations of microbial parasites.

In the following paragraphs the historical development of the human-oriented fields dealing to a considerable extent with parasitism will be very briefly reviewed.

Early Beginnings

Because many parasitic worms are visible to the unaided eye, man probably recognized helminth parasites at an early stage of his development. Hoeppli (1954) investigated certain primitive tribes in Southeast Asia and found that the majority of these people were aware of small and large intestinal roundworms, presumably *Ascaris* and *Enterobius*, and a few had some knowledge of tapeworms. Hoeppli concluded that early man probably had such knowledge also.

There is not much doubt that civilized man recognized long ago that the presence of certain worms in man was an undesirable state of affairs. The Ebers Papyrus, an Egyptian medical book written about 1550

B.C., clearly discusses *Ascaris* and tapeworm infections, with a description of drugs used in treatment. Schistosomiasis was described as a disease but without convincing evidence that the role of a trematode worm was known. *Ascaris* and tapeworms were independently recognized and briefly described by physicians in the early cultures of Palestine, Greece, Rome, India, and China. In several instances, the free segments of tapeworms were regarded as separate species, a mistake still made occasionally by twentieth-century American physicians. Assyro-Babylonian physicians were familiar with scabies (mites) and pediculosis (lice). Although these ancient physicians apparently did not recognize the parasitic nature of scabies, they used sulfur, a treatment still employed in modern times.

Many historians agree that the Israelites were familiar with the guinea worm, *Dracunculus*, and that the "fiery serpents" mentioned by Moses (Num. 21:6–9) represent a direct reference to this worm. There seems to be little basis for the idea that the Hebrew prohibition of the eating of pork originated in the recognition that pork tapeworm and *Trichinella* infections were possible public health problems. The poor keeping qualities of pork for a society living in a warm climate without refrigerators and the possible role of the pig as a totem animal seem to be more likely reasons for the rule.

From early antiquity to the Renaissance little progress was made in the way of new information on parasitism. Certain physicians, Rhazes in the Near East (A.D. 850–932) and Avicenna in Persia (A.D. 980–1037), made contributions, the latter being the first to correlate clearly the presence of worms with symptoms produced in humans.

End of the Dark Ages

During the fifteenth and early sixteenth centuries several epidemic diseases swept through Europe. Smallpox, measles, syphilis, influenza, and typhus appeared and were disseminated with great rapidity. This led to a general appreciation that contagion was involved and, in 1546, Girolamo Fracastoro of Verona advanced, on epidemiological grounds, the conception of a *contagium vivum* as the cause of infectious diseases.

By 1600 several authors had recorded parasitic worms from game birds and had noted their similarity to forms found in man. As with other aspects of biology the development of the microscope lent new impetus to the study of parasitism. Shortly thereafter, a remarkable man appeared on the parasitological scene. This colorful personality was Francisco Redi (1626–1697) who, with his colleague Cestoni, demonstrated the role of the itch mite, *Sarcoptes*, in causing scabies. He showed that males and females existed and studied transmission from host to host. After these discoveries, his information on scabies was neglected for the next hundred and fifty years. Redi is best known for his experimental evidence that lower animals do not arise by spontaneous generation. He clearly recognized the separate sexes of the nematode *Ascaris* and described reproductive organs and eggs. He was an indefatigable collector and described 108 kinds of helminth parasites.

The Dutch microscopist Leeuwenhoek (1632–1723) not only played a major role in promoting the use of the instrument but turned his inquisitive eye on anything which came his way. In 1674, Leeuwenhoek made the first observations on a parasitic pro-

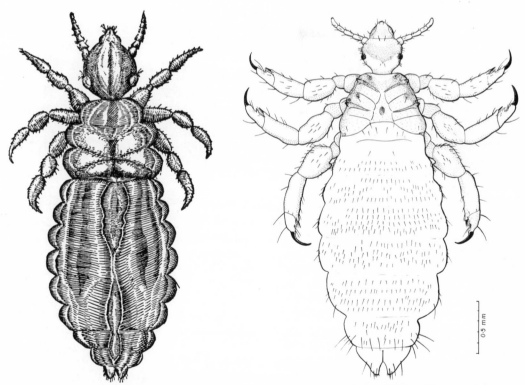

Fig. 1–2 Comparison of Redi's figure of the human louse *(left)* with a modern drawing of the same organism *(right)* shows the accuracy of Redi's observations. (Figure on left from Redi, 1688.)

Fig. 1–3   Antoni van Leeuwenhoek (1632–1723), in a portrait by Verkolje. (Courtesy of the Rijksmuseum, Amsterdam.)

tozoan, a coccidian from the rabbit. In this same period, he observed many bacteria which were undoubtedly commensal organisms in various animals, including himself. Subsequently, this amazing man reported observations on the parasitic protozoans *Giardia*, *Opalina*, and *Nyctotherus*. What is perhaps most astonishing is that Leeuwenhoek worked with the *simple* microscope rather than the compound one. His success as a microscopist is attributable to his unusual skill as a lens maker, as well as to his insatiable curiosity. After Leeuwenhoek, isolated observations on microbial parasites were made by Brassi, Pollender, Davaine, and others. In 1729, Micheli published evidence that fungi developing on plants were not spontaneously generated, and Tillet (in 1755) and Tessier (in 1783) furnished experimental proof that wheat bunt disease is contagious. The two latter authors failed to appreciate that their "black dust" was a living organism. Needham described and drew for the first time a nematode parasite of plants, the wheat eelworm, in 1745. In the mid-eighteenth century, Muller made further observations on parasitic Protozoa, but not until the nineteenth century was there a real burst of activity in this field.

Nineteenth Century

This century had an auspicious beginning, for, in 1807, Bénédict Prévost published his remarkable studies showing that bunt disease of wheat is caused by a fungal organism. This publication was the first to record, with adequate experimental proof, that a microorganism "causes" a disease. Prévost's work was extremely important and laid the foundation for nearly all branches of modern plant pathology. He developed methods for culturing the fungus and expressed his disbelief in spontaneous generation. He regarded the bunt fungus as the direct cause of bunt disease but clearly recognized that disease appeared only under certain conditions. This appreciation of a causal relationship of environment to disease symptoms has proven to be extremely important. Prévost's work was rejected by his contemporary academicians, for, as Keitt (1959) remarked, Prévost was too far ahead of his time. Nearly a half century elapsed before the scientific world was prepared to accept the essentials of Prévost's work. The devastating outbreaks of infectious disease of potatoes in the middle of the nineteenth century (1845–1846) stimulated interest, and there were heated debates over the cause of the pestilence. The causal role of a fungus was proven by Speerschneider in 1857 and De Bary in 1861. All during this period, Prévost's neglected researches held the essentials of a solution to the problem.

In 1834, Agostino Bassi showed experimentally that a fungus, *Beauveria bassiana,* was the cause of an infectious disease in silkworms. The great importance of Bassi's work has not been appreciated until recent years. The role of fungi in some plant diseases had been widely accepted for almost twenty-five years before a similar role for bacteria was proven. The brilliant researches of Louis Pasteur led him to the proof. In the memoir of his work on the importance of microorganisms in the health and disease of beer and wine (1855–1865), it is clear that Pasteur considered the possibility of applying his findings in the study of infectious animal diseases. He was invited to study pébrine, a disease of silkworms and, in 1860, reported his studies showing the role of a protozoan, *Nosema,* as the causal factor. This was the first scientific study of a protozoan which resulted in effective methods of controlling the parasite. This work was followed by Pasteur's studies of the role of bacterial parasites in producing anthrax and chicken cholera. In Germany, Koch independently investigated anthrax (1876) and later the tubercle bacillus and the cholera vibrio. New information literally poured forth from the laboratories of Pasteur, Koch, and their followers. Meanwhile, in America, Burrill showed that bacteria caused blight disease of pears, and, shortly thereafter, the Dutchman Wakker discovered the bacterial parasite producing yellows disease of hyacinths.

In the meantime, many worm and protozoan parasites had been described. Rudolphi in 1819 summarized his researches on worms, describing many new species from all kinds of animal hosts. Dujardin, Diesing, Schneider, Cobbold, and many other biologists made similar contributions. In 1835, Owen described the larva of the nematode *Trichinella* from human muscle, and shortly thereafter Leidy discovered the same form in pigs. New concepts were introduced by the discovery of Leuckart and Metchnikoff, in 1856, that the nematode *Rhabdias* showed an alternation of free-living and parasitic generations and that *Camallanus* passed through a portion of its larval development in an arthropod intermediate host, *Cyclops*. Following the latter lead, Fedtschenko in 1871 showed that the guinea worm *Dracunculus* also develops in *Cyclops*. Leuckart published his great treatise on animal parasites in 1876, and, a year later, Manson showed that the filarial nematode *Wuchereria bancrofti* was transmitted from vertebrate host to vertebrate host by a mosquito. This investigation provided the first evidence that an arthropod can transmit a parasite by biting a vertebrate. Grassi, Calandruccio, and others (1887–1890) showed that the nematodes *Ascaris* and *Trichuris* infect the vertebrate when the eggs are ingested. However, twenty-nine more years elapsed before the extra-intestinal migrations of *Ascaris* were discovered. Knowledge of the transmission of parasites by biting insects was extended in 1893, when Smith and Kilbourne proved that the protozoan *Babesia*, which causes Texas fever in cattle, is transmitted by ticks. Shortly thereafter, Bruce implicated tsetse flies in transmission of trypanosome protozoans, and Ross and Grassi showed that malarial parasites are passed to the vertebrate host by mosquitoes. The first report of an insect-transmitted plant parasite was that of Waite in 1891, who showed that the bacteria causing fire blight of pears are mechanically transmitted by bees and wasps.

During the latter half of the nineteenth century, other complications of animal parasitism were being unfolded. In 1883 Thomas solved the essentials of the riddle of the trematode life cycle by demonstrating the stages in the development of *Fasciola hepatica*. As the nineteenth century came to a close Loeffler and Frank showed that the parasite of foot-and-mouth disease of cattle was a filtrable virus and Beijerinck in Holland announced that tobacco mosaic was a virus. In the same year, Bolle implicated a virus in polyhedrosis disease of silkworms. It was the year 1898, and virology had begun.

Twentieth Century

This century has seen a fantastic development of science, and the special branches of symbiology have been in the forefront of some of these advances. Not the least of these strides has been the growth and maturation of public health science, including the accompanying concept that government must encompass within its responsibilities active concern for the health of the governed. Whole arrays of infectious diseases of man have been brought under control in the industrialized countries of the world. Applications of knowledge in symbiology have led to unprecedented yields of food from plant and animal resources. The sheer volume of new information in symbiology acquired in this century makes it impractical to review it completely in a single small volume, but subsequent chapters will be concerned largely with work developed in the twentieth century.

GENERAL REFERENCES

The following list includes larger reference works dealing with groups of symbiotes or with some major category of symbiosis. In most cases, the reference cited contains a large number of references to specific literature in the area concerned.

If reference gives only author's name and date, see Literature Cited, at the end of this work, for the complete reference.

AHMADJIAN, V. 1967. *The Lichen Symbiosis*. Blaisdell Publishing Co., Waltham, Mass.

AINSWORTH, G. C., and P. H. A. SNEATH (eds.). 1962. *Microbial Classification*. Cambridge University Press, London and New York.

ALLEE, W. C., et al. 1949.

ARTHUR, D. R. 1961. *Ticks and Disease*. Row, Peterson, & Co., Evanston, Ill.

BAER, J. G. 1951. *Ecology of Animal Parasites*. University of Illinois Press, Urbana, Ill.

BAWDEN, F. C. 1964. *Plant Viruses and Virus Diseases* (4th ed.). The Ronald Press Company, New York.

BISSETT, K. A. 1959. Characters associated with parasitism in gram-positive bacteria. *Nature* 184:29.

BOYD, M. F. 1949. *Malariology.* W. B. Saunders Co., Philadelphia.

BRAND, T. VON. 1952.

BRAND, T. VON. 1966.

BUCHNER, P. 1965.

BURNET, F. M. 1960.

BURNET, F. M., and W. M. STANLEY (eds.). 1959. *The Viruses* (3 vols.). Academic Press, New York.

BURNET, M. 1966. *Natural History of Infectious Disease* (3rd ed.). Cambridge University Press, London and New York.

CALKINS, G. N., and F. M. SUMMERS (eds.). 1941. *Protozoa in Biological Research.* Columbia University Press, New York.

CAMERON, T. W. M. 1956. *Parasites and Parasitism.* John Wiley & Sons, New York.

CAULLERY, M. 1952. *Parasitism and Symbiosis.* Sidgwick & Jackson, London.

CHANDLER, A. C., and C. P. READ. 1961.

CHEN, T. T. (ed.). 1967. *Research in Protozoology* (2 vols.). Pergamon Press, New York.

CHENG, T. C. 1964. *The Biology of Animal Parasites.* W. B. Saunders Co., Philadelphia.

CLAUSEN, C. P. 1940. *Entomophagous Insects.* McGraw-Hill, New York.

CORLISS, J. O. 1961. *The Ciliated Protozoa: Characterization, Classification, and Guide to the Literature.* Pergamon Press, New York.

CORLISS, J. O. 1967. Systematics of the phylum Protozoa. In *Chemical Zoology,* Vol. 1 (ed., G. W. KIDDER). Academic Press, New York.

CROFTON, H. D. 1966. *Nematodes.* Hutchinson & Co., London.

DE BARY, A. 1879.

DOBELL, C. 1932. *Antony van Leeuwenhoek and His "Little Animals."* J. Bale Sons & Danielsson, London. (Also in paperback: Dover Press, New York.)

DOGIEL, V. A. 1966. *General Parasitology.* Academic Press, New York.

DOWSON, W. J. 1957.

DUBOS, R. J. 1950. *Louis Pasteur: Free Lance of Science.* Little, Brown & Co., Boston.

DUBOS, R. 1954.

DUCLAUX, E. 1920. *Pasteur, the History of a Mind* (transl. E. F. SMITH and F. HEDGES). W. B. Saunders Co., Philadelphia.

FAUST, E. C., P. C. BEAVER, and R. C. JUNG. 1968. *Animal Agents and Vectors of Human Disease* (3rd ed.). Lea & Febiger, Philadelphia.

FAUST, E. C., and P. F. RUSSELL. 1964. *Clinical Parasitology* (7th ed.). Lea & Febiger, Philadelphia.

FLORKIN, M., and B. T. SCHEER (eds.). 1967. *Chemical Zoology* (2 vols.). Academic Press, New York.

FOSTER, W. D. 1965. *A History of Parasitology.* Balliere, Tindall & Cox, London.

GÄUMANN, E. 1950.

HALL, R. P. 1953. *Protozoology.* Prentice-Hall, New York.

HEGNER, R., and J. ANDREWS. 1930. *Problems and Methods of Research in Protozoology.* Macmillan Co., New York.

HENRY, S. M. (ed.). 1966–67. *Symbiosis* (2 vols.). Academic Press, New York.

HERMS, W. B., and M. T. JAMES. 1961. *Medical Entomology* (5th ed.). Macmillan Co., New York.

HOEPPLI, R. 1954.

HOEPPLI, R. 1959.

HORSFALL, J. G., and A. E. DIMOND (eds.). 1959. *Plant Pathology* (2 vols.). Academic Press, New York.

HUFF, C. G. 1956.

HUNGATE, R. E. 1966.

HUNTER, G. W., W. W. FRYE, and J. C. SWARTZWELDER. 1966. *A Manual of Tropical Medicine* (4th ed.). W. B. Saunders Co., Philadelphia.

HUTNER, S. H., and A. LWOFF (eds.). 1955. *Biochemistry and Physiology of Protozoa.* Vol. 2. Academic Press, New York.

KLIENEBERGER-NOBEL, E. 1964.

KLUYVER, A. J., and C. B. VAN NIEL. 1956.

KUDO, R. R. 1966. *Protozoology* (5th ed.). Charles C Thomas, Springfield, Ill.

LAPAGE, G. 1958. *Parasitic Animals.* Heffer & Sons, Cambridge.

LEE, D. L. 1965.

LEVINE, N. D. 1961. *Protozoan Parasites of Domestic Animals and Man.* Burgess Publishing Co., Minneapolis, Minn.

LURIA, S. E., and J. E. DARNELL, JR. 1967.

LWOFF, A. (ed.). 1951. *Biochemistry and Physiology of Protozoa.* Vol. 1. Academic Press, New York.

MANN, K. H. 1962. *Leeches (Hirudinea), Their Structure, Physiology, Ecology, and Embryology.* Pergamon Press, New York.

MANSON-BAHR, P. 1966. *Tropical Diseases.* Williams & Wilkins, Baltimore, Md.

MARAMOROSCH, K. (ed.). 1962. *Biological Transmission of Disease Agents.* Academic Press, New York.

METCHNIKOFF, E. 1905.

MOULDER, J. W. 1964.

NOBLE, E. R., and G. A. NOBLE. 1964.

NUTMAN, P. S., and B. MOSSE. 1963.

ODUM, E. P. 1959.

OLSON, W. O. 1962. *Animal Parasites: Their Biology and Life Cycles.* Burgess Publishing Co., Minneapolis, Minn.

PAVLOVSKY, E. N. 1966. *Natural Nidality of Transmissible Diseases* (transl. N. D. LEVINE). University of Illinois Press, Urbana, Ill.

PONTECORVO, C. 1955. Principles of microbial classification. *J. Genl. Microbiol.* 12:314.

RIVERS, T. M., and F. L. HORSFALL. 1959. *Viral and Rickettsial Infections of Man* (3rd ed.). J. B. Lippincott Co., Philadelphia.

ROGERS, W. P. 1962.

ROTHSCHILD, M., and T. CLAY. 1953. *Fleas, Flukes and Cuckoos.* Philosophical Library, New York.

SMITH, W. (ed.). 1963. *Mechanisms of Virus Infection.* Academic Press, New York.

SMYTH, J. D. 1962. *Introduction to Animal Parasitology.* English Universities Press, London.

SMYTH, J. D. 1966. *The Physiology of Trematodes.* W. H. Freeman & Co., San Francisco.

SOULSBY, E. J. L. (ed.). 1966. *Biology of Parasites.* Academic Press, New York.

STANIER, R. Y., and C. B. VAN NIEL. 1941.

STEINHAUS, E. A. (ed.). 1963. *Insect Pathology.* Academic Press, New York.

THORNE, G. 1961. *Principles of Nematology.* McGraw-Hill Book Co., New York.

TRAGER, W. 1960.

WALKER, J. C. 1957.

WARDLE, R. A., and J. A. McLEOD. 1952. *The Zoology of Tapeworms.* University of Minnesota Press, Minneapolis, Minn.

WENYON, C. M. 1926.

WHETZEL, H. H. 1918. *An Outline of the History of Phytopathology.* W. B. Saunders Co., Philadelphia.

WILSON, G. S., and A. A. MILES. 1957.

ZINSSER, H. 1935. *Rats, Lice and History.* Atlantic Monthly Press, Boston.

2

Symbiosis and Disease

Symbiosis may have a variety of consequences for hosts. Such effects may be categorized very roughly as injurious, neutral, or beneficial. It should be obvious that in any particular symbiosis all of these effects may be present. However, one type of consequence will usually be quantitatively dominant and will characterize the relationship.

In addition to consequences for the individual host, we readily recognize that parasitism may affect populations, species, or even groups of species. These effects have biological implications somewhat different from those involving individuals. In this chapter injurious effects of parasitism on individuals will be briefly considered.

WHAT IS A DISEASE?

The term *disease* is not always easy to define. We recognize that an afflicted animal or plant is diseased; indeed, most of us have been diseased at one time or another. Disease is not a simple physiological state. The physiological state is a manifestation of disease and is a complex of symptoms (a syndrome). We frequently confuse the disease and the parasite. For example, the terms *smut* or *mildew* or *malaria* are used almost interchangeably for certain diseases and the symbiotes which are involved in the diseases. A disease is not simply an injury, which may be a result of disease. Disease is a departure from a norm and might be defined, in thermodynamic terms, as a change resulting in an unusual increase in the entropy of the living system. *disorder* Although this may appear to be a somewhat theoretical definition, it seems better to defer a definition in other terms until we have considered various aspects of disease phenomena. It should be kept in mind that disease in which a symbiote is involved is a set of manifestations of the host-symbiote association. There is no typhoid fever in a typhoid bacterium or in an uninfected host. Typhoid fever is a manifestation of an association pattern of the two kinds of organisms.

INFECTION VERSUS DISEASE

The terms *infection* and *disease* are frequently confused. The term "infection" does not indicate a malfunctioning process. It only means that a host is harboring a symbiote, sometimes a parasite. The duration of the association may be so short that it escapes notice. Infection frequently escapes notice because no disease results. (In another chapter we shall discuss the phenomena of infectiousness, or the capacities of the symbiote to infect.) From the practical standpoint, it is of considerable importance to differentiate infection from disease. This need is particularly pointed in the case of metazoan animal parasites. For example, a population of humans may be widely infected with hookworms, but the actual number of worms per person may be so low that *hookworm disease* is not common. Thus, two populations may contain the same number of infected persons but differ considerably in the proportion who can be called diseased (see p. 69).

A number of other symbiotes, frequently regarded as dangerous, may exist within a majority of the members of a host population yet only occasionally produce overt disease. The polio virus is a good example. Before a vaccine was developed, most young adults had been infected with the virus, but only in rare individual cases did the disease, poliomyelitis, appear. A number of other viruses apparently live in millions of humans, producing disease only rarely. Similarly, various bacteria commonly identifiable on the surfaces of animals, or in their mouths or noses, produce disease occasionally. Even in those instances in which a bacterium provokes disease with high frequency, some hosts will show no signs of disease. The typhoid bacillus is a good example; some individuals harbor a flourishing population of the symbiote for extended periods but show no evidence of typhoid fever. In the case of the typhoid organism, such hosts are referred to as "carriers," since they may serve as a source of infection for other hosts who do subsequently show symptoms of disease. As will become more apparent, it is sometimes difficult to draw a sharp demarcation between symbiotes involved in the genesis of disease and those not so implicated.

This brings us to the general problem of determining whether a given symbiote species is involved in the genesis of a given disease in a population of hosts. Almost a century ago Robert Koch enunciated a set of basic rules which may guide an experi-

mental approach to a specific symbiosis. These rules, usually called Koch's postulates, state that: (1) a particular parasitic organism is always found in hosts showing the specific disease; (2) the parasitic organism can be isolated in pure culture outside the host; (3) after introduction of the pure cultured parasite into uninfected hosts, the disease ensues; and (4) with the experimentally produced disease, the parasitic organism should be continuously associated with the host. It will become clear that there are instances in which it has not been possible to satisfy all of Koch's postulates, but they have furnished a working method for many proofs of the genesis of disease. As a matter of fact, these rules can be adapted for the general experimental proof of the causal relationship between any biological or chemical agent and an observable phenomenon.

HOW SYMBIOTES PRODUCE DISEASE

We are now primarily concerned with examining the kinds of processes involved in producing disease. As might be expected, this is not a simple matter; there are many factors which may be concerned in determining whether the presence of a given parasite will result in overt disease. We have already indicated that the number of parasites in a host is important. Examining this further, we may ask what determines the numbers of parasites in a host. Generally speaking, the metazoan parasites do not multiply within host animals. Thus, in the case of the helminth parasites, the number in a particular host will most certainly be partly dependent on the rate at which new worms get into the host and the average length of life of the worm. The survival of the worm will in turn be determined by a variety of factors, including the capacity of the host to evict the parasites. Among the protistan and viral parasites, we find that multiplication within the vertebrate host is a common pattern. In many instances, the introduction of only one or a few individual parasites results in the production of a large number of individual parasites within the host. Plainly, disease produced in vertebrates by worms and protistans will be differently determined as far as the frequency of infection is concerned. This point will be discussed further in Chapter 11. Multicellular parasites of plants, on the other hand, frequently multiply within the host and the determinants of plant diseases invoked by uni- and multicellular parasites are not so clearly differentiated.

If there are sufficient numbers of parasites to result in the appearance of disease, analysis of what occurs in the host body invariably shows that there is cell damage and cell death. The specific symptoms involved in a particular disease seem to be functions of (1) what types of cells are affected, (2) where affected cells are located, (3) numbers of cells affected, and (4) the rate at which cells are affected. It is of interest to examine some of the mechanisms by which parasites can produce damage to cells, tissues, and organisms. It may be emphasized that, although we may classify these damage mechanisms, a given disease can almost never be attributed solely to a single underlying set of events. In many cases, the damage can be recognized as having joint origins in host and parasite and representing a compounding of effects. The parasite acts and the host reacts; in turn parasite reacts to host. This cybernetic aspect of disease will be discussed further in other parts of the book.

MECHANICAL INJURY AT THE TISSUE LEVEL

Direct mechanical injury seems to be a very common feature in disease involving larger animal parasites; and it is frequently associated with the food-gathering processes of the parasite or with the action of hold-fast structures which serve to maintain contact between host and parasite. Puncturing or wounding of the host's tissues is a very common form of mechanical injury. Direct perforation of the external surface and underlying cells, with subsequent feeding on tissue juices and blood, is observed in the behavior of such parasites as fleas, lice, bedbugs, some flies and mosquitoes, ticks, mites, and leeches. Many of these organisms are known to secrete anticoagulant substances into the bite wound. Some parasites may literally chew at external tissues. The mallophagans, or bird lice, feed on skin, hair, and feathers in this manner. In some of these cases, disease is associated with the reactions of the host rather than the actual *quantity* of tissue directly damaged. This is discussed below under *Irritation*.

Some of the helminths which are endoparasites bite into and destroy tissues in various parts of the host body. The intestinal mucosa is probably the internal tissue most commonly affected in this way. Some intestinal nematodes, such as the hookworms and their relatives, bite the intestinal mucosa (Figs. 2–1 and 2–2) and suck blood

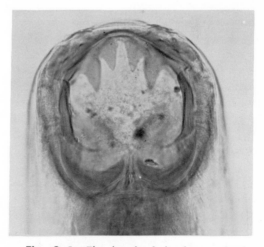

Fig. 2–1 The head of the human hookworm, *Ancylostoma duodenale*. Note the heavily sclerotized buccal capsule with two pairs of teeth in the upper portion.

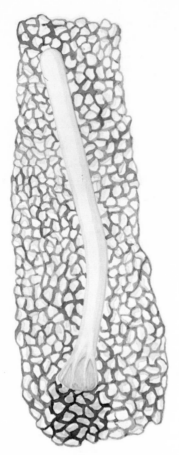

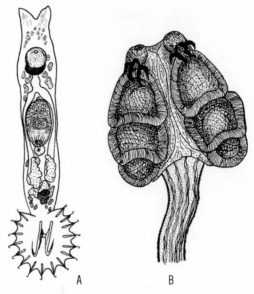

P.31 **Fig. 2–3** Holdfast organ development in a monogenetic trematode, *Gyrodactylus* (A), and a cestode, *Acanthobothrium* (B). (A, redrawn from Mueller and Van Cleave, 1932; B, redrawn from Alexander, 1953.)

Fig. 2–2 A male hookworm (*Ancylostoma duodenale*) attached and feeding on the mucosa of the human small intestine.

from the bite wound. This results in direct loss of blood and tissue fluids. In addition, movement of the individual worm to a new feeding site in the host may leave a bleeding wound. Many of the diseases associated with such parasites have anemia as a characteristic feature.

Mechanical damage due to the action of holdfast organs is often seen in hosts parasitized by flatworms. In some this may be associated with feeding, as in the trematodes, but may only be incidental to an action serving to maintain the parasite at a favorable site in or on the host (Figs. 2–3 and 2–4). In a few instances, protozoan

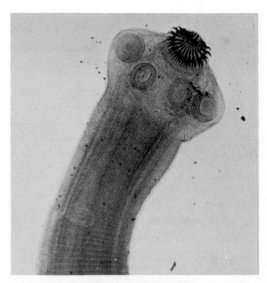

Fig. 2–4 The holdfast organ, or scolex, of *Taenia pisiformis*, a tapeworm symbiote of dogs and other carnivorous mammals.

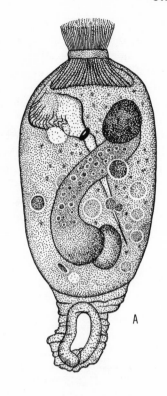

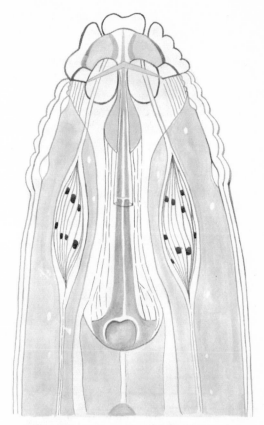

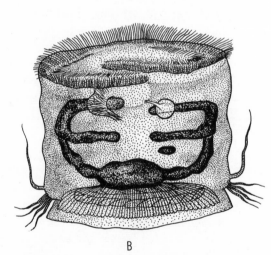

Fig. 2–6 The anterior region of the nematode *Heterodera glycines*, showing the mouth stylet used in penetrating host-plant tissues. (Redrawn from Hirschmann, 1960, *Nematology*, University of North Carolina Press, Chapel Hill, N. C.)

Fig. 2–5 Holdfast organelles of protozoan symbiotes of mollusks. In *Caliperia brevipes* (A), the symbiote is attached to the gill filaments of the host. In *Cyclochaeta (Urceolaria) korschelti* (B), the base of the cell is a cup-like attachment structure supported by radially arranged ribs. (A, redrawn from Laird, 1959; B, redrawn from Zick, 1928.)

holdfast organs may produce mechanical damage (Fig. 2–5). Some of the nematodes parasitizing plants are equipped with a mouth stylet which may function as a puncturing instrument (Fig. 2–6); there are several descriptions of the puncturing of host plant cells by the nematode *Heterodera*, and Dickinson (1959) has described the mechanical penetration of non-living membranes by this worm.

Some parasites produce mechanical damage at one site in the host during one portion of their lives and at another site at some later time. For example, *Ascaris lumbricoides,* a large nematode parasite of pigs and man, undergoes a migration in the vertebrate host during its early life (see p. 95). Damage to the liver involving small hemorrhages and the death of groups of cells is sometimes observed. Later, the young nematodes cause damage in the lungs when they break out of the capillary bed into the pulmonary alveoli. Bleeding and accumulation of fluid occur. Similarly, the hookworms and their relatives may produce damage in the lungs during migration (see p. 96).

Another type of damage which may be regarded as mechanical is observed in infections with the redworm of horses, *Strongylus equinus.* During the migration of this species in the horse, damage is done to the intimal lining of arteries. This results in the formation of aneurysms (blowouts) in large arteries.

Parasites living in hollow organs, such as the intestine, bile duct, or vascular system, may mechanically occlude these organs and actually prevent the normal flow of secretions or body fluids. The nematode *Ascaris* occasionally enters such ducts as those from the pancreas, blocking them and producing serious consequences for the host. The tracheal nematode of birds, *Syngamus,* produces the characteristic symptoms known as "gapes" by occluding the air passages of the bird host. Blockage of bile ducts by the trematode *Fasciola* is sometimes observed, although this may be due primarily to host reaction to the flukes. Certain parasites may produce disease by the exertion of pressure. The large larval stage of the tapeworm *Multiceps multiceps* develops in the brain or spinal cord of sheep, goats, cattle, horses, or even man. The pressure exerted by the developing cyst interferes with the functioning of the nervous system and, depending on the precise location, various symptoms of this interference appear.

Parasitic worms may get into what may be called an aberrant or unusual host. In such a host, they may behave very differ-

ently than they do in their usual hosts and may produce unusual mechanical damage. Gnathostome nematodes, for example, behave like bulls in a china shop in unusual hosts, wandering about in the tissues of such organs as the liver and producing extensive mechanical disruption; in their usual hosts these worms remain in the digestive tract. There has been considerable recent interest in the occurrence in humans of parasites which are characteristically parasites of other host species. In these human infections, larval nematodes of species normally occurring in such hosts as dogs may wander in the tissues of the human, producing mechanical damage, as well as irritation, in various locations. If this wandering occurs in an organ such as the eye, it may of course cause irreparable damage (Beaver, 1956). (This is discussed further on page 83.)

Generally speaking, mechanical damage imposes a burden of reconstruction on the host body, and the host may fail to keep pace with the rate of new damage. Further, the processes of reconstruction practically never result in restoration of tissues to their original form (discussed further on page 28). Another important consideration is that mechanical injury frequently destroys a barrier to the invasion or activity of some other parasite species. For instance, damage to the intestinal mucosa by nematodes may increase the opportunities for invasion of this tissue by bacteria which may be present; apes parasitized by certain worms are readily infected with typhoid bacilli, whereas unparasitized apes are not infected by the bacteria (or at least in the latter case the bacilli do not produce disease). Similarly, in plants, wounding by one symbiote may predispose to infection with another (see Yarwood, 1959).

INJURY AT THE CELLULAR LEVEL

Under this heading we differentiate a large number of injuries produced by protistan organisms and viruses that live in-

[handwritten margin note: results in dissolution of traces & accumulation of polyhedral granules in the resulting fluid]

side cells and whose activities result in cell destruction. Typically, a particular type of cell seems to be favored as a site for a particular intracellular parasite. In vertebrates they are often cells of what has been termed the lymphoid-macrophage system, and it seems likely that parasites are readily absorbed on these cells and taken in. When cells of a particular type are favored by a given parasite, it is not surprising to find that the symptoms of disease produced are referable to some extent to this specificity. For example, in some kinds of coccidiosis (see p. 94) many of the symptoms of an acute infection can be referred to the fact that a particular portion of the digestive tract is parasitized. Not all symptoms can be so explained, however (see p. 28). In a few instances this cell destruction is essentially synchronized so that large numbers of cells are destroyed almost simultaneously (see discussion of malaria parasite life cycle on page 104). Our knowledge of the mechanisms by which cells are damaged by such parasites is quite deficient.

We have some information on the action of viruses on host cells. In the lytic bacterial viruses, the synthesis of host-cell nucleic acid is quickly inhibited after entry of the virus. During multiplication of virus, the major synthesis of nucleic acids is directed to replication of virus rather than host. As the virus matures into a new infectious particle, an enzyme appears which is capable of hydrolyzing constituents of the host cell wall. Lysis of the host cell is thought to be mediated by this enzyme. On the other hand, viruses which produce lysis of animal cells do not seem to cause the early striking depression of host nucleic acid synthesis.

Special mention may be made of the nuclear-polyhedrosis viruses which live in the cells of insects. These viruses develop within the nuclei of the host cells and cause the formation of polyhedral inclusion bodies in the infected nucleus. The nucleus swells and eventually breaks down. Cell death follows.

In the cytoplasmic polyhedrosis virus infections of insects, the cytoplasm becomes completely filled with virus particles, and it seems likely that cell death occurs by gross interference with the metabolism required to maintain cell integrity.

IRRITATION AND ALLERGY

These two elements of disease are dealt with together because there are practically no instances in which they do not occur together and they may be indistinguishable. Irritation is used here in a physiological rather than a psychological sense. Irritation and local inflammatory reaction are extremely common phenomena in parasitisms involving vertebrates.

Most persons have suffered the highly localized inflammatory reactions which occur during and after the feeding activities of certain arthropods. Fleas, flies, mosquitoes, bedbugs, lice, mites, and certain other insects frequently cause an inflammation in the neighborhood of the bite wound. There are two common causes for such reactions; both may occur. First, the salivary secretions of the arthropod may contain substances which have a direct irritating effect on cells. Second, the individual may have been rendered immunologically sensitive by previous bites, and the irritation response may be allergic in nature. If the response is primarily allergic, the individual may eventually be desensitized (if he can tolerate a sufficient number of bites). The writer has several times passed through an allergic to a non-allergic state with regard to the bites of culicine mosquitoes.

Some indirect effects of skin irritation are seen in parasitisms involving mallophagan lice and various birds and mammals. Most of the species of mallophagans feed on feathers, down, skin-scurf, or hair. They are very active and annoying to their hosts. The hosts are stimulated to peck or bite at the skin or to rub against solid objects. This results in the loss of hair or feathers, and the skin may be markedly abraded, resulting in a mangy appearance. The sucking lice, on the other hand, are much less active and less annoying to their hosts, although they feed on blood and tissue fluids.

The widespread importance of allergic responses to endoparasites in causing manifestations of disease has only been appreciated in the past few years. It has long been known that, in many helminth infections, an increase in the eosinophile blood leucocytes is observed. However, it required some time to appreciate that this eosinophilia has its basis in allergy. In some acute diseases attributable to helminths, generalized allergic responses seem to be quite important. For example, many of the symptoms in acute trichinosis (caused by the nematode *Trichinella*), in ascariasis (*Ascaris*), and in other nematode diseases are clearly allergic in nature. Recently, considerable evidence has been adduced to support the idea that a number of obscure diseases having eosinophilia as a prominent feature are due to the presence of worms which are living in an unusual host and tend to wander about the body (see p. 83).

Many of the inflammatory responses can be discussed more properly in connection with the resistance of hosts to establishment and maintenance of symbiosis (see p. 77 et seq.).

TOXIC EFFECTS AND TOXINS

Chemical injury to the host may involve more direct effects of specific chemical substances, usually referred to as *toxins*. The best known of such effects are those produced by certain microbial parasites other than parasitic animals.

Roux and Yersin first demonstrated a bacterial toxin, that of the diphtheria organism, in 1888, although earlier workers had suggested that toxins were involved in disease. Within the next two years, the tetanus toxin was discovered; and in the ensuing decade microbiologists quickly adopted a general view that all infectious diseases were due to toxins. In the following sixty years, a number of other bacterial toxins were discovered and some were purified and studied in detail. However, much of the earlier enthusiasm has cooled, and there have been only a few fundamental discoveries concerning the role of toxins in the pathology of infectious disease.

Since it has often been assumed that toxins produced by a parasite have an influence in producing disease, it is appropriate to review the criteria which must be rigorously applied to judge that a toxin is involved. Van Heyningen (1955) has outlined the criteria which would be ideally fulfilled: (1) the organism is known to produce a toxin; (2) virulent variants of the organism produce toxin and avirulent ones do not; (3) injection of the toxin separately from the parasites produces symptoms that mimic the disease; (4) the infecting organism produces the disease without multiplying profusely or spreading extensively, and organs at a distance from the seat of infection are affected; (5) the disease can be prevented by immunization against the toxin.

It is obvious that a toxin may play a role in producing a disease without satisfying all the criteria. Failure to demonstrate toxin production by a parasite *in vitro* may not mean that the organism will not produce toxin. Some organisms only produce toxin outside a host under specialized culture conditions. For example, virulent diphtheria organisms will only produce toxin in media which are deficient in iron. The case of the anthrax organism illustrates the fact that failure to demonstrate toxin, even after exhaustive experiments, cannot be used to conclude that toxin production is unimportant. For many years investigators diligently sought but failed to find a toxin produced by the anthrax organism; but in a brilliant set of experiments, Smith and Keppie showed that toxin is produced in the host and can be recovered from the plasma of infected animals. Of the criteria laid out above, (2) has not been fulfilled with the anthrax organism, but the student may appreciate the technical difficulties involved in satisfactorily proving that virulent strains produce toxin and avirulent ones do not when experiments must be carried out with living hosts rather than cultures (Smith, 1960).

To say that a substance is a toxin is insufficient since it says nothing about how the material is toxic. The mode of action, of course, is fundamental to understanding the role of a toxin in a disease. It is thus pertinent to examine some examples for which there is evidence concerning the mechanism of toxicity.

The toxins produced by the bacteria of the genus *Clostridium*, causing tetanus and botulism, have the most exceptional lethality known. These substances act on the nervous system of the vertebrate at extremely low concentrations. The substances seem to be proteins, and only a few molecules per nerve cell are lethal. Each milligram of the purified toxins will kill about ten million mice. The site of action is thought to be the motor nerve endings, by interference with the release of acetylcholine. There is reason to believe that there are specific effects differing with the specific toxin since botulism and tetanus differ to some extent in the manifestations of disease, but the nervous system as the site of action seems to be well established. The toxin produced by the dysentery bacillus also acts on the nervous system. Curiously, although its action is on the central nervous system, damage is indirectly manifested in the intestinal mucosa by effects mediated through the autonomic nervous system. The dysenteric symptoms are not due to direct irritation of the digestive tract.

A different and interesting mechanism of toxin action is seen in the case of the toxin produced by the virus-infected diphtheria bacillus. Earlier studies indicated that the toxin interfered in the synthesis of a component of the cytochrome system. However, more recent work has shown that there is a more generalized effect on protein synthesis (Collier and Pappenheimer, 1964; Moehring et al., 1967).

A fungus, *Fusarium*, which causes a wilting disease of tomato plants, produces at least two chemical products which are thought to be responsible for symptoms. These substances have been called fusaric acid and lycomarasmin. Both substances cause wilting and browning of tomato cuttings. Lycomarasmin, a polypeptide composed of several amino acids, modifies the permeability of cells to water and increases the rate of water loss from plants. Fusaric acid has similar effects. It seems probable that these metabolites contribute to the altered water economy of infected plants and final death of the host (Gäumann, 1956).

A related bacterium, causing wild-fire disease of tobacco, produces a toxic substance called tabtoxinine (β-hydroxy-diaminopimelic acid). This is an amino acid which the tobacco plant is apparently incapable of utilizing. It closely resembles the amino acid methionine, a normal plant metabolite, and its toxic effect seems to be exerted through its interference with methionine metabolism (Braun, 1955).

Evidence for a most interesting virus toxicity has been accumulated by Racker and his associates. This involves the Theiler virus, which produces a fatal disease in mice. The evidence supports the concept that the virus causes the liberation of iron in the tissues of the brain. This free iron activates a proteolytic enzyme, normally relatively inactive in this tissue, which *digests* an enzyme important in the carbohydrate metabolism of the tissue. The evidence is rather complicated, but the interested student may read Racker's review (1954) of the brilliant researches supporting this concept.

Daugherty and Herrick (1952) reported that in infections of chickens with the pro-

tozoan *Eimeria tenella* a substance is produced which was shown to interfere with
the phosphorylation of glucose. This finding was correlated with the very high blood
glucose levels seen in birds suffering acute
infections.

Perhaps the simplest toxin known is hydrogen cyanide, which is produced by the
snow mold organism, a symbiote of barley
plants (Lebeau and Dickson, 1953). This
is in contrast with the bacterial botulinum
toxin, which has a molecular weight of
about 900,000. It is plain that toxins vary
enormously in their chemistry, and it is not
surprising that there are a variety of ways
in which toxins may act to injure a host.
We may expect that other unexpected
mechanisms will turn up. There seem to
be many instances in which the production
of toxins by animal symbiotes has been suggested, but there is little evidence that
such materials are produced by the living
symbiotes in such a manner as to affect
hosts. Toxic substances have been demonstrated to be present in the tissue fluids of
nematodes such as *Ascaris,* cestodes such as
Moniezia, trematodes such as *Schistosoma,*
and in protozoans such as *Sarcocystis.*
However, it has not been shown that these
substances are released by the parasite nor
that they are important in producing pathology. A number of animal parasites have
been shown to secrete anticoagulant substances which interfere with the normal
clotting of blood. In most cases these are
parasites which feed upon blood; they include such diverse organisms as nematodes,
leeches, polychaetes, fly maggots, and lice.
Little is known of the chemical nature of
these anticoagulants nor of the mechanisms
by which they prevent clotting. Some other
aspects of chemical effects of parasites on
hosts are discussed in Chapter 7.

EFFECTS ON HOST-CELL GROWTH

Stimulation of host-cell growth is frequently seen in symbiosis. This is sometimes associated with cellular reaction
which walls off or limits the development
of the symbiote. This type of reaction will
be more fully treated in connection with the
resistance of hosts to symbiotes (Chapter
4).

Several parasites of vertebrates cause
hyperplasia of host tissues (increase in the
number of cells without an increase in cell
size). Such effects are not restricted to any
particular host organ. Hyperplasia may occur in the liver of rabbits infected with the
protozoan *Eimeria stiedae,* or of cattle infected with the trematode *Fasciola hepatica.*
Such changes are frequently seen in the
bladder of humans infected with the blood
fluke, *Schistosoma haematobium,* or in the
noses of cattle harboring *Schistosoma
nasalis.*

In some instances the presence of a parasite causes a change in cell character. In the
lungs of man and carnivores infected with
the lung fluke *Paragonimus,* the normal
cylindrical cells of the bronchioles are re-
placed by flattened squamous epithelial
cells (Yokagawa, Cort, and Yokagawa,
1960). In many instances parasites may be
"walled off" by fibrous connective tissue not
normally present in quantity.

Symbiosis and Cancer

The scientific literature furnishes numerous examples of neoplasia, or tumor formation, attributed to the presence of animal
parasites. Many of these examples are not
well documented and have not been studied under experimental conditions. The
few experimental studies carried out suggest that this may be a fertile field for investigation. For example, the tapeworm
Taenia taeniaeformis lives as an adult in the
intestine of cats. Rodents become infected
by eating eggs which are voided in the
feces of the cat. In the rodent, the embryonic tapeworms migrate to the liver and
grow into a relatively large larval form
called a strobilocercus. For completion of

the life history, the rodent must be eaten by a cat. It has been observed on numerous occasions that rats harboring *Taenia* larvae have cancerous growths of the liver. It was shown experimentally that if rats are infected with the tapeworm, they will, after a lapse of time, develop liver tumors. Further, if the tissue of the worm is ground up and this soupy material is injected into the body cavity of the rat, tumors develop in the body cavity. This latter observation opens up the distinct possibility that the tumor-inducing principle might be isolated from the worm and studied to determine whether it may be a chemical carcinogen or an oncogenic virus transmitted to the host by the worm.

Schistosoma mansoni infections sometimes cause cauliflower-like tumors in the wall of the intestine. Some species of nematodes living in the lungs of domestic animals produce tumors which may become malignant and affect other organs. Cancer has been attributed to a number of other animal parasites, but these require study since it seems probable that in some cases the occurrence of parasites and tumors in hosts is coincidental.

Interestingly, bacteria have never been identified with cancerous growth in animals. There has been great interest in a number of virus-induced tumors of vertebrates, and some virologists feel that viruses will ultimately be shown to be most important as causative agents of human cancers. Rous demonstrated in 1910 that a muscle cancer in chickens was transmissible by cell-free filtrates; and this disease, Rous sarcoma, has been studied by a number of investigators. Other virus-induced cancers of animals include leukemia, polyoma, and mammary tumors of mice; lymphocystis disease of fish; myxoma and papilloma in rabbits; renal cancer in frogs; and others. One interesting finding in recent years is that an adenovirus isolated from humans will cause tumors in some laboratory animals. A number of benign tumors of ani-

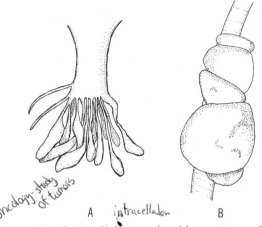

Fig. 2–7 Clubroot of cabbage (A) and crown gall of apple (B).

mals, including man, are considered to be the result of virus infection. Warts are examples of such tumors. The genetic aspects of virus relationships to cancer will be discussed in Chapter 9.

Plant Tumors

Plants are known to react by cellular proliferation to a variety of stimuli, including chemical and mechanical injury and the presence of insects, nematodes, bacteria, fungi, and viruses. Two well-known examples involving symbiotes are the plant diseases, clubroot and crown gall (Fig. 2–7). These are instances in which the stimuli of infection induced essentially unregulated growth of host tissue. Clubroot is caused by a fungus, *Plasmodiophora*, which is an intracellular parasite of turnips, cabbages, and mustards. The organism stimulates cell multiplication in the host root tissue, resulting in a clubbed appearance of the root. The rapid growth of club tissue is inimical to the normal development of protective layers on the outside surface, and secondary invasion of the tissue by other organisms occurs. Death of the tissue results and ultimately the host dies (Kunkel, 1918).

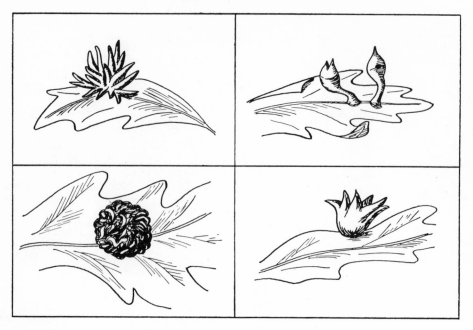

Fig. 2–8 Four morphologically distinct galls produced on leaves of the California white oak by four closely related species of insects. (From Braun, 1960, courtesy of Academic Press.)

Crown gall is caused by the bacterium *Agrobacterium*, which is an intercellular parasite of a variety of plants, including many which man uses for food or decorative purposes. Rapid cell division occurs around the points where bacteria are present in intercellular spaces. There is an accompanying decrease in the normal differentiation of cells in the tumorous growth. After tumor growth has begun, the presence of bacteria is no longer required for continuation of uncontrolled growth. Needless to say, this disease has been of great interest to those interested in the problems of cancer (Braun, 1959).

A quite common class of growth abnormalities seen in plants are the galls associated with the activity of certain insects. It has been suggested that these highly specialized growths are examples of dependent differentiation (Felt, 1940). The forms of galls are highly specific in that a given species of gall insect is responsible for the formation of a gall having specific morphology (Fig. 2–8). There is evidence

that the specific morphogenetic stimuli involved are chemical in nature. The specificity of gall morphology extends from one host plant to another. For example, the galls produced by the sawfly, *Micronematus gallicola*, on four different species of willow are bright red in color and very similar in morphology. Experimentally, Plumb (1953) showed that injection of a glycerol extract of salivary glands from the Norway spruce aphid, *Adelges abietis*, produced a gall resembling that produced when the insect is present. Other experimental evidence of this type is available, although the chemical nature of the growth-modifying substances does not appear to have been determined.

Like insect galls, the root nodules arising on leguminous plants infected with bacteria of the genus *Rhizobium* are also highly organized and specialized structures. The specificity of the response with different strains of *Rhizobium* and the nature of the growth response is discussed on pages 53 and 197.

[handwritten margin note, top:] polyembryony: equiv. to identical twinning; zygote divides several times - each separate cell gives rise to complete individual

Mention must be made of the abnormal growths on a variety of trees and shrubs identified as witches'-brooms. Diseased plants exhibit an overproduction of branches and the formation of broom-like structures. A variety of rust fungi and viruses have been shown to be concerned in the formation of this type of abnormal growth. The witches'-brooms associated with fungal symbiotes live somewhat independently and almost appear to be parasitic on the plants from which they grow. Growth of shoots and buds on the broom is often out of phase with growth of the host. It has been suggested that this peculiar growth pattern is due to a deficiency of auxin, but conclusive evidence has not been obtained.

A number of observations indicate that the growth of mollusks may be affected by developing larval stages of trematode flatworms. Strangely, this effect is one of enhanced growth; infected mollusks may grow faster and attain larger body size than uninfected ones, although more often growth is inhibited. The causes of such effects are not known, although it may involve the production of endocrine substances mentioned earlier in this chapter. Digenetic trematode infections may also have marked effects on the shape and color of the shell of snail hosts; the incorporation of dark pigments is a common effect in certain species. Deposition of pigment in the soft tissues, such as the foot, of snails as a consequence of trematode infection also occurs.

CASTRATION AND ALTERATION OF SEX CHARACTERS

In a number of instances, parasites effect destruction of the gonads of the host. Those stages of digenetic trematodes which undergo polyembryony in mollusks are known to destroy all or portions of the gonads. In some cases this is attributed to the actual devouring of tissue by the parasite, while in others it is considered to be largely a physiological effect due to the nutritional demands of the parasite or elaboration of inhibitory chemical products by the parasite. There is some evidence that infection with larval trematodes may induce sex reversal in certain mollusks.

The parasitic crustacean *Sacculina* produces a rather remarkable effect on the host, a crab (Figs. 2–9 and 2–10). When male crabs are parasitized by *Sacculina*, the secondary sex characteristics of the

[handwritten margin note, left:] Digenea — life cycle includes 3 or 4 successive larval stages and up to 4 different hosts.

Monogenea: class w/out intermediate hosts mainly ectoparasitic

[handwritten margin note, right:] larvae are free swimming (recognizably crustacean) St. Cirripedia (barnacles) g. Sacculina

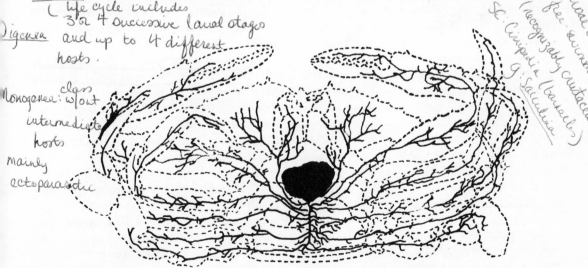

Fig. 2–9 *Sacculina,* a crustacean parasite of crustaceans. The parasite is drawn with solid lines and the host outlined in broken lines. (Adapted from Smith, 1906.)

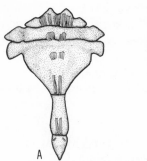
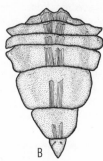

A   B

Fig. 2–10 The effects on male crabs (*Cal-linectes*) of parasitism by a sacculinid crus-tacean (*Loxothylacus texanus*). A. Abdomen of a normal male *Callinectes* showing dorsal muscles and fusion of segments. B. Abdomen of a male parasitized by *Loxothylacus*. Its musculature and segmentation are like those of a normal female. (Redrawn from Reinhard, 1950, *Biol. Bull.*)

crab are modified. The abdomen assumes the shape seen in the female crab, egg-bear-ing appendages appear, and the claws un-dergo modification. Endocrine balance is obviously upset. If the parasitism is inter-rupted early enough, the male crab may regain its sexual function; but, in this al-tered state, it may also gain female func-tion and become hermaphroditic. On the other hand, if a female crab is parasitized, the ovary is destroyed; and when the para-site leaves the host, sexual function is not resumed (see Day, 1935). There is some evidence that in a male host there is com-pensatory tissue hypertrophy and subse-quent disappearance of the androgenic hormone or the secretion of an inhibitor which interferes with hormone production in the androgenic gland (Charniaux-Cot-ton, 1962).

Similar castration effects are known among the insects, for example, the squash bug, *Anasa*, when parasitized by a tachinid fly, *Trichopoda*, suffers a degeneration of the reproductive organs. The maggot of the parasite attaches itself to the tracheae

of the host on either the right or left side. The only apparent injury involves the re-productive organs. In these organs a pro-gressive atrophy occurs, being confined at first to the gonad on the side to which the parasite is attached. Eventually the other gonad shows evidence of degeneration. If the early parasite is surgically removed, the single degenerating gonad does not recover, although the intact gonad develops nor-mally. The affected ovary shrinks and un-dergoes degeneration. This atrophy is not due to mechanical injury since the parasite is not in contact with the gonad. There are other parasitic arthropods producing similar effects in invertebrate hosts (Beard, 1940; Doutt, 1963).

Among insect hosts, various symbiotes are known to produce changes in secondary sex characteristics. The symbiotes include protozoans, nematodes, and insects (strep-sipterans, hymenopterans, and dipterans). In many cases direct mechanical damage to the gonads does not seem to be involved, but the mechanisms of symbiote effects are not well understood (Wülker, 1964). One of the most astonishing parasitisms involves an isopod crustacean, *Liriopsis pygmaea*, which causes atrophy of the ovary of its cir-ripede crustacean host, *Peltogaster*, which is itself a parasite of a hermit crab, *Pagurus*, and causes a castration of the crab (Smith, 1906).

Among vertebrates, a few examples of the effects of symbiotes on gonadal function have been recorded. Arme (1968) has shown that the larval tapeworm *Ligula intestinalis* living in the body cavity of fishes produces a functional sterility of the host. Oogenesis or spermatogenesis is ar-rested and observable changes in the hy-pophysis suggest that the effect probably involves an interference with the normal gonadotropic function of that organ. Sur-prisingly, the closely related worm *Schisto-cephalus* does not produce this kind of effect, even in heavy infections (Fig. 2–11).

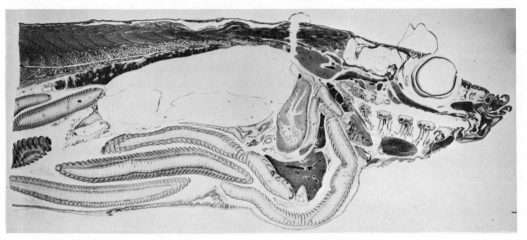

Fig. 2–11 Section through a fish (*Gasterosteus aculeatus*) infected with plerocercoid larvae of the tapeworm *Schistocephalus solidus*. (Courtesy of Dr. C. Arme and *Parasitology*.)

ENDOCRINE SUBSTANCES PRODUCED BY PARASITES

In a few cases it has been shown that parasitic organisms produce substances which are identical in physiological activity with hormones produced by the host. The excess hormone of parasite origin may be involved in producing a disease associated with the parasitism.

One of the best worked-out relationships of this type is seen in a rice plant disease known in Japan as "Bakanae." Sixty-five years ago it was shown that the disease is caused by a fungus of the genus *Gibberella*. A striking characteristic of infected plants is an unusual degree of growth, the tall, spindly, diseased plants being readily seen in a field. In 1926, Kurosawa showed that sterile filtrates of *Gibberella* cultures would cause the peculiar overgrowth of plant stems. However, later studies showed that some fungus strains caused retardation of growth rather than stimulation. It was shown that the growth-retarding substance was fusaric acid, a toxic substance produced by plant pathogens (p. 27). The growth-stimulating substance was named "gibberellin" by Yabuta. There was much fur-

ther work on gibberellin during World War II, but much of the information did not become available in the United States until 1950. Since 1950, work in Japan, Britain, and the United States has resulted in the isolation and characterization of several gibberellins (see Stodola, 1958). Further, it has now been established that these are natural hormones of higher plants (MacMillan and Suter, 1958). This, then, is a disease in which at least one of the characteristics is attributable to the production of an excess quantity of a plant growth hormone by a parasite.

In several relationships involving insects and their parasites, there is evidence that parasite-produced hormones are involved in producing abnormalities of host development (see Fisher, 1963). The ichneumon fly, *Diplazon*, causes premature pupation of its arthropod host by secretion of excess molting hormone (Schneider, 1951). More recently, Fisher and Sanborn (1963) have studied the effects of a protozoan, *Nosema*, on certain insect hosts. Infected grain beetle larvae pass through a number of extra molts and attain much larger size than unparasitized animals. This observation suggested that the parasite might produce a substance with juvenile hormone activity or induce the host to produce excess amounts of juvenile hormone. To study this experimentally, Fisher and Sanborn surgically removed the corpora allata from roaches. This treatment results in cessation of juvenile hormone production, and at the next molt such insects have adultoid characteristics. When *Nosema* was transplanted into allatectomized roaches, development of adultoid characteristics at the molt was prevented. When parasites were confined in a small chamber opening into the hemocoele or separated from the hemocoele by a very fine filter, the allatectomized nymphs did not develop adultoid characteristics at the molt but remained nymphal. Further, it was shown that extracts of *Nosema* spores have juvenile hormone activity in tests on cercropia moths and on allatectomized roaches. These observations strongly indicate that *Nosema* produces juvenile hormone or at least manufactures a substance having such biological activity.

Attention may be directed to observations of Mueller (1963), who showed that, with moderate infections of the larval tapeworm *Spirometra,* mice become quite obese. This phenomenon may involve an endocrine relationship. Harlow and Mertz (1967) showed that the larva of *Spirometra* contain an agent which stimulates glucose utilization and lipogenesis in rat tissue. The observation that the entry of sugar into cells was increased suggested that the site of action may be the cell membrane.

MODIFICATION OF METABOLISM

In addition to those cases already mentioned, there are other instances in which intracellular symbiotes alter the metabolism of the host cell. In the lytic bacterial viruses, host-cell metabolism is grossly altered during the early phases of virus development (see Stent, 1963, and p. 208). Of particular interest is the finding that

a bacterial virus containing 5-hydroxymethyl cytosine in its nucleic acid causes the appearance in its host cell of the enzyme, deoxycytidylate hydroxymethylase. The enzyme is necessary for the synthesis of virus nucleic acid but is not normally present in the host cell. It can be detected 2 minutes after infection (Flaks et al., 1959). Several of the neurotropic viruses of animals stimulate the incorporation of radiophosphate into brain tissue (Kimura et al., 1955). Monkey kidney tissue in culture shows a stimulation of energy metabolism after it is infected with polio virus and before any new virus is formed (Levy and Baron, 1957). Similar observations have been made with embryo chick tissues and rabbit myxoma organisms. At least one of the enzymes of glycolysis in embryo tissues is increased after infection with any one of seven animal viruses. A great variety of enzyme changes have been recorded in plant tissues after infection with intracellular symbiotes (see review by Uritani and Akazawa, 1959).

CHEMICAL COMPETITION

In addition to chemical injury by toxic effects or by feeding directly on host substance, there are a few recognized instances in which parasites compete with the host for available food materials after food has entered the host's body but before it has been assimilated into host tissue.

It has been recognized for a considerable time that certain humans infected with the broad tapeworm, *Dibothriocephalus,* develop an anemia which is indistinguishable from the non-parasitic disease known as pernicious anemia. Various suggestions were made concerning the mechanism by which the tapeworm might produce this effect. One such suggestion by Chandler was that the worm may absorb some vitamin which is important in the normal formation of blood cells. Careful researches carried out by Bonsdorff and his associates in Finland have demonstrated that this is indeed the correct explanation. The broad tapeworms compete with their hosts for vitamin B_{12}, a cobalt compound which is now known to be necessary for normal production of red blood cells. It is important to note that not all humans infected with this worm show anemia. This point will be discussed further in connection with susceptibility (p. 73). It is of interest that other species of tapeworms are not known to precipitate pernicious anemia. Nyberg (1958, 1963) has shown that the explanation is that *Dibothriocephalus* has an unusually high affinity for the vitamin. Correlated with this is the observation that *Dibothriocephalus* contains more vitamin B_{12} in its tissue than other helminths examined. In many other parasitisms involving helminths, symptoms suggest that vitamin deficiencies may be involved, but there is no clear-cut evidence implicating the worms as precipitating agents.

Competition and Disease

Under the term "competition" we might also include a variety of instances in which a parasite devours host body components at such a high rate that it interferes with the functioning of the host. In a given host without the parasite there is a characteristic quantitative level of synthesis of particular body constituents. If a parasite enters a host and feeds on tissues, such as the blood, the host must be able to make up the deficit if a state of health is to be maintained. As the intensity of infection increases, it is a matter of simple arithmetic that the host is required to make up the deficit to an increasing extent. In many hosts in a state of good nutrition, it is often astonishing to what size such deficits may grow before the appearance of symptoms of disturbed body chemistry. In hosts in a more limited nutritional state, the presence of parasites above a certain level cannot be

handled by the body, and symptoms of chemical distress appear.

In some cases, this robbing of host tissue may be fairly generalized. In hookworm and *Haemonchus* infections (see pp. 92 and 96), the worms literally remove blood from the host mucosa. Some of the materials seem to pass through the body of the hookworm and may be resorbed by the intestinal mucosa. There is considerable evidence, however, that the vitally important material, hemoglobin, and perhaps other protein constituents, are not recovered completely by the host. In a host on a diet which is inadequate or barely adequate, the presence of hookworms may push the individual over into a deepened state of malnutrition, and a nutritional anemia will make its appearance. Obviously, the *number* of hookworms in such an individual becomes a very important consideration. Furthermore, the loss of protein may have important effects in determining the resistance of the host to the parasite. (This matter is discussed further on page 84.)

In addition to the direct devouring of host tissue, as in the blood-sucking activities of hookworms, the body stores may be robbed in more subtle ways. In the intestinal tract of the vertebrate, there is a constant secretion of materials which may be visualized as a part of the body protein. This includes the digestive enzymes and the nitrogenous materials of intestinal juice. There is evidence that much of this secreted material is normally resorbed in the digestive tract. A parasite which lives in the intestine and which does not feed on tissues nevertheless has access to those secreted materials as well as to the food ingested by the host. Such parasites as ascarid nematodes and tapeworms undoubtedly fulfill a large part of their nutritional requirements from this exocrinoenteric circulation. Hosts on a poor diet continue to secrete and resorb nitrogenous materials, and parasites in the lumen are not deprived of food. In the case of *Ascaris*, the amount removed may be enough to push the individual over into a state of protein malnutrition (see also p. 70).

PARASITOID RELATIONSHIPS

Many insects are subject to a peculiar form of predation by other insects. Most of these relationships involve the deposition of eggs by a female insect in or on an insect of another species. Typically, the eggs hatch and the "host" is devoured from inside. The predator species is referred to as *parasitoid*, but the relationship could also be termed delayed predation. Most parasitoids are hymenopteran insects, usually wasps, and the prey, in many instances, are symbiotes of plants. These latter relationships may resemble hypersymbiosis (discussed on p. 61). Doutt (1963) has reviewed the pathology produced by various parasitoid species, and Berg (1964) has presented a thorough discussion of the terms *parasite* and *parasitoid*.

digger wasps

TRANSMISSION OF INFECTIOUS AGENTS

Numbers of viral, bacterial, fungal, protozoan, and helminth parasites of animals and plants are transmitted from one host to another by parasitic arthropods, particularly members of the orders Insecta and Acarina. The special relationships of some of these arthropod-transmitted parasites are discussed in Chapter 5. Within the past ten years, it has begun to be appreciated that the arthropods do not have a monopoly on transmission of other parasites.

In several instances helminth parasites have been shown to be involved in transmitting some other species of parasite to a vertebrate host. There is some evidence that the fowl nematode *Heterakis* transmits the protozoan *Histomonas*, which is evidently incorporated into the shelled embryo of the worm. A rickettsial disease of dogs is apparently transmitted by the trematode

Nanophyetus. The nematodes known as lungworms transmit or precipitate influenza in swine. *Trichinella* will transmit lymphocytic chorio-meningitis virus to rodents. Some recent evidence indicates that nematodes parasitic on plants may transmit bacterial, fungal, and viral infections.

Special mention may be made of an association between a fungus parasite of plants and the tobacco necrosis virus. The virus particles may be incorporated into the zoospores of the fungus and thus be transmitted from infected to uninfected plants. Other associations of this type should be sought (Teakle, 1962; Kassanis and MacFarlane, 1965).

localized tissue death

EFFECTS IN LOWERING RESISTANCE

One of the facets of parasitism that is most difficult to analyze is the lowering of resistance to other parasitic agents. In parasitisms in which the external tissues— e.g., skin—are wounded, the wound represents a potential site for entry and establishment of bacterial parasites. A number of animal parasites, such as the protozoan *Schizotrypanum cruzi*, habitually enter the host through a bite wound made by an arthropod such as a triatomid bug, in which the parasite has developed (pp. 100 and 104). Wounding of the intestinal mucosa by endoparasites also creates possible entry points for protistan parasites.

multiple symbiotic series is host to smaller symbiote

Mechanical damage and resulting cell death may allow the proliferation and production of diseases by agents already present. For example, the damage to the liver of sheep by the trematode *Fasciola hepatica* may allow development of spores of the anaerobic bacterium *Clostridium oedematiens*, already present in the liver. The bacteria then produce what is called "black disease," which affects sheep in England and Scotland.

In producing pathology, parasitic organisms tend to reduce the capacity of the host to develop resistance mechanisms (see p. 70). Scrimshaw et al. (1959) have pointed out the need for study of the effects of parasitism on host nutrition. This admonition is pertinent to the present considerations because it is recognized that lowered nutritional status generally results in lowered resistance (p. 84).

TIME AND DISEASE

It has long been recognized that certain parasitic organisms characteristically produce disease if the host is infected at a certain time in its life span. We are all familiar with what are called the diseases of childhood. Sometimes they can be attributed to the development of mechanisms of resistance through contraction of the disease. This will be discussed further in Chapter 4. However, in other cases there is actually a differential effect associated with age which cannot be attributed to previous contact with the parasite. Parasitologists take advantage of the fact that young animals can sometimes be infected in the laboratory with species of parasites to which the adult animal of the same species is completely refractory. Kittens, for example, can readily be infected with the dysentery ameba, whereas adult cats are extremely resistant to infection with this parasite. We have little understanding of such phenomena, although some work of Ackert and his colleagues must be mentioned (references in Read, 1950). These workers showed that the resistance to initial infection of chickens with a nematode parasite, *Ascaridia galli*, increases with age. This resistance is correlated with the increase in the number of goblet cells in the digestive tract of the birds; and Ackert and his associates actually showed that mucus, presumably from goblet cells, is toxic to the worm. The chemical nature of the toxic substance has not been elucidated.

Mention must be made of the fact that very young animals are also quite often resistant to parasitic agents. In some instances, this has been shown to be due to the passage of protective substances in the milk of the mother or in the yolk of the egg in the case of birds. However, that this mechanism is not always involved was shown by study of the insusceptibility of nursing rodents to the malaria parasite, *Plasmodium berghei*. It was shown by Hawking (1954) and others that young rodents are protected from the parasite by the fact that the milk is quite deficient in p-aminobenzoic acid, which the parasite requires for growth. Ingenious experiments in which the nipples of the mother animals were smeared with p-aminobenzoic acid showed that addition of the vitamin allowed the parasite to grow in young animals and produce disease (see also p. 160).

Among plant hosts, insusceptibility associated with age is quite common. There are a number of instances in which parasitism and ensuing disease can only occur if plants are infected during a very particular state of growth. For example, stage-specific susceptibility of wheat to the stem rust fungus, *Puccinia graminis*, has been known for about seventy-five years. Lines of wheat which are markedly susceptible as seedlings may show marked insusceptibility as mature plants. It gradually became common knowledge among plant pathologists that the insusceptibility of mature wheat plants and of seedling wheat was inherited independently (Walker, 1957). Yarwood (1959) cites many other examples of stage-specific susceptibility in plants (see also p. 258).

THE BENEFITS OF DISEASE

We do not ordinarily think of disease agents as having effects which can be construed as beneficial; we tend to think of disease in reference to ourselves or to our domestic animals. However, it is important to recognize that disease produced by parasitic agents is not restricted in this fashion. Among populations of "wild" animals, disease has effects on populations which may be likened to the effects of predators. The removal of the usual regulators of population numbers may have quite disastrous long-range effects. For example, it may be shown quite easily that in theory the removal of predation and disease in certain wild populations would result in such a rapid increase in numbers that the food supply of a given species would soon be limiting and starvation would ensue. As a matter of fact, we now have many very good examples of such effects when predators have been removed. The indiscriminate killing of wolves in North America has created very real problems for deer populations, which have difficulty in getting enough to eat because there are *too many* deer.

In some cases, the disease produced by a parasite (or parasites) may save the situation. For example, if the predators are removed, populations of hosts tend to increase quite rapidly. The resulting increase in the density of potential hosts may allow transmission of parasitic agents at a higher rate and result in the appearance of more disease. In addition, there is evidence that the increase in population sets up what are known as stress reactions in the hosts and may render them more susceptible to the attacks of parasitic agents. (This subject is discussed further on page 261.) All of these factors operating together may result in sufficient disease to prevent the destruction of the hosts' food supply and may ultimately result in saving the host species from extinction.

Among domestic animals, it has been pointed out that disease attributed to animal parasites may serve to eliminate constitutionally inferior animals before they attain reproductive age. Whitlock (1962) has pointed out that the blood loss in sheep infected with the nematode *Haemonchus* may even have a physiological advantage in warm wet climates.

GENERAL REMARKS

It may be seen that the specificity of disease-producing mechanisms will determine the overall character of the entity which may be diagnostically recognized as "Disease A" or as "Disease B." The possible number of mechanism combinations is very large indeed since it will depend not only on the actions of the symbiote but also on the reactions of the host. Other host reactions are discussed in Chapter 4.

As will be apparent, disease is not necessarily a "bad" state of affairs. In many instances, it appears to have adaptive value for populations, particularly animal populations, and may serve as a mechanism for natural selection.

SUGGESTED READING

BAWDEN, F. C. 1964. *Plant Viruses and Virus Diseases* (4th ed.). The Ronald Press Company, New York.

BURNET, M. 1966. *Natural History of Infectious Disease*, 3rd Ed. Cambridge University Press, New York.

BURNET, F. M., and W. M. STANLEY (eds.). 1959. *The Viruses*. Academic Press, New York.

CARPENTER, P. L. 1965. *Immunology and Serology*. W. B. Saunders Co., Philadelphia.

DUBOS, R. 1954.

FELT, E. P. 1940.

FIENNES, R. 1965. *Man, Nature and Disease*. New American Library, New York.

FISHER, F. M., JR. 1963.

GRESHAM, G. A., and A. R. JENNINGS. 1962. *An Introduction to Comparative Pathology*. Academic Press, New York.

HORSFALL, J. G., and A. E. DIMOND (eds.). 1959. *Plant Pathology*. Academic Press, New York.

HOWIE, J. W., and A. J. O'HEA (eds.). 1955. *Mechanisms of Microbial Pathogenicity*. Cambridge University Press, New York.

RACKER, E. 1954.

REINHARD, E. G. 1956.

SMITH, H. 1968. Biochemical challenge of microbial pathogenicity. *Bacteriol. Rev.* 32:164–84.

SMITH, T. 1934. *Parasitism and Disease*. Princeton University Press, Princeton, N.J.

SMITH, W. (ed.). 1963. *Mechanisms of Virus Infection*. Academic Press, New York.

WALKER, J. C. 1957.

WRIGHT, C. A. 1966. The pathogenesis of helminths in the Mollusca. *Helminth. Abstr.* 35: 207.

3

Symbiosis Without Disease

The living world furnishes quite an astonishing variety of examples of two or more species of organisms living together in varying degrees of intimacy with negligible evidences of disease resulting from the associations. The degree of integration, or what might be termed physiological intertwining, in these associations seems to vary from highly complex physical and chemical relationships, with the resulting appearance of many new features not characteristic of either partner, to quite simple integrations in which few—perhaps even a negligible number—new properties seem to result from the association. As a matter of fact, it is possible to interpret disease itself as simply one special type of manifestation of integration (or lack thereof) between a host and a symbiote. As will become apparent, both host and symbiote are participants in the genesis of disease. The symbiote acts and the host reacts. The overall effect is that the host is harmed in the relationship.

It is difficult to find a very strong justification for treating disease as an outside special feature of symbiosis, and it may be argued that it is an overemphasis resulting from our tendency to refer things to ourselves. However, disease has been regarded as something more than that and may merit special treatment. We can leave the question open for the moment since it will become apparent that these relationships may be looked at from more than one point of view and differences in treatment are not truly mutually exclusive. In this chapter we shall try to briefly review some relationships in which disease is not a prominent feature. As will also become apparent, a number of cases have been freely cited as interesting examples from various areas of symbiology without particular regard to the taxonomic position of the organisms involved.

METHODS OF STUDY

Any study of these relationships might be carried out by one of several plans. Historically, they have often been arranged according to the taxonomy of the symbiotes. Occasionally, they have been arranged according to the host, in veterinary parasitology, for example. In other instances, they have been arranged in terms of the presumed reciprocity of benefits, or the lack thereof. (Table 1–1 is of this type.) It may be desirable to arrange the relationships according to what appears to be the complexity of interaction of organisms in symbiosis. This analysis is difficult to make in a systematic fashion because of rather glaring deficiencies in our knowledge of most of the associations in which disease is not a feature. Such relationships have simply attracted less scientific attention. In the ensuing discussion, relationships have been roughly grouped as follows: (1) simple integration, in which the interaction between the partners has a relatively low order of complexity; (2) intermediate integration, in which a moderate degree of functional interrelationship is apparent. Many of the relationships of this second type are obligate for the symbiote, but the host may be little altered by the association; (3) complex integration, in which there is a high degree of incorporation of function, and the symbiosis shows many new properties not observed in its separable components.

It may be that some currently regarded as simple or intermediate integrations may not be simple at all, and it is to be hoped that future work will clarify such cases. In attempting to discuss functional integration, grouped in this fashion, it immediately becomes obvious that it is most simple to discuss the extremes, that is, the simple and complex integrations. These are the ones that are the most clear-cut and, since they are the extremes, are most easily distinguished one from another. For this reason, in most of our discussion below, we shall deal with simple or complex integrations.

SIMPLE INTEGRATION

Loose associations (in the physiological sense), involving bodily contact but a rather low order of integration, are extremely common. A close examination of the bed of organisms living on pilings or rocks at the seashore will often reveal myriads of species in close association. Although many of these are obviously related to each other as prey and predator, many are not. Any large sponge or piece of coral

taken from the sea will show worms, crustaceans, nematodes, and various other organisms living in tubes or cracks or on the surface. Most of these seem to have negligible effects on the "host" and are probably not physiologically integrated to a significant extent with the host.

The dorsal surfaces of many species of organisms, such as spider crabs, are commonly covered with a veritable forest of living plants, hydroids, sponges, and other small organisms. It has been assumed in the past that some of these are actually placed in position by the crabs and, at least in the case of spider crabs, the associates belong to species which are commonly not associated with other hosts. Although some of these crabs may occasionally browse on their symbiotes, there seems to be no real evidence that the symbiotes are of any specialized particular nutritional significance to the host. It has also been asserted that the sessile associates may serve to camouflage spider crabs. Again, this view may be anthropocentric. This type of association may have a physiological significance of the same order as seen in the case of a worm hiding in a tube in a sponge. An amazing example of a loose association is the green alga which lives on the long grooved hairs of sloths, often being sufficiently abundant to impart a greenish color to the animal. Similarly, the green alga *Basicladia* grows only on the backs of freshwater turtles. In this latter case, the alga seems to require keratin for growth; and this protein is in fact a major constituent of turtle shells (Leake, 1939).

In some cases a low order of physiological integration is more apparent than in those instances mentioned above. Classical examples frequently cited are the associations between species of hermit crabs and anemones (Fig. 3–1). Some of these show definite interaction. There may be actual sharing of food or protection of the crab by an anemone, which has secreted a foot, causing a functional prolongation of the shell.

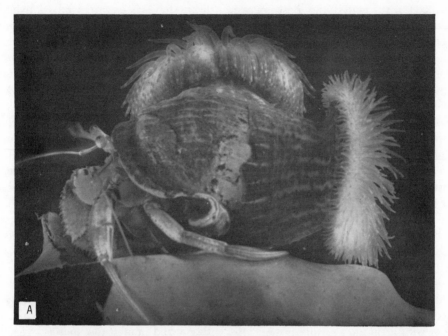

Fig. 3-1 Associations of hermit crabs and anemones. (A) *Calliactis parasitica* on a shell inhabited by the hermit crab, *Pagurus bernhardus,* from the English Channel. (B) *Calliactis polypus* on a shell inhabited by the crab, *Dardanus gemmatus,* from Hawaii. The crab is prodding another *Calliactis* on a stone. This is the first stage in a behavior pattern by which the anemone is transferred to the shell. (Photographs by courtesy of Dr. D. M. Ross, University of Alberta.)

Ross (1960) investigated the best known of these relationships, that between the European hermit crab, *Eupagurus bernhardus,* and the sea anemone, *Calliactis parasitica.* The anemone plays the major role in consummating the relationship. When an unattached anemone contacts a shell occupied by *E. bernhardus,* the tentacles explore the shell briefly and adhere to it. The oral disc of the coelenterate is then applied to the shell, operating as a sucker and firmly anchoring it to the host shell. This is followed by a slow bending of the body column and an attachment of the pedal disc to the shell. After the pedal disc is firmly anchored, the tentacles and oral disc release their hold on the shell and the animal assumes its normal extended posture. The entire operation represents an amazingly coordinated behavior pattern for an organism with a simple nervous system. In an association between a crab *Hepatus* and an anemone, the cnidarian is reported to initiate the association, literally climbing onto the back of the host (Burger, 1903).

A number of species of annelids live in association with echinoderms and crustaceans, and the behavioral responses of these symbiotes to substances which are associated with their specific host demonstrate that there is indeed some physiological integration in these associations (see p. 118). One of the most astonishing associations is that of the crab *Melia* with certain anemones. The crab actually carries an anemone in each of its chelipeds. The crab apparently "uses" the anemones to capture food and the coelenterates probably serve a defensive function (Duerden, 1905).

Some very interesting relationships involving fishes and certain invertebrates have been described. A small fish, *Carapus acus,* is known to live in the intestine or respiratory chamber of sea cucumbers, emerging for short intervals to feed (Fig. 3–2). The sea cucumber tolerates its uninvited guest without any obvious inconvenience. In several other instances small fishes have been reported to live in close association with large sea anemones; the very complex behavioral conditioning involved in the development of tolerance by the symbiotes and hosts has been described by Davenport and Norris (1958). Similarly, small fishes are constantly associated with the pelagic, colonial coelenterate *Physalia,* and some fishes and amphipods live in the umbrellas of large jelly fishes. There are obvious behavioral integrations in such relationships, although these have rarely been studied in any detail. Dales (1966) has reviewed a variety of such associations among marine organisms.

Insects and Their Ectosymbiotes

Many insects have loose ectosymbiotic relationships with other organisms. Among the wood-inhabiting insects, many have such relations with microorganisms, which most often are yeasts or fungi. These relationships take different forms.

Among the ambrosia beetles, the insects tunnel in trees but feed mainly on fungi which are cultivated in the galleries ex-

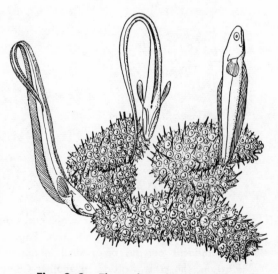

Fig. 3–2 The endosymbiotic fish *Carapus,* which enters and leaves through the cloaca of its sea-cucumber host. (Redrawn from Emery.)

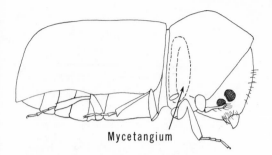

Mycetangium

Fig. 3–3 A female ambrosia beetle, *Xyloterus,* showing the fungus sac (mycetangium) in the thorax. (Modified from Francke-Grosmann, 1967.)

cavated in the wood. There is evidence that neither the fungi nor the beetles can live in wood without each other. The transmission of fungi from one host plant to another is effected by storage of the fungus spores in bag-like sacs of ectodermal origin in the thorax of the beetle associate (Fig. 3–3). Bark beetles sometimes have similar fungus-bearing organs. Special mention may be made of the association between elm bark beetles and *Ceratocystis ulmi,* the pathogenic fungus involved in Dutch elm disease. The fungus is transmitted to healthy trees by the beetle and, because of the lethal effect of *C. ulmi* on the host tree, it accelerates the growth of beetle populations.

In the beetles known as ship timber worms, pouches associated with the ovipositor serve as organs for the storage of fungus spores. The fungi are transmitted to the young beetles by contamination of the eggs during oviposition. Similarly, among the wood wasps whose larval forms develop in trees or fresh cut logs, the fungal associates of the larvae are injected into the wood along with the egg. These and similar associations have been discussed by Francke-Grosmann (in Henry, 1967).

The social ants harbor an astonishing variety of symbiotes, which typically share the ant nest. These include mites, spiders,

bristletails (Thysanura), isopods, crickets, cockroaches, aphids, scale insects, leaf hoppers, flies, lepidopteran caterpillars, beetles, and other species of ants.

The associations of ants and aphids (plant lice) are probably the most publicized. The aphids excrete a clear liquid, honeydew, which is rich in nutrients, particularly sugars (Gray and Fraenkel, 1954). Ants feed on this material and in turn furnish protection to their aphid symbiotes. Similar relationships between ants and scale insects are known, the latter producing honeydew, referred to in the Bible as "manna" (Bodenheimer, 1951).

Certain ants live in mutualistic relationship with certain fungi. The fungi are furnished with food by the ants who also appear to remove other microorganisms which might compete with the symbiote species. In turn, portions of fungi are eaten by the ants. Weber (1957) has carried out experimental studies of one of these symbioses and has shown that fungi other than the species usually in association are not acceptable to the ants.

In some ants of the North Temperate Zone, the habit of slave-making—the capture and enslavement of other species of ants—is well developed. In some cases, functions have been transferred to the slaves to such an extent that the slave-maker species is completely dependent on the slaves. This has been referred to as social parasitism but may actually be mutualism. In the slave-making Amazon ant *Polyergus,* the mandibles are so modified that the animal depends on a slave species of the genus *Formica* to feed it (Fig. 3–4). Some of the symbiotes of ants do appear to have rudimentary parasitic relationships with their hosts. The association of the larval fly *Metopina pachycondylae* with its ant host *Pachycondyla vorax* is a case in point. The larval fly fastens itself by a posterior disc to the anterior end of an ant larva. The symbiote bends its body around that of the host, forming a collar

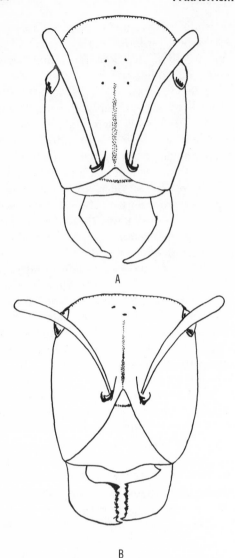

A

B

Fig. 3–4 The heads of the slavemaker ant, *Polygerus rufescens* (A), and its slave ant, *Formica fusca* (B). The mandibles of *Polygerus* have lost their cutting edge; the slavemakers are completely dependent on *Formica* or other slave species to feed them. (Redrawn from Bondroit.)

(Fig. 3–5). When a worker ant presents food to the larval ant, the symbiote extends its head and is fed. The ant workers treat the fly larva as though it were an ant, cleaning and grooming the symbiote along with the larval host (Wheeler, 1901).

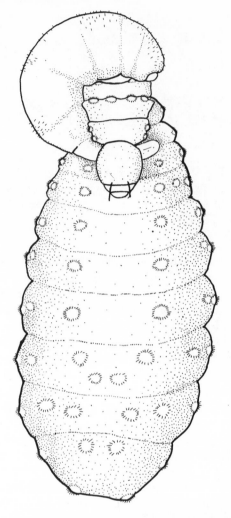

Fig. 3–5 A larval ant, *Pachycondyla vorax*, bearing the fly larva, *Metopina pachycondylae*. (Redrawn from Wheeler, 1901.)

Cleaning Symbioses

There is a class of simple integrations in which one of the associates cleans the other, removing dead tissue, bacteria, fungi, and animal ectoparasites. The behavior of the cleaning organisms varies from very simple to complex but the physiological integration is of a low order. Many species of fishes serve as "hosts" and about forty-five species of fish are known to serve as cleaners. A half dozen or so species of shrimps and at least one crab are known to act as cleaners of fish. In some cases, the cleaner species stays in one spot and is regularly visited by various species of fish which may wait their turn to be cleaned. These relationships have been reviewed by Feder (1966).

Although apparently less common among terrestrial animals, similar cleaning symbiosis is known. Pseudoscorpions, for example, have been reported to clean reptiles and large insects. One of the best known of such relationships is that of a bird, the African oxpecker (*Buphagus*), with large game animals such as buffalo, rhinoceros, giraffe, and various antelopes. The bird removes ticks and lice from the host animals and also serves as a sort of warning system, emitting alarm notes at the approach of the host's enemies (Moreau, 1933).

The Egyptian plover cleans ectoparasites from the surface of crocodiles and has even been reported to enter the open mouths of these reptiles and pick leeches from between the teeth.

INTERMEDIATE INTEGRATION

Large numbers of symbiotic associations seem to fall within our arbitrary category of intermediate integration. When these associations are considered in detail, the difficulties involved in applying such terms as mutualism, commensalism, or parasitism to specific cases become obvious. For example, while we stated that both partners derive benefit from the association in mutualism, it is often difficult to distinguish such relationships from parasitisms. Mutual beneficence may be at the molecular level, with each partner furnishing a valuable chemical to the other or furnishing some substitute for a homeostatic mechanism. If we fail to detect the fact that one partner provides some benefit to the other, we classify the relationship as parasitism. Clearly, in parasitism the host participates in the association, furnishing the symbiote with substances necessary for survival. The host also makes various adjustments in response to the parasite. These physiological responses are integrative in character, although they may appear to be quite different in significance when treated in anthropocentric terms as "contracts" between two parties. Our definitions require that we know something of a given relationship on a profit-loss basis.

Parasitologists have tended to claim certain groups of symbiotes as parasites, although in many of these cases the clauses in the contracts are not known. One reason for this is that if some members of a large taxonomic group of symbiotes are implicated as producing harm in hosts, the remaining symbiotic members have been assumed to be parasitic—a case of guilt by association. The flatworms are a good example; very few parasitologists would care to entertain the notion that many digenetic trematodes may have mutualistic relationships with vertebrates, although they would be forced to admit that only a small minority have been shown to produce evident pathology (and are thus presumably parasitic). Even species which cause disease may do so only at times.

It is tempting also to make the assumption that, in what may appear to be parasitism, the symbiote requires the association. However, as already indicated (p. 7), we know of many parasitic organisms which seem to be facultatively so. On the other hand, we may find cases which clearly seem to be instances of mutualism in which the symbiote cannot live without the host; these become difficult to distinguish from parasitism. The obligateness of the relationship, then, does not appear to be the most valuable criterion as to the terms of the contract. What the foregoing seems to lead to is the conclusion that significant aspects of the relationships may be found in determining the level of integration rather than the degree to which the physiological exchange may be mutually beneficial. Failure of the mechanisms of integration may result in what we call disease, and the failure itself, or rather the events resulting in such failure, have considerable interest, as pointed out later.

Intermediate integration may be examined from other standpoints, from that of feedback mechanisms, for example, from which it becomes very obvious that host reaction in this sense must be involved in the maintenance of the new entity that the host-symbiote system represents. In all those cases in which chemical pathology is not present, the host *must* make physiological compensations for the presence and the demands of the symbiote. Since many of the relationships dealt with in other portions of this book are in the category of intermediate integration, further examples will not be cited in this chapter.

THE NATURE OF COMPLEX INTEGRATION

Under this heading we may place a large number of associations in which the functional relationships are several, and in which the symbiosis shows properties that are new and characteristic of the association rather than of either organism separately. In some cases the integration even involves interaction of the genetic components of members of the association. In the most complex of these relationships, the symbiote is intracellular. We may examine a few examples of these relationships to obtain an idea of integrative complexity. However, it should be borne in mind that many of these have been inadequately analyzed, in that we cannot obtain as yet a full evaluation of the degree of integration.

PHOTOSYNTHETIC SYMBIOTES

In a wide variety of instances, photosynthetic organisms are associated in symbiosis with heterotrophic plants or animals. Yonge (1944) reviewed a number of cases involving invertebrate hosts. In most instances the animals involved are those which typically have intracellular digestion. This might imply that a frequent requisite for the establishment of symbiosis

in these cases is resistance of the symbiote to digestion by the host.

Zooxanthellae

Among marine animals the protistans that are most often involved have been called zooxanthellae and are usually yellow or brown in color. The zooxanthellae are widely distributed in invertebrates, particularly in the warmer oceans of the world. They are abundant in the endoderm of the tentacles of coral zooids and other coelenterates, in radiolarian protozoans, and even in some mollusks. In the coelenterates it is known that the symbiotes are transmitted from the parent to the planula larvae. In 1944, Kawaguti cultured zooxanthellae from a coral and showed that they were identical with dinoflagellate protistans. McLaughlin and Zahl (1959) cultured three species from coelenterates and these have also proven to be protistans of the dinoflagellate group (see also Freudenthal, 1962).

Some of the most impressive monuments to symbiosis are the frequently immense marine structures known as coral reefs. The coelenterates responsible for the erection of these structures, as well as some other coelenterates, harbor the unicellular tissue symbiotes discussed above, the zooxanthellae. The precise nature of the relationships of these symbiotes to their hosts has not been clearly understood. They seem to possess photosynthetic pigments, but there have been differences of opinion concerning the extent to which the host may benefit from the associations. The studies of Sargent and Austin (1954), the Odums (1955), and the Goreaus (1960) indicate that the physiology of coral coelenterates and their contained zooxanthellae may be closely integrated, leading to increased metabolic efficiency in warm oceans, which tend to be poor in nutrients. McLaughlin and Zahl (1959; 1966) pointed out that the complexities involved in the coral structure are not completely resolved and warn against making generalizations at this point.

Symbiotes and Giant Clams

Some very interesting modifications for symbiosis have been described in the giant tropical clams of the family Tridacnidae. These clams have a greatly thickened and laterally extended mantle edge which contains vast numbers of zooxanthellae (Fig. 3–6). The edge of the mantle with its

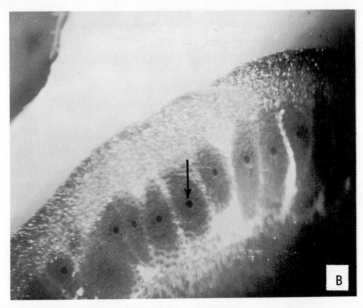

Fig. 3–6 *Tridacna maxima* Röding, from Eniwetok Atoll, Marshall Islands. *A*, a dorsal view of the animal with the mantle expanded. *B*, the edge of the mantle, showing the hyaline organs (*arrow*) at the centers of aggregated zooxanthellae. (Photographs by courtesy of Dr. Joseph Rosewater and the Smithsonian Institution.)

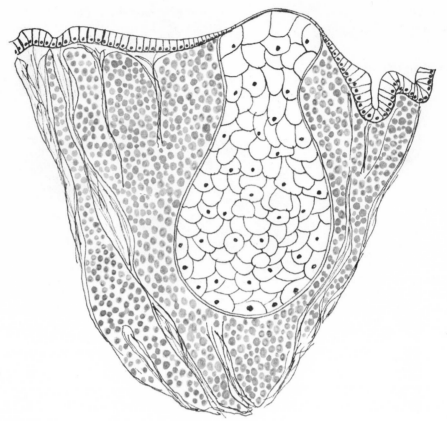

Fig. 3–7 A hyaline organ from the mantle of the giant clam *Tridacna*. Note the zooxanthellae aggregated around the organ. (Redrawn from Yonge.)

protistan contents is topographically uppermost and is invariably exposed to whatever light may be available in the environment. The host animals occur in shallow water, usually in the upper portions of coral reefs, and light is focused into the mantle tissue with the aid of hyaline organs (Fig. 3–7). These latter organs have been referred to in some of the earlier literature as "eyes," but they have neither pigment nor special innervation. Zooxanthellae gather around these organs in maximum concentration in the tissues (Fig. 3–6). The symbiotes are contained in what have been called phagocytic blood cells in the mantle and are also found in similar cells around the diverticula of the digestive tract. The host animals certainly feed on phytoplankton, but Yonge (1944) suggested that the extra food represented by the protistan associates may account for the immense size attained by these clams, enabling them to exceed the size limits imposed by ciliary feeding.

Protistans in Cnidarians

An unusual function has been suggested for the zooxanthellae living in gorgonians (sea fans). The symbiotes seem to produce large amounts of terpenes which are highly toxic to fishes, many invertebrates, and bacteria. This may explain why gorgonians remain clean and are not coated with other invertebrates nor are they often food for fishes. Unusual sterols were also found to occur in zooxanthellae-containing gorgonians but were absent from zooxanthellae-free forms (Ciereszko, 1962).

There are many other examples in nature of animal organisms which are green in

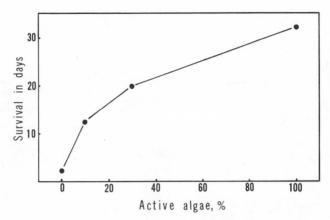

Fig. 3–8 The survival of starved hydra as a function of the number of photosynthetically active algae in the tissues. (From Muscatine and Lenhoff, 1965, *Biol. Bull.*)

color, due to the presence in the tissues of chlorophyll-bearing symbiotes. Among fresh-water coelenterates and sponges it is quite common to find that the animals are green because of the presence of zoochlorellae. Small green hydras are familiar to most students who have had elementary training in zoology. In algae-bearing *Chlorohydra,* 10 to 20% of labeled carbon fixed by the algae is transferred to the animal partner and incorporated into nucleic acids, proteins, and other constituents. The specific radioactivity of labeled carbon compounds in algae-bearing hydra tissues is 50 to 100 times greater than that in albino hydra controls (Lenhoff and Zimmerman, 1959; Muscatine and Lenhoff, 1963). Further, Muscatine and Lenhoff (1965) related survival of starved *Chlorohydra* and number of algae in the tissues (Fig. 3–8).

Green Worms and Protistans

One of the most famous associations of this type involves the acoel turbellarians of the genus *Convoluta,* which have associations with photosynthetic microorganisms. In *C. convoluta,* the symbiotes are found in large numbers in the subepidermal cells. The host is said to be dependent on lipids synthesized by the symbiotes and does not develop normally without them. If the host

is starved, it digests its symbiotes but can be reinfected (Keeble, 1908). In the closely related *C. roscoffensis* (Fig. 3–9),

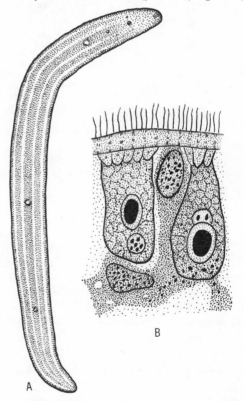

Fig. 3–9 The acoel turbellarian flatworm *Convoluta roscoffensis.* A, Whole animal. B, Section through outer tissues showing the algal symbiotes. (Redrawn from Keeble, 1912.)

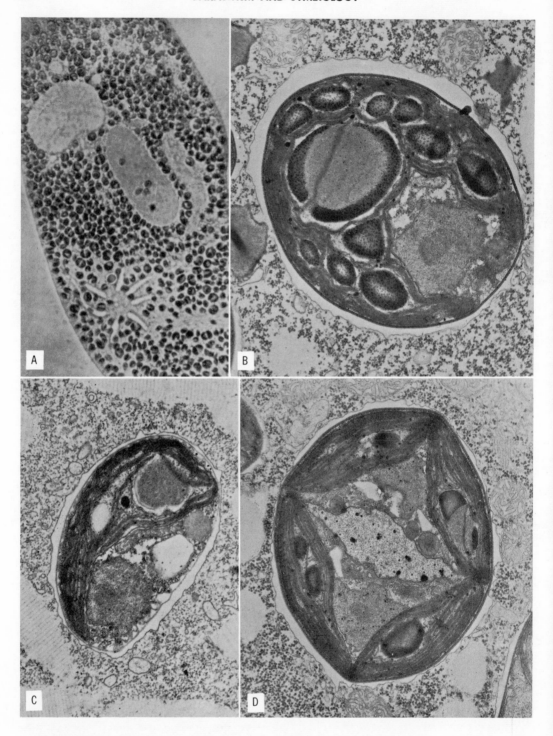

Fig. 3–10 *Paramecium bursaria* and its algal symbiote, *Chlorella*. A. A living *P. bursaria* which has been compressed between the slide and coverslip. Anterior and posterior contractile vacuoles are visible, as is the macronucleus, and on the right the

the mature turbellarian actually feeds only on its symbiotes. Eventually, it entirely consumes its algal companions, reproduces, and dies. In both species of *Convoluta* the young worms are not infected, but, according to Keeble and Gamble (1907), the algae are chemotactically attracted and infect the worms at an early age. These associations are amenable to further laboratory study but do not seem to have drawn the attention of modern workers, except for studies on ultrastructure.

There are many other examples of such associations between invertebrates and protistans. Welsh (1936) investigated the relationship between the marine turbellarian *Amphiscolops langerhansii* and its contained protistan associates. Gilbert (1944) obtained evidence for an integrated relationship between the embryos of the amphibian *Ambystoma* and green protistans. Embryos containing symbiotes had a lower mortality and a higher growth rate and, as a result, hatched earlier than embryos without symbiotes. The larval amphibians developing from "infected" embryos were larger and more advanced than those from "uninfected" individuals.

Associations of photosynthetic algae with other unicellular organisms are known but have not been extensively investigated. In one case investigated by Pascher in 1929, a colorless cryptomonad flagellate harbors three to five blue-green algae per cell. The algae were found to be capable of independent growth when freed from the host cell. When host-cell division occurs, the symbiotes are distributed in approximately equal numbers to the daughter cells. When only one symbiote is present, symbiote-free host cells arise at cell division. Interestingly, Pascher found that cells carrying the symbiote showed a positive phototaxis while symbiote-free cells did not. A real difference in the metabolism of infected and uninfected cells was indicated by the observation that starch accumulated in cells bearing symbiotes but not in uninfected cells.

While the foregoing symbiosis is maintained by heredity, an association between a blue-green alga of the genus *Nostoc* and a phycomycete fungus is not so maintained. In this case, the algae are taken up by each new generation of fungal cells by a curious process. When the hypha contacts an algae, the hyphal membrane dissolves and the algae are taken in by a mechanism which seems to resemble phagocytosis. This association shows some resemblances to lichens (described below).

Some ciliated protozoans characteristically harbor green symbiotes (Fig. 3–10). Those in *Paramecium* are described further on pages 61 and 207.

micronucleus. Symbiotic algae are scattered throughout the cytoplasm. *B.* A mature alga enclosed within a vacuole in the host cytoplasm. The massive chloroplast is cup-shaped and contains a large pyrenoid basally and numerous starch grains. The nucleus and a mitochondrial profile are visible in this alga also. *C.* An alga which has recently divided. The chloroplast is comma-shaped, with a pyrenoid at one end. The nucleus is eccentrically located, and there is a long mitochondrion adjacent to the chloroplast. The algal cytoplasm also contains a vacuole and an inclusion which is probably lipid. In the cytoplasm of the paramecium exploded trichocysts show a characteristic periodicity. *D.* An alga in division. The cell has divided once, and each cell contains two chloroplasts—a sign that a second division is impending. The nuclei of the daughter cells are especially prominent, and in two of the chloroplasts new pyrenoids can be seen to be forming. There is a large amount of intercellular material, which may condense during wall formation. (By courtesy of Dr. Stephen Karakashian and the *Journal of Protozoology*.)

Of some interest in this connection are Buchsbaum's (1937) experiments on the relationships between *Chlorella* and embryonic connective tissue cells in tissue culture. These associated cells both grew better together, when exposed to light, than they grew separately. This experimental symbiosis should be studied further, using improved methods for biochemical analysis.

LUMINESCENT SYMBIOTES

Among the most curious cases of symbiosis are those in which the host harbors microorganisms in tissues which are luminescent. Certain of the luminescent squids, teleost fishes, and tunicates have been found to owe their emitted light to the presence of certain bacteria. In some of the squids the luminescent bacteria are harbored in accessory glands near the ink sac, and are discharged by the animal with the ink. The frequent associations of luminescent bacteria and marine teleosts are quite variable in character. Many of the hosts are abyssal in habit and have apparently evolved specialized tissues in connection with the symbiosis. The bacteria are borne in what are called light organs, usually epithelial in character and often well vascularized. In these instances, the luminescence is emitted continuously. Harvey (1952) presented a very thorough review of this type of symbiosis.

MICROBES IN THE GUT

There is a large scientific literature dealing with the synthesis of vitamins by intestinal bacteria. All of the water-soluble vitamins are synthesized to some extent in the intestines of birds, rodents, rabbits, horses, and men. Evidence for this is of several types: (1) In a number of instances, it has been shown that the quantity of a vitamin appearing in the urine and feces far exceeds that in the food and vitamin synthesis in the tissues fails to account for the extra quantities. (2) When animals are fed certain sulfonamide drugs to depress the numbers of intestinal bacteria, symptoms of vitamin deficiency may appear. Feeding of the vitamin relieves the symptoms. (3) Germ-free animals show greatly increased requirements for several vitamins. (4) Some animals show evidences of vitamin deficiency when they are not allowed to eat their own feces.

In some cases, the relationship of the bacteria to host may involve substances utilized in large quantity by the host. For example, the African birds known as honey-guides feed on beeswax. These birds cannot themselves digest beeswax, but harbor symbiotic intestinal bacteria and a yeast which degrade the wax to products that can be utilized by the host.

In a number of herbivorous animals, such as horses, elephants, and various rodents, fermentation of cellulose in the cecum by bacterial and protozoan symbiotes allows utilization of the fermentation products by the host. Fermentation of forage by symbiotes also occurs in the stomach of herbivorous marsupials, hamsters, and certain monkeys. However, the best-known relationships of this type are those involving ruminant hosts and their bacterial and protozoan symbiotes. The rumen is a highly specialized part of the digestive tract in these mammals; and this organ may be described as an open fermentation system. It is now quite firmly established that the ruminant and the rumen microbial population live in a reciprocally beneficial relationship. Much of the plant material ingested by the mammal is digested and fermented by the rumen organisms to form methane, carbon dioxide, and volatile fatty acids. The acids are absorbed and metabolized by the host. In addition, the microorganisms themselves serve as a source of food for the host. The relationships of rumen organisms and the host are complicated, due to the fact that numbers of species of symbiotes are involved. Thus,

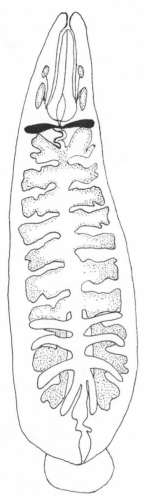

Fig. 3–11 The leech *Placobdella.* The evaginations of the esophagus occupied by symbiotes are in black. (Redrawn from Reichenow.)

there are interactions between the various elements of the total symbiote population. The biology and chemistry of the rumen have been examined by Hungate (1966) in his very excellent monograph on the subject.

It may seem surprising that the medicinal leech *Hirudo,* an animal which feeds on blood, apparently depends on symbiotic bacteria for the digestion of this highly specialized food (Fig. 3–11). Further, the bacterium *Pseudomonas hirudinis* produces

an antibiotic which renders the leech gut virtually free of other species of microorganisms. When *Hirudo* is treated with chloromycetin to clear it of *Pseudomonas,* the leech loses the ability to digest blood (Büsing et al., 1953). The bacterial associate probably synthesizes compounds of nutritional significance to *Hirudo,* but this does not appear to have been investigated.

MICROBIAL MUTUALS IN PLANTS

A well-known mutualism, or parasitism in some instances, is the relationship between the legume-nodule bacteria of the genus *Rhizobium* and many species of leguminous plants, such as beans, clover, and alfalfa. The bacteria live in nodules on the roots of the host, and are sometimes of benefit because they can fix atmospheric nitrogen, thus making it available to the plant. In return, the host is the source of certain nutrients for the microorganisms. It may be noted that not all strains or species of *Rhizobium* possess efficient mechanisms for trapping atmospheric nitrogen. In such cases the host receives little or no benefit from the association and the relationship is clearly parasitic (see p. 197). There are a number of other plant-bacterial symbioses in which nitrogen fixation is thought to occur (Lange, 1966).

A somewhat different type of relationship is known among plants of the genus *Ardisia* and bacteria. Large numbers of bacteria occur in the terminal buds of *Ardisia crispa.* Regularly spaced bacterial nodules subsequently form on the margins of the leaves. Plants lacking the symbiotes are termed "cripples" and are severely dwarfed. During host reproduction the symbiotes are enclosed in the mature seed and are thus transmitted to the next generation (de Jongh, 1938). The nutritional exchange between the host and symbiotes is inadequately understood but appears to involve some other factors in addition to nitrogen fixation.

FRIENDLY VIRUSES

This heading is borrowed from an article by Maramorosch (1960), who cited examples of beneficial effects wrought by viruses on hosts. Some of the most interesting virus infections are found among the bacterial viruses (bacteriophages: Fig. 3–12). These viruses may produce infections

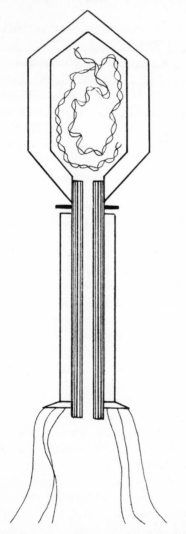

Fig. 3–12 Diagrammatic representation of a bacteriophage in optical section. The tail is about 1000 Å in length. (Adapted from various authors.)

which result in the death of the bacterial host. However, in some instances, bacteriophage infects bacteria and produces disease (as manifested by cell lysis) only in an occasional cell. Within the infected cell, the virus behaves as though it were part of the genetic apparatus and is reproduced in successive daughter cells. Occasionally, when such a virus produces disease and death in a bacterial cell, it may escape from the lysed host cell, carrying with it genetic information from the bacterial cell—genetic material which the phage ancestor did not possess. When this virus infects a new host cell it introduces this new genetic information into the host. The host may thus gain the capacity to resist an antibiotic or to synthesize a nutrient substance. This carrying of genetic information from one bacterial host to another has been termed *transduction.*

The relatively benign relationships of certain of the bacteriophages led the virologists to refer to them as lysogenic phages, in contrast to the lytic phages which cause acute disease and death in the majority of the bacterial hosts which they infect. The role of lysogenic phages in causing bacterial cells to produce toxins, which in turn cause disease in animal hosts harboring these bacteria, is discussed on page 27. Research on the bacteriophages has been carried out with great intensity in a number of laboratories, furnishing valuable material for the investigation of the molecular basis of heredity (see p. 207).

A well-known class of beneficial virus infections must, of course, include those which, when administered to a host, produce little or no disease but stimulate host resistance to subsequent infection by viruses which are capable of producing serious disease. The live-virus vaccines against yellow fever, smallpox, and polio are familiar examples.

One interesting aspect of the rapid advances in our knowledge of viruses is the fact that large numbers of viruses have been recovered from the tissues of various healthy organisms and that, in many cases, these viruses cannot be identified as being involved in the genesis of disease. It has become apparent that viruses are relatively common inhabitants of cells. It may be only the occasional one, rather than the usual one, which is involved in inducing disease in hosts.

A most curious effect of virus infection in an animal has been produced in the laboratory by infecting an insect, the corn leaf-hopper, with the aster yellows virus. Uninfected corn leaf-hoppers are quite finicky animals and cannot be induced to feed on plants other than corn *and* virus-infected asters. After becoming infected with the virus, however, the leaf-hopper will feed on healthy asters, carrots, and even rye. The insect seems to suffer no ill effects from infection, but the infection definitely increases the range of host food plants. When infected insects are kept at 87° F for eight days, they are "cured" of the virus infection and, at the same time, lose the ability to feed on healthy asters and other typical food plants (Maramorosch, 1960). It seems probable that many such beneficial virus-host relations exist in nature; however, they will not be simple to demonstrate.

VIRUSES AS ORGANISMS

Viruses show some of the important properties of organisms. They contain nucleic acids and proteins and have the capacity to reproduce. In addition to reproduction, they have genetic characteristics—the offspring of a given virus are like the parent, rather than like some other kind of virus. They show mutations such as we see in other entities which are referred to as organisms. In other words, they show hereditary continuity. The difficulties arise because biologists are accustomed to thinking of the cell as a unit, whereas the viruses have a subcellular organization. Insofar as it is known, they are obligate parasites with extremely limited synthetic capacities. Although the virus particle carries genetic information which in part specifies the synthesis of more virus, it is dependent on the host cell to carry out energy function catalysis and thus furnish the necessities for reproduction. It behaves like an organism only with the essential aid of the host cell. As a matter of fact, the viruses in the early stages of their infection of a cell cannot be truly distinguished from the elements of the host cell itself.

Detection of viruses has usually depended on the fact that they may alter the appearance or behavior of the host cell—in the most obvious instances, killing it. Also, the viruses are infectious in that they may be transferred from cell to cell in some kind of contagious way. Contagion itself may go unnoticed if there are no effects on the cell, and it is certainly possible that many viruses do indeed go undetected for this reason. If we have effects on a cell without contagion, it is difficult to differentiate the virus from the hereditary characteristics of the host cell. Such viruses, if we may call them that, would have to pass from one generation to another through the reproductive products of the host, and it would be quite difficult to distinguish the effects from those of the host genetic material.

There are cases in which virus-like particles are present in cells and are contagious only under very special conditions. Lysogeny in the bacterial viruses, mentioned above, is a case in point. Another such instance is carbon dioxide sensitivity in certain flies. In 1937 L'Héritier and Teissier discovered carbon dioxide sensitivity in the fruit fly, *Drosophila melanogaster,* and the sensitivity showed evidence of being a case of cytoplasmic inheritance. Subsequently, it was found that the cytoplasmic character was infectious and fitted the characteristics of a virus. The stable carbon dioxide-sensitivity virus is maternally inherited and produces no other known effects than this sensitivity to carbon dioxide. Sensitive flies seem to live as long as resistant ones and reproduction is not affected (L'Héritier, 1958).

In a number of cases, insects are infected by viruses without showing any evidence of disease. These have been referred to as *occult viruses*. Such an occult virus may be induced to cause overt disease without introducing additional virus particles into the host organism. Various physical and chemical agents will act as inducers. Excessive cold, excessive heat, sharp changes in temperature, ultraviolet and X-irradiation, and even sonic treatment have been reported to induce occult viruses. Further, the rate of induction of nuclear polyhedrosis in silkworms is determined by several factors: (1) the temperature used, (2) the genetic makeup of the silkworm strain, (3) the developmental stage of the silkworm larva, and (4) the nutritional state of the silkworm.

A variety of chemical agents have been reported to induce occult insect viruses. These include formalin, potassium nitrite, hydroxylamine, deoxyribonucleic acid (DNA) preparations, hydrogen peroxide, sodium cyanide, sodium fluoride, iodoacetic acid, sodium azide, mercuric chloride, and nitrogen mustard. Some of these agents act in the case of one kind of virus but not of another. It seems evident that there is a considerable lack of specificity in these inductions (Aruga, 1963). It may be pointed out that the induction of lysogenic bacterial viruses clearly shows some similarity to the above.

Symbiotic Relations Between Viruses

There are several instances in which beneficial effects of one virus upon another have been described. Rous sarcoma virus requires the presence of another virus for synthesis of the protein coat. (This point is discussed further on page 220.) Some

tobacco necrosis virus preparations actually consist of two unrelated viruses, one of which can multiply only in the presence of the other. Under some conditions the advantages are mutual (Kassanis, 1963).

Among the bacterial viruses, one phage may derive benefit from another phage in the same host cell. Phages may be inactivated by certain doses of ultraviolet irradiation so that they will infect bacterial cells but fail to reproduce. If several inactivated phages infect the *same* bacterial cell, multiplication may ensue. This has been explained as the recombination of different parts of phage genomes, resulting in a new viable genome (Stent, 1963). A different phenomenon has been called phenotypic mixing: Two related but not identical phages multiplying in a single bacterial cell may exchange protein coats without an alteration of the genome. Since the attachment of phage to a new host cell depends on the properties of the protein coat, these recoated particles may infect host cells which their parents failed to infect. In short, it may result in a change of host range.

MICROORGANISMS IN INSECTS

There is a voluminous literature dealing with the bacterial and fungal organisms considered to be symbiotes in insects (see Buchner, 1965, for a detailed review of the older literature). The broad distribution of symbiotes among the insects suggests that such symbiosis has arisen on many independent occasions in insect evolution. In some instances, the importance of mutualism seems apparent. Thus, insects which feed on such materials as blood, wood, stored grain, or plant sap often harbor special microorganisms. It is commonly concluded that the symbiotes permit the use of foods which would otherwise be nutritionally inadequate. In some instances, removal of the symbiotes has little effect on

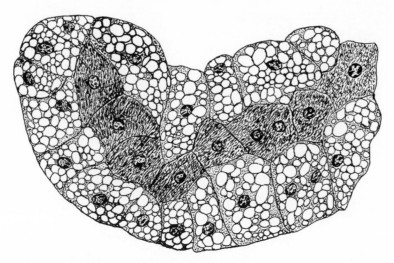

Fig. 3–13 Mycetocytes surrounded by fat cells from the cockroach *Blatta orientalis.* ×225. (Redrawn from Blochmann.)

the host but in other cases, as will be indicated below, removal of symbiotes has deleterious effects on the host.

Mycetomes and Mycetocytes

Although obvious modifications of host tissue for holding symbiotes are not always observed, in many insects, the host differentiates a special organ, the mycetome, which contains the symbiotes. Visibly differentiated host cells for holding symbiotes are called mycetocytes. The mycetome may be made up of distinctly separate cells (Fig. 3–13) or of a syncytium of mycetocytes. When mycetocytes are interspersed in the fat body of the insect, they may be separated from each other or they may be aggregated in a layer near the outside of the fat body. The mycetocytes are usually large cells and are reported to be highly polyploid in some instances. Baudisch estimated that mycetocytes of cockroaches range from tetraploid to 512-ploid! "Empty" mycetomes or mycetocytes have been produced experimentally in a number of insects and, in some scale insects, cells

which appear to be mycetocytes but which contain no symbiotes have been found in nature.

Microbial symbiotes are usually incorporated into mycetocytes at the time these cells are differentiated in the developing embryo. There is great variation in the pattern of incorporation and differentiation, even in closely related insects. In a number of forms, the microorganisms have been seen penetrating the ovarian follicle in the female insect (Fig. 3–14). In some insects the mycetocytes tend to degenerate in the adult insect, a process that has been attributed to lowered nutritional demands of the adult. When the symbiotes are maintained in the adult, it is frequently assumed that they are in some way essential for reproduction. This assumption has been shown to be valid for the German cockroach (Brooks and Richards, 1955). It has been suggested that in some cases microbial symbiotes may be involved in endocrine function of the host. This relationship has been demonstrated rather conclusively in at least one case (see p. 33). Conversely, effects of host endocrine secretions on symbiotes

transmitted thru egg to next generation

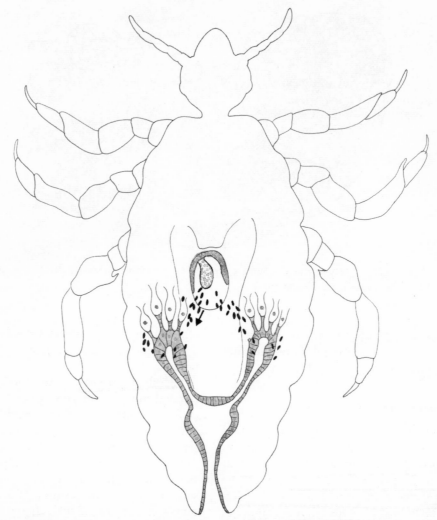

Fig. 3–14   The movement of symbiotes from a mycetome on the gut of the human body louse *Pediculus* to the ovarian ampules. Infection of oocytes ensues, and the symbiotes are transmitted to the next generation of lice. (Modified from Ries, 1931.)

have been quite clearly demonstrated with protozoan symbiotes of the wood roach *Cryptocercus* (see p. 65).

Special mention may be made of an astonishing relationship between symbiotes and host described by Buchner. In insect species of the coccid genus *Stictococcus*, mycetocytes invade the ovary but infect only a portion of the oocytes. Two kinds of eggs, infected and uninfected, are produced. The eggs develop parthenogenti-

cally, and infected eggs give rise to females while uninfected eggs develop into males.

Experimental Studies on Insects

Experimental elimination of microbial symbiotes from insects has allowed examination of the nature of the relationship in a number of instances. Much of this work has been reviewed by Koch (1960) and by Richards and Brooks (1959). In some species, such as the hemipteran bloodsucking insect *Rhodnius*, transmission from one generation to another may be interrupted by keeping the breeding cages sufficiently clean. In some species transmission occurs by contamination of the outer surface of the egg shell and transmission to the young can be prevented by sterilizing the surface. In a number of instances, elevated temperature, inadequate diets, antibiotics or sulfonamide drugs, or surgical removal of mycetomes may be used to "cure" insects of their symbiotes. Of the hundreds of insect-symbiote associations known, less than two dozen have been studied by experimentally breaking the association. These cases, however, have been revealing. In one case, removal of symbiotes seems to have no effect at all. In another insect, *Sitophilus*, symbiote-free (aposymbiotic) individuals are smaller and lighter in color. On the other hand the bloodsucking bugs *Rhodnius* and *Triatoma* are markedly affected; aposymbiotic *Triatoma* shows a high mortality and prolonged time for development while *Rhodnius* usually dies before attaining adulthood. It may be remarked that, of the arthropods which feed on blood, only those that are strict blood-feeders throughout the life cycle seem to harbor intracellular symbiotes of nutritional significance. Forms whose larvae feed on other diets, such as mosquitoes, tabanid and muscid flies, and fleas, do not seem to contain mutualistic intracellular symbiotes.

In the most clearly analyzed cases, it has been found that symbiotes supply most of the B vitamins and sterols (reviewed by Lipke and Fraenkel, 1956, and Richards and Brooks, 1959). There is clear evidence that the intracellular bacterial symbiotes of the cockroach *Blatella* can synthesize the sulfur amino acids, cystine and methionine, from $Na_2S^{35}O_4$. Synthesis occurred only in insects containing the symbiotes (Henry and Block, 1960). Further, the incorporation of carbon from C^{14}-glucose into amino acids was limited to non-essential ones when

the cockroaches were "cured" of their symbiotes by aureomycin treatment. Untreated insects showed incorporation of glucose carbon into both non-essential and essential amino acids (Henry, 1962).

Some experiments on exchanging the symbiotes of two host species have been revealing. Pant and Fraenkel (1954) cultivated the microbial symbiotes from each of two beetles, *Lasioderma* and *Stegobium*, and then fed them to the opposite larval host. The symbiotes became established in each "abnormal" host. However, it was observed that the symbiotes of *Stegobium* are less capable of synthesizing water-soluble vitamins and this host with its normal symbiotes requires thiamine in the diet. Hence, it is not surprising that the symbiotes of *Lasioderma* substituted very adequately in sustaining *Stegobium* but that the converse was not true. *Lasioderma* harboring the symbiotes from *Stegobium* required thiamine.

Digestion and Symbiotes in Insects

Cleveland (1923) showed that there is a correlation between the woodeating of termites and the presence of flagellate protozoans in the gut. In some termites, such as *Zootermopsis*, the gut is literally packed with flagellates, and in nymphs of this insect the protozoans may constitute one-third to one-seventh of the total weight (Hungate, 1955). It was suggested that the protozoans had the capacity to digest wood, and Cleveland showed that termites "cured" of their protozoans failed to survive on a diet of wood. Subsequently, Trager showed that the termite protozoans contained the enzyme cellulase, and Hungate demonstrated that the major digestion of cellulose occurs in that portion of the termite gut in which the protozoans live.

A most interesting utilization of intestinal flora for digestive function is seen in the larva of the fly *Hylemyia cilicrura*, also known as the seed-corn maggot. The adult fly deposits its eggs on or in the ground around potato plants. When the larvae hatch, they move through the soil to the surface of a potato. During the next 24 hours, they creep about on the potato surface, scratching it repeatedly with two prominent mouth hooks and inoculating it with bacteria. As bacterial decomposition proceeds, the larval fly feeds on the decaying material. After 2 or 3 weeks of feeding, pupation occurs. It should be remarked that during this period, the bacteria enter the stem of the potato plant, producing the disease known as potato blackleg. There is good evidence that the bacterial decomposition is required by the fly larva since they will not develop on potato tissue in the absence of the bacteria. Various research

workers seem to agree with the concept that microbial symbiotes usually function in making marginal diets adequate. Thus, demonstrating a beneficial effect of symbiotes may commonly necessitate placing the aposymbiotic insect under suboptimal conditions.

Symbiotes of Protozoans

There is an extensive literature dealing with what commonly have been regarded as symbiotes of protozoans (reviewed by Kirby, 1941). These have been of variable morphology and have been interpreted as bacteria, yeast, fungi, or other protozoans. The bulk of these reports are concerned with seeing bodies of various kinds in the

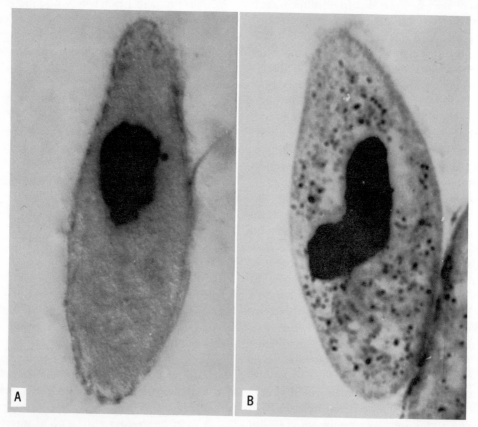

Fig. 3–15 *Paramecium aurelia:* (A) sensitive and (B) killer. Note the kappa particles in the cytoplasm of the killer. These specimens are Syngen 4, stock 51. The sensitive has a genotype kk and the killer a genotype KK. (Photographs furnished by courtesy of Dr. Ruth V. Dippell, Indiana University.)

cytoplasm or nucleus of a protozoan cell, but the interpretation of these particles as symbiotes has rarely been supported by other evidence. It seems probable that many of these inclusions, indeed, are symbiotes and that symbioses involving protozoans as hosts are extremely common in nature. However, such a conclusion can only be tentative in the absence of supporting evidence beyond that presently available. A recent example of a bacterial endosymbiote in a protozoan is found in the case of some strains of the trypanosomatid flagellate *Crithidia oncopelti*. The endosymbiote apparently furnishes metabolites to the protozoan, which explains the simple nutritional requirements of some strains of this protozoan as compared with others. As a matter of fact, this protozoan may be "cured" of its symbiote with penicillin (Gill and Vogel, 1963).

Some years ago it was found that certain individuals of the ciliated protozoan *Paramecium aurelia* extruded into the medium a factor which was toxic to other individuals of the same species. Sonneborn carried out a fascinating series of studies of this phenomenon, primarily as a genetic problem (discussed in more detail on page 204). The work of Sonneborn and his associates has shown that the formation of the so-called killer substances is due to the presence of what appears to be a bacterial symbiote, which has been termed *kappa* (Fig. 3–15). What has proven to be of great interest from the standpoint of the integrative level of this association is the finding that the capacity to harbor and to allow the reproduction of a given number of kappa particles in a host cell requires a given host genetic constitution. Similarly, Siegel, Karakashian, and associates have carried out studies on the symbiosis of *Paramecium bursaria* and zoochlorellae (see Karakashian and Siegel, 1965) and have also found that the capacity to support zoochlorellae has a genetic background (see p. 207).

Independent evidence that the strains (or species?) of the green alga *Chlorella*

living in symbiotic associations are physiologically specialized is found in the observation that such strains synthesize the sugar maltose, liberating it into the surrounding medium. Free-living strains of *Chlorella* do not liberate significant amounts of sugar (Muscatine et al., 1967).

HYPERSYMBIOSIS

There are numerous instances in which symbiotes serve as hosts to smaller symbiotes. This relation is referred to as hypersymbiosis. In the scientific literature many of these associations have been referred to as hyperparasitism. However, the nature of the relationships is generally unexplored and their specific characterization as hyperparasites should be avoided.

There are a number of examples of hypersymbiotic protozoans living in association with protozoan symbiotes (Figs. 3–16, 3–17, 3–18). For example, the suctorian *Allantosoma* (Fig. 3–16) lives on ciliates in the large intestine of horses. Several workers have described amebas living in opalinid protozoans from the gut of amphibians (Fig. 3–17). Carini and Reichenow suggested that these amebas are identical with species living free in the gut of amphibians. Stabler and Chen (1936) found the amebas in opalinid cysts.

Microsporidians have been reported as hypersymbiotes in gregarine and ciliate protozoans but, in addition, are symbiotic in trematodes, tapeworms, and nematodes from the intestines of vertebrates and in

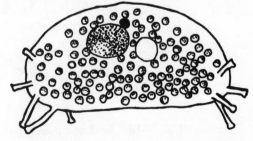

Fig. 3–16 *Allantosoma intestinalis* from the cecum of a horse. (Redrawn from Hsiung, *Iowa State Coll. J. Sci.*)

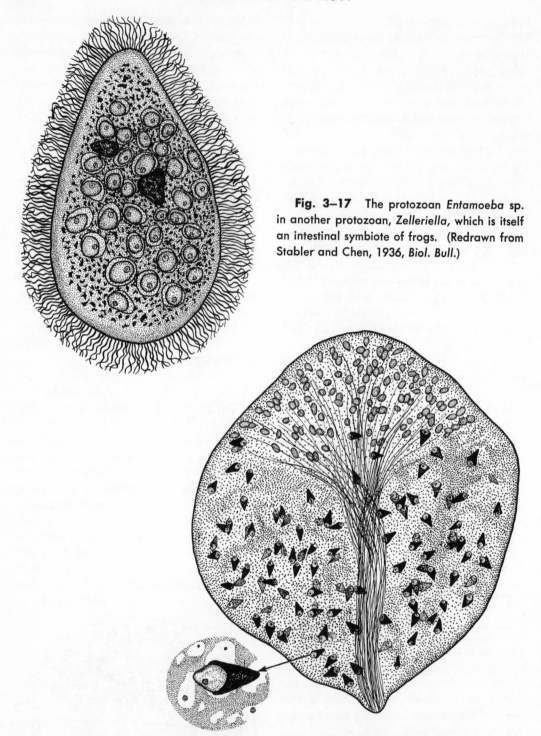

Fig. 3–17 The protozoan *Entamoeba* sp. in another protozoan, *Zelleriella,* which is itself an intestinal symbiote of frogs. (Redrawn from Stabler and Chen, 1936, *Biol. Bull.*)

Fig. 3–18 Symbiotic microorganisms in the protozoan *Stephanonympha* sp., which is itself a symbiote of the termite *Kalotermes jeannelanus.* (Redrawn from Kirby, 1949, *Protozoa in Biological Research,* Columbia University Press, New York.)

trematode larvae in mollusks. It may be remarked that some of these helminth hosts live in mammals which do not themselves serve as hosts of microsporidians. Thus, these associations are probably not cases of facultative symbiosis.

Flagellate protozoans have been reported as hypersymbiotes of trematodes and nematodes. Of particular interest is *Histomonas*

meleagridis, which is said to live in association with the nematode *Heterakis gallinae* in the gut of turkeys. *Histomonas* also infects the avian host, sometimes resulting in a fatal disease, and birds are reported to become infected with the protozoan by ingesting infected nematode eggs. This phenomenon bears some resemblance to the virus-nematode relationship in swine influenza (see p. 111).

One of the most astonishing examples of symbiotic integration has been described by Cleveland and Grimstone (1964). The large protozoan *Mixotricha paradoxa,* which lives in the gut of a primitive Australian termite, has two kinds of hypersymbiotic microorganisms living on the cell surface (Fig. 3–19). What were at one time thought to be cilia were shown to be spirochaete microorganisms. The movements of these microorganisms are amazingly well coordinated, and the protozoan is propelled by the undulations of its attached surface symbiotes. The spirochaetes are attached to brackets on the protozoan surface and a second kind of bacterial symbiote is also associated with each bracket (Fig. 3–20). Kirby (1941) reviewed many other examples of microorganisms living on the surfaces of protozoans.

Occasionally helminths have been described as hypersymbiotes of other helminths, but more often helminths live in association with ectoparasitic arthropods, such as fleas, mallophagan lice, isopods, and copepods.

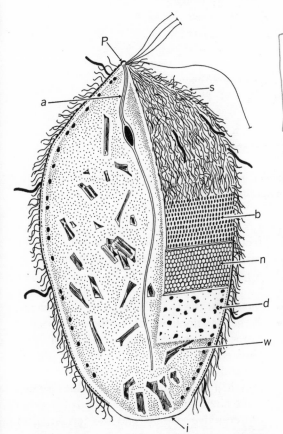

Fig. 3–19 A diagram of the protozoan *Mixotricha paradoxa,* a symbiote of the Australian termite *Mastotermes darwiniensis.* The organism is drawn in optical section on the left. On the right the surface structures are shown at progressively deeper levels passing downward: *a,* axostyle; *b,* bacterium; *d,* dictyosome; *i,* ingestive zone; *n,* fibrous network; *P,* papilla; *s,* spirochaete; *w,* wood particles. Spirochaetes are drawn as they appear in fixed material and the brackets (Fig. 3–20) are not shown. (From Cleveland and Grimstone, 1964.)

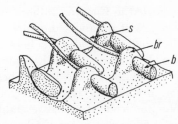

Fig. 3–20 A reconstruction of a small area of the *Mixotricha* cell surface showing the brackets (*br*) and the arrangement of bacteria (*b*) and spirochaetes (*s*). (After Cleveland and Grimstone, 1964.)

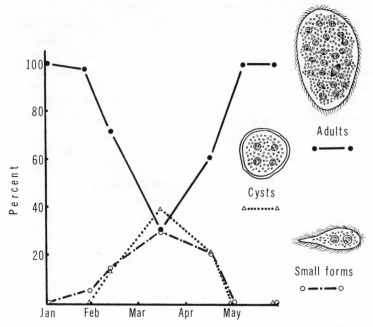

Fig. 3–21 The life cycle forms of *Opalina ranarum* during the winter and spring months. The frog host (*Rana temporaria*) oviposits in mid-February. (Drawn from data of El Mofty and Smyth, 1964.)

Among the arthropods, many crustaceans are hypersymbiotic, frequently associated with other crustaceans (see p. 32). However, insects are the most common hypersymbiotic arthropods and other insects commonly serve as hosts in these associations. Many of these hypersymbioses are clearly parasitism or are parasitoid in character (see p. 36).

SOME ENDOCRINE RELATIONSHIPS

As indicated in Chapter 2, there are several examples of instances in which a symbiote is known to produce a hormone or hormone-like substance which results in a diseased condition of the host. These are instances in which the host is affected by a symbiote-produced substance, resembling or identical with substances which are normally produced by the host. There are other interesting examples of complex integration of symbiotes and host, in which the reproduction of the symbiote is affected by the endocrine balance of the host and the effects can be related to other aspects of the biology of the symbiote. The protozoan *Opalina ranarum*, living in the rectum of the frog, *Rana temporaria*, shows cyclic development of cystic stages, small forms, and the so-called adult form. The character of this cycle is shown in Figure 3–21. Experimental studies by Mofty and Smyth (1959) and McConnachie (1960) leave no doubt that the induction of a sexual reproductive pattern and the formation of cysts in *Opalina ranarum* are associated with the level of gonadal hormones in the host. However, the precise action of host hormones in initiating reproductive activity of the symbiote is not yet elucidated.

The amazing life pattern seen in the monogenetic trematode *Polystoma* (Fig. 3–22) is probably one in which host hormones play a significant role. Adults of this worm develop as ectosymbiotes on the external gills of young frog tadpoles or in the urinary bladder of adult frogs after a preliminary development on the internal gills of advanced tadpoles. If the young worm infects the external gills of a young tadpole, it rapidly develops into a small adult and produces eggs before the external gills are resorbed during tadpole metamorphosis. On the other hand, if the young worm enters the gill chamber of an advanced tadpole, it lives on the internal gills for a period of several weeks and, as metamorphosis is completed, the worm migrates down the digestive tract and enters the urinary bladder. Here it may require three years to attain sexual maturity. Miretski (1951) has shown that the trematode may be induced to produce eggs in about a week by injecting the host with pituitary extract, suggesting that the maturation pattern of the worm is under the control of host hormones.

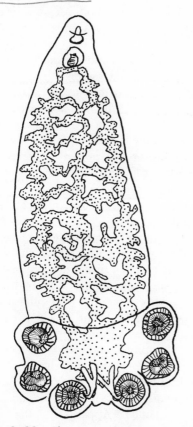

Fig. 3—22 The monogenetic trematode *Polystoma.*

Reproduction in the rabbit flea *Spilopsyllus* seems to be sharply regulated by host hormones. Ovarian maturation in the flea is stimulated by elevated corticosteroids in the pregnant doe rabbit. Shortly after the birth of young rabbits, the fleas move from doe to the young. The fleas are stimulated to copulate by pituitary growth hormone in the young hosts and egg-laying rapidly ensues. About 10 days after birth of young rabbits, the fleas return to the lactating doe and regression of the insects' ovaries occurs (Rothschild and Ford, 1966).

One of the most interesting and instructive patterns of relationship between host endocrine conditions and reproductive activity of symbiotes has been worked out by Cleveland and his associates (see Cleveland, 1960). The wood roach *Cryptocercus punctulatus* harbors a great abundance of protozoan flagellates in the gut. A dense population of the symbiotes belonging to over thirty species is maintained throughout the life of the insect. During the development of *Cryptocercus,* when the roach is undergoing periodic molts, there is a definite synchronization of the sexual cycles of the protozoan symbiotes with the molting cycle of the host. Upon removing certain neurosecretory cells from the brain (pars intercerebralis), sexual cycles of some of the protozoans are arrested or aborted and in others the protozoans undergo degeneration. Further work showed that this effect was indirect; a hormone produced in the brain controls the production of molting hormone, ecdysone, by the prothoracic glands, and ecdysone is the substance which exerts an effect on the reproduction of the flagellates. Of great importance was Cleveland's demonstration that the host does not have to actually go through molting for the protozoans to carry through their sexual cycles. The morphological and physiological changes of the host are not involved at all. As a matter of fact, it was shown that the protozoans are more sensitive to ecdysone, from the standpoint of concentration, than are their hosts. Further, some genera of flagellates were found to be more sensitive to ecdysone than other genera. Of interest was the experimental observation that in the presence of too much ecdysone the sexual maturation of the flagellates may be so much accelerated that degeneration results in death for many of the protozoans. Cleveland carried out very ingenious transfaunation experiments in which flagellates were transplanted from insect hosts having a low titer of ecdysone to hosts having a high titer of the hormone and vice versa. The student is urged to examine the original papers detailing these very ingenious experiments (references in Cleveland, 1960). DeGiusti (1963) also found evidence that sexual reproduction of a gregarine symbiote is coordinated with the molting cycle of its amphipod host.

PLANT GRAFTING AS SYMBIOSIS

It is appropriate to point out that the well-known procedure in plant husbandry known as grafting results in many instances of symbiosis—in this case man-made. In a successful graft there is little doubt that the integration of the graft and the root stock is of a very high order. There is a complex exchange of nutrients, water, and plant hormones, and the association may be of quite long duration. Many species of plants cannot be successfully grafted to one another; these are clearly instances in which integration cannot be achieved, although our detailed understanding of why a pair of plants fail to make the necessary integration is not equally clear.

MYCORRHIZAE AND HIGHER PLANTS

In a large number of cases, relationships between fungi and rhizoids, or roots, of bryophytes, pteridophytes, and angiosperms have been recognized to be symbiotic in character; such fungi are characterized by the term *mycorrhizae*. Endotrophic mycor-

rhizae enter into a close physical relationship with root systems by means of hyphae penetrating between and into cells (Fig. 3–23). Those in which the mycelium is mainly external to the roots are referred to as ectotrophic mycorrhizae. In the endotrophic form the fungus is in the tissues and the host digests portions of the mycelium. In some cases, mutualism has been definitely demonstrated: in the presence of appropriate fungi there is greatly enhanced growth of seedlings. According to Sadasivan and Subramanian (1960), the probable mechanisms involved in this increase are: the fungi alter insoluble carbon compounds to soluble form, change the pH around the root, or produce vitamins or auxins.

Some of the more recent experimental work on mycorrhizae has been summarized by Melin (1963) and Mosse (1963). In discussing mycorrhizal relationships, Gäumann (1950) pointed out that in many cases these grade from mutualism to parasitism. The nature of an association seems to depend on the environmental conditions under which the relationship develops. Ectotrophic mycorrhizae are quite common on many deciduous and coniferous trees, being almost universally present on some kinds. There is considerable specificity in these relationships; the same fungus is usually associated with a limited number of tree species.

Endotrophic mycorrhizae are commonly found associated with orchids, the seeds of some species requiring the presence of a fungus for germination. One of the Japanese orchids is reputed to require a fungus for flowering to occur. In this case, the orchid plant is an underground tuber without chlorophyll and without leaves. It produces a flower-bearing shoot only when it is invaded by *Armillaria*, the shoestring mushroom, which is parasitic on certain woody plants. Apparently, the fungus derives some nutrients from the orchid and in turn produces metabolites, probably

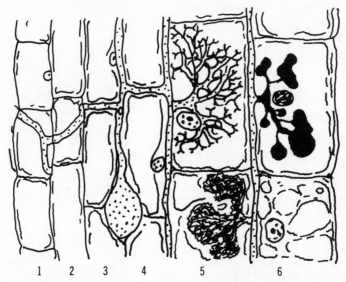

1 2 3 4 5 6

Fig. 3–23 The course of infection of *Allium* root by a mycorrhizal fungus. There is an intracellular penetration of epidermal cells (*1, 2*). In the third cell layer the fungus is intercellular (*3*), and between (*3*) and (*4*) it forms a storage organ. An intracellular arbuscule is formed (*upper 5*). Eventually the host cell begins digestion of the fungus arbuscule (*lower 5*), and undigested remains of the fungal structure persist (*6*). (Redrawn from Burgeff, 1943, *Naturwissenschaften.*)

auxins, which stimulate the host to flower. Of great interest is the elaboration of fungus-inhibiting substances by orchids in response to the presence of a fungus. Various orchids have been shown to elaborate fungistatic dihydrophenanthrene derivatives when a fungus is present, although these substances are absent from the tissues of orchids grown without fungi (Nüesch, 1963).

LICHENS

Among plant symbioses, lichens are outstanding examples of the creative attributes of interspecific associations. A lichen is an association of a fungus and an alga (Fig. 3–24), and the union of the two results in new and unique morphological and physiological properties not observed in either separate organism. Sometimes other organisms, such as bacteria, are also present in a lichen but their role in these associations is quite unclear. There is evidence that products of photosynthetic carbon dioxide fixation by the algal symbiote are available to the fungal symbiote. Identified products produced by the algae include mannitol and ribitol.

Lichens grow extremely slowly, many of them growing less than a millimeter per year, and may live for very long periods of time (Fig. 3–25). In alpine-arctic areas some lichens are estimated to be 4500 years old (Beschel, 1961). Many lichens carry on photosynthesis at low temperatures. During winter there is an increase in the chlorophyll content which may be related to an increase in the number of algal cells. The slow growth of lichens does not appear to be explained solely on the basis of low photosynthetic capacity but is rather attributed to the low water content. The lichen thallus dries rapidly and photosynthesis is inhibited by a low water content.

For many years lichen physiologists have

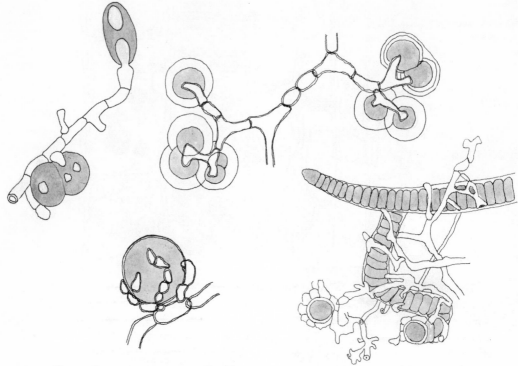

Fig. 3–24 Several types of relationship between fungal and algal associates in lichens. Algae are shaded and fungi unshaded. (From De Bary, 1884.)

attempted to cultivate a new lichen from the algal and fungal components previously isolated in culture. Lichen fungi and algae do not have obligate relationships, and the relationships are readily broken under laboratory conditions. Any factors promoting independent growth of either member will prevent their union, and reestablishment of the lichen symbiosis has not proven to be a simple matter of mixing the organisms together. Ahmadjian had some success in reconstituting these associations and concluded that the most important stimuli for lichen formation are nutrient-poor conditions and slow drying. Ahmadjian (1966) has reviewed available information on lichen biology.

CELL ORGANELLES AND SYMBIOTES

A word must be said concerning the concept that certain components of cells may be derivatives of symbiotic organisms. It was suggested many years ago that mitochondria and various plastids were symbiotes. Overenthusiastic supporters of this idea identified these cell components with bacteria; some workers claimed that they could be readily cultured outside of cells. The idea fell into disrepute (see discussion in Buchner, 1965).

The discovery that mitochondria and chloroplasts contain DNA produced a reconsideration of the possibility that such strucutures are indeed symbiotes. The case for the blue-green algal symbiotes as precursors of chloroplasts is not unreasonable. In addition to the morphological similarities between symbiotic blue-green algae and chloroplasts (Hall and Claus, 1963; Lang and Rae, 1967), chemical studies on DNA from chloroplasts indicate that it more closely resembles DNA from blue-green algae than it resembles nuclear DNA from the cell containing the chloroplast. The subject is being actively pursued by a number of investigators and has been reviewed in some detail by Sagen (1967).

THE INTERGRADE FROM NO DISEASE TO DISEASE

It is commonly observed that many animals harboring parasitic symbiotes show no evidence of disease. Evidently, parasite and pathogen cannot be precisely equated. In the laboratory, well-fed rats, mice, hamsters, and the like infected with tapeworms or nematodes may be kept for long periods without showing symptoms of infection when compared with their parasite-free brethren in neighboring cages. In defining different kinds of symbiosis, we stated that when one member of a symbiosis

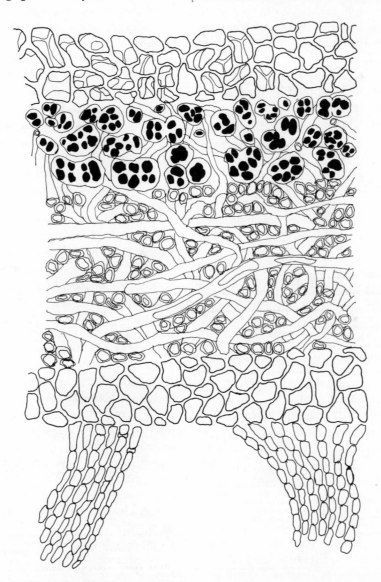

Fig. 3–25 A transverse section through a foliaceous lichen. Algal components are black. (Redrawn from De Bary, 1884.)

profits at the expense of the other the relationship is termed parasitism. This definition implies that we may observe evidence that one partner profits to the other's detriment. One obvious evidence may be the appearance of disease. However, if the host can efficiently counterbalance the effects of the symbiote by maintaining a more than adequate intake of nutrients, disease will not necessarily appear. Thus, a host may simply eat enough to support itself and its symbiotes, and so avoid the appearance of dysfunction.

In addition to satisfying the nutritional requirements of a host and its symbiotes, the intake of sufficient food by the host has other effects on the association. In some cases of symbiosis, maintenance of adequate nutrition is essential to the fullest development of the resistance of the host (see p. 84). Thus, the animal host on an inadequate diet may have an impaired capacity for the production of antibodies, whereas the host with an adequate food intake may be capable of sharp responses to the presence of the symbiote.

In sum, maintenance of a high level of nutrition may prevent the occurrence of disease in two ways: (1) the host feeds the symbiote without detriment to its own nutrition and (2) the host is capable of resisting the activities of the symbiote by the development of specific defenses, such as antibodies. The aspect of resistance has other consequences than that of simply protecting the host from the effects of already established symbiotes. A high capacity for the development of resistance mechanisms may also determine the number of additional symbiotes which may become established. In the case of the metazoan symbiotes, it may be emphasized that they do not reproduce new individuals within the vertebrate host, Hence, the appearance of new individual symbiotes in such a host indicates that new entry and new establishment of symbiotes has occurred. It has been shown with some metazoan symbiotes, e.g., nematodes, that in a host in a good state of nutrition fewer individuals become established than in a host suffering from malnutrition. Similar phenomena have been observed in hosts harboring protistan symbiotes which, of course, do multiply within the host. In many such cases the reproduction of protistan organisms cannot keep up with the rate of mortality, due to the effects of host resistance mechanisms, and the number of symbiotes is reduced. This matter is discussed in somewhat more detail in Chapter 4.

Returning to the original question, we may ask whether "parasite" and "pathogen" can be considered related terms. When we are dealing with living organisms, pathogens are generally parasites; but a parasite may be a potential pathogen rather than an actual one. Given the proper circumstances, it seems plain that almost any symbiote may become a pathogen. The circumstances seem frequently to involve the nutritional state of the host. When we speak of "nutritional state" in this way we must look at the meaning carefully. As far as the effects of the outcome of a parasitism are concerned, we must be prepared to examine nutrition at the cellular as well as at the organismic level. Adequate nutrition requires not only that the organism get enough to eat but also that the foods be properly balanced in quality with respect to carbohydrates, proteins, fats, vitamins, and trace elements. Further than this, the process of utilization must be operating with adequate efficiency. A host animal which is suffering gross fatigue, for example, may not have adequate nutrition at the cellular level. This altered state may influence the outcome of a given symbiosis.

The classical instance in which the level of nutrition modifies the outcome of parasitism may be found in the history of hookworm disease in Puerto Rico. Around the turn of the century it was discovered that the devastating anemia found in much of the human population of Puerto Rico was related to the activities of a nematode parasite, the hookworm (*Necator americanus*). After a considerable expenditure of money and time in attempting to eradicate the infection, it began to be appreciated that the nutritional state of the host had a great deal to do with determining whether or not the individual showed disease. The disease could be treated by improved nutrition in many cases. It was also shown that the number of hookworms present bore a relationship to whether or not overt disease was characteristic of the parasitism. The picture of the relationship which has finally emerged is that the degree of disease produced by a given number of worms is related to the nutritional state of the host. Moreover, the number of worms harbored is, at least in part, related to the capacity of the host to resist the establishment of new worms, which establishment rate is, in turn, related to the nutritional state. This is clearly a set of feedback mechanisms. As presented, the foregoing description is oversimplified. There are other complicating factors in the hookworm-human ecology. However, the point is made that this is a feedback mechanism, with the nutritional state as a central feature through which the components operate. At present, the hookworm-human parasitism is quite common in Puerto Rico but hookworm disease is not. Other examples illustrating the importance of environment in determining the nature of a symbiosis are discussed in Chapter 11.

GENERAL REMARKS

In this chapter an attempt has been made to touch on a few meaningful examples of symbiotic integration, ranging from the simple to the complex. Those termed complex seem to involve homeostatic devices which sharply regulate the association at the level of the individual host and thus at the population level. Factors which interfere with operation of a homeostatic device may change the character of an association and, as in marriage, it may be for better or worse. Associations that appear to be simple may involve complex behavior.

SUGGESTED READING

AHMADJIAN, V. 1967. *The Lichen Symbiosis.* Blaisdell Publishing Co., Waltham, Mass.

ALLEN, E. K., and O. N. ALLEN. 1958. Biological aspects of symbiotic nitrogen fixation. In *Handbuch der Pflanzenphysiologie* (ed., W. RUHLAND), Vol. 8. Springer Verlag, Berlin.

BUCHNER, P. 1965.

CLEVELAND, L. R. 1960.

DOWSON, W. J. 1957.

X GARRETT, S. D. 1956. *Biology of Root-Infecting Fungi.* Cambridge University Press, London and New York.

HALE, M. E. 1961.

HARLEY, J. L. 1959. *The Biology of Mycorrhiza.* Leonard Hill, London.

HARVEY, E. N. 1952.

X HENRY, S. M. (ed.). 1966–67. *Symbiosis.* Academic Press, New York.

HUNGATE, R. E. 1966.

KARAKASHIAN, S. J. 1968. Invertebrate symbioses with *Chlorella.* In *Colloquium in Biology.* Oregon State University Press, Corvallis, Ore.

KIRBY, H., JR. 1941.

MARAMOROSCH, K. 1963.

MUSCATINE, L. 1961.

NUTMAN, P. S., and B. MOSSE. 1963.

SAGEN, L. 1967.

YONGE, C. M. 1936.

4

Host Defense and Predisposition

In this chapter we are concerned with those properties of the host, both static and dynamic, which determine whether or not a parasite becomes established in a host and whether it persists if it does succeed in becoming established.

The terms *susceptibility* and *resistance* have frequently been used as though they were opposites. The author has discussed elsewhere the desirability of carefully defining these terms so that they represent, not opposites, but two different qualities in the host-parasite relationship. "Susceptibility" would thus be defined as a physiological state of the host in which a given parasite is furnished with its life needs, and "insusceptibility" as the state in which these life needs are not satisfied, neither state involving a response of the host to the presence of the parasite. This latter point is extremely important in differentiating insusceptibility and resistance. "Resistance" is defined as those alterations of the physiological state of the host which represent a physiological response to previous or present experience with the parasite or a chemically related entity. Using these definitions, we may see that an individual host may be highly susceptible and become highly resistant (Read, 1958).

There are of course genetic determinants of susceptibility-insusceptibility and of the capacity of a host to show resistance to a parasite. These genetic factors are discussed in Chapter 9.

SUSCEPTIBILITY

There are usually static barriers to the entry of a given parasite. In vertebrates, the skin and the mucous membranes of the open cavities of the body represent barriers which may have to be penetrated. Some parasites have evolved mechanisms for gaining entrance through these barriers by the activity of a vector organism which punches or scrapes a hole in the barrier through which the parasite can enter. In still other cases, the parasite has other mechanisms for penetrating the barriers, or may depend on chance for entry. The tetanus and gas gangrene bacteria are parasites of this latter sort. They gain entry when injury to the skin barrier allows their introduction. In plants, the same sort of static defense of a morphologically recognizable type is also found.

In addition to what may be called purely mechanical defenses, many potential hosts are equipped with static chemical defenses.

These may be chemical substances which interfere with the metabolism of an entering parasite. There are few well-recognized ones in the case of animal hosts; examples which may be cited are the effects of specific bile salts which inhibit certain tapeworm larvae (p. 133), the effects of urea on flatworms, rendering them incapable of parasitizing elasmobranch fishes (p. 235), and the effect of host hemoglobin type on susceptibility to malaria parasites (p. 226).

Sharks, rays

Certain plant hosts have well-recognized non-specific chemical defenses against parasites. The classical example is seen in the insusceptibility of some onions to the smudge parasite *Colletotrichum*. This fungus begins its relationship with the host by a saprophytic development on the outer, non-living scale of the plant. Eventually it penetrates the underlying living scales and becomes a parasite. Onion varieties in which the bulb scales are pigmented are highly insusceptible to smudge. Associated with the colored flavone compounds in the dry outer scales are colorless, water-soluble phenols, catechol and protocatechuic acid. These phenols are toxic to the smudge organism, preventing germination and penetration. That this protection is afforded by the dry outer scales is shown by the fact that if the outer scales are removed and the underlying fleshy scales are exposed to the fungus in a moist chamber, parasitism ensues. In some plants, antifungal substances are found on the surface of the leaves. Brief washing of the leaves with water yields extracts which inhibit the germination of fungus spores (Martin et al., 1957). Other chemical substances have been shown to occur in corn and potatoes which have an antiparasitic effect and afford those plant strains possessing them some protection from parasites and thus from the disease produced by certain plant parasites (Beck, 1957). Some examples of insusceptibility due to lack in host tissues of metabolites required by symbiotes are discussed in Chapters 7 and 10.

Alteration of Susceptibility

Changes with age of the host in susceptibility to the establishment of symbiotes is widely recognized in plants and animals. Among insect hosts, age and state of nutrition may be critical in determining whether or not a symbiote may be established. Most bacterial and viral symbiotes become established more readily in insect larvae than in adults. Terzian et al. (1956) showed that, with advancing age, the mosquito *Aedes aegypti* grew less susceptible to the avian malaria organism *Plasmodium gallinaceum*. When aging mosquitoes were given blood meals on humans before being fed on infected avian blood, there was an increase in the number of parasites established.

Wijers (1958) studied the effect of age on the infection of the fly *Glossina palpalis* with the hemoflagellate protozoan *Trypanosoma gambiense*. When flies of various ages were fed on an infected monkey, 21% of newly emerged flies and 4% of two-day-old flies became infected. Older flies did not become infected. This change has been attributed to the development and hardening of the peritrophic membrane in the digestive tract of the fly (Willett, 1966). In examining the susceptibility of snails to two trematodes of the genus *Fasciola*, it was found that immature snails, belonging to species which are insusceptible as adults, can often be infected (Kendall, 1964).

The development of malaria parasites in mosquitoes may also be affected by the presence of other organisms in the insect gut. Several years ago, Terzian showed that addition of sulfonamides or antibiotics increased the apparent susceptibility of mosquitoes to *Plasmodium gallinaceum*, and Micks and Ferguson (1961) increased the number of *P. relictum* developing in the arthropod host by adding chloramphenicol and streptomycin to the diet. Garnham (1956) noted that microsporidian infections in mosquitoes reduced the numbers of *P. cynomolgi* developing in these hosts.

Environment and Susceptibility

In plants, a number of cyclic alterations in susceptibility, induced by the environment, have been recognized. Various trees show enhanced susceptibility to infection by fungi during certain times of the year. In several instances it is known that there are diurnal fluctuations in the susceptibility of various plants to infection by bacterial and fungal symbiotes. Sometimes this variation is correlated with the diurnal opening of the stomata on the leaves of the host or with fluctuating chemical changes in the tissues (Yarwood, 1959).

Temperature change is known to change susceptibility. The classical demonstration was that of Pasteur and his collaborators in 1878. It was shown that chickens with a body temperature of 42° C were insusceptible to anthrax bacteria. However, if birds were chilled so that the body temperature fell to 37 to 38° C they became susceptible to anthrax. There are probably numerous other examples of such alterations, but they have not been scientifically established in many cases. Dubos (1954) discussed some of the difficulties.

In plant hosts, temperature has long been recognized as a factor altering susceptibility. Plants exposed to high or low temperatures often show an increased susceptibility when subsequently exposed to fungal symbiotes. Humidity too seems to play a role in plant susceptibility. There are also instances in which there is a correlation between the establishment of a symbiote in animal hosts, e.g., filarial nematodes in man, and humidity. However, it is not clear whether this is an effect on susceptibility of the host or a direct effect on the symbiote. In many cases, it is necessary to distinguish the possibilities but this is often easier said than done.

Cyclic manifestations of susceptibility are sometimes associated with patterns of feeding in animals. Differences in the establishment of helminths under different host feeding regimes are known (see below). Addition of vitamins to the diet has been shown to affect the susceptibility of mosquitoes to the malaria parasite *Plasmodium gallinaceum,* and according to Terzian and Stahler (1960), the administration of certain acids, bases, or salts markedly altered the rate of establishment of *Plasmodium* in the mosquito host. In plants, alterations of mineral nutrition, light intensity, and soil pH (all of which have general nutritional effects) have been shown to have effects on susceptibility to viral, bacterial, and fungal symbiotes.

Mention may be made of genetic modifications of susceptibility. Such modifications are clearly indicated in some of the examples cited above, and a number of such instances are discussed in Chapter 9.

Insusceptibility Involving Host Behavior

The most obvious behavioral insusceptibilities are those in which the host behaves in such a way that it is simply not available at the same time as the parasite. In some cases, it has been shown that a particular host may be insusceptible because of defenses which cannot accurately be called static but which are not resistance. For example, Godfrey has published a series of studies showing that the inclusion of cod-liver oil in the diet of laboratory animals has a markedly deleterious effect on a variety of protozoan parasites, including sporozoans (*Babesia* and *Plasmodium*) and hemoflagellates (*Trypanosoma* spp.). This suppression of the parasites was antagonized by adding certain antioxidants to the diet, such as ascorbic acid or vitamin E. The evidence seems to indicate that the effect of cod-liver oil is attributable to the presence of unsaturated fatty acids which form organic peroxides in the tissues of the host. These peroxides in turn inhibit the parasite. It seems obvious in this case that a host having a predilection for certain items of food containing large amounts of unsaturated fatty acids might be relatively insusceptible to some animal parasites (Godfrey, 1957). Along another line, Chu and Oguri showed that ducks are only susceptible to infection with the trematode *Parorchis* if they are maintained on a diet containing mollusks, in this case squid. The normal hosts of the trematode are mollusk eaters. Squirrels are highly susceptible to the tapeworm *Hymenolepis nana* if maintained in the laboratory on a diet of dog biscuits. However, the author and his colleagues were unable to establish this worm in wild populations of gray squirrels in the Baltimore area. Subsequent laboratory study showed that if squirrels are fed on acorns or mushrooms, natural foods of these animals, they cannot be infected with *Hymenolepis nana*. It seems probable that the squirrel may be protected from *H. nana* infection in nature by virtue of its choice of foods, although other factors may also be involved.

RESISTANCE IN VERTEBRATES

Most of our information on the development of resistance in animals has been obtained with mammals. However, it will be clear that the reactions described in vertebrate hosts have evolved from mechanisms in lower animals. Some of these may represent such modifications that a straightforward evolutionary story may never be fabricated.

During the mid-nineteenth century it was noticed by several investigators that when foreign particles, such as carmine, were injected into mammals, the particles were deposited in certain organs, such as spleen, liver, and lymph nodes, where they could be found for several days. In later years many other substances were found to be deposited in this fashion. Metchnikoff (1905) recognized the importance of the cells carrying out this capture of foreign particles and called them *macrophages*. Some are more or less fixed in position,

while others seem to wander in the tissues. The most active of the fixed macrophages are those in the vascular system, liver sinusoids, sinuses of the spleen, the bone marrow, and the lymph glands. Wandering macrophages are found throughout the body, including the blood. The common capacity to accumulate foreign materials, notably dyes, led several workers to consider such cells as an integrated system, which Aschoff in 1924 called the *reticuloendothelial system*. Unfortunately, this terminology implied that the true endothelium of the vascular system engaged in phagocytosis. There is virtually no evidence for such activity; this cellular system is more properly termed the *lymphoid-macrophage system* (Taliaferro and Mulligan, 1937).

As noted above, Metchnikoff recognized that the phagocytic activity of macrophages could serve as a defense mechanism through the capture of invading micro-parasites and the lymphoid-macrophage system may be regarded as a functional unit of the body having phagocytic activity as a common characteristic. The distribution of phagocytic cells is not the same in all vertebrates. For example, the bone marrow of the mouse is much less active than the bone marrow of the rabbit. In birds, most of the phagocytic cells are in the liver.

There is considerable evidence that the removal of small parasitic organisms, such as bacteria, from the blood of a vertebrate resembles what is observed with non-living particles. Macrophages take up bacteria injected into the blood. One difference is seen in that the polymorphonuclear blood cells seem to phagocytize bacteria much more readily than non-living particles. Such blood cells are in turn phagocytized by fixed or wandering macrophages. The blood is frequently cleared of microorganisms in very short periods of time. Bull (1915) found that bacteria fell from 10 million per milliliter 1 minute after intravenous injection to 40 per milliliter 15 minutes later. This drop in numbers is seen

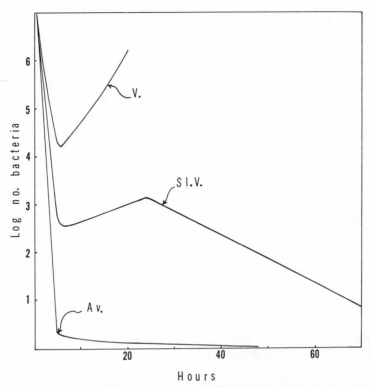

Fig. 4–1 The change with time in numbers of bacteria (pneumococci) per milliliter of blood after intravenous inoculation of rabbits with virulent (V), slightly virulent (Sl.V.), and avirulent (Av.) strains of the symbiote. (Drawn from data of Wright, 1927, *J. Pathol. Bacteriol.* 30.)

even though the injected organisms are highly virulent, in which case the number in the blood may later increase (Fig. 4–1). It may be pointed out that the intravenous injection of large numbers of bacteria is a laboratory procedure and would rarely occur in nature (an interesting exception to this was the spread of an infection among drug addicts in New York). However, it has been shown in various infections that phagocytosis of microorganisms does indeed occur.

Although parasites may be removed from the extracellular fluids of the body by phagocytosis, this may not result in the death of the parasites. In some cases, the microorganisms are killed in macrophages but in other instances they are not, or rather only some of them are. The tuberculosis and leprosy bacilli and certain protozoans, for example, seem not to be seriously inconvenienced by phagocytosis. Our detailed information on how microorganisms are killed in tissues is very limited. It is known that some are killed by intracellular digestion; but it would be very helpful if we knew why some are digested and some are not.

The Vertebrate Responses

It may be pertinent to consider what happens to microorganisms entering the body through epithelial layers, such as skin or the respiratory or intestinal mucosa. The parasite is first lodged in the subepithelial tissues and the host tissues show what is called an *inflammatory response*. There is dilation of capillary blood vessels with a local increase in blood flow. Leukocytes leave the capillaries and enter the tissues. Fluid collects in the extracellular spaces, due to increased permeability of the blood vessels, and this fluid may form a clot. These reactions tend to localize microorganisms and prevent their movement into other parts of the body. If they are indeed localized but not all destroyed, death of cells may occur and the formation of a local pocket or abscess may be the result. (Compare these events with the clotting response in some invertebrates, page 85.)

Second Lines of Defense

The speed with which inflammation occurs seems to vary with different invading organisms, and this rate of response will have a bearing on whether the microorganisms are localized. (Our knowledge of the value of the early inflammatory reaction as a defense is very incomplete.) If reaction is slow, some microorganisms escape this line of defense and enter the lymphatics or spread widely in the subcutaneous tissues.

In the lymphatics, local clotting may occur, which again tends to localize invading organisms. Further trapping of microorganisms by phagocytosis also occurs, particularly in lymph nodes. The latter occurs quite frequently when entry is through the intestinal mucosa.

In the cases of parasites with high invasive power or virulence, the clearing mechanisms described above may be relatively ineffective. On the other hand, in an animal which has been immunized by previous exposure of the tissues to the particular parasite, the responses are of heightened intensity and the parasite may be rapidly overwhelmed.

Up to this point we have been dealing with host responses which occur almost immediately after the parasite has entered the host tissue. The cells of the body have further resources for defense, provided that the host is not overcome by the growth of the parasite. The presence of foreign materials, either the parasite itself or toxic materials produced by the parasite, stimulates the production of specific globulin proteins, antibodies, by cells of the lymphoid-macrophage system. Antibodies are capable of combining with the substances which stimulated their production, the antigens, and reaction of antigen and antibody may result in precipitation of the complex, which would be of obvious defensive value in the case of a toxin. If the antigen is actually associated with the body of the parasite, the reaction of antigen and antibody may cause clumping of the organisms or even lysis of the parasite. In some instances the reaction alters the parasite in a fashion facilitating phagocytosis and intracellular digestion of the invader. There are other instances in which the combination of antibody with the parasite cell interferes with cell function so as to slow or even halt growth of the parasite (see p. 214). This latter effect has been called "ablastic."

Wood (1953) gave a detailed description of human recovery from pneumococcus pneumonia which will serve as an example of the modes of resistance in an acute infectious disease. In a well-established lung infection, the first area of defense is in a fluid-filled local area in which bacteria are multiplying. Here, in an outer ring, are found numerous leukocytes containing phagocytized microorganisms. Central to this is a zone of pus cells containing very few intact bacteria. In the center of the lesion, macrophages are abundant and the bacteria have been cleared. The second area of defense involves the tracheobronchial lymph nodes which drain the pulmonary system. If bacteria reach these nodes, inflammation quickly occurs and numbers of polymorphonuclear leukocytes accumulate. The leukocytes in these lymph nodes remove bacteria very efficiently and may keep them from entering the subclavian veins and the general circulation.

Third Lines of Defense

Bacteria escaping phagocytosis in the lymph nodes may cause a fatal bacteremia if the third area of cellular defense is inadequate. This third area is capillary phagocytosis; the normally free circulating polymorphonuclear leukocytes attach to the walls of capillaries and small arteries and veins and remove bacteria from the blood. This process also goes on in the liver, spleen, and lungs. Most of the bacterial population may be destroyed and, when antibodies appear later, destruction of the microorganisms may be complete. The pneumococci are representative of the extracellular microbial symbiotes which do not survive inside phagocytic cells. They incite violent inflammation, which results in rapid phagocytic host response.

Humoral Immunity

Immune reaction involving globulins is generally termed *humoral immunity*. Its efficacy will be determined by the speed with which it is brought into play, by the concentration of antibody in tissue fluids, and by the availability of circulating (blood) antibody to the antigen. These factors seem to vary quite widely in various organs of the animal. Once an animal has produced a specific antibody, production may continue long after the parasite has been apparently exterminated. Even in those cases in which it disappears, a second infection at some later time by the same parasite results in a stronger and more rapid production of antibody than was seen in the original infection; the body seems to remain geared up for production of specific antibody.

Immunity based on actual response to a parasite or parasite antigen is called *active immunity*. The administration of specific antigens from parasites or of weakened parasites for the purpose of stimulating antibody production is the basis for the procedure known as *vaccination*.

Additional evidence for the role of humoral factors in immunity is that when serum from an immune animal is injected into a non-immune animal it will frequently confer some protection against the parasite. This phenomenon is known as *passive immunity* since it is not due to a response of the recipient animal. Passive immunity is also seen in the young animal whose female parent has an active immunity. Antibodies from the parental source may be deposited in the yolk of bird eggs, rendering the young bird insusceptible to specific symbiotes for several weeks after hatching. In mammals, passive transfer of antibodies occurs through the placenta and in the colostrum.

Animal Antibodies

The formation of specific protein antibodies in vertebrate animals is of general significance in biology, as well as in the framework of resistance to symbiotes. The natural configuration of globulin proteins, specified by the genetic makeup of the particular vertebrate, has imposed on it a specificity relating to the character of the particular antigen with which it reacts. Three general theories have been used to explain the origin of what is termed the *immunological specificity* of antibodies.

In the first of these, sometimes called the *direct template theory*, the antigen is utilized as a template in determining the secondary configuration, or folding, of the protein molecule. This theory preserves the idea that the coding for protein synthesis rests in the genetic makeup of the host. Pauling, a major proponent of this theory, postulates that the ends of the protein chain are primarily concerned and that each antibody thus has two specific combining regions, each of which fits a particular portion of the antigen molecule. The significance of this resulting bivalence will become apparent when we discuss the events of antigen-antibody reaction.

The second theory, sometimes called the *indirect template theory,* postulates that the antigen produces its effect on the genetic material of the vertebrate and thus modifies the specifications for globulin synthesis. This theory would explain why the animal may continue to produce specific antibody after the antigen has apparently disappeared. Corollaries of this theory are used to explain why the organism does not usually make specific antibodies which combine with its own proteins and would predict the phenomenon known as immunological tolerance. Simply stated, the latter suggests that an organism does not distinguish an antigen as "foreign" if it contacts the antigen before birth or under other special circumstances. The animal thus "tolerates" the antigen, not producing specific antibody in response to its presence. Studies by Burnet, Fenner, Medawar, and others have shown that this is indeed the case with some antigens.

A third theory, usually called the *clonal selection theory,* owes much to the discarded side-chain theory postulated by Ehrlich many years ago. Ehrlich speculated that reactive side chains were available in the organism *before* antigen was introduced and that antigen simply stimulated the production of the specific reactive groups. Jerne (1955) postulated that there is normally a very diverse population of globulin molecules, representing all antigenic determinants. When antigen is introduced into the body, enhanced production of the appropriate member of the globulin population ensues. Burnet modified Jerne's theory and proposed clonal selection. Simply stated, this theory postulates that lymphoid cells vary in surface

makeup with respect to specific sites which may combine with antigens. Each cell type is capable of giving rise to a clone of cells with a specific site *and* with the capacity to make and liberate globulins bearing this specific site.

None of these theories can be considered proven. All of them have weaknesses, but they furnish a valuable framework for studying this problem.

There is good evidence that antibodies are produced in cells of the lymphoid-macrophage system. Chemical or physical agents which interfere with the function of the system interfere with antibody production. When cells of the lymphoid-macrophage system from an immunized animal are transplanted to another animal, the ability to produce antibodies is also transferred. Such cells will also produce antibody in tissue culture.

Antigen-Antibody Reaction

The union of antigen and antibody has been the subject of intensive investigation for more than fifty years; the student is referred to Kabat and Mayer (1962) for a sophisticated survey of the development of this knowledge. The power of antibody to combine with antigen is its most important feature in acquired immunity. The reaction of antigen and antibody is specific and reversible and the complexing is thought to involve van der Waals forces. Some of the visible effects of antigen-antibody reaction, such as precipitation of soluble antigen or agglutination of microorganisms, are explained on the basis of bivalence. That is, each antibody has at least two reactive sites. Thus, after one site has reacted with an antigen molecule, the second site may react with a second antigen molecule. The ultimate result of the repetition of such reactions is precipitation or agglutination. Lysis of symbiote cells after combination of antibody with cell surface antigens also involves the participation of other serum components, collectively called *comple-ment*. It may be reiterated that the foregoing is highly abridged and the student should consult other sources, such as Carpenter (1965), for detailed discussions of antigen-antibody reactions.

An Application of Koch's Postulates

Koch's postulates (see p. 20) may be adapted to the problem of criteria for determining whether a chemical substance is involved in resistance to a symbiote: (1) the substance is associated with resistance to the symbiote at the site in which the symbiote occurs; (2) the substance can be isolated from hosts responding to the presence of a symbiote; (3) introduction of the substance to the appropriate organ or fluid of a healthy host confers some enhanced protection against establishment of the symbiote; and (4) the character of the induced protection resembles that observed in the resistant animal or plant. It may be seen that, with slight modification, these criteria can be applied to problems of insusceptibility.

RESISTANCE TO ANIMAL PARASITES

Thus far, we have described the responses of the host as though the outcome would be either pro or con; the host would overcome the parasite or succumb to the effects of the parasite. Actually this dichotomy is the course only in very acute disease. More often, the relationship does not have such a final black-or-white outcome but ends up in varying shades of gray. This outcome is the biological "compromise," which may be arrived at quite soon after the parasite enters the host. We may cite certain examples of resistance resulting in suppression rather than extermination of animal parasites.

Immunity to Some Protozoans

The very extensive studies of resistance to malaria infections have shown that there is considerable destruction of the parasites from the very beginning of an infection. (See page 104 for discussion of the life history of the malaria parasite.) Huff and his colleagues obtained evidence that the acquired immunity to the blood stream stages of malaria parasites of birds has little effect on the exoerythrocytic stages of the parasites. Such observations have been used to explain the relapses (reappearance of disease) seen in infections with some malaria parasites.

Taliaferro and his colleagues (1937) have demonstrated the general mechanism of immunity to malaria parasites in the blood. The parasites and infected red blood cells are phagocytized by reticulo-endothelial cells, mainly in the liver, spleen, and bone marrow, and destroyed. The destruction of parasitized red cells by the reticulo-endothelial cells is thought to contribute to the anemia observed in malaria infections. As the infection goes on, the host's phagocytic activity increases, due to an increased activity of individual cells *and* an increase in the number of phagocytes. Eventually the rate of destruction of parasites exceeds the rate of their production and the parasites are no longer found in the blood.

However, the exoerythrocytic stages may continue to live and reproduce. In a healthy individual, the parasites released into the blood from this exoerythrocytic population serve to stimulate, more or less continuously, the immunity of the host, and the parasites are destroyed as they appear in the blood. Anything serving to interfere with the functioning of the immunity reactions, e.g., poor nutrition or another disease, may allow the development of a new population of blood stream forms, and a relapse, with the appearance of disease, results. It may be pointed out that the immunity is highly specific and not only fails to protect the host from the activities of another species of malaria parasite but may not even affect other strains of the same species (see p. 202).

Immune reactions of various hosts to trypanosome infections have been studied in some detail. Some of these are of interest in showing the alterations of the immunological properties of parasite populations and are discussed on page 214.

Immunity to Metazoans

The development of immunity to nematodes, particularly those feeding on the tissues of the gut, has been studied for about thirty years. It has been shown that some host immunity to reinfection occurs with a number of nematode parasites and that this immunity may be passively transferred. Some years ago, Sarles demonstrated that when the nematode *Nippostrongylus* is incubated in serum from an immune host, precipitates form around the mouth, anus, and excretory pore. Thorson and others made similar observations with the dog hookworm, *Ancylostoma caninum*. Later Thorson (1956b) found that the catalytic activity of proteolytic enzymes from the esophagus of *Ancylostoma* is inhibited by immune sera. In general, these and other researches support the idea presented by Chandler (1937) that immunity to these nematodes may involve reaction of the host to enzymes concerned in the feeding activities of the worms. Immunity against nematodes may have very different aspects, however. The so-called "self-cure" phenomenon in certain nematode infections appears to differ from resistance developed to the antigens of adult worms (see p. 83). Many details of the basis of immunity to nematodes require further study.

The development of resistance to *Trichinella* has been the subject of much investigation since the studies of Ducas in 1921. During the early stages of a *Trichinella* infection the host first becomes allergic to nematode antigens (see p. 84 and p. 127). As the allergic symptoms of the host subside the host develops some

immunity to *Trichinella*, and there is evidence that host antibodies are formed against "metabolic products" of the worm (Campbell, 1955; Chipman, 1957).

Host resistance to several flatworm parasites has been demonstrated. The development of partial immunity to such infections has been demonstrated with schistosome trematodes. In addition to the observations on resistance of the host, a variety of immunological responses have been found (Kagan, 1958). It is difficult from information available to determine how many types of antibodies are formed and whether any or all are involved in the actual resistance of the host. Similarly, the resistance of hosts to the mouse tapeworm, *Hymenolepis nana*, and to the larval forms of several other tapeworms has been reported, but considerable work remains to be done to establish the mechanisms involved in these cases of acquired resistance.

It may be pointed out that there is evidence that immunity is not developed by the vertebrate in response to parasites which live *only* in the lumen of the gut. Most of the tapeworms and acanthocephalans live in this fashion and may not stimulate the resistance mechanisms of the host. On the other hand, ectoparasites may stimulate an immune response in the host. Such have been recorded for monogenetic trematodes from fishes (Nigrelli, 1937), and various biting arthropods (Gaafar, 1966). Maggots living in the skin also stimulate immunity in the host (Blacklock, Gordon, and Fine, 1930; Esslinger, 1958).

HYPERSENSITIVITY IN VERTEBRATES

We have discussed antibodies as defensive agents of the vertebrate. Mention should be made of the fact that the combination of antigen and antibody can produce considerable damage to the host. This situation is seen in the individual who is *hypersensitive* to an antigen. This state is also known as *allergy*. What appears to

eosinophils - leucocytes, w/ cytoplasmic or other granulocytes

inclusions readily stained by the dye eosin

be involved is that there is only a small amount of free antibody circulating in the body fluids but relatively large amounts attached or fixed to cells of the host body. When antigen combines with fixed antibody it causes damage to the cell, perhaps resembling the damage to a parasite when circulating antibody combines with an antigen fixed on the parasite cell. Stewart (1950–1953; 1955) has furnished evidence that, in certain nematode infections, local hypersensitivity of the intestinal mucosa may serve as an effective mechanism for what is called "self-cure." In this case, the host becomes sensitized to molting fluid produced by the larval nematode in connection with the third molt (see p. 92). In a host harboring worms, the introduction of a new batch of larval nematodes results in the release of molting fluid and a consequent hypersensitive response of the gut mucosa. This results in marked hyperemia and most of the nematodes including those already resident in the gut are swept out, producing a "self-cure" effect. This type of allergic response to molting fluid produced by a *new* inoculum of infective larval nematodes should be carefully differentiated from the development of resistance to adult nematodes, which may produce a marked reduction in the number of symbiotes (see p. 129).

Hypersensitivity as Part of Disease

Although allergy may have "value" as a part of the host's resistance in that it hastens the local inflammatory response, it may be most inconvenient for humans when the antigen is a substance in foods, pollen, or house dust. The reactions of hypersensitivity vary considerably; some are known by such well-recognized names as asthma, hives, and hayfever.

In a number of vertebrate diseases attributed to animal parasites, allergy appears to play a rather prominent role. The specific allergic manifestations vary, depending on the species of parasite (differing antigens?) and on the location of the parasite in the host. In the case of aberrant parasites which behave in an unusual manner in an unusual host, allergic manifestations are the major indication that parasites are present. For example, the human disease known as *cutaneous larva migrans* is recognized by what appear to be allergic responses in the skin to the presence of foreign worms, such as the dog hookworm.

In *visceral larva migrans,* caused by the wanderings of dog or cat nematodes or other "foreign" helminths in the interior of the human body, the allergic symptoms may be much more generalized and may include eosinophilia, fever, coughing and pulmonary difficulty, enlargement of the liver, and kidney disease (nephrosis) (see Beaver, 1956). A widespread set of tropical human diseases (pulmonary eosinophilia, tropical eosinophilia, and others) are now thought to be primarily due to hypersensitive reactions to "foreign" species of helminths. A cosmopolitan human disease known as swimmer's itch is an allergic dermatitis due to penetration of the skin by larval trematodes of species which normally develop in non-human hosts.

Infections of "usual" hosts by animal parasites frequently result in the appearance of allergic symptoms at one point or another. Repeated exposure of vertebrates to species of parasites which enter the body through the skin often results in the appearance of dermatitis. This sensitivity has been observed with various hosts parasitized by nematodes, schistosome trematodes, and arthropods. In the latter case the disease may consist mostly of hypersensitive reaction. For example, the skin afflictions of man, cats, dogs, cattle, goats, sheep, camels, pigs, foxes, lions, wolves, wombats, and many other animals caused by itch mites seem to be primarily manifestations of allergy to the mites or their products. This seems to be true also of symptoms associated with the presence of sucking lice (Peck et al., 1943) and of the discomfort produced by the bites of many mosquitoes, flies, fleas, etc. Some components of flea saliva combine with skin proteins to form an active antigen (Young et al., 1963).

In a number of protozoan infections allergy may be suspected because of the symptoms which may appear. In many hemoflagellate infections there are local responses associated with the point of entry into the body. In the early development of pathogenic trypanosomes in various hosts there are responses, such as enlargement of lymph nodes, edema, skin rashes, and fever, suggesting the development of hypersensitivity.

Allergic manifestations are commonly observed in helminth infections. Most of the early symptoms (several weeks) produced by *Trichinella* are clearly those of hypersensitivity, with edema, fever, eosinophilia, hives, and pulmonary difficulties as prominent features, and treatment for generalized allergy yields results. The symptoms of disease produced by filarial nematodes are certainly in part allergic; such effects include "Calabar swelling" caused by *Loa*, "mu-mu" caused by *Wuchereria*, elephantiasis caused by *Wuchereria*, the skin lesions of "poll ill" caused by *Onchocerca*, and probably others.

Hypersensitivity reactions are quite common in infections with ascarid nematodes. As a matter of fact, humans readily become sensitive to *Ascaris* without being infected. One of the author's colleagues is so sensitive that contact with *Ascaris* precipitates asthma and urticaria, once requiring hospitalization. Much of the cellular reaction in the lungs of pigs infected with *Ascaris* has been attributed to hypersensitivity.

"NATURAL" RESISTANCE

There is some evidence that hosts may show resistance, due to previous exposure to antigens which are chemically related to those of a given parasite. This immunity arises from a sort of natural vaccination. For example, Warren and Borsos (1959) studied in chicken sera the antibody against the protozoan *Schizotrypanum cruzi*. Antibody against the protozoan was present in the newly hatched chick, apparently from maternal sources, but disappeared a few days after hatching. After several weeks the antibody titer again rose in normal chicks but not in germ-free chicks. The actual source of antigen was not discovered, but it seems certain that it does not involve infection with *S. cruzi*.

EFFECTS OF HOST DIET ON RESISTANCE

There is abundant evidence that the quality and quantity of the host diet may have sharp effects on the capacity of the host to develop or maintain resistance to parasites. Such effects have been observed with a great variety of parasitic agents, including worms, protozoans, bacteria, and viruses. A poor diet may affect the development of resistance in at least two ways: by interference with normal antibody production and, in some cases, by suppressing the production or activity of phagocytes. Antibodies are of course proteins, and the normal production of these substances requires the presence of the appropriate amino acids, the enzymes for activation, and an energy source with the coupling mechanisms at a high level as a minimum for the synthesis. If the required materials are not present in the diet, an animal may utilize its protein reserves. However, in the undernourished animal on a low protein or otherwise deficient diet the reserves may not be sufficient. Antibody production in such a host is lowered. Resistance to a parasitic agent is retarded or stopped and resistance already developed may be quickly lost. When such an individual animal is placed on an adequate diet, antibody production may increase with astonishing rapidity.

EFFECTS OF STRESS ON RESISTANCE

It is known that increased secretion of the hormones from the vertebrate adrenal cortex results in depression of inflammatory responses and antibody production. Further, it is known that various forms of stress may cause enhanced adrenal cortical activity. Thus, it follows that stress might be expected to produce effects on resistance to symbiotes. Indeed, it has been shown that crowding and fighting lower resistance to the nematode *Trichinella*, the tapeworm *Hymenolepis nana*, the protozoan *Trichomonas*, and the poliomyelitis and rabies viruses. Cold and certain other forms of stress also affect resistance to various symbiotes. The possibility that such stress responses may be important in the regulation of rodent populations has been discussed by Christian and Davis (1964).

It was mentioned in an earlier paragraph that state of nutrition may have effects on the state of resistance. There is the possibility that nutritional stress may involve endocrine factors. It is somewhat surprising that the significance of the host endocrine system in the decreased resistance occurring in most types of malnutrition is unknown (WHO, 1965). Stress is discussed further on page 261 in terms of ecology.

RESISTANCE AND SUSCEPTIBILITY OF INVERTEBRATE HOSTS

Phagocytosis, already mentioned as an important aspect of vertebrate resistance, is an important mechanism for food-getting in the lower metazoan animals. It is a common feeding method in sponges, flatworms, and coelenterates, and it seems probable that this was its primitive role. It may be noted that, in an organism such as a sponge, it would seem almost impossible to differentiate resistance from food-gathering.

In his original observations of phagocytosis, Metchnikoff (1905) noted the phenomenon in arthropods, echinoderms, and certain other invertebrates exposed to foreign agents. We have not made sweeping advances in the subject since Metchnikoff's day. Recent studies by Bang and his associates suggest that clotting of the blood with a consequent trapping of foreign organisms may be an important resistance mechanism in marine arthropods. When this is accompanied by autotomy, or shedding, of a limb, the host not only traps the foreign agent, but effectively sheds it from the body.

Immunity in Arthropods

The walling off of foreign bodies by the migration of macrophage-like cells and the subsequent deposition of chitin has been observed on many occasions in various arthropods. Particles of foreign material may be surrounded by blood cells that complete the encapsulation process with formation of a nodule within 24 hours (Metalnikov and Chorine, 1930; Cameron, 1934).

Salt (1960–1963) studied the reactions of the blood cells of certain insects to various foreign bodies, including parasites. Very marked activity of the blood cells resulted in encapsulation of parasites within a few hours. Of great interest was the finding that the surface properties of parasites determine whether or not the hemocytic reaction occurs. In addition to other observations supporting such a conclusion, Salt found that a surface to which an insect host does *not* react can be altered in such a way that a hemocyte response will be elicited. Larvae of the parasitoid insect *Nemeritis* do not stimulate a hemocyte reaction in the usual moth host *Ephestia*. However, when young larvae of *Nemeritis* were removed from the host, washed in certain fat solvents, and implanted in new hosts, a hemocytic reaction was observed.

Controls, washed in salt solution, developed in the second host without evoking a response. Quite clearly, in its usual host, *Nemeritis* has surface characteristics which either fail to evoke a hemocyte response or inhibit such a response.

There is some evidence that the extent of cellular reactions to entering trematode larvae may determine whether or not establishment of the worms in a molluscan host will occur. Newton (1952) investigated the infection of various strains of the snail *Australorbis glabratus* by the blood fluke *Schistosoma mansoni* and found that the worm readily penetrated all strains. However, in unsuitable strains, the symbiotes were destroyed within 24 to 48 hours by a marked cellular infiltration. This was followed by the formation of fibrous host tissue.

In many insects, a common reaction to the presence of a symbiote is the deposit of melanin. This is sometimes regarded as a mechanism for detoxifying phenolic compounds. The formation of melanin is thought to be the result of action of the enzyme phenolase on hydroxylated amino acids. Such development of melanin is not clearly a defense reaction to the presence of parasitic organisms, and it has been suggested that the deposition of melanin may fortuitously act as a defense when it is deposited in such a way as to prevent a vital activity of the parasite. In some cases, however, the general deposition of melanin does not seem to affect the parasite at all. This matter has been discussed by Salt (1961).

In some cases, there seems to be a humoral insusceptibility of insects to certain symbiotes. For example, the malaria organism *Plasmodium gallinaceum* will complete its development in the mosquito *Aedes aegypti* but will not develop in *Culex pipiens*. The lethal effect of the *C. pipiens* hemocoele fluid on the symbiote was elegantly shown by Weathersby (1963), who joined individuals of the two mosquito species by a plastic tube. In such preparations with a common hemocoele fluid, *P. gallinaceum* fails to develop when the mosquitoes feed on a bird infected with *P. gallinaceum*.

The viruses developing in arthropods frequently show a very broad capacity to infect different species. However, tissue susceptibility, which determines whether or not an ingested virus will establish itself, seems to relate to the capacity of gut cells to support virus multiplication. Although virtually nothing is known of the basis for such insusceptibility to animal viruses, it has been postulated that virus inhibitors present in the salivary secretions of aphids account for the apparent specificities of certain aphid-borne viruses of plants. This may be the case with other viruses.

Michajlow (1951) observed what appears to be differential susceptibility of various species of copepod crustaceans to larvae of pseudophyllidean tapeworms. When eaten by some copepods, larvae were killed by the digestive juice. In others, most but not all larvae were killed, while in a third species group of copepods the tapeworm larvae were not injured by the digestive juices. Such differential susceptibilities are probably quite common though they have been demonstrated rather infrequently. Similarly, some mosquitoes are rendered insusceptible to larval filarial nematodes by the lethal effect of host digestive secretions on the worms (Kartman, 1953).

Although there is little evidence for antibodies of the globulin protein type in insects, there is no question that humoral immunity is a reality. Insect "antibodies" do not agglutinate or precipitate antigens or microorganisms; however, the development of antibacterial substances in insect blood has been demonstrated. Unlike vertebrate antibodies, the antibacterial factors in insects are heat-stable (Briggs, 1958). A number of investigators have shown that insects can acquire immunity to bacterial toxins and to bacteria, although the immunity appears to be considerably less specific than the immune responses of vertebrates (Briggs, 1958; Stephens, 1959, 1962). Briggs showed that conventional serological procedures were not useful in demonstrating acquired immunity in insects. He showed that an increase in the immunity was paralleled by an increase in a heat-stable antibacterial substance which could be extracted from insects a few hours after vaccination. Aizawa (1954) produced an acquired immunity to nuclear polyhedrosis virus in silkworms, using a vaccine prepared from infected insect blood.

There is a quantity of circumstantial evidence that closely related invertebrates may differ in susceptibility to a given parasite. Such differences are best known in those instances in which invertebrates serve as intermediate hosts. For example, the species of *Plasmodium* causing human malaria infect only mosquitoes of the genus *Anopheles*. However, a given strain of *Plasmodium* will infect only a limited number of species or strains of *Anopheles*. Similar observations have been made on filarial worms and mosquitoes, as well as various other parasite-arthropod combinations. While we cannot be certain that we are dealing with variations in susceptibility rather than variations in the capacity to resist, the former seems most likely to the author (see p. 202).

Molluscan Reactions

The formation of pearls in Mollusca is a well-known result of cellular reaction to foreign agents, the foreign body frequently being a larval cestode or trematode in the case of natural pearls. Man, of course, has learned to introduce other types of foreign bodies to induce the reaction and consequent formation of pearls. In general, we can say that our knowledge of resistance mechanisms in invertebrates is woefully inadequate when compared with the quantity of information on vertebrates.

RESISTANCE IN HIGHER PLANTS

There is a considerable literature dealing with defense reactions of plants to invading parasites. During the early part of the century, the impact of new findings on immune reactions of vertebrates stimulated researches on the occurrence and basis of plant immunity. A great body of work was done to determine the basis of plant immunity before it was even established that plants can acquire immunity! Much of this early work sought to demonstrate antigen-antibody reactions and is inconclusive. This work was reviewed by Chester in 1933 and little has been done since. There is no adequate evidence for antigen-antibody reactions in plants and the existence of such in plants still remains unproven.

There is sound evidence that higher plants can produce chemical inhibitors in response to the presence of symbiotes. Such substances seem to be of low molecular weight. Important early studies were carried out with orchids and the fungi which live in symbiotic association with them. A French worker, Noel Bernard, showed in 1909 that the fungi grow freely in association with the orchid for a time, but fungus growth is then retarded and the orchid is immune to a subsequent infection. Later studies by Magrou, Nobecourt, Gäumann, Nüesch, and others showed that a diffusible chemical inhibitor is produced (Nüesch, 1963). Although this association of fungus and orchid is mutualistic, the significance of these observations for parasitic associations was recognized. Mueller and his associates studied the production of antifungal materials in strains of potatoes and beans which were resistant to a fungus causing late blight disease. Interestingly, the antifungal substance was produced in the presence of avirulent fungus strains and the toxic material once produced did not seem to be specific for a particular microorganism (see Mueller, 1950, 1956).

Whenever a plant is locally injured certain defense reactions can be observed. Injured cells apparently release substances, perhaps hormones, which stimulate cell division and sometimes the formation of cork tissue. In many instances this type of generalized response to injury is the same with parasitic and nonparasitic injury. There is also some evidence that injury allows the liberation of phenolic compounds from cells and that a parasite may be sharply inhibited by such compounds. It seems questionable whether the latter phenomenon should be considered a specialized response to injury by parasites.

HYPERSENSITIVITY REACTION IN PLANTS

Plant pathologists recognize another type of defense mechanism known as hypersensitivity, but differing sharply from what is called hypersensitivity in animals. The phenomenon was first observed with fungal parasites of plants and has been most studied with them. In essence, the reaction is as follows: The parasite penetrates host tissues and there is a rapid death of host cells in the neighborhood of the parasite. Local host-cell death and necrosis occur and the growth of the parasite is inhibited. The infection is limited to a local necrosis and the plant escapes the disease. The rapid breakdown of host cells indicates that the tissues have some kind of increased sensitivity to the parasite. The earlier that host-cell breakdown occurs, the greater is the chance that minimal symptoms of infection will be observed.

In nonresistant plants, host reaction and necrosis occur more slowly. Such hypersensitivity reactions have been observed in parasitisms involving bacteria and viruses, as well as fungi. The hypersensitivity reaction does not seem to be simply ascribed to the rapid starvation of the symbiote but may involve release of antibiotic materials.

The phenomenon is not completely understood (Mueller, 1959).

INTERFERONS

The term *interferon* has been applied to certain cell products which act as virus inhibitors. In 1957, Isaacs and Lindenmann discovered that when pieces of chick chorio-allantoic membrane were exposed to heat-inactivated influenza virus, an antiviral factor was produced. The factor, named "interferon," was shown to be a protein; there was evidence that it exerted antiviral effects by making cells incapable of supporting virus multiplication rather than by interacting directly with virus. Subsequent studies have shown that interferons are formed in many other virus–host-cell systems, many of them in tissue cultures.

Interferons show antiviral activity with a remarkable number of unrelated viruses but show considerable species specificity, with respect to host cells. For example, interferon produced by chick cells may fail to show any protective effect when placed in a virus–mouse-cell system, although a single interferon preparation may show antiviral activity with either DNA or RNA viruses.

Interferons appear to produce antiviral effects by inducing changes in host-cell metabolism. Agents which inhibit RNA or protein synthesis prevent the antiviral effects of interferon. There is considerable evidence to support the hypothesis that a specific RNA is made by the host cell in response to interferon; this may then serve as messenger for synthesis of a cell protein which has antiviral activity (Sonnabend and Friedman, in Finter, 1967). In reacting with cells to induce an antiviral substance, interferons seems to resemble hormones. These antiviral systems have been identified in all major groups of vertebrates and may occur in plants. Careful search for interferons in invertebrates does not seem to have been made.

GENERAL REMARKS

It is apparent that living organisms respond to the presence of symbiotes in a variety of ways. The responses are of broad significance since they are involved in the emergence of new properties during symbiosis. The appearance of new and unique properties, not characteristic of the isolated partners in a given symbiosis, is observed in *all* types of symbiosis.

In many cases, host responses in symbiosis are chemical in nature. They may be relatively specific responses, as in the case of antibody production, or relatively non-specific, as in the responses of plants and some chemical events of inflammation in animals. It is also apparent that there are time-dependent and cyclical changes in what we have chosen to term "susceptibility." The basis for these cyclic changes differs in various groups of hosts and symbiotes and may be altered by environmental factors. Some additional aspects of resistance and insusceptibility in populations of hosts and symbiotes and in their evolution will be considered in Chapters 10 and 11.

SUGGESTED READING

ALLEN, P. J. 1959. Physiology and biochemistry of defense. In *Plant Pathology* (eds., J. G. HORSFALL and A. E. DIMOND). Academic Press, New York.
BURNET, F. M. 1959.
CARPENTER, P. L. 1965.
CHESTER, K. S. 1933.
CHRISTIAN, J. J., and D. E. DAVIS. 1964.
CORT, W. W. 1950. Studies on schistosome dermatitis. II. Status of knowledge after more than twenty years. *Amer. J. Hyg.* 52:251.
DUBOS, R. 1954.
FINTER, N. 1967.
HELLER, J. H. (ed.). 1960. The reticuloendothelial system (R.E.S.). *Ann. N.Y. Acad. Sci.* 88:1.
HIRSCH, J. G. 1960. Antimicrobial factors in tissues and phagocytic cells. *Bacteriol. Rev.* 24: 133.
JERNE, N. K. 1955.
KABAT, E. A., and M. M. MAYER. 1962.
MARTIN, J. T., R. F. BATT, and R. T. BURCHILL. 1957.
METCHNIKOFF, E. 1905.

MUELLER, K. O. 1959.
NÜESCH, J. 1963.
POYNTER, D. 1966. Some tissue reactions to the nematode parasites of animals. *Adv. Parasitol.* 4:321.
READ, C. P. 1958.
ROGERS, D. E. 1960. Host mechanisms which act to remove bacteria from the blood stream. *Bacteriol. Rev.* 24:50.
SALT, G. 1961.
SCHNEIDER, T. A. 1951. Nutrition and resistance-susceptibility to infection. *Amer. J. Trop. Med.* 31:174.
SPRENT, J. F. A. 1963. *Parasitism*. Williams and Wilkins, Baltimore.
STEPHENS, J. M. 1963. Immunity in insects. In *Insect Pathology* (ed., E. A. STEINHAUS). Academic Press, New York.
TALIAFERRO, W. H., and H. W. MULLIGAN. 1937.
WALKER, J. C., and M. A. STAHMANN. 1955. Chemical nature of disease resistance in plants. *Ann. Rev. Plant Physiol.* 6:351.
WOOD, W. B. 1960.
YARWOOD, C. E. 1959.

5

Adaptations for Reaching Hosts

Symbiotes reach their hosts in such varied ways that the task of generalizing is bewildering. The intricate and ingenious modifications of several general patterns have so fascinated biologists that great effort has been expended in the past hundred years in prying out the secret details of how symbiotes get about from host to host. Many of the scientific accounts of symbiote life histories sound like detective stories: until all the data were in, wrong guesses concerning the modus operandi have sometimes been made.

A primary problem for symbiotes is that of reaching new hosts, since this is necessary to perpetuate the species. This problem of getting to a fresh habitat is a pressing one for the symbiote since the environment itself, the host, has a very limited mortal duration. It has been remarked elsewhere that parasites do not eat to live, but eat to reproduce. Transfer to new hosts is intimately involved with biological reproduction. In considering the mechanisms by which symbiotes reach hosts, it is frequently a temptation to present the "simplest" ones first and then to proceed to those which are more "complicated." However, it should be kept in mind that these terms, "simple"

and "complicated," are merely expressions of how these cycles appear to us. In some instances, we know that some which appear to be simple and straightforward affairs contain all sorts of subtleties which may be easily overlooked. Some of the physiological subtleties are treated elsewhere in the book. In this chapter we shall try to outline briefly the general types of life cycles seen in certain groups of symbiotes and some of the special attributes associated with getting from host to host. It should be emphasized that ours is not an exhaustive treatment of this subject since it would require several books to present the life histories in the scientific literature. Many of the references at the end of this chapter will serve for further exploration of the literature on various aspects of the subject.

The commonest point at which symbiotes enter animal hosts is through the mouth, usually in company with food or drink. The second commonest path of entry is probably through the surface of the body. In the latter case, symbiotes may be brought to the host by another organism, a vector, or may reach and penetrate the host without being carried there. There is frequently some kind of development of symbiotes outside of hosts, although this is by no means invariably true. It has become customary to refer to the host in which a given symbiote undergoes sexual reproduction as the *definitive* host and to other hosts in the life history as the *intermediate* hosts. In most cases, the definitive host is a higher metazoan than the intermediate host. However, some forms violate our definitions. For example, the malaria parasites and some of their close relatives undergo sexual reproduction in invertebrates and asexual reproduction in a vertebrate. It has been customary in such cases to stretch a point and refer to the invertebrates as intermediate hosts.

LIVING IN ONE HOST

When we say that a life history involves only one kind of host, we actually mean that only one species of host is required for the completion of the life cycle. We know in fact that many symbiotes can utilize more than one species of host although there may be only one common one. In fact, we may generalize by saying that animal symbiotes always seem to have the physiological capacity to live in more kinds of hosts than they are usually found to inhabit.

FORMS ENTERING THROUGH THE HOST'S MOUTH

All groups of symbiotic organisms having representatives living in the digestive tract of hosts have some species that enter the host through the mouth. Many of these, as we said, enter with food or drink; a few are actually eaten as food items by the host. Most of those entering the mouth are taken in unintentionally by the host, and most commonly the parasite is enclosed in a sheath, a shell, or protective cyst of some kind. The life histories of certain proto-

zoans and worms follow this general pattern.

Life Pattern of *Haemonchus*

The life history of *Haemonchus contortus*, the stomach nematode of sheep and cattle, will serve as an example (Fig. 5-1). The sexually reproducing adults of this worm live in the abomasum of the host and are red-colored animals about 10 to 25 mm long. The presence of the worms causes inflammation of the gastric mucosa and constitutes a serious economic problem in some areas. The life cycle appears to be relatively simple but is complicated by the phases of growth and development involved. The female lays from 5,000 to 10,000 eggs per day, and these pass out of the host in the droppings. On the ground under the proper conditions of temperature and humidity, the cells of the embryonic worm undergo repeated divisions to form a first larval stage. This tiny worm emerges from its shell and feeds on microorganisms. After a period of feeding, it molts and the second larva continues to feed for a second period. It finally molts, forming a third stage, but does not shed the molted skin, which is retained as a sheath. Only after attaining this third larval stage is the young nematode capable of infecting a vertebrate host. If the earlier stages get into a vertebrate, they are incapable of becoming established. This third larval stage does not feed and persists for a considerable period of time on pastures which are moist and moderately cool. The ruminant hosts become infected by inadvertently devouring larvae when grazing. In the stomach the larva emerges from the sheath and begins to feed on mucosal tissue. It molts twice more in this host as it grows to maturity. Within three or four weeks after entering the host the adult females will begin to produce eggs, and the cycle may be repeated.

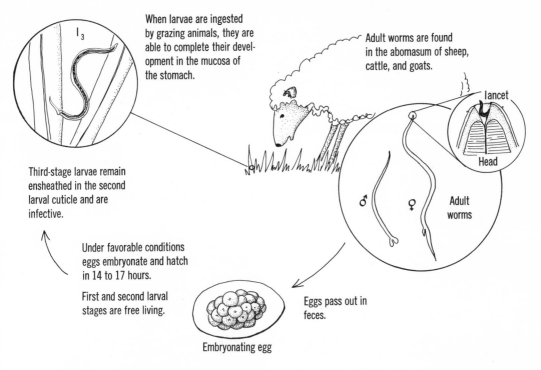

When larvae are ingested by grazing animals, they are able to complete their development in the mucosa of the stomach.

Adult worms are found in the abomasum of sheep, cattle, and goats.

lancet

Head

Third-stage larvae remain ensheathed in the second larval cuticle and are infective.

♂   ♀   Adult worms

Under favorable conditions eggs embryonate and hatch in 14 to 17 hours.

First and second larval stages are free living.

Eggs pass out in feces.

Embryonating egg

Fig. 5–1 The life pattern of the barber pole worm, *Haemonchus contortus*. (Redrawn from various authors.)

A number of other nematode symbiotes follow this general pattern, although some of them may actually burrow deeply into the host mucosa after entering the host and reenter the lumen of the gut after a period of development in the tissues immediately adjacent to the intestine. Many of them, also, do not hatch outside the host. For example, the large group of nematodes living in the cecum and large intestine of vertebrates and known as pinworms do not hatch until the shelled infective larvae are ingested by the vertebrate host.

Life Pattern of *Entamoeba*

A protozoan having a direct type of life history is the dysentery ameba, *Entamoeba histolytica* (Fig. 5–2). This parasite lives in the intestine, feeding on bacteria or on host tissue components. Periodically, certain individuals in the population round up and produce an external cyst. These cysts, as well as some unencysted individuals, pass out of the host in the feces. The encysted stages undergo rapid nuclear division, typically producing a tetranucleate form in this species. This quiescent, non-feeding encysted stage is highly resistant to environmental conditions and is immediately infective for another human host. To reach another host, it depends on the contamination of food or water by feces or by the feces-contaminated hands of its first host. On reaching the intestine of a new host, the ameba emerges from the cyst, rapidly undergoes cell division, and begins to produce a new population of amebas by fission. Although this life pattern seems simple, it is enormously successful.

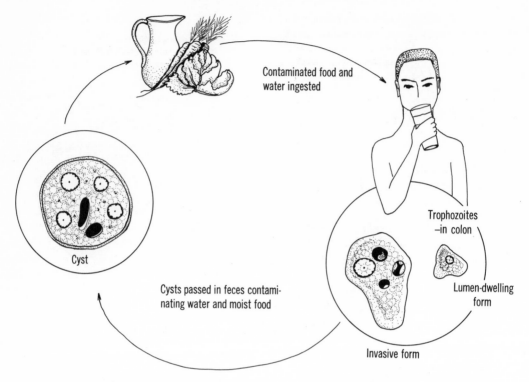

Fig. 5–2   The life pattern of the dysentery ameba, *Entamoeba histolytica.* (Redrawn from various authors.)

Life Pattern of *Eimeria*

A somewhat more complicated life history is seen in the protozoan *Eimeria tenella,* a sporozoan symbiote of chickens (Fig. 5–3). This organism passes out of its bird host in an encysted, resistant stage, known as an *oocyst.* Outside the host, this encysted stage undergoes cell division, producing eight sausage-like *sporozoites.* These sporozoites are capable of infecting a new bird host if the oocyst is ingested. These oocysts are extremely resistant to a variety of environmental conditions; it is common practice to incubate them in the laboratory in potassium dichromate solutions which inhibit and kill the accompanying bacteria. When the ripe oocyst is eaten by a host, the sporozoites are liberated. These sporozoites enter epithelial cells lining the intestine, where they grow until each invaded host cell is essentially filled by the parasite, which is now termed a *trophozoite.* The trophozoite now undergoes rapid cell division, producing a number of small cylindrical *merozoites.* These leave the now exhausted host cell, and each of them enters a fresh epithelial cell and grows, producing a second generation of trophozoites. Each of these trophozoites grows and again divides repeatedly, producing a second crop of merozoites. There are at least two cycles of this type, and it will be plain at this point that the number of host cells which may be damaged by the progeny of a few sporozoites will be considerable. At this stage, the members of the last crop of merozoites enter cells and grow, but they do not undergo division to produce another batch of merozoites. They differentiate into sexual cells, the *gametocytes,* some of which divide, producing motile male gametes which proceed to fertilize large female gametes. The zygote quickly forms an external cystic structure, and this is an oocyst. The oocyst leaves the battered host cell in which it formed and is passively carried out of the host in the feces.

Some Unusual Patterns

A peculiar pattern of migration in the vertebrate host is seen in certain ascarid nematodes. Development of the shelled larval worm occurs outside the host. Hatching does not occur until the egg is ingested by a vertebrate host. In the vertebrate, the young nematode penetrates the wall of the intestine and undergoes a migration in the body. In the case of *Ascaris lumbricoides* of man and pigs, the worms are carried in the vascular system to the liver, thence to the heart, and finally to the capillary bed of the lungs. Here they break out into pulmonary alveoli and are carried passively to the pharynx, where they are swallowed by the vertebrate. Upon reaching the intestine for the second time, the worms settle down and grow to sexual maturity (Fig. 5–4). The biological significance of this migration was not apparent until it was shown by Tiner and by Sprent to be related to the behavior of other ascarid nematodes in

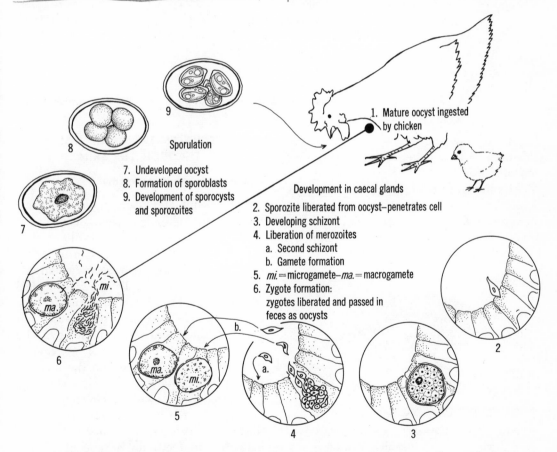

Fig. 5–3 The life pattern of the coccidian protozoan *Eimeria tenella.* (Adapted from various authors.)

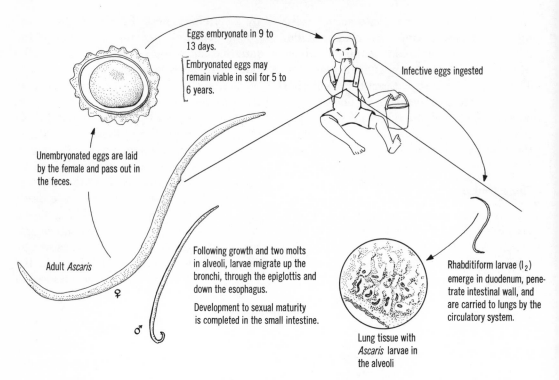

Eggs embryonate in 9 to 13 days.

Embryonated eggs may remain viable in soil for 5 to 6 years.

Infective eggs ingested

Unembryonated eggs are laid by the female and pass out in the feces.

Adult *Ascaris*

♀

♂

Following growth and two molts in alveoli, larvae migrate up the bronchi, through the epiglottis and down the esophagus.

Development to sexual maturity is completed in the small intestine.

Rhabditiform larvae (l_2) emerge in duodenum, penetrate intestinal wall, and are carried to lungs by the circulatory system.

Lung tissue with *Ascaris* larvae in the alveoli

Fig. 5–4 The life pattern of *Ascaris lumbricoides*. (Adapted from various authors.)

which an intermediate host is part of the life cycle. (This matter is discussed further on page 232.)

An unusual form of _direct transmission_ is observed in some social termites. Young termites become infected with the symbiotic flora and fauna of the adults by proctadeal feeding (Fig. 5–5).

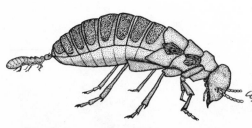

Fig. 5–5 A one-day-old nymph of the termite *Kalotermes flavicollis* receiving _proctadeal food_ from the adult female, illustrating the manner in which symbiotes are transmitted to the young in this form. (Redrawn from Goetsch, 1936, Z. Morphol. Okol. Tiere.)

SPECIES ENTERING THE HOST THROUGH THE SKIN

Life Pattern of Hookworms

Some symbiotes can _enter the host through the unbroken skin._ The nematodes known as hookworms have this capacity, and the human hookworm, *Ancylostoma duodenale*, will serve as an example (Fig. 5–6). The morphological stages of the life history are quite similar to those of *Haemonchus* (pp. 92–93), but there are sharp differences in biology. The adult worms live in the small intestine of the host, where they feed on the mucosa, sucking blood quite voraciously. The eggs (actually zygotes with a covering shell) produced by the female worms pass out of the host in the feces. The embryo develops, hatches, and feeds for a time as a free-living form. It passes through the process of molting twice and, like *Haemonchus*, retains its larval skin when it reaches the third larval stage. Again, it may be noted that the third stage must be attained before the young worm is capable of infecting a new vertebrate host. In other words, a period of life as a free-living organism is an obligate part of the life cycle. These third-stage larvae tend to crawl to the highest point of the environment in which they find themselves, which may be a particle of dirt or a blade of grass.

If the skin of a host comes into contact with these third-stage larvae, the worms react by shedding the sheath and boring into the skin. In the subcutaneous tissues, the larvae enter lymph or blood vessels. They are carried with the venous blood to the heart and then pumped out to the lungs. Most of the larvae are trapped in the capillary bed of the lung. They break out of the capillaries into the alveoli of the lung and are carried, presumably in the mucous stream, up the bronchi to the trachea and eventually to the pharynx. They are then swallowed by the host. On reaching the small intestine, the young worms begin to feed and grow, molting twice more before they attain sexual maturity. Within a few weeks after entry, eggs are again produced and the cycle is completed. In this journey through the body, there are some hazards for the developing worm. It may make a "wrong turn" and fail to reach the pharynx and thus the digestive tract. Such wanderers are lost in the body and probably die after a period of time. Further, if the worm gets into a host

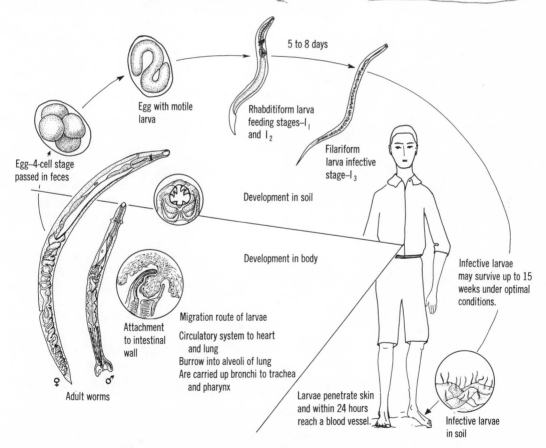

5 to 8 days

Egg with motile larva

Rhabditiform larva feeding stages–I_1 and I_2

Egg–4-cell stage passed in feces

Filariform larva infective stage–I_3

Development in soil

Development in body

Infective larvae may survive up to 15 weeks under optimal conditions.

Migration route of larvae

Attachment to intestinal wall

Circulatory system to heart and lung
Burrow into alveoli of lung
Are carried up bronchi to trachea and pharynx

Larvae penetrate skin and within 24 hours reach a blood vessel.

Infective larvae in soil

♀ ♂
Adult worms

Fig. 5–6 The life pattern of the Old World hookworm, *Ancylostoma duodenale.* (Adapted from various authors.)

which is not its usual one, it may wander extensively and produce disease. Some of the dog hookworms, for example, produce a variety of human diseases known by the general name of *larva migrans* (see p. 83).

It might seem that this ability to penetrate the host offers certain advantages over the type of cycle seen in *Haemonchus*, which has to wait for the prospective host to eat it. However, it is also plain that *Haemonchus* is doing very well with the cycle it has adopted, and this is the ultimate test of whether a pattern of development is satisfactory.

Larval Symbiotes

There are a number of forms belonging to various groups in which immature stages live a symbiotic life in a host, whereas the adults are free-living. In many cases the adult actually brings the eggs or young to the host and deposits them in or on the host body. This is a well-known phenomenon in the insects, particularly in the Hymenoptera and Diptera. (It is of interest that the biologist Alfred C. Kinsey gained his first reputation studying insects having this type of life history before he became more publicly known for his researches on certain behavior patterns of human beings.) The life history of the fly *Callitroga hominovorax*, also known as the screwworm, will serve to illustrate (Fig. 5–7). The adults are large, greenish-blue flies which deposit their eggs in fresh wounds of animals. The wound need not be a large one; a tick bite or a small scratch in the skin will attract the flies, and the larvae (maggots) will be deposited. The larvae enter the host tissues and feed on living material. Considerable damage may be suffered by the host. They grow to a length of 12 to 15 mm, at which time they leave the host and drop to the ground, where they pupate. A week or so later the adult fly emerges from the pupa.

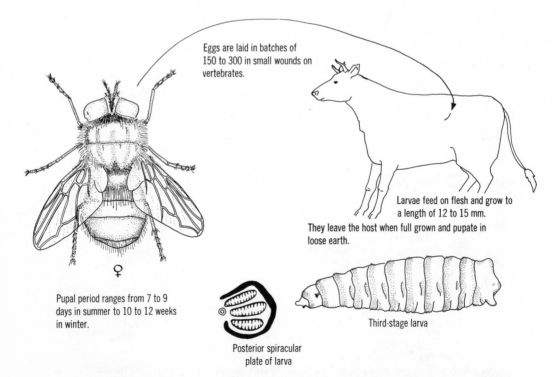

Eggs are laid in batches of 150 to 300 in small wounds on vertebrates.

Larvae feed on flesh and grow to a length of 12 to 15 mm. They leave the host when full grown and pupate in loose earth.

Pupal period ranges from 7 to 9 days in summer to 10 to 12 weeks in winter.

Posterior spiracular plate of larva

Third-stage larva

♀

Fig. 5–7   The life pattern of the screwworm, *Callitroga hominivorax*. (Adapted from various authors.)

"PASSIVE" ADAPTATIONS

Generally, the fungal and bacterial parasites of plant hosts reach new hosts by what are essentially passive modes. The principal factors involved in spreading these symbiotes to new hosts are wind, water, insects, and man. Air movements may carry spores hundreds or even thousands of miles. Insects are the main vectors of many viruses and of some bacteria and fungi, while man has contrived to continually spread various symbiotes by carrying plant parts or products from one part of the world to another. In general, the mechanisms for getting from host to host appear to be less "complicated" for plant symbiotes than animal symbiotes. Major adaptations for transmission, seen in many bacterial and fungal parasites of both plants and animals, are the capacity to survive outside a host for some period of time and the production of enormous numbers of offspring.

The aerial transmission of fungal parasites of plants has been known for more than a hundred years. These organisms produce spores which are highly resistant to environmental conditions and are also light enough to be readily carried by wind currents. Spores of the wheat stem rust fungus, *Puccinia graminis* var. *tritici*, have been recovered as high as 14,000 feet above an infected field. By knowing the rate of fall of such spores, Stakman and Christensen (1946) estimated that spores at a height of 1 mile could be carried 740 miles by a 20-mile-per-hour wind. Assuming updrafts, the distance covered could be much greater. Since "finding" a new host is a matter of chance for spores of *Puccinia,* it is not surprising that the number of spores released is enormous. Stakman and Harrar indicate that an acre of rusted wheat may yield 50,000 *billion* uredospores! It is perhaps fortunate that most of these do not come into contact with a new host.

Among passive modes of transmission we may include a number of symbiotes that are directly transmitted by contact of host and potential host. Skin contact, for example, may allow passive transmission of itch mites or pubic lice. In the same category is venereal transmission of *Trypanosoma equiperdum* in horses, *Trichomonas foetus* in cattle, or of the syphilis spirochete, the gonorrhea bacterium, and the protozoan *Trichomonas vaginalis* in humans. A number of viral and bacterial agents are transmitted between animals and between human beings in close proximity by direct contamination of food or aerosol cough spray.

LIVING IN TWO OR MORE HOSTS

As indicated above, there are a number of instances in which parasitic organisms are mechanically carried from one host to another. Many parasites living in the skin or the oral or nasal mucosa may be transferred this way on occasion, but a few forms regularly depend on such mechanical transmission. The hemoflagellate protozoans *Trypanosoma evansi* and *Trypanosoma equinum* are usually carried from one horse to another by flies and similar insects whose feeding may be interrupted.

A number of bacterial and fungal parasites of plants are similarly transmitted by arthropods. It may be recalled that Waite showed in 1891 that bees and wasps transmit the bacteria responsible for fire blight of apples and pears. Insects are major agents for the transmission of some fungi and, although transmission is mechanical, serve a special role. Fungi produce gametes of different sex on separate mycelia, and insects may serve to bring the gametes together. This is particularly true in the case of those fungi known as "rusts" (see p. 107). The fungus *Endoconidiophora fagacearum,* causing oak wilt disease, is another example. The mycelial pads of the parasite exude an odor which attracts insects, particularly nitidulid beetles. In feeding on the fungus, the insects become contaminated with gametes which they carry to other mycelia, allowing sexual reproduction of the fungus. In addition, the beetles carry spores to wounds on other hosts and thus mechanically transmit the symbiote.

When a second host organism plays some part in the life of a parasite, beyond allowing it to hitchhike, the process is called *biological transmission.* Huff (1931) proposed a classification for different types of biological transmission, which was modified by Chandler and Read (1961).

1. *Propagative:* The organisms undergo no cyclical changes but do multiply. Examples: plague, yellow fever, aster yellows virus.
2. *Cyclopropagative:* The organisms undergo cyclical changes and also multiply. Examples: malaria parasites, trypanosomes, digenetic trematodes, black stem rust.
3. *Cyclodevelopmental:* The organisms undergo developmental changes but do not multiply. Examples: filariae, guinea worm, tapeworms.

4. *Transport* (in vertebrates as well as arthropods): The symbiotes invade and may become encysted in or on some host, specific or non-specific, after developing elsewhere, and are transported by this host to the final host. Example: the nematode *Syngamus.*

PROPAGATIVE DEVELOPMENT OF *PASTEURELLA*

There are a number of symbiotic organisms which multiply in intermediate hosts without obvious physiological or morphological changes. Many viruses undergo reproduction in arthropods which may, in turn, transmit viruses to animal or plant hosts. In the animal or plant, reproduction occurs and the virus may be transmitted to an arthropod. Some bacterial symbiotes similarly grow in numbers in an intermediate host. The plague bacillus, *Pasteurella pestis,* is a well-known example. In nature,

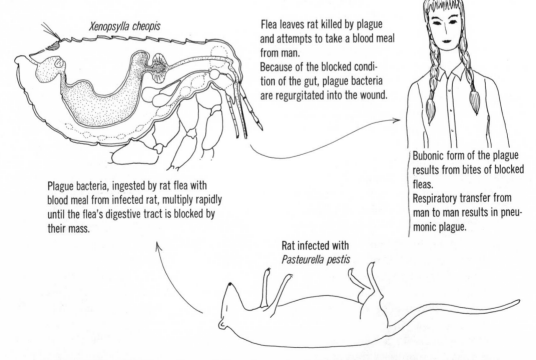

Xenopsylla cheopis

Flea leaves rat killed by plague and attempts to take a blood meal from man.
Because of the blocked condition of the gut, plague bacteria are regurgitated into the wound.

Plague bacteria, ingested by rat flea with blood meal from infected rat, multiply rapidly until the flea's digestive tract is blocked by their mass.

Bubonic form of the plague results from bites of blocked fleas.
Respiratory transfer from man to man results in pneumonic plague.

Rat infected with *Pasteurella pestis*

Fig. 5–8　The life pattern of the plague bacterium, *Pasteurella pestis.* (Adapted from various authors.)

plague is transmitted from infected to uninfected rats by fleas. After being taken in with a meal of blood from a plague-infected rat, plague bacilli multiply in the midgut of the flea. This growth produces a plug of bacilli which blocks the proventriculus (Fig. 5–8). Apparently there is interference with the feeding of the flea, and such blocked fleas tend to attempt feeding more often than usual and also wander from host to host. The blocked flea regurgitates material from the proventriculus when it tries to feed, and a new host may become infected. Species of fleas vary in the ease with which they become blocked and so there is variability in their capacity to transmit the plague organism.

It may be interpolated at this point that we occasionally see forms which have developed a secondary means of getting from one host to another. The plague organism is such a case. Although the transmission may occur by the development in a flea as outlined above, there is a second pattern of transmission. When repetitive infection occurs (epidemics), some individuals have what is called a *pneumonic* form of the disease. That is, the plague bacilli are associated with disease of the respiratory system. As such, the organisms may now be transmitted to other hosts in a more direct fashion, somewhat after the manner of the common cold.

OTHER PROPAGATIVE SYSTEMS

Among plant hosts, bacteria may show propagative relationships with insects. For example, the cucumber wilt bacterium, *Erwinia tracheiphila*, has an obligate ecological relationship with cucumber beetles. It is obligate because the organism persists through the winter in the insect hosts during periods when plant hosts are not available. Infections occur in the spring, when the bacteria are introduced into plants during the feeding of the beetles.

There is evidence that, in some cases, viruses of both plant and animal hosts undergo reproduction in an arthropod vector. In some cases, they are transovarially transmitted from one generation of arthropod to the next. A general feature of virus infections is the phenomenon known as *eclipse*. Following infection of the host cell, viruses literally disappear for a time; sometimes for 2 or 3 hours but sometimes longer. Reproduction seems to occur in part during this phase. Burnet (1960) considered eclipse to be a general property of viruses and included it in his definition of what a virus is. In Figure 5–9, intracellular multiplication

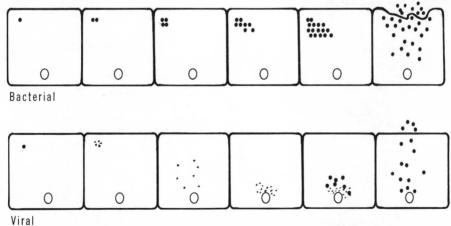

Bacterial

Viral

Fig. 5–9   A comparison of the life pattern of a virus and an intracellular bacterial parasite. The virus undergoes an "eclipse" period, during which it is not detectable. (Modified from Burnet, 1960.)

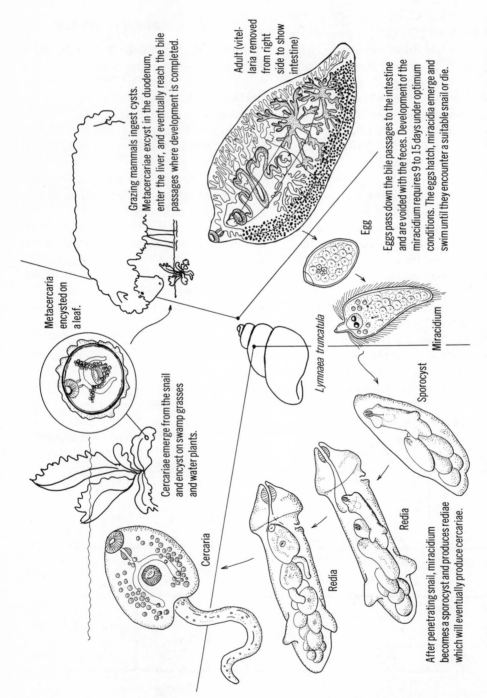

Grazing mammals ingest cysts. Metacercariae excyst in the duodenum, enter the liver, and eventually reach the bile passages where development is completed.

Adult (vitellaria removed from right side to show intestine)

Eggs pass down the bile passages to the intestine and are voided with the feces. Development of the miracidium requires 9 to 15 days under optimum conditions. The eggs hatch, miracidia emerge and swim until they encounter a suitable snail or die.

Egg

Miracidium

Metacercaria encysted on a leaf.

Lymnaea truncatula

Sporocyst

Cercariae emerge from the snail and encyst on swamp grasses and water plants.

Redia

Redia

Cercaria

After penetrating snail, miracidium becomes a sporocyst and produces rediae which will eventually produce cercariae.

Fig. 5–10 The life pattern of the liver fluke, *Fasciola hepatica*. (Adapted from Thomas, 1883, and various other authors.)

of a bacterium and a virus are diagrammed to show the eclipse phenomenon. The tiny symbiotic bacteria known as rickettsiae also show a phenomenon resembling eclipse. When infected ticks are kept in the cold, the number of infectious rickettsiae sharply decreases; on warming for a short time at 37° C, the number of infectious rickettsiae in a tick increases. Such changes are not simply due to death of rickettsiae on cooling, followed by rickettsial multiplication on warming; they even occur in homogenates of tick tissue and the effect of warming can be mimicked by adding coenzyme A at room temperature.

CYCLOPROPAGATIVE DEVELOPMENT IN INTERMEDIATE HOSTS

Symbiotes belonging to various groups undergo cyclic morphological and physiological changes in intermediate hosts and undergo multiplication. In many cases, the intermediate host serves a function as a place for the symbiote to develop but plays no active role in carrying the symbiote to the definitive host. Species belonging to quite different taxonomic groups may serve as examples.

Cyclopropagation of Trematodes

The liver fluke *Fasciola hepatica* is a digenetic trematode living in the bile ducts of herbivorous animals, including cattle, sheep, rabbits, and occasionally, man. The hermaphroditic adult produces shelled embryos which pass out of the host in the feces. During a period of growth within the shell, the embryo develops into a ciliated larval form called a *miracidium*. The miracidium leaves the shell as a free-swimming organism. If a snail of an appropriate species is present, the miracidium penetrates the soft tissues of the mollusks, shedding its ciliated covering in the process, and forms a saclike *sporocyst*. This sporocyst grows in the tissues of the snail, and cells

contained within it give rise to organized balls of cells which undergo differentiation to another larval form, the *redia.* A number of rediae develop within a sporocyst, and these are liberated into the tissues of the snail. Each redia in turn undergoes growth and germ cells within the body undergo differentiation into a second generation of rediae. These leave the parent rediae and grow. Further formation of redial generations does not continue indefinitely. The germ cells of the second generation of rediae develop into a quite different larval form, the *cercaria.* This tailed cercaria shows more evident relation to the adult worm, since it bears sucker-like structures and has the rudiments of certain other adult organs. The cercaria leaves the snail host and becomes a free-swimming animal for a short period of time. Unlike the miracidium, its swimming is performed with the aid of the tail, which it may beat quite vigorously. After a brief swimming life, sometimes a few hours, the cercaria settles down on vegetation, sheds its tail, and proceeds to produce a cyst over the body. It undergoes some further differentiation in the cyst and now truly resembles a miniature, sexually immature trematode. This encysted stage is called a *metacercaria.* When the metacercaria is eaten by the herbivorous vertebrate, along with the grass on which the metacercaria is encysted, the young worm emerges from its cyst and enters the wall of the intestine. The larval trematodes are thought to pass out into the peritoneal cavity of the host and enter the liver on its peritoneal surface. They make their way to the bile ducts and develop to sexual maturity. The events of this life pattern are shown in Figure 5-10. Nothing is known of the factors which guide the worm through its migration in the vertebrate. It is difficult to believe that, unlike worms which enter the blood stream, these worms are passively carried about.

It is plain that the process of development in a snail has resulted in a very large number of young trematodes as the product of a single zygote. In a general fashion, other trematode life histories resemble that of *Fasciola*. There are, however, many variations on this theme. Some species encyst as metacercariae in some second species of intermediate host. Such is the case in the life history of *Dicrocoelium dendriticum*, a trematode parasite of sheep and other ruminants in Europe, Asia, and, to a limited extent, North America. The cercariae develop in small land snails (*Cionella lubrica* in the United States), and these collect in the respiratory chamber of the snail. They are ejected from the snail in balls of slime, each ball containing hundreds of larval trematodes. Such slime balls are regarded by ants as choice food items and are carried by these insects to their nests. Metacercariae develop in the ants, and the definitive host becomes infected by ingesting infected ants along with vegetation. Interestingly, the presence of *Dicrocoelium* metacercariae sometimes produces changes in the behavior of the ant hosts, such that infected ants remain out on the grass overnight. This would appear to enhance the probability that an infected ant would be eaten by a sheep.

The second intermediate host may be a food item for the definitive host rather than being accidentally ingested as above. The trematodes found in carnivores typically reach the definitive host in this fashion. *Paragonimus*, the lung fluke of carnivores and man, utilizes such a second intermediate host. The short-tailed cercariae of *Paragonimus* develop in aquatic snail (*Pomatiopsis*, and perhaps *Thiara*, in the United States). After leaving the snail, the larval trematodes creep about until they encounter a crayfish or freshwater crab. They pierce the cuticle of the crab and make their way to the heart or gills where they encyst, forming metacercariae. The definitive host becomes infected by eating the crayfish or crab. In the definitive host, the young worms excyst in the gut and make their way to the lungs (Fig. 5–11).

There are a variety of modifications in the patterns of trematode life histories. In the schistosomes, or blood flukes, the quiescent metacercarial stage is not present; the cercaria penetrates the skin of the definitive host and grows rather directly into an adult. The great variety of ingenious modifications of the basic pattern of digenetic trematode development and utilization of intermediates has been a never-ending source of wonderment to fascinated parasitologists.

Cyclopropagation of Sporozoans

The cyclopropagative development of the protozoans which cause the diseases collectively known as malaria is fairly well understood. The life history of species of *Plasmodium*, first described in 1898–1899 by Ross, Grassi, and their colleagues, is complex, involving mosquitoes and vertebrates as hosts. The general pattern is shown in Figures 5–12 and 5–13. The parasite passes from the mosquito to the vertebrate when the mosquito feeds. The

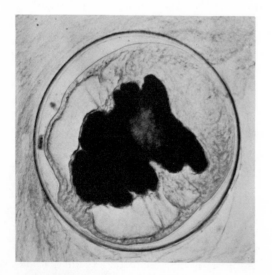

Fig. 5–11 The encysted metacercaria (×85) of the lung fluke, *Paragonimus westermani*. (Photograph through courtesy of Dr. Mariano Yogore.)

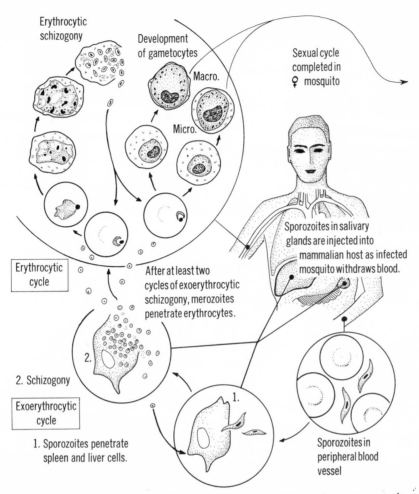

Erythrocytic schizogony

Development of gametocytes

Macro.

Micro.

Sexual cycle completed in ♀ mosquito

Sporozoites in salivary glands are injected into mammalian host as infected mosquito withdraws blood.

Erythrocytic cycle

After at least two cycles of exoerythrocytic schizogony, merozoites penetrate erythrocytes.

2.

2. Schizogony

Exoerythrocytic cycle

1. Sporozoites penetrate spleen and liver cells.

1.

Sporozoites in peripheral blood vessel

Fig. 5–12 The life pattern of the malaria parasite *Plasmodium vivax* in the mammalian host after injection of sporozoite stage by the mosquito host. (Adapted from various authors.)

spindle-shaped *sporozoites* are injected into the blood of the vertebrate along with the secretions of the insect's salivary glands. Within a few minutes, the sporozoites leave the blood and enter tissue cells where they undergo multiplication as *pre-erythrocytic forms*. Depending on the species, intracellular multiplication in the tissues may occur repeatedly without the appearance of parasites in the blood of the host. After some days, some of the parasites leave the fixed cells of the body and enter erythrocytes. The earliest forms seen in the blood

have the appearance of a signet ring. With the usual blood stains, Giemsa or Wright, the ring stains a pale blue and the "setting" (the nucleus) is ruby-red.

As the parasite grows, it becomes rounded or irregular in shape and the nucleus undergoes repeated division. This multiple division of the nucleus without cytoplasmic division has been referred to as schizogony, and the multinucleate form is termed a *segmenter*. The cytoplasm around each nucleus separates from the remaining cytoplasm, and the small cells or *merozoites*

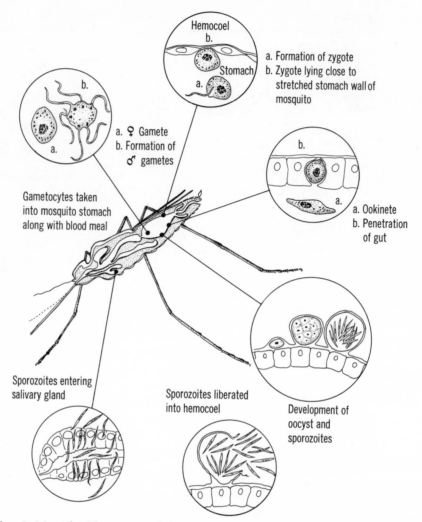

Fig. 5–13 The life pattern of the malaria parasite *Plasmodium vivax* in the mosquito host. (Adapted from various authors.)

eventually break out of the cell. These free parasites enter fresh erythrocytes and undergo merogony. The growth of the parasites and their release from the red blood cells are more or less synchronized, so that the bursting of red cells tends to occur simultaneously. This synchrony is thought to be the basis for the paroxysms of chills and fever which are periodically characteristic of malaria. The species differ in the time table of these events but are quite similar in general pattern. In some species,

merozoites may enter fixed cells of the body as well as erythrocytes and undergo reproduction outside the blood. Such stages are referred to as exoerythrocytic. Parasites from exoerythrocytic stages may reenter the blood cells at irregular intervals.

After the first few generations in the blood, some of the merozoites show a different pattern of development after entering a red blood cell. They grow rather slowly into large, uninucleated cells. These are *gametocytes*, which circulate for a time

in the blood but undergo no further development in the vertebrate. Two types
of gametocytes are distinguishable and are
referred to as male or female on the basis
of their behavior when they are ingested
with the blood meal of a mosquito. If the
gametocytes are sucked up by a mosquito,
the male (*microgametocyte*) quickly shows
nuclear division, which is followed by the
extrusion of several flagellate-like micro-
gametes. These break free and undergo
union with the female (*macrogametocyte*),
which has undergone little change. After
union of the male and female cells, the
zygote is a rounded, pigmented cell which
transforms in an elongated, motile ookinete.
This form penetrates the stomach wall of
the mosquito. In the stomach wall, the
zygote becomes lodged under the outer
limiting membrane, produces a cyst wall,
and grows rather rapidly, with repeated
nuclear division followed by cytoplasmic
divisions, to form sporozoites. These are
contained for a time in what is termed an
oocyst, which eventually breaks down,
liberating the sporozoites into the body
cavity of the mosquito. The parasites make
their way to the salivary glands, in the
anterior region of the mosquito, where they
assemble in the cells lining the glands.
There may be as many as a quarter of a
million in one mosquito. When the mosquito feeds on a vertebrate, the parasites
are injected into the bite wound. A number
of factors may influence the time required
for development in the mosquito. These
are discussed elsewhere (pp. 254–256).

Cyclopropagation of Rust Fungi

Cyclopropagative patterns appear to be
less common among symbiotes of higher
plants. However, in some cases, alternate
hosts are clearly essential for completion of
the life history. The stem rust fungus,
Puccinia graminis, living on wheat, oats,
barley, and other small grains is an example (Fig. 5–14). Development on bar-

berry, or related plants, with a sexual phase
is essential. As in the case of the malaria
protozoans, the "wild" barberry host is
sometimes called an intermediate host, although, by our previous definition, it is more
properly termed the definitive host.

The mycelium of *Puccinia*, composed of
binucleate cells, lives in the tissues of the
wheat plant host. It ruptures the surface of
the host and forms clusters of binucleate
one-celled summer spores, or *uredospores*.
These are rough-walled and reddish in
color, giving the infected wheat leaf a rusty
appearance. The uredospores may be carried to a new wheat host and germinate,
producing a new invasive mycelium. Toward the end of the growing season, clusters of another type of spore are produced
at the surface of the host. These are black,
composed of two cells, and are called
teliospores. Each cell of the teliospore differs from uredospore cells in having a single
diploid nucleus, due to nuclear fusion.
These spores survive through the winter
season. In spring, each teliospore cell gives
rise to a delicate four-celled promycelium.
Meiosis occurs during the growth of this
promycelium and each of the four cells becomes a haploid *basidiospore*. These basidiospores will not develop on wheat plants
but require the barberry, or a related plant,
as a host for further development.

On the leaf of the barberry, the basidiospore germinates and forms a penetrating
mycelium, composed of uninucleate haploid
cells. Such mycelia are heterothallic, belonging to one of two sexual types designated as "plus" or "minus." Small flask-like
structures, the *pycnia*, soon appear on the
upper surface of the barberry leaf. The
pycnium produces numbers of flexible protruding hyphal structures, and many very
small *pycniospores* are formed and extruded from the pycnium in a drop of liquid. This liquid is attractive to insects,
which mechanically disperse the pycniospores. When a pycniospore comes into
contact with a hypha protruding from a

pycnium of the opposite sexual type, fusion occurs and a new mycelium develops, each cell containing two nuclei. This new mycelium undergoes new growth in the barberry tissues and forms a peculiar cup-shaped structure called an *aecium, or cluster cup,* on the lower surface of the barberry leaf. Long rows of binucleate *aeciospores* are formed in the aecium. These aeciospores do not reinfect the barberry but, after aerial dispersion, will develop on wheat plants.

Germination on wheat results in development of a binucleate mycelium, and the life cycle is thus completed.

This astonishingly complex type of life history is known for some other rust fungi. White pine blister rust, for example, forms uredospores on currants and gooseberries and develops its pycnia and aecia on the white pine. Apple rust forms uredospores on the red cedar and other stages on apple trees.

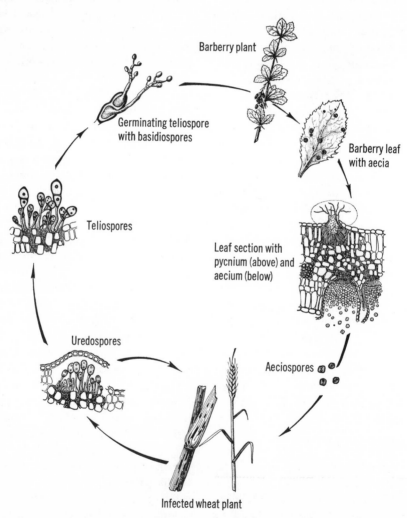

Barberry plant

Germinating teliospore with basidiospores

Barberry leaf with aecia

Teliospores

Leaf section with pycnium (above) and aecium (below)

Uredospores

Aeciospores

Infected wheat plant

Fig. 5–14 The life cycle of the wheat rust symbiote, *Puccinia graminis.* See the text for description of stages in the life pattern. (From *Botany,* 5th ed., by E. W. Sinnott and K. S. Wilson. Copyright © 1956 by McGraw-Hill Book Company, Inc. Used by permission of McGraw-Hill Book Company.)

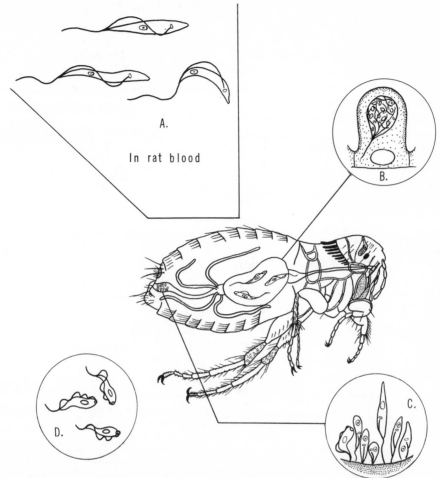

Fig. 5–15   The life pattern of the hemoflagellate protozoan *Trypanosoma lewisi*. The trypanosomes (A) in the blood of a rat host are ingested by the flea *Ceratophyllus fasciatus*. In the stomach epithelium of the flea, the protozoan undergoes repeated divisions (B). These emerge into the gut lumen, giving rise to forms in the rectum (C) and to the forms (D) capable of infecting the rodent when the flea or its feces are eaten. (Adapted from Minchin and Thompson, 1915.)

Cyclopropagation of Trypanosomes

The cyclopropagative patterns outlined above involve a sexual phase. However, among the Protozoa, there are forms which show such patterns without sexual reproduction. Many hemoflagellates have such a development; *Trypanosoma lewisi*, a common parasite of the rat, will serve as an example (Fig. 5–15). This species lives in the blood of rats and in the gut of rat fleas all over the world. When the trypanosomes are taken into the stomach of the flea, along with the rat's blood, the protozoans undergo a physiological change. After about 6 hours, they are incapable of infecting the vertebrate host if re-injected. Some of the parasites enter cells lining the stomach and undergo repeated cell divisions. By rupture of the cells, the flagellates escape into the stomach. Some of them may reenter other cells and repeat the process. This may go on for 4 or 5 days.

The next phase involves migration backward to the hind gut and rectum with changes in the morphology of the protozoan cell. In the rectum, several flagellate cell types are seen (Fig. 5–15). The small infective forms (*metacyclic*) which appear are trypanosome-like but have very short, free flagella. Cell divisions continue to occur in the rectum of the flea, and many of the flagellates pass out of the flea in the feces. The rat becomes infected by eating the feces of the flea, probably during its flea-chasing efforts. How the trypanosomes pass from the digestive tract of the rat to its blood system is not known, but trypanosomes appear in the blood of the rodent in a few days. The flea apparently remains infected and continues to eject trypanosome-laden feces for the remainder of its life. The period from the ingestion of trypanosome-laden blood to the appearance of infective metacyclic stages in the feces of the flea is about 6 days (Wenyon, 1926).

CYCLODEVELOPMENTAL PATTERNS— NEMATODES

As was indicated on page 100, some symbiotes undergo developmental changes but do not multiply in an intermediate host. The filarioid and spiruroid nematodes exhibit this mode of development. In the filarioids, the worm is typically transmitted to the vertebrate host during the period in which a biting insect is feeding on the host, and the insect host becomes infected with the worm by ingestion of the larval form in the blood or tissue fluids. On the other hand, the spiruroid nematodes usually enter the vertebrate host when the infected insect intermediate host is devoured by the vertebrate. The insect is infected by eating the shelled embryos of the worm, which leave the vertebrate host in the feces. As might be expected, the filarioids live in the

extra-intestinal tissues of the vertebrate and deposit their young in the blood, lymph, or intercellular fluids, while the spiruroids usually live in the digestive tract. The life history of the filarial nematode *Wuchereria bancrofti* will serve as a more detailed example (Fig. 5–16).

The adult worms of *W. bancrofti* live in the lymph glands and ducts, and the females deposit unshelled vermiform embryos, or *microfilariae*, in the tissue fluids of the host. These embryos get into the circulatory system and are periodically found in the peripheral blood. No further development of these young worms will occur in the vertebrate. They must be taken up along with a blood meal by a mosquito. After ingestion by a mosquito, the microfilariae penetrate the stomach wall and migrate to the thoracic muscles of the insect. Here the body of the worm becomes shortened and thickened, and the digestive tract of the parasite undergoes differentiation. The worm then begins to grow in length as well as in thickness until it is several times as large as the original microfilaria.

During this sojourn in the muscles of the insect, there are two molts. The young worm has now reached a stage at which it is capable of infecting a vertebrate and migrates to the proboscis of the insect host. If and when the mosquito feeds on a moist, warm skin, the larval worm breaks free from the labium of the insect and penetrates the bite wound or other abrasion in the skin. Little is known of the details of development after the worms enter the vertebrate in this manner, except that they eventually end up in the lymphatics and develop to sexual maturity after a period of several months' growth.

CYCLODEVELOPMENTAL PATTERNS— CESTODES

Most tapeworms show cyclodevelopmental patterns, frequently, but not always, in-

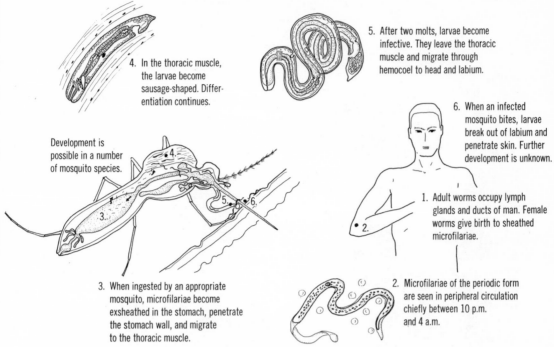

4. In the thoracic muscle, the larvae become sausage-shaped. Differentiation continues.

5. After two molts, larvae become infective. They leave the thoracic muscle and migrate through hemocoel to head and labium.

Development is possible in a number of mosquito species.

6. When an infected mosquito bites, larvae break out of labium and penetrate skin. Further development is unknown.

1. Adult worms occupy lymph glands and ducts of man. Female worms give birth to sheathed microfilariae.

3. When ingested by an appropriate mosquito, microfilariae become exsheathed in the stomach, penetrate the stomach wall, and migrate to the thoracic muscle.

2. Microfilariae of the periodic form are seen in peripheral circulation chiefly between 10 p.m. and 4 a.m.

Fig. 5–16 The life pattern of the filarial nematode *Wuchereria bancrofti.* (Adapted from various authors.)

volving an arthropod. The cosmopolitan rat tapeworm, *Hymenolepis diminuta,* will serve as an example (Fig. 5–17). The adult worm lives in the small intestine of the rodent host and sheds embryo-filled pieces of the growing strobila. Most of these strobilar fragments break down, liberating the shelled embryos, which pass out in the feces. If these embryos are eaten by an appropriate arthropod, commonly grain beetles of the genera *Tribolium* and *Tenebrio,* the embryo is liberated from its shell and penetrates the gut wall of the arthropod host. Upon reaching the hemocoele, the embryonic worm grows and differentiates, forming a cystic structure containing a scolex. It is only now capable of infecting another rat. If and when the infected beetle is eaten by a rodent, the scolex is freed from its cyst and in the small intestine generates a new strobila, which comes to sexual maturity in a little over two weeks.

Many other examples of cyclodevelopmental growth in an intermediate host could be cited. This pattern is not at all uncommon among animal symbiotes.

COMPOUNDED PATTERNS

In some cases in which a symbiote is transmitted to a host by a symbiote, the life history may be difficult to fit into the categories discussed in preceding pages. An example is found in the interrelations of pigs, earthworms, a nematode, and a virus.

Pigs are highly susceptible to a virus which produces a disease known as swine influenza. It has recently been recognized that there is more than one kind of swine influenza, but for purposes of this discussion, we shall refer to it as a single disease. The course of the infection in pig populations is strikingly like that of human epidemic influenza, and it has actually been

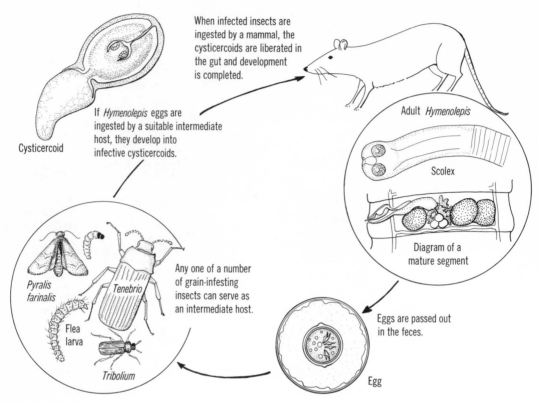

Fig. 5–17 The life pattern of the rat tapeworm, *Hymenolepis diminuta*.

suggested that the origin of the pig disease may have been humans in the great human influenza pandemic of 1918.

It was more or less assumed that the disease was transmitted only by contact of pigs until Shope (1940–1942) began a series of studies on the disease. It seemed peculiar that, in the fall of the year in the United States, there were epidemics among pigs which had been quite healthy and shown no sign of the disease during preceding months. There was a popular belief among some farmers that the earthworm had something to do with the spread of certain other diseases of pigs, and Shope wondered whether earthworms might have anything to do with swine influenza. Although this conjecture may have been pure guesswork, there was another relationship between earthworms and pigs which was known

to be true at that time. The earthworm is the intermediate host for a nematode, *Metastrongylus*, the pig becoming infected after devouring earthworms which harbor the infective larval stage. After entering the pig, this nematode moves to the lungs, where it develops to sexual maturity. It was reasoned that these lungworms might carry a virus to the respiratory system of the pig and thus transmit the virus. Shope performed careful experiments to determine whether this might be so. Three pigs were inoculated with the virus of swine influenza and one was killed on the third, fourth, and fifth days after the appearance of disease symptoms. The lungworms were removed from these pigs and chopped up to release the eggs. This material was then mixed with pig feces and placed in a barrel of soil along with about 400 earthworms; several weeks later the earthworms were examined and found to be infected with the larvae of the lungworm.

Some of the infected earthworms were now fed to healthy pigs and, during ensuing days, the pigs remained healthy. However, some of the same pigs were being given injections of bacteria, *Hemophilus influenzae suis,* which is quite often found in pigs with swine influenza. Pigs which had eaten the infected earthworms and were injected with the bacterium came down with swine influenza. It might be reasoned that this result may only suggest that the bacteria produce the disease. However, when bacteria are injected into healthy pigs, they do not show signs of influenza. Further, it was shown that the injection of heat-killed bacteria to pigs which had eaten the earthworms was just as effective in causing the appearance of the disease. The answer seems to be that the virus is definitely present in the pigs after they have eaten infected earthworms, but some stimulus is required to provoke the appearance of disease.

Shope (1940–1942) showed that the virus can persist in the lungworm for at least 2 years, and it has been possible to produce swine influenza in pigs during fall, winter, or spring. Oddly enough, it has not been possible to produce the disease during summer, and more research is required to work out the finer details of the natural history of this parasite of pigs which is transmitted by a parasite of pigs.

The Complex Pattern of *Histomonas*

Another example of complex integration in symbiosis involves the protozoan *Histomonas meleagridis* (Fig. 5–18), the nematode *Heterakis,* turkeys, and perhaps bacteria. In addition, earthworms are sometimes involved. A disease of turkeys, most often referred to as *blackhead,* has been associated with the presence of *Histomonas*

and is characterized by inflammatory processes of the liver and gut. In 1920, Graybill and Smith showed that embryonated eggs of the nematode *Heterakis,* externally sterilized, could harbor and transmit *Histomonas meleagridis* to turkeys. This has been verified by a number of later investigators; and it has been shown that the protozoan will survive for as long as 150 weeks within the worm eggs. Experiments with bacteria-free birds have indicated that bacteria may also be essential for the appearance of disease in turkeys. However, it is not clear whether this is a generalized effect, the bacteria altering the environment of the protozoan, and thus stimulating its growth, or a more specific effect, involving a parasitic role for the bacteria. Earthworms become involved when they serve as transport host for the nematode *Heterakis.* Lund and his colleagues (1966) showed that embryonated eggs of *Heterakis* hatch in earthworms and remain viable in these hosts. Feeding either infected earthworms or larval *Heterakis* from earthworms to turkeys produced histomoniasis. Reid (1967) has furnished a com-

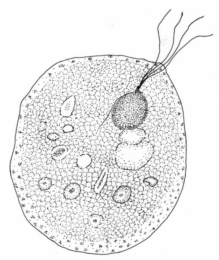

Fig. 5–18 *Histomonas meleagridis* from a turkey. The cell is about 20 microns in diameter. (Drawn from a stained preparation.)

prehensive review of histomoniasis and the complications of this symbiosis.

TRANSPORT HOSTS

Some animal parasites may use an intermediate host on occasion, but this intermediate may be essential neither for the completion of morphological development nor for completion of the life history. In other instances, the intermediate may actually be essential for transmission but does not serve as a significant source of food for the symbiote. Such intermediates are called *transport hosts*. The nematode *Syngamus trachea,* a relative of the hookworms, is a well-known form which may utilize earthworms as transport hosts. The adult parasites live in the tracheae of birds, and the shelled embryos leave the host in the feces. Development of the larval nematode with molting occurs within the shell, and the young nematode hatches as a third-stage larva which is infective for the vertebrate. If the larva is eaten by a vertebrate, development to adulthood occurs. If, on the other hand, the larva is eaten by an earthworm, the nematode encysts in this host; and completion of development and maturity depends on the infected earthworm being eaten by a bird. In *Syngamus*, utilization of a transport host may occur with considerable frequency, depending on local circumstances and the kind of birds involved. Some other species of parasites may use transport hosts only occasionally.

Another type of intermediate host relationship which appears to be essential for transmission of a symbiote is observed in the life history of the fly *Dermatobia hominis,* whose larvae are obligate parasites in the skin of warm-blooded vertebrates. The gravid free-living female fly captures a bloodsucking insect, typically a mosquito, and deposits eggs on the mosquito's abdomen (Fig. 5–19). When the mosquito bites a vertebrate host, the young larvae of *Dermatobia* leave the arthropod

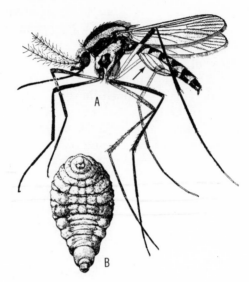

Fig. 5–19 A. *Dermatobia hominis* eggs (*arrow*) deposited on the abdomen of a mosquito. B. A mature larva of *Dermatobia* from the skin of a mammalian host. (After Sambon.)

host and enter the skin of the vertebrate through the bite wound or other break in the integument. Here the larvae feed on the subcutaneous tissues and leave the vertebrate host when ready to pupate. The adult flies are free-living.

TAXES AND KINETIC RESPONSES

Many animal parasites are known to show taxes in response to physical factors. It is frequently recognized that these responses are of specific importance in allowing the parasite to reach or enter a host.

The free-living infective larval stages of hookworms and their relatives show temperature responses which are important in their biology. When a warm body is brought into contact with the larvae, they respond by what may be called a "penetration response." This kind of response seems to be more complex in some nematodes, which pass from an arthropod to a vertebrate host. The spiruroid nematode *Habronema* undergoes larval development in flies which habitually feed on the fluids about the nose and mouth of such mammals as horses. When the hungry fly alights on such a wet, warm surface, the larval nematodes leave the body of the fly and remain on the vertebrate when the fly has had its fill. For completion of the life history, the nematode must be swallowed by the vertebrate.

In certain filarioid nematodes, the larval worms develop in the hemocoele of a blood-sucking arthropod. When the arthropod feeds on a vertebrate, the young nematode leaves the cold-blooded host by breaking through the membranous portion of the mouth parts and enters the host through the wound made by the arthropod or through other skin abrasions.

It seems probable that the schistosome trematodes (Fig. 5–20 and Fig. 6–12, p.

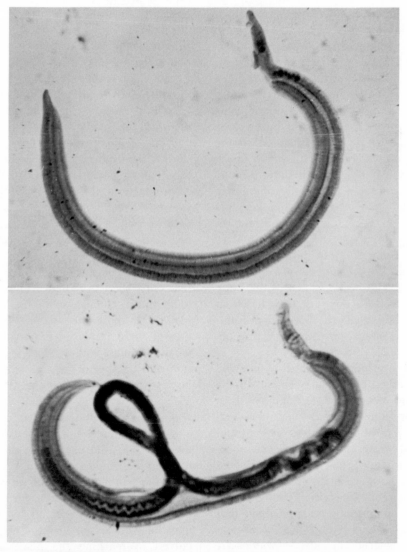

Fig. 5–20 The adult phase of the human blood fluke, *Schistosoma mansoni.* The upper figure is a male worm; the lower figure is a male and female *in copula.*

136), which reach the vertebrate host by penetrating the skin, may also show responses to temperature; but this may not have been studied in sufficient detail.

Temperature, as a triggering stimulus for some response in a parasite, may be extremely important in steps in a life history. It has been shown, for example, that the excystment of tapeworm larvae in mammals is a complex phenomenon, and that an increase in temperature is an extremely important factor (p. 133). Many parasitic helminths produce shelled embryos which leave the body of the vertebrate in a state of arrested development. In many of these cases (e.g., the hookworms, ascarids, etc.), it has been shown that a lowering of the temperature and oxygen seem to be essential for further development. Environments of lower temperature may be found in some poikilothermic host, such as an arthropod, or in soil or water. There may be doubt that parasitic symbiotes will show positive behavioral responses to lower temperatures in a thermal gradient (see p. 142).

Some parasites may show significant responses to alterations of osmotic pressure or to ionic composition of the environment. For example, the shelled embryos of schistosome trematodes do not hatch in the body fluids of the host, nor will they hatch in normal saline outside the host. Upon dilution of such media, however, hatching occurs very quickly.

Some such response is probably involved in the observed effects of seawater on the free gravid segments of tetraphyllidean tapeworms from sharks. When such segments are placed in seawater, swelling and subsequent expulsion of "eggs" occurs almost immediately. This reaction might be thought to be an osmotic effect, since the tissue fluids of the host (elasmobranch fishes) have an osmotic pressure above that of seawater. However, when such segments are placed in 30% seawater—70% distilled water, they fail to show the response. The latter might argue for a chemical effect, which may complicate an osmotic one.

SERIATED RESPONSES

In a few cases it has been shown that the responses of a symbiote are compounded, being a summation of reactions. For example, the host-finding mechanisms of certain parasitoid flies have been studied in some detail. It was shown that a fly may be attracted to the environment where the host is likely to be. Thus, the fly *Alysia* is attracted by olfactory stimuli emanating from decomposing meat. This species normally lays its eggs in the body of blowfly larvae, likely to be found in such an environment. The stimulus which seems to trigger the actual laying of eggs is the movement of the blowfly larva. The negative geotaxis of infective hookworm larvae is of similar significance. These larvae climb to the highest possible point in the microenvironment and "wait" for a host. The previously mentioned response to the temperature which follows, if a warm host is near, aids in completing the process of host-finding.

Ticks have been shown to have a complex series of responses to light, contact, gravity, temperature change, vibration, and chemistry of the host integument. The summation of these responses is of value in survival or in host-finding, since it results in a sufficient number of ticks reaching hosts to insure the perpetuation of ticks (Lees, 1948).

It may be concluded that, in many cases, a symbiote reaches a particular environment outside a host by responses which are frequently complex. Within this environment the symbiote may then show a second series of responses, which result in its entering the habitat represented by a host. It may be emphasized that the responses involved in reaching the place where the host is may be quite different from those directly involved in getting in or on a host.

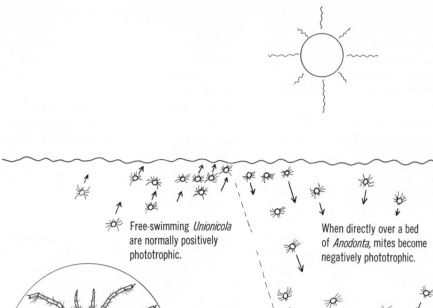

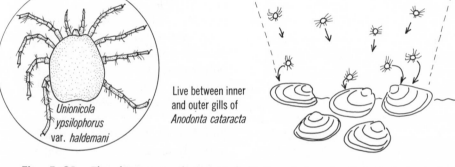

Free-swimming *Unionicola* are normally positively phototrophic.

When directly over a bed of *Anodonta*, mites become negatively phototrophic.

Unionicola ypsilophorus var. *haldemani*

Live between inner and outer gills of *Anodonta cataracta*

Fig. 5–21 The changes in phototactic behavior of the mite *Unionicola* in the presence of a substance produced by its mussel host, *Anodonta*.

Another interesting complex of responses was studied by Welsh, who found that *Unionicola*, a mite symbiotic in the mantle cavity of mussels, gave a negative response to light in the presence of a chemical substance from the tissues of its host. When the mites were washed free of the unidentified substance, a positive response to light was observed. Adding the host factor restored negative phototaxis. Later, Welsh (1931) made similar observations on three species of symbiotic mites and showed that the reversal of phototaxis could be accomplished only by a factor from the host on which each species lives. These responses would obviously have high adaptive value in host-finding (Fig. 5–21).

TRIGGERING RESPONSES IN PLANT SYMBIOTES

The specific effects of host substances in triggering the activity of a parasite are well demonstrated in the case of the golden nematode, *Heterodera*, a symbiote of potatoes, tomatoes, eggplant, and related plants. The nematodes enter the roots of susceptible plants. As eggs begin to develop in the female, the animal begins to swell. As swelling continues, the host surface is broken through and the cuticle of the worm becomes golden and finally reddish-brown in color. The female dies and larvae develop in this tough, cyst-like structure formed from the female body. Many of these cysts remain dormant but viable for several years. It has been shown that soluble chemical material secreted by the roots of potatoes and numerous other plants stimulates "hatching" and migration of the larvae. A similar phenomenon occurs with some ectosymbiotic trematodes in which larval hatching occurs only when a potential fish host of the appropriate species is in the immediate vicinity (Euzet and Raibaut, 1960).

There is some evidence for the role of chemical mediators from the plant host in stimulating the formation of a penetration structure of fungal symbiotes. While these phenomena are not strictly "behavior," they may be mentioned at this point since they are of similar biological significance. For example, infection of seedling plants by the fungus *Pellicularia filamentosa* (= *Rhizoctonia filamentosa*) requires the formation of a hyphal cushion on the host surface. When susceptible seedlings of lettuce or radish are grown aseptically in cellophane bags, the fungus forms hyphal cushions on the outer surface of the cellophane. On the other hand, when insusceptible seedlings are similarly grown in bags no cushions are formed (Kerr, 1956). Sterile exudates from suitable hosts also induce formation of infection cushions when added to cultures of the fungus (Kerr and Flentje, 1957). There are a few known cases of this type of responsive integration in symbioses between different species of fungi. The spores of the parasitic *Calcarisporium* secrete a substance which evokes a growth response in the host fungus *Physalospora*. The host sends out hyphal branches toward the parasite. A specialized cell is then formed by the parasite at the tip of each hyphal branch in contact with the host.

RESPONSES OF COMMENSALS

A number of commensal organisms are known to show tactic responses to hosts, apparently responding to chemical substances from the host. For example, observations on the pinnotherid crabs which live in certain mollusks have shown that these arthropods respond to materials diffusing from the host body (Sastry and Menzel, 1962) and that commensal bivalve mollusks are activated by substances from their echinoderm or annelid hosts (Gage, 1966). The ectosymbiotic trematode *Entobdella soleae* responds to material in the skin of its fish host (Kearn, 1967).

Of great interest are the specific responses of various species of polychaetous annelid worms which live in symbiotic relationships with other invertebrates (Davenport, 1955). In the case of *Polynoe*, which lives on another polychaete, the worm responds to the host if it is brought into physical proximity; it follows if the host is moved away. It does not respond to four other species of polychaetes belonging to families other than that of the host, nor to three other species belonging to the same family as that of the host, and responds very weakly to two species of annelids on which it is not normally found. The attracting material is apparently not present in the mucous secretions of the host; Davenport found that external tissues removed from the host elicited a response but that internal tissues, such as gonad and gut, did not. When the host is placed in bolting cloth and the commensal is brought near it, there is a response. The attracting material is sensitive to heat, the attracting property being lost after heating it to 60° C.

Of great interest are Davenport's observations on three populations of the polychaete species *Harmothoe lunulata*, which occur on the echinoderms *Acrocnida* and *Leptosynapta*, the terebellid annelid *Amphitrite*, or the annelid *Arenicola*. Individuals from each of these populations responded to their own host species but *not* to those species of hosts on which they were not normally found. (This would obviously be of interest in terms of genetic isolation and population problems, discussed elsewhere in this text.) It was significant that the attracting substance was found to act only over very short distances, keeping the symbiote very close to the host. If it worked at long distances, the symbiote might well wander. Also, the attraction of the host is removed if the symbiote for some reason or other is dislodged, and the symbiote might then exploit new habitats.

Questions arise from the above which bring to mind earlier work of Thorpe (1939). Thorpe demonstrated that, among certain insects found as parasites on other insects, the selection of the host depends upon the conditioning of the early stage of the parasite to host substances; that is to say, the adult insect which has spent its larval life in contact with a particular species of insect host will, when it comes to lay its eggs, tend to be attracted to that same host species. This inclination can be altered experimentally by removing parasitic larvae from one host species and transplanting them into another host species. Such transplanted insects will, upon attaining sexual maturity, seek to lay the eggs upon the host species to which they were transplanted. A similar situation might well obtain in the case of the annelid *Harmothoe*, mentioned above. Although experimental evidence to support this point is not available, Spooner (1957) distinguished the *Harmothoe* populations, using morphological criteria. Davenport (1966) extensively discussed the role of behavior in symbiosis.

It may be remarked that the chemical trail-marking substances, or pheromones, produced and utilized by ants are also utilized by some symbiotes associated with ants. This appears to be the case with symbiotic millipedes migrating with columns of army ants and has been demonstrated conclusively with a cockroach symbiote of the town ant, *Atta texana* (Moser and Blum, 1963).

PERIODIC RESPONSES

Many parasites show various types of periodicity in their behavior which are probably tropic in nature. For example, we might consider the case of the filarial nematode worms. Several species of these animals are known to show a peculiar form of periodicity which is diurnal in character. In these species, the larval worms are deposited by the adult worms in the vascular system of the vertebrate host. The appearance of these microfilariae in the peripheral host fluids is often periodic in nature. It seems to be correlated with the periodic feeding behavior of the intermediate host, usually a mosquito, and may vary with the same species in different geographical locations. It is easy to see how this variation might have occurred by selection, but the nature of the periodicity itself is not well understood. Hawking and his colleagues found that if microfilariae are injected into the blood stream of the vertebrate, they continue to appear and disappear periodically from the blood. Since no new microfilariae are produced under such conditions, it follows that the periodicity is in some measure a physiological property of the larvae.

Similarly, the periodicity in the migration of the human pinworm, *Enterobius*, is well recognized. *Enterobius* usually leaves the anus of the host during the night hours, producing the well-known symptoms associated with the migration. The migration itself is recognized to be associated with the reproductive activity of the worm. However, the physiological factors involved in eliciting migratory behavior are not known. In the case of a protozoan symbiote, *Leucocytozoon*, living in the blood of birds, a very well-developed seasonal periodicity is generally recognized. Again, this regularity is correlated with the activities of the intermediate host, a biting fly. It corresponds to the spring season, in which the particular fly involved appears in great numbers. During this period the number of protozoan parasites found in the blood is quite high, whereas at other seasons of the year it may be difficult to find them even in blood removed from such a host. One of the most fascinating instances of periodicity, which is probably tropic in nature, is periodicity in reproduction of the flagellate Protozoa occurring in the wood roach, *Cryptocercus*. This periodicity is correlated with the secretion of the molting hormone in the host. Since the insect physiologists have furnished quite a body of information on the endocrinology of molting, we may soon have more information on the nature of the tropic response of the flagellates (see p. 65).

REPRODUCTIVE RATE OF SYMBIOTES

It has been said that many parasitic organisms show an increased rate of reproduction associated with the necessity for reaching a new host (habitat). Such reproductive function appears to be highly wasteful, in the sense that most of the progeny do not reach the prospective host. In other words, the organism must reproduce at a high rate in order to "beat the odds," and there has been an evolution, with selection for high reproductive capacity.

The increased reproductive capacity of parasitic organisms seems to take a number of different forms. Obviously, these capacities have independent evolutionary origins. In the case of tapeworms, for example, high reproductive rate is maintained in most of the species by a repetition of reproductive organs along the body or strobila of the animal. The reproductive organs are produced in a multiple fashion. Each segment is composed essentially of a bag of reproductive organs, and this is the major function observable in the animal. The number of the eggs produced may be

enormous. For example, in the case of the rat tapeworm, *Hymenolepis diminuta*, a single worm may produce over 200,000 eggs per day during the life of the rodent host, which may be eighteen months or more in the laboratory. The total corresponds to a number approaching a billion young tapeworms, which would amount to about 120 tons of tapeworm tissue if all mature.

Repetitive Twinning

A rather curious form of increased reproductive capacity, known as polyembryony or multiple twinning, is observed in some symbiote groups, such as the digenetic trematodes and a number of parasitic wasps. In the case of the digenetic trematodes, this process of multiple twinning may be seen to have advantages from two different standpoints. First, it would be advantageous in the simple sense that a single larval trematode encountering the intermediate host could give rise to a number of individuals. On the other hand, there is a certain chance that the cercaria emerging from the mollusks will not encounter the vertebrate host. Thus, the multiple twinning in the mollusk host increases the number of individuals having the possibility of reaching a vertebrate host.

These two aspects are obviously not separable from each other from a biological standpoint. In the case of the wasps, chance phenomena again are probably involved in selection for multiple twinning. The chances are very great that a female wasp will not encounter the proper arthropod host in which to lay her eggs. By laying a single egg which will give rise to numerous individuals, the female wasp is then free to move on to another host that may be close at hand. This enhancement would be of great importance if numerous females of the species failed to find suitable hosts in which to lay the eggs.

Various Patterns for Increased Reproduction

We know that in many cases there has been a purely quantitative increase in the rate at which eggs are produced without repetition of reproductive organs or polyembryony. This is particularly well illustrated in the case of the nematodes. *Ascaris*, for example, produces an enormous number of eggs during the life of the female worm. Unfortunately, our information on the rate of reproduction of free-living nematodes is not sufficient for us to make real quantitative comparisons. In the case of many flatworm parasites, increased reproductive capacity, or at least the opportunities for increased reproductive rate, are furnished by adoption of hermaphroditism. This is commonly seen in tapeworms, superimposed on the repetition of reproductive organs, and is also common among the trematodes. On the other hand, few nematodes and no Acanthocephala are known to be hermaphroditic. There are some instances among the nematodes in which parthenogenesis may occur. This pattern has obvious advantages in terms of production of new individuals of the species without the necessity for sexual union.

One form of increased reproductive capacity that seems to have been generally overlooked is the relatively short generation time seen in many parasitic Protozoa. It might be argued that this is due to the higher temperatures obtaining in warm-blooded vertebrates, and it is true that most of our data on the growth of parasitic protozoans have been obtained with those species living in warm-blooded vertebrates. For example, good data are available on mammalian trypanosomes belonging to several species and on some of the trichomonad Protozoa from birds and mammals. In the present context the question of whether rapid growth is due to the increased temperature is of little importance, since the organisms do reproduce faster than their free-living relatives living at low temperatures, which are not capable of tolerating these elevated temperatures.

We might examine the question as to whether these forms of increased reproductive capacity are actually adaptations for parasitism. If we examine free-living organisms, we may find any or all of these different mechanisms for increased reproduction in various groups. The high rate of production of the young in those marine invertebrates that cast their reproductive products upon the waters is well known. Polyembryony is not unknown among free-living organisms, occurring in both vertebrates and invertebrates. Hermaphroditism occurs in various free-living animal groups, particularly in groups whose young have high mortality rates. However, the fact that these phenomena occur among free-living organisms does not negate the fact that these same mechanisms are useful and represent adaptations associated with the adoption of symbiosis. The pressures which lead to increased reproductive capacity in symbiotic and non-symbiotic organisms differ somewhat, but these are simply examples of convergent evolution.

A CYBERNETIC PRINCIPLE IN ANIMAL SYMBIOSIS

One of the most fascinating controversies among biologists of an earlier day took place between those who were termed "vitalists" and those termed "mechanists." One of the basic differences between these two schools of thought had its origin in the difficulty of explaining how the vast quantity of information required for the operation of a living system could be stored within the germ cells. While it cannot be said that the difficulties have been resolved in a satisfying manner, discovery that information can be stored and transmitted in macromolecules allows us to view a variety of biological phenomena in terms quite different from those of even a few years ago.

If we regard the development of an organism as a "reading out" in time of coded information, mainly from endogenous sources, it is of course obvious that not all the information in the storage system is being read out at any given time. While the information required for branching of the gut is undoubtedly present in the redia of *Fasciola,* there is no evidence of this information in the morphology of the redia; we know it is there because we have seen such a structure appear in the adult of *Fasciola.*

Readout and Feedback

Further data available on the development of organisms indicate that the reading out of information involves sets of feedback mechanisms. Experimentally, it is sometimes possible to garble the information by altering the environment: Studies by Voge and Turner (1956) on the effects of temperature on the development of certain cestodes furnish an example of raising the "noise" level to a degree which interferes with operation of feedback systems of development. Experimentally, it is also possible to produce a partial replaying of a developmental feedback sequence (Williams, 1961).

With these few general introductory remarks, the author wishes to present the proposition that the feedback systems for playing out information or information content of obligate symbiotes show a striking common difference from the information systems of other organisms. In the reading out of information in the life of free-living organisms, we may visualize a series of feedback mechanisms of the closed-loop type although in some instances we may recognize that an open loop occurs. For example, the necessity that pupae of some insects be chilled for development to proceed may be interpreted as an open loop which is closed

by a physical factor from the non-living world. There are other instances in which such a physical factor may be required to close an open-loop feedback in a developmental sequence. On the other hand, in the development of obligate symbiotes open loops in developmental feedbacks are the rule, and these are closed by components which are characteristic of the living organism, the host. In other words, development can proceed in obligate symbiotes at one or more points in development *only* if an open loop is closed by the insertion of information from a host. This information is of a specialized type in that it occurs in the living world and is itself produced as a result of information stored in a host genotype. Examples may be cited to illustrate the general distribution of this characteristic among obligately parasitic organisms.

Open Loops in Worms

Rogers has described the events of exsheathment in a number of trichostrongyle nematodes. Stimuli involve the interaction of temperature and oxidation-reduction potential with a CO_2–carbonic acid system and may involve the action of certain salts which affect the CO_2–carbonic acid system (Rogers, 1960; Taylor and Whitlock, 1960). Rogers has compared this with the metamorphosis of insects in which hormone interactions are involved in the events of differentiation and molting; in the case of the nematodes, the host furnishes what is physiologically equivalent to a hormone to set off the next train of developmental events (Rogers, 1962). In more general terms, this may be interpreted as a class of phenomena in which the host closes an open feedback loop. The excystment of cestode larvae in the definitive host requires the action of gastric juice followed by specialized action of the salts of bile acids, alterations of pH, action of proteolytic enzymes, and temperature change, the precise requirements varying with different species (reviewed by Read and Simmons, 1963). Again, each of these phenomena may be viewed as examples of an open feedback loop in development of an adult cestode.

The events occurring in many trematode cercariae when they penetrate a host or are eaten by a host are similar examples, although our data on the physiological signals which result in the shedding of the tail, encystment, and the development of a metacercaria in or on a host are quite inadequate. There is an open loop which is closed by information from the host. A second open loop in most trematode life cycles is immediately apparent. The metacercaria typically does not develop into an adult until it has entered a definitive host, at which time encystment occurs and maturation proceeds. It will be seen that, in these stages, some trematodes possess at least two open loops and some only a single obvious one which must be completed by information from another living system (the host). The digenetic trematodes possess an additional open loop. The changes in the miracidium triggered by contact with molluscan host tissues is a manifestation of the closing of such a loop by information from the host. The shedding of the ciliated plates and almost instantaneous transformation into a sporocyst is a most dramatic case (Dawes, 1960).

Open Loops in Protozoans

The necessity for signals or information from the host to induce excystment is widely recognized to occur among the parasitic amebas, coccidians, and flagellates living in the gut of animals. These cases may also be construed as involving open loops; the loop is closed by the host, excystment occurs, and cell division ensues with or without entering a host cell. Some dramatic examples of the necessity for chemical mediators of host origin for development are found in the opalinid pro-

tozoans living in amphibians and the flagellate symbiotes in the wood roach *Cryptocercus*, and in the life cycle pattern observed in the monogenetic trematode *Polystoma integerrimum* (see p. 64). Among some hemosporidian sporozoans, the completion of development and formation of gametocytes clearly require information from a host to close an open loop. A completely different type of information is required to close a separate open loop for gametogenesis and fertilization in an invertebrate host. Similarly, the morphogenetic changes observed in the hemoflagellates seem to require information from a living system when the symbiote passes into a vertebrate host. In the hemoflagellate *Trypanosoma mega* the nature of this information has been clarified. In this instance, the compound urea induces morphogenesis. At a concentration of only 0.016 M urea, a certain number of crithidial forms of *T. mega* transform into trypanosomes. Only in the stationary phase of growth do these flagellates become competent to make this morphological modification. Subsequently, it was discovered that the addition of urea blocks the uptake of tritiated thymidine by those cells which transform but does not affect thymidine uptake by incompetent cells (Steinert, 1958; Steinert and Steinert, 1960). Transformation to the trypanosome form seems to involve elevation of temperature with the hemoflagellates *T. conorhini* and *Schizotrypanum cruzi*. In the former, pH also seems to be important.

Other Open Loops

Among such symbiotes as the filarioid nematodes, contact with a vertebrate and stimuli of unknown nature are required for further development; in some cases, exsheathment is also involved. Again, this involves the closing of an open-loop feedback, with the vertebrate furnishing a specialized input. Perhaps the simplest input which we can recognize is seen in the sexual maturation of the cestode *Ligula*. In this case an elevation of temperature to about 40° C induces maturation (Smyth, 1949).

An Interpretation

If it is postulated that feedback loops are not involved at the specific points in development indicated above, but that the readout is linear in form, this condition has a negligible effect on the general hypothesis, which may be stated as follows: *Obligate symbiotes show interrupted coding of information for development and hosts furnish information which fills the gaps in the readout operation.*

It must be emphasized that the evidence available thus far indicates that the information obtained from the host does not possess the specificity residing in the macromolecular information storage system. The information is presented in low-molecular-weight compounds plus physical factors and operates within the framework of the readout operation constituting the host phenotype. Direct interaction of symbiote and host genotypes has been demonstrated to occur only among the viruses, although such may ultimately be shown to occur with certain intracellular protozoan and bacterial symbiotes. We may even find that symbiotes repress or derepress expression of host genetic information.

The argument for the occurrence and significance in symbiotes of open feedback loops which are functionally closed by the host is considerably strengthened by studies on temperature-gradient responses of a number of symbiotes (Mellanby et al., 1942; McCue and Thorson, 1964). These organisms, belonging to several groups, showed no negative feedback response in a temperature gradient. These are of the open-loop type, and survival of the symbiotes clearly depends on the homeostatic functions of the host. In reviewing the physiology and biochemistry of tapeworms, Read and Simmons (1963) concluded that these parasites seem to lack many functions usually associated with maintenance of a steady state. Further accumulation of evidence may show that open loops are found generally in systems required for homeostasis of obligate symbiotes, with hosts supplying the necessary systems for closing such loops and thus maintaining what approximates a steady state in the symbiote.

GENERAL REMARKS

It will be apparent that the entire life history of a symbiote is integrated in time and space with the life of its host. The patterns of integration vary greatly. It now seems evident that understanding the nature of such integrations will require a systems approach with an emphasis on host-symbiote, rather than on host or symbiote.

SUGGESTED READING

CHANDLER, A. C., and C. P. READ. 1961.

COLE, L. C. 1954. The population consequences of the life history phenomena. *Quart. Rev. Biol.* 29:103.

DAVENPORT, D. 1966.

DOGIEL, V. A. 1966. *General Parasitology*. Academic Press, New York.

FAUST, E. C., P. C. BEAVER, and R. C. JUNG. 1968. *Animal Agents and Vectors of Human Disease* (3rd ed.). Lea & Febiger, Philadelphia.

HUFF, C. G. 1931.

McCUE, J. F., and R. E. THORSON. 1964.

OLSEN, O. W. 1962. *Animal Parasites: Their Biology and Life Cycles*. Burgess Publishing Co., Minneapolis.

REID, W. M. 1967.

ROGERS, W. P. 1962.

THORPE, W. H. 1939.

WALKER, J. C. 1957.

6

Adaptations for Entry
and Establishment

With evident adaptations for getting from one host to another, a symbiote will be faced with a new, or at least different, set of problems. Gaining entry to the new habitat (the host) may require a set of adaptations quite different from those required in the previous life of the individual symbiote. However, the functions discussed in the previous chapter form a continuum with those to be considered here. In some cases, no new adaptations for entry are obvious; a symbiote which is brought to and enters a host by the activity of a biting arthropod may not have special separable adaptations for entry, nor will those forms which enter the host by being eaten with food or drink. However, as will be indicated, just getting into the mouth, the stomach, or the blood can be construed as only the first step in the entry process. It is frequently very difficult to dissociate the events involved in the entry and the establishment of a symbiote. Hence we will treat these two aspects concurrently.

SOME HOST-ADJACENT REACTIONS

Among the symbiotes of plants are many species which are passively carried to the vicinity of potential hosts. Reactions to the host would be of positive value in culminating a host-symbiote association. Such reactions were mentioned in Chapter 5 but are considered now in a slightly different context.

Much study has been devoted to factors responsible for "hatching" of the cysts of the golden nematode, *Heterodera rostochiensis*, a parasite of potatoes. It has been well established that chemical substances diffusing into the soil from host roots actively stimulate emergence of larval nematodes from their cysts and migration to the host roots. There is evidence that the active principle is an organic molecule, a cardiac glycoside (Ellenby and Gilbert, 1957). It has also been shown that root diffusates from appropriate plants will induce molting of larval *Paratylenchus projectus*, a nematode symbiote of plants (Rhoades and Linford, 1959).

The spores of some fungal symbiotes of plants show characteristics which are adaptations for association with a host. If spores of various rust fungi are present in very high concentration on host leaves, germination is inhibited. This phenomenon, called *self-inhibition*, is apparently caused by chemical mediators, tentatively identified as 2-methyl-butene-2 (trimethylene) in the case of *Puccinia graminis tritici.* Self-inhibition has the advantage that spores will not germinate before attaining a certain degree of dispersal.

A factor commonly occurring in soils and acting as an inhibitor of fungus spore germination has received considerable attention. It occurs in the upper layers of soil and is destroyed by high temperatures. However, certain plant materials antagonize the inhibitor and allow germination to occur. For example, in the case of *Helminthosporum sativum,* a fungus associated with seedling blight in wheat, the effect of the germination inhibitor is reduced in the presence of susceptible plants. This inhibition reaction represents a mechanism by which spores would be conserved until they are in an environment adjacent to a host. The discovery that plant substances antagonize the antigermination soil factor led to suggestion of a method for control of certain fungal parasites of plants. If spore germination can be stimulated in the absence of suitable hosts, the fungi will fail to develop and will die. A reduction of the fungal "inoculum potential" would result (Chinn and Ledingham, 1957).

SPECIALIZATIONS FOR BEING EATEN

In addition to those symbiotes which are eaten inadvertently or which are in or on the body of an intermediate host, a few symbiotes have adaptations which allow them to be "mistaken" for food by potential hosts. In other words, the symbiote itself is the bait. One of the most interesting of these is seen in the life history of *Leucochloridium,* a trematode symbiote of birds. The cercariae of this species develop in terrestrial snails and remain within sporocysts; these sporocysts develop most astonishing features, actually growing *out* of the snail and being decorated with brightly colored bands. The pulsating, highly col-

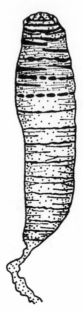

Fig. 6–1 The colored, pulsating sporocyst of *Leucochloridium.* (After Wesenberg-Lund.)

ored sporocysts are attractive to birds which eat them and obtain a ration of metacercariae (Fig. 6–1). There are several instances in which cercariae are eaten as ostensible food items by carnivorous aquatic animals which serve as second intermediate hosts. Of these, the cercaria of *Phyllodistomum solidum* is an excellent example (Fig. 6–2). The movements of this cercaria attract the attention of aquatic carnivores and, when eaten, encysted metacercariae develop in such different hosts as salamanders or immature damsel flies (Groves, 1945).

PROTECTION AFTER BEING EATEN

Many symbiotes enter an animal host by way of the mouth and are swallowed by the host. Almost at once the symbiote is brought into contact with the contents of the stomach. Typically, this is a most peculiar aquatic environment for the incoming organism. Free hydrochloric acid is frequently present with a resulting low pH.

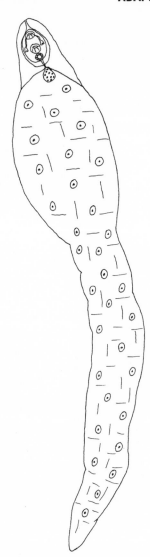

the host. This is evidently the case with trichomonad flagellate protozoans, which show no evidence of protective structures, and is known to be the case with typhoid bacilli. Of course, there are a few species that not only tolerate the stomach but settle down quite happily and live there.

A number of symbiotes show evidence of specialization for tolerance or protection from the stomach juices while passing through that organ. The larval forms of the nematode *Trichinella* (Fig. 6–3) furnish an excellent example of tolerance. These tiny worms are encysted in the muscle tissue of mammals and are taken into the definitive host along with a meal of meat. In the stomach, digestion of the meat is initiated and at least some of the larvae are liberated from their cysts. They are not killed by gastric juice but pass on into the small intestine with the partially digested food.

Some species have developed structures which serve to protect them during passage through the stomach. There is reason to believe that in some forms there is a new second function for the structure in the definitive host and that the same structure may have had a differing function in a previous stage of the life cycle. For example, many of the nematodes entering the host through the mouth are covered by a cuticular sheath remaining from the previous molt, and this sheath remains on the

Fig. 6–2 The cystocercous cercaria of *Phyllodistomum solidum.* (Redrawn from Groves, 1945, *Trans. Am. Microbiol. Soc.*)

Conditions are excellent for the denaturation of protein and for the death of living plant or animal cells. An organism entering the gut must have a mode of protection from the stomach juices and tolerate them or it must die. In some cases, most symbiotes entering *are* killed and relatively large numbers must be ingested for a few to slip past the stomach barrier and infect

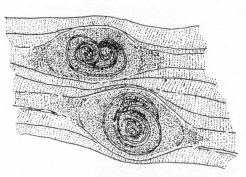

Fig. 6–3 The larval stage of the nematode *Trichinella spiralis* encysted in mammalian muscle.

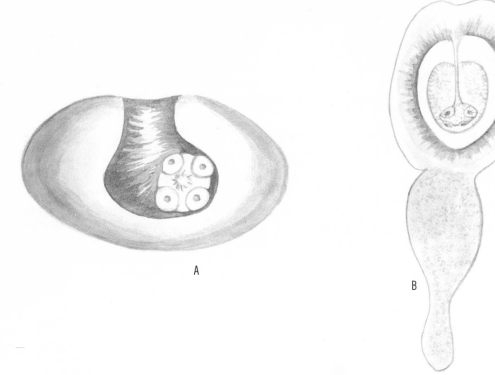

Fig. 6–4 Encysted tapeworm larvae. A. Cysticercus larva of *Taenia solium*. (After Blanchard.) B. Cysticercoid larva of *Hymenolepis diminuta*.

worm during its passage through the stomach. This sheath may also function as a protection against desiccation of the larva in the period preceding its entering the host. Many helminths and protozoans develop inside an eggshell or cyst outside the host and are taken in by the host in this condition. *Ascaris* (p. 95) or *Entamoeba* (p. 93) are such cases. The shell or cyst wall serves to protect the young parasite from desiccation or from the action of chemical substances in the environment (substances in decomposing feces, for example) during the period outside a host and later protects the young parasite from the action of gastric juice. In a few cases, notably tapeworms' "eggs" (*Taenia*), it has been shown that the action of gastric juice actually changes the structure of the shell and more or less prepares it for the chemical

action of the digestive juices of the small intestine.

There are some symbiotes in which the development of a cystic structure may be primarily associated with protection from the chemical and physical action of the anterior parts of the host's digestive tract. The cystic structures seen in tapeworm larvae may serve mainly this end (Fig. 6–4). On the other hand, it may be argued that such cystic structures would also function in protecting the larval tapeworm from resistance mechanisms of the intermediate host, and, in one case, there is evidence that the cyst may have a trophic function in the intermediate host.

In at least one case, a symbiote may enter the host while enclosed within the egg of another species and thus be protected from the action of stomach juices. The protozoan *Histomonas meleagridis* commonly enters its avian host enclosed in the egg of the cecal nematode *Heterakis*. *Histomonas* is quite sensitive to low pH; research workers often have great difficulty in infecting turkeys by feeding free protozoans (see also p. 113).

In the case of symbiotes entering the bodies of warm-blooded vertebrates there is an obvious sharp increase in environmental temperature (except in tropical situations). The symbiote must have attained a certain level of development in order to tolerate the change as well as the absolute level of temperature elevation. The effects on development produced by temperature are clearly demonstrated in Voge and Turner's studies (1956) of the effects of temperature on the early development of tapeworm larvae in arthropod hosts. Those species, such as *Hymenolepis diminuta,* which are not capable of larval development in a warm-blooded host show marked derangements of development when the intermediate host is maintained at 37° C. On the other hand, when larval development has proceeded to that stage capable of infecting the warm-blooded vertebrate, the symbiote has developed a tolerance and, as will be subsequently indicated, elevated temperature is probably involved in events of establishment in a host.

LIBERATION OF SYMBIOTES IN HOSTS

We have considered various ways in which symbiotes may get into hosts and some aspects of the protection of symbiotes during their initial contacts with hosts. We may now consider certain physicochemical effects which may result in the symbiote being liberated in the host. If a trophic stage of a symbiote is found in a host, we know that the organism has been liberated from its cyst, shell, or larval membranes. The assumption has sometimes been made that liberation is accomplished by the sim-

ple action of digestive enzymes of the host. However, there is a body of evidence supporting the view that, among the helminths, the mechanisms involved are not so generalized but may differ from one species to another. There are not only differences between species of different phyla but even between species of the same genus. Among the protozoan symbiotes we know very little of the physiological stimuli for excystment.

Exsheathment of Nematodes

After being taken into the mouth and swallowed by the vertebrate host, the infective larvae of some nematodes, such as *Haemonchus* (see p. 92), quickly shed the previously molted cuticle which had been retained as a sheath (Fig. 6–5). There

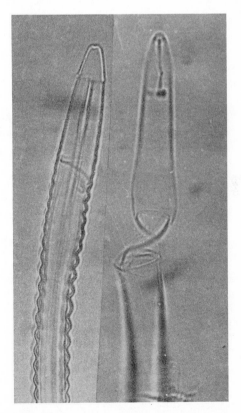

Fig. 6–5 The fourth-stage larva of *Haemonchus* and its freshly shed sheath. (Courtesy of Dr. Paul Silverman.)

has been considerable interest in studying the stimulus for such exsheathment. According to results obtained by Sommerville, Rogers, Silverman, Whitlock, and others, the major stimulus involves carbon dioxide–carbonic acid. When infective larvae are incubated at 37° C in a salt solution containing bicarbonate, to serve as a buffer, and carbon dioxide is present in the system, exsheathment occurs. Inorganic salts are also involved and, according to Rogers (1960), oxidation-reduction potential is important, the response being enhanced at low oxidation-reduction potentials. Taylor and Whitlock (1960) found that various ions have enhancing effects. Since the data of Rogers (1960) show that the stimulus is probably undissociated carbonic acid, it is of interest that the relative effects of different ions studied by Taylor and Whitlock are correlated with their activity as catalysts in the reaction $H_2CO_3 \rightarrow H^+ + HCO_3^-$. Rogers (1966a) furnished evidence that the receptor of the exsheathment stimulus has active sulfhydryl groups.

Silverman and Podger (1964) showed that the stimuli for exsheathment of three species of nematode larvae were different. *Dictyocaulus viviparus*, which lives as an adult in bovine hosts, had an absolute requirement for the gastric enzyme pepsin. *Trichostrongylus colubriformis*, which normally exsheaths in sheep, had a relative requirement for pepsin, with pepsin and carbon dioxide having complementary effects in inducing exsheathment. *Haemonchus contortus*, on the other hand, was quite indifferent to the action of pepsin. Christie and Charleston (1965) reported that *Nematodirus battus*, a nematode symbiote of bovines, is stimulated to exsheath by HCl and is indifferent to the presence of carbon dioxide. It would seem that the stimulus initiating exsheathment of various trichostrongylid nematodes is not restricted to a single common one as envisaged by Rogers and Sommerville (1963), although all stimuli appear to be of biological origin.

In the exsheathment of larval tricho-strongyle nematodes such as *Haemonchus*, the free larval forms retain the shed cuticle as a sheath when they reach a stage which is capable of infecting the vertebrate host. It has been known for a considerable time that, when such infective sheathed forms are eaten by the vertebrate, exsheathment occurs and worm development proceeds. A stimulus furnished by the host apparently results in production of an exsheathing factor by the nematode. This factor, which may contain more than one enzyme entity but includes a leucine aminopeptidase (Rogers, 1965), attacks the sheath in a circular area behind the head and the anterior portion of the sheath finally becomes detached. The effects of oxidation-reduction potential may also be related to this reaction.

As Fairbairn (1960) pointed out, no change in permeability of the larval sheath, as a preliminary step, seems to be necessary for stimulation of the exsheathment process. The site of the receptors in the nematode and the precise origin of the exsheathment fluid are not known. The secretion may be involved as an antigen in the "self-cure" phenomenon (see p. 83). It may be noted that elevation of temperature is required for exsheathment of *Haemonchus* and those of its relatives which live in homoiothermic hosts. The foregoing discussion would suggest that the exsheathment of these larval nematodes is a relatively non-specific affair and that appropriate conditions might pertain in the gut of a wide variety of hosts.

However, Sommerville (1957) showed that, for a given species of trichostrongyle nematode, the exsheathing stimulus was first received by the larvae at a level of the intestinal tract which is anterior to the site at which the worms live during parasitism (Table 6–1). Thus, larvae exsheathing in the rumen become established in the abomasum, those exsheathing in the abomasum develop to maturity in the small gut, and a form which establishes in the large intestine undergoes exsheathment in the small intestine. Clearly, there are

Table 6–1

Relation Between Site of Exsheathment of Trichostrongyle Nematode Larvae and Site of Establishment in Intestinal Tract of Sheep [a]

Species	Exsheathment	Maturation
Haemonchus contortus	Rumen	Abomasum
Trichostrongylus axei	Rumen	Abomasum
Ostertagia circumcincta	Rumen	Abomasum
Trichostrongylus colubriformis	Abomasum	Small intestine
Nematodirus spp.	Abomasum	Small intestine
Oesophagostomum columbianum	Small intestine	Large intestine

[a] From Sommerville, 1957.

greater subtleties in the exsheathment stimulus and reaction than would first appear. There may be factors which modify the ionization of carbonic acid, as well as independent effects of pH and oxidation-reduction potential. Of some interest is the report of Madsen and Whitlock (1958) that, in gastric pouches of sheep having a genetic factor for insusceptibility to the nematode *Haemonchus*, there is decreased exsheathment of infective larvae.

Hatching of Nematodes

Vertebrates become infected in some cases by ingesting shelled "eggs" containing infective larval nematodes such as *Ascaris* (see p. 95), *Ascaridia*, and *Toxocara*. The nematode larva must emerge from a casing which has an inner layer of lipid, a central chitin-containing layer, and an outer coat of protein-mucopolysaccharide. Eggs kept in salt solutions or water do not hatch and are relatively impermeable to solutes. When placed in the small intestine of a warm-blooded vertebrate, hatching occurs. None of the enzymes found in the vertebrate gut will induce hatching, but, if the eggs are exposed to a carbon dioxide-bicarbonate buffer in the presence of a reducing agent, hatching occurs. An increase in temperature (above 36° C) seems to be essential for hatching. The leakage of material from

the egg after stimulation, but before evidence of changes in the eggs can be observed, indicates that one primary change induced by the stimulus is a change in permeability (Fairbairn, 1960). The events of hatching seem to involve dissolution of the chitinous and outer shells followed by rupture of the vitelline membrane enclosing the worm (Fig. 6–6). Rogers (1958) identified a chitinase, a lipase, and possibly a proteolytic enzyme in hatching fluids obtained from *Ascaris*. Eggs of *Ascaridia* from birds and *Toxocara* from cats show similar responses (see Rogers, 1963). Among those nematodes whose larvae hatch from the egg outside the host there is evidence that special stimuli from the external environment are probably not required to induce hatching (Wilson, 1958). This independence is probably also true of those cestode eggs normally hatching outside hosts (Pseudophyllidea and Trypanorhyncha).

Liberation of Juvenile Cestodes

The stimuli concerned in inducing hatching of tapeworm eggs or excystment of tapeworm larvae seem to differ considerably from those discussed above. The eggs of the taeniid tapeworms (*Taenia* and its close relatives), which normally hatch in the digestive tract of vertebrates, seem to require the action of gastric juice to remove

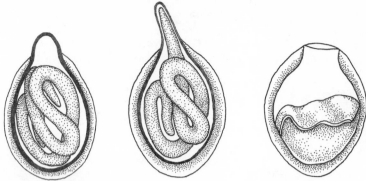

Fig. 6–6 The hatching of the shelled embryo of *Ascaris*. (Redrawn from Fairbairn, 1960.)

the outer portion of the shell (Fig. 6–7). Subsequent exposure to bile salts and cholesterol activates the tapeworm embryo. It shows enhanced movement, and Silverman and Maneely (1955) demonstrated glandular secretion of material, which is probably concerned in penetration of the host mucosa. The eggs of tapeworms which develop in invertebrate hosts differ from those of taeniids. In some species, mechanical rupturing by the action of host mouthparts liberates the embryos.

When the infective larval form of a cestode is taken into the digestive tract of a vertebrate, the scolex or head is typically invaginated and is usually surrounded by a cystic structure of one sort or another (Fig. 6–4, p. 128). The reactions of these larval forms may determine whether or not establishment in a given definitive host species will occur. Early workers noted that bile or bile salts induced evagination of the scolices of *Taenia* species, and in 1936 De Waele reported that the conjugated bile

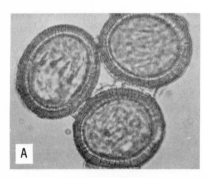

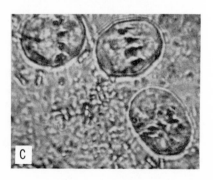

Fig. 6–7 Hatching of the shelled embryo of *Taenia* in the gut of the vertebrate intermediate host. *A.* Intact shelled embryos. *B.* Action of gastric juice in disintegrating the outer shell. *C.* Freed oncospheres still enclosed by the inner shell membrane. (Courtesy of Dr. Paul Silverman.)

acid, glycocholic acid, is toxic to *Taenia pisiformis* whereas the conjugated taurocholic acid is not; this was correlated with the fact that this worm species inhabits carnivores whose bile acid conjugates are mainly taurocholic. In herbivorous vertebrates, glycocholic acid is the main bile acid, and *T. pisiformis* dies in such hosts.

More recently, Smyth and Haslewood (1963) examined the effects of bile from various vertebrates and of specific bile acid salts on the scolices of *Echinococcus granulosus*. The adult of this tapeworm develops in the small intestine of carnivores. The worms tolerated dog bile, but sheep, pig, ox, and fish (*Gadus* sp.) bile were toxic, being increasingly so in the order named. Salts of conjugated bile acids were less toxic than the salts of deoxycholic or chenodeoxycholic acids. The data suggest that bile acids may be of significance in determining host specificity of *Echinococcus*.

The influence of salts of bile acids, digestive enzymes, and temperature on tapeworm encystment has been examined with several species. In the case of *Hymenolepis diminuta* (see p. 111), five physiological effects involved in excystment were noted (Read, 1955). These were a "priming effect" on the outer cyst effected by pepsin at a low pH, an "irritability effect" induced by salts of bile acids and manifested by movements of the scolex, a "surface alteration effect" effected by bile salts and manifested by the effects of trypsin on bile salt-treated larvae, a "proteolytic effect" of trypsin, and a "temperature effect" in that excystment will only occur at elevated temperatures. Rothman (1958; 1959) extended these studies to several other species. There may be doubt about the "priming effect," in the case of *H. diminuta*. Observations of the effects of some of these factors are summarized in Table 6–2.

Table 6–2

Qualitative Aspects of Some Factors Contributing to Larval Tapeworm Excystment *in vitro*[a]

	Effect of Acid Pepsin on Cyst Digestion	Effect of Bile Salts on Excystment	Effect of Trypsin on Excystment	Effect of Temperature on Excystment	
				Room Temperature[b]	37°C
Oochoristica symmetrica	Unessential	Excyst	None	Excyst	Excyst
Hymenolepis diminuta	Initiates	Some excystment	None[c]	None	Excyst
H. citelli	Initiates	Activation only	None[c]	None	Excyst
H. nana	Initiates	Activation only	None[c]	None	Excyst
Taenia taeniaeformis	Essential	Some excystment	None	Excyst	Excyst
T. solium	Essential	Excyst	None[c]		Excyst
T. saginata		Excyst		Excyst	Excyst
T. tenuicollis		Excyst		Excyst	Excyst
T. pisiformis	Unessential	Excyst		Excyst	Excyst
Raillietina kashiwariensis	Unessential	Some excystment	Excyst[d]	None	Excyst[e]

[a] From Read and Simmons, 1963.
[b] Temperature, 18 to 26°C.
[c] Produces excystment if bile salts present.
[d] Pancreatin active; lipase relatively inactive; amylase not tested.
[e] Temperature, 40 to 42°C.

It may be seen that there are some differences between species, but it is not yet possible to relate these differences directly to the question of whether these excystment reactions may determine the establishment of a particular tapeworm species in a particular vertebrate host.

Excystment of Trematodes and Protozoans

Bile or bile salts have been shown to effect excystment of several trematodes, including *Paragonimus westermani*, *Metagonimus yokogawai*, *Fasciola hepatica*, and *Cryptocotyle lingua*. In some cases, increased carbon dioxide tension and proteolytic enzymes appear to act synergistically with bile salts in producing excystment. In a careful study of the excystment of *Fasciola hepatica* metacercariae, Dixon (1966) distinguished two stages, activation and emergence. Activation is brought about by high concentrations of carbon dioxide, reducing conditions, and a temperature of about 39° C. Emergence is triggered by bile, and Dixon furnished evidence that the metacercaria secretes an enzyme which degrades a portion of the cyst.

Over thirty years ago, Pratt showed that bile or the bile salt sodium taurocholate stimulated excystment of the coccidian protozoan *Eimeria tenella*. Later work with six other species of *Eimeria* has indicated that bile promotes excystment. In at least one species, carbon dioxide also appears to be a necessary stimulus (Jackson, 1962).

MECHANISMS FOR PENETRATING HOSTS

We have already indicated that some symbiotes enter the host by penetrating the skin or outer covering of animal hosts. As might be expected, penetration of the outer covering is even more commonly observed among symbiotes of plants. In addition, many animal symbiotes which are

Fig. 6–8 Mouth stylet in the cercaria of the trematode *Prosthogonimus macrorchis*, a parasite of birds. (Redrawn from Macy, 1934.)

taken in by mouth penetrate the mucosal membranes. Some of these forms have structures suggesting that entry may be at least partly mechanical. Some trematode larvae, some nematodes, and larval pentastomids are equipped with cephalic stylets (Fig. 6–8) which are probably used in penetration. Gordiacean larvae (Aschelminthes) have a complex retractile perforating apparatus (Fig. 6–9) used in penetrating the gut of insect hosts; this structure disappears after the larva has passed into the host's body cavity. The oncosphere larvae of tapeworms are equipped with three pair of hooklets which seem to be used in penetrating the gut of the intermediate host (Fig. 6–10). In many of these instances penetration is not effected by mechanical means alone but may also involve secreted chemical effectors. Among the metazoan parasites, one which is demonstrably capable of penetrating membranes by purely mechanical means is the plant-parasitic nematode *Heterodera schachtii*. Dickinson (1959) studied the ability of *H. schachtii* to penetrate nitro-cellulose membranes having different physical properties. It was found that the nematode could penetrate membranes having hydrophobic properties but could not penetrate hydrophilic ones. Dickinson related this finding to the necessity for obtaining leverage without a water film between the mouth of the parasite and the membrane. Taylor and Murray (1946) described what appeared to be mechanical penetration of skin by the scabies mite *Sarcoptes*. The mite attaches to the skin by the suckers on its anterior legs, raises the hind end of the body until it is essentially perpendicular to the surface, and then cuts into the skin. Penetration requires less than 3 minutes.

Host Surface Properties

The properties of surfaces seem to be important in the mechanical entry of some fungal symbiotes of plants (Fig. 6–11).

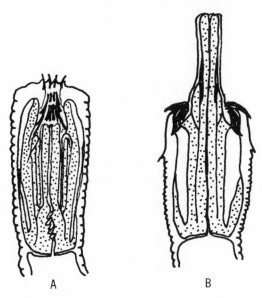

Fig. 6–9 The perforating apparatus of a gordiacean larva, inverted (A) and everted (B). This is used in penetrating an arthropod host. (Redrawn from Dorier, 1930.)

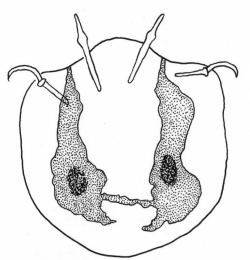

Fig. 6–10 The oncosphere larva of the tapeworm *Raillietina cesticillus* showing the "penetration glands." (Redrawn from W. M. Reid.)

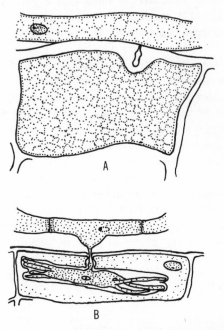

Fig. 6–11 The fungus *Erysiphe graminis* on barley. A. Penetration after formation of an appressorium. B. Intracellular haustorium developed after penetration. (Redrawn from G. Smith.)

Many such fungi form specialized organs, known as *appressoria,* when hyphae come in contact with surfaces. There is a resulting close adhesion of the apposite surfaces. A new growing point now arises in the adherent area and, if the angle of adhesion is high, this point penetrates the external surface of the host. Leverage is furnished by the cohesive forces between the fungal appressorium and the host surface. In some instances, chemical factors are also involved in softening the host tissues inside, but the fact that some of these fungi penetrate films of cellophane, paraffin wax, collodion, and gold indicates that purely mechanical modes are involved in the penetration of the outer barriers (Dickinson, 1960).

Chemical Aids to Penetration

In the past few years some information has accumulated to show that a variety of animal symbiotes possess chemical aids for host penetration. Many helminths possess rather limited physical equipment for mechanical entry, although the importance of leverage against a very thin layer of water may be involved in some instances. Some helminths, e.g., the cercariae of schistosomes and larvae of some rhabditoid nematodes and hookworms, rapidly pass through the epidermis of vertebrates. Glandular structures in these forms were long thought to be involved in penetration of hosts, but only in the past few years have attempts been made to critically determine the role of chemical aids to penetration. Lewert (1958) and Stirewalt (1966) reviewed the available information on penetration by helminths.

Skin Penetration by Worms

The mechanisms of skin invasion by the cercaria of the blood fluke *Schistosoma mansoni* have been described in considerable detail (Stirewalt, 1966) and demonstrate the complexity of entry mechanism. The first recognizable feature is exploration of the skin by the larval worm. This is followed by secretion of a mucus droplet from the postacetabular glands (see Fig. 6–12). The worm is anchored by this secretion and

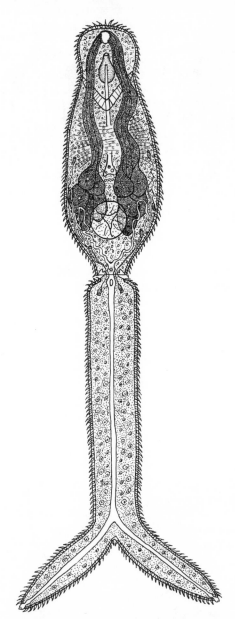

Fig. 6–12 The cercaria of the trematode *Schistosoma.* (Redrawn from Faust and Meleney, 1924, *Am. J. Hyg. Monographs No. 3.*)

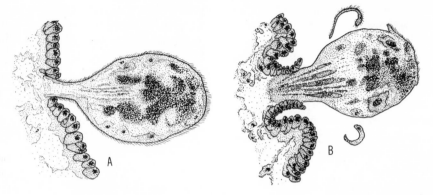

Fig. 6–13 Penetration of the molluscan host by the miracidium of *Fasciola*. A. Early stage of penetration. B. Later stage of penetration accompanied by shedding of the symbiote's ciliated surface epithelium. (Redrawn from Dawes, 1959, 1960.)

orients itself perpendicularly to the skin surface. It now undergoes vigorous muscular contraction, abrading the skin surface with the cuticular tips of the acetabular gland ducts and pouring an alkaline secretion onto the entry site. This activity softens the horny outer keratin and allows partial penetration. The worm then deposits the preacetabular gland secretion, which is regarded as enzymatic in nature.

During skin penetration by schistosome trematode cercariae or larval nematodes of the genera *Strongyloides* and *Nippostrongylus*, alterations of the basement membrane and of the ground substance, presumably glycoprotein, have been demonstrated by histochemical techniques. Similar effects were observed in the penetration of intestinal mucosa by the embryos of the tapeworm *Taenia*. Secretions of the living larvae of schistosomes and *Strongyloides* are capable of digesting gelatin films and releasing dye from azo-dye-bound collagen substrates, and there is adequate evidence that the activity is enzymatic. Lewert has referred to these as collagenase-like enzymes, but studies by Millemann and Thonard (1959) on the activity of schistosomes against pure collagen casts some doubt on the specific identity of the substrate for these secretions. Collagenases

have been reported from the parasitic maggots of flies (*Hypoderma* and *Lucilia* spp.). Lewert pointed out that the chemical mechanisms differ with different species; the substances produced by the nematode *Nippostrongylus* do not act on azo-dye-bound collagen substrates, and it has been postulated that in *Nippostrongylus* a lipolytic enzyme is involved in penetrating the host.

Other Examples of Penetration

Dawes described the entry of the miracidium of the trematode *Fasciola* into the molluscan host. A preliminary attachment of the parasite to the host occurs, followed by what appears to be cytolysis of host tissue. The parasite sheds its coat of ciliated epithelial cells and enters the host tissue as a sporocyst (Fig. 6–13). It would be of great interest to determine whether ciliated plate shedding is initiated by specific substances released from host tissue by the cytolytic action of miracidia or whether this is a reaction to endogenous stimuli. It may be suspected that it is the former (see Dawes and Hughes, 1964).

Steiner and Christie independently concluded that certain plant parasitic nematodes probably enter the host with the aid of enzymes, and there is evidence that species of *Ditylenchus* and *Pratylenchus* do produce cellulolytic enzymes (Tracey, 1958; Krusberg, 1960). However, in discussing the chemical aids to host penetration utilized by plant parasitic fungi, Wood (1960) concluded that the penetration of the outer host cuticle is mechanical and does not depend on substances produced by the hyphae of the symbiotes.

Among the viruses, we find that the only enzymes known seem to be concerned with entry into host cells (see p. 139). Bacteriophages and some of the animal viruses possess enzymes which act on components of host cell walls or cell membranes (Burnet, 1960).

MOVEMENT OF SYMBIOTES IN HOSTS

Though a considerable number of parasites penetrate the outer covering or mucosa of hosts, an even larger number move about in the tissues of hosts. Lewert (1958) showed that, in the movements of the larval nematode *Trichinella* and the cestode *Taenia taeniaformis* in the rat host, there are changes in the host's extracellular glycoproteins, these changes probably involving the action of enzymes. However, these have not been characterized. The Hungarian worker Balo has reported that the nematode *Spirocerca* secretes an enzyme, elastase, which acts on the principal component of elastic tissue.

A very "popular" enzyme factor frequently suggested as having a role in the invasive activities of parasites in animal hosts is the enzyme hyaluronidase, often referred to as "spreading factor." This enzyme was first demonstrated in bacterial parasites and acts on a specific component of the ground substance, or intercellular matrix, of tissues (Duran-Reynals, 1950). Although it has been thought that hyaluronidase functions in allowing microorganisms to spread in the body, the evidence for such a function is not convincing. Anti-

hyaluronidase serum seems to have no influence on the spread of parasitic bacteria in the host body (see discussion by Wilson and Miles, 1957, pp. 1153–55). "Spreading factor" (hyaluronidase) has been reported from extracts of several helminths and from the protozoan *Balantidium,* and it has been suggested that it occurs in the dysentery ameba *Entamoeba histolytica* and the hookworm *Ancylostoma.* However, there seems to be no clear evidence that an enzyme acting on polymerized hyaluronic acid is involved in the invasive activity of any animal parasite. Lewert (1958) gave a more detailed discussion of this point.

Various other enzymes have been assumed to be involved in the invasion of host tissues by bacterial parasites. These enzymes include the deoxyribonuclease, or streptodornase, produced by certain streptococci, and a cholera vibrio enzyme desquamating epithelial cells. In the latter case, it has been argued that since the cholera organism enters the host through the intestine, removal of the presumably protective layer of the gut would be of obvious advantage to the parasite. Unfortunately, the cholera vibrio enzyme appears to act only on dead tissues and, as a matter of fact, it was shown in 1960 that the mucosa is not desquamated during a cholera attack. The enzyme coagulase, produced by *Staphylococcus,* seems to be an agent for which an invasive role is reasonably well established. This enzyme causes the coagulation of plasma by converting fibrinogen to fibrin, and there is evidence that coagulase-producing organisms form a layer of fibrin on their own cell surfaces, rendering them resistant to phagocytosis.

The gas gangrene bacillus, *Clostridium welchii,* produces an enzyme, *lecithinase,* which hydrolyzes or splits certain phospholipids that are widely distributed as structural elements of tissues. This enzyme, formerly referred to as *alpha* toxin, is thought to be a major factor in producing the unpleasant effects of gas gangrene disease. The antitoxic sera used in treating the disease are inhibitors of the enzyme activity. Lecithinases are produced by other species of *Clostridium,* but not all of them possess the same kind of toxic activity. Thus, the enzyme from *C. welchii* lyses and destroys red blood cells from the sheep but not blood cells from the horse. On the other hand, the enzyme from *C. oedematiens* destroys horse cells but is essentially without effect on sheep cells. This result is enigmatic, at the moment, since the enzyme from either bacterial species acts on the same phospholids, at the same chemical bond, and both require the presence of calcium for their enzymatic action.

In plant hosts, certain parasitic microorganisms produce alteration of the cell wall and separation of individual cells, usually followed by death of the protoplasts. This pathology was studied in detail with the fungus *Botrytis cinerea* some years ago (Brown, 1936). It was shown that this fungus macerates plant tissue by secreting an enzyme, *protopectinase,* which hydrolyzes protopectin, an important intercellular cementing substance in plant tissues. Death of the cells is produced by the enzyme or some other agent closely associated with it. In more recent years a number of species of bacterial and fungal parasites of plants have been shown to produce protopectinases. The enzymes produced by different species have somewhat different properties, but the end result is essentially similar. In addition to the role of pectic enzymes in invasion, these factors are associated with toxic effects of a more general nature (see p. 26).

ENTRY OF SYMBIOTES INTO CELLS

Many parasites seem to be taken in mainly by the activities of the host cell itself. This passive mode is particularly important for smaller organisms such as the tubercle and leprosy bacilli (Shepard, 1955), leishmania, and rickettsiae. The only necessity seems to be an adsorption of the parasite, which behaves like a particle on the cell surface. On the other hand, there are instances in which the entry into the host cell involves some activity by the parasite. The entry of certain rust fungi into host cells would fall into this category (see p. 107). One of the most remarkable adaptations is seen in the spores of the microsporidian protozoans. These organisms contain a coiled structure, the polar filament. When ingested by an appropriate host, extrusion of the polar filament occurs; and attached to the distal tip of this extruded filament is a minute amoeboid cell which initiates infection in the new host. It seems likely that the extrusion of the filament may aid in penetration of the cell in the host (Trager, 1937; Dissanaike and Canning, 1957). Although the entry of malaria protozoans has been observed, both with erythrocytes (Trager, 1956) and in chick embryo cells in tissue culture (Huff et al., 1960), the descriptions do not adequately tell us whether there is active entry on the part of the parasite or some other type of non-specific mechanism. Trager (1960) pointed out that the entry might be analogous to entry into the egg of the sperms of some invertebrates.

The initial attachment of viruses to cells is probably due to electrostatic attraction between a definite pattern of charged groups on the virus surface and some complementary pattern on the host-cell surface. Thus, some specificity for initial attachment may be imposed and is indeed observed. For example, polio virus will attach to certain primate cells but will not be adsorbed on chick embryo cells. The entry of the bacterial viruses has been studied by several workers and involves the active alteration of the host cell wall and subsequent injection of virus nucleic acid (see p. 207). There is similar interaction between some other viruses and host cells. The viruses of the influenza group interact with red blood cells, attaching to specific receptor sites on the surface of the cell. The attached virus then initiates a change in the surface which increases the permeability of the cell and also apparently destroys receptor sites for other viruses. Substrates on which the virus enzyme acts are apparently mucoproteins. The same viral enzymes may be involved with escape from, as well as with penetration into, the host cell.

The events involved in the establishment of viruses within cells after initial entry probably differ widely with different viruses. The events of infection with bacterial viruses are discussed in Chapter 9 (p. 207). The events thought to occur after entry° of vaccinia, an animal virus, will serve as an example of a complicated interaction between virus and host cell. The processes of establishment lead to the release of viral DNA, a process termed "uncoating." The first step of uncoating is the loss of phospholipid, followed by release of what has been termed an inducer protein in the virus coat. This inducer protein apparently de-represses a host gene, resulting in synthesis of new messenger RNA. During this process, the virus has moved into the cell nucleus. The new messenger RNA codes for a new protein, which is responsible for the final release of virus DNA (Joklik, 1966).

ESTABLISHMENT AT SPECIFIC SITES IN HOSTS

The symbiotes living in the digestive tract typically show a predilection for a particular part of the gut. Forms characteristically found in the small intestine are usually found only in that region. Further, there is good evidence that a particular smaller segment of the gut may be favored by a given species of symbiote (for example, see Holmes, 1961). On the other hand, forms which show considerable localization as long as they are limited to

the digestive tract may live quite well in a variety of locations outside the digestive tract. *Entamoeba histolytica,* for example, does not colonize the small intestine but lives in the cecum and colon. However, if this parasitic ameba invades the extraintestinal tissues of the host, it may colonize the liver, brain, skin, the genitalia, spleen, pericardium, and kidneys, and has even been found in a nasal polyp. The most common extraintestinal site is the liver, probably because the ameba is carried there after bumbling into the portal circulation.

In a similar fashion, the flagellate *Trichomonas gallinae* is more or less restricted to the anterior part of the digestive tract in its bird host, as long as it remains in the digestive tract. However, it frequently spreads to extraintestinal sites and may then be found in almost any soft tissue of the body.

Many other cases might be cited to indicate that symbiotes of the digestive tract tend to be limited in their ability to colonize various portions of the tract. This limitation is not surprising when the properties of the gut lumen are examined in detail. As is well known, the stomach is typically an organ whose contents are at a relatively low pH. Below the pylorus, the pH rapidly rises to values just under neutrality; there is a gradient of increasing pH from the pylorus to the posterior end of the small intestine. The chemical constitution of the contents of the gut undergoes change along the course of the tract. The obvious changes involve hydrolysis and absorption of food materials, the secretions of the glandular structures associated with the gut, the absorption of some components of these secretions at different levels of the tract, and the chemical activities of microorganisms in the lower parts of the tract. A gradient in oxidation-reduction potential has been demonstrated in several species. All things considered, it appears that the gradients along the digestive tract are of greater magnitude and involve more variables than the differences between any of the extraintestinal tissues. We know very little concerning the factors which determine what parts of the digestive tract allow the establishment of particular symbiotes, although this is critical to understanding such symbioses. Rothman's observations on the effects of pH on the inhibition by bile salts of tapeworm metabolism suggest that the intestinal gradients may have interdependent effects on symbiotes (Rothman, 1958, 1959).

Most symbiotes which live outside the digestive tract show some predilection for particular organs. We know very little about why this is so. In some instances, parasitologists have tended to overemphasize organ specificity and to assume that the organ is a sort of target for a parasite after it enters a host. There is reason to believe that organ specificity is frequently not an absolute affair. For example, the trematode *Paragonimus* is frequently referred to as a lung fluke. However, this worm turns up in a variety of locations in the vertebrate body although it is evident that the lungs are probably the commonest site (Yokagawa, Cort, and Yokagawa, 1960). This is not peculiar to *Paragonimus*. Many animal symbiotes turn up in locations in the body other than "where they are supposed to be." This suggests that while symbiotes may have behavioral responses tending to produce specific localization in the host, these responses may be variable or not completely specific and indirectly related to determination of the final location in the host.

In some cases specific location in the host may involve little or no behavioral response on the part of the parasite. For example, the sporozoites of the malaria parasites (see p. 105) are probably taken up by phagocytic activity of cells of the reticuloendothelial system, and development proceeds in certain of such cells. The specific capacity of these and other intracellular agents to be adsorbed on host cells may be construed as a specialization for organ localization. Our knowledge of these specializations is quite inadequate.

TIMING AS INTEGRATION

It will be obvious at this point that many of the adaptations in the life histories of symbiotes are useful to the organism during a very limited portion of its life span, and there is a considerable amount of circumstantial evidence that some of the adaptations for entry and establishment may be present *only* during a very limited stage of the life history. Certain examples may be cited: It has been the experience of many workers that trematode cercariae dissected from snails are not capable of establishing an infection in the second intermediate host or in the definitive host; tapeworm larvae with scolices apparently fully developed will not infect the definitive host unless they have spent a sufficient period of time in the intermediate host to have fully elaborated cystic structures (and perhaps other adaptive functions: see page 128); the embryos of many animal parasites require a period of development outside a host or in an intermediate host before they are capable of establishing themselves in a new definitive host (see p. 92 et seq.).

These and other observations support this general concept: At certain points in the life history, parasites develop specializations for entering hosts and other specializations for establishment in hosts. Some of these specializations involve sensitivity to physicochemical stimuli supplied by the host, the sensitivity manifesting itself as a physiological response by the parasite. Such changes in responsiveness may be construed as a very delicate development of integration in the symbiotic relationship. Rogers (1960, 1962) has pointed out that the exsheathment mechanisms of nematode larvae may be likened to an endocrine relationship in which the host furnishes the "hormone" to set off a physiological response in a target organ.

In somewhat more general terms, development of symbiote responses may be compared with the sequence of events in development of non-symbiotic organisms. Development may be regarded operationally as a series of feedback systems. In the forms just discussed, we may visualize a series of feedback mechanisms from which a component has been deleted. The host furnishes the missing component. Interesting examples of this are seen in work from Thorson's laboratory (McCue and Thorson, 1964). It was shown that a number of animal symbiote species show a positive kinetic response in a temperature gradient, moving toward regions of higher temperature. However, they continue to exhibit a positive response until the temperature reaches the lethal point. These organisms seem to possess open-loop feedback systems. In free-living organisms such a system would have ultimately fatal consequences, and free-living organisms generally have closed-loop systems. That is, the organism reacts positively in a temperature gradient until a position is reached at which the operation of negative feedback results in depression of the response. The free-living organisms thus tend to congregate at some given temperature point in a gradient, and this point is usually well below lethal temperatures. In symbiotic forms, the host controls the temperature at which the symbiote will live, either by physiological regulation of temperature or by responses to a temperature gradient.

CODING, ESTABLISHMENT, AND DEVELOPMENT

As indicated in Chapter 5, modern appreciation of the meaning of the transmission of information by coded sets of molecules called nucleic acids allows us to think of a variety of phenomena in somewhat dif-

ferent terms than those of a few years ago. As a matter of fact, the advances in this area of genetics have been so rapid and sweeping that one is forced to catch one's breath periodically and wonder if the breakneck speed of this research can continue. However, it is apparent that we can now look at problems of development and of inheritance in quite different terms than was possible even ten years ago. The communications engineer and the physicist have much to tell us about the theoretical handling of this new knowledge. The disadvantage from which the engineer and the physicist suffer is a lack of appreciation of biological problems; there is always the danger that the central problem of biology may be lost in the shuffle. The central problem is, and of course always has been, the organism.

If we think of development of the organism in terms of the coded information available in its genetic material, we are immediately aware of the fact that not all of the information in the code is played out in expression. This fact is often overlooked. In its most obvious form, we are made aware of it in studies on enzyme induction. However, it is even more obvious than that. It is pertinent to point out that if something is obvious, it is frequently important. For example, it will be quite evident that the genetic information for the characters of an adult animal are present in the genetic material of the organism throughout its life but there may be little obvious sign of the presence of this information in the larval form. Although no one would doubt that the information for the branching of the intestine is present in the redia of the trematode *Fasciola,* there is no evidence of this coded information in the morphology of the redia. We therefore may envision the genetic information not as a simple message which is independent of time, but rather as a message which is "read out" on a time scale, be it a physiological or a chronological time scale.

It has become plain in the development of many organisms that the information which is coded is played out through sets of feedback mechanisms which will determine the next sequence to be played in the series. These feedback mechanisms usually seem to involve the production of chemical substances which in turn produce an effect and determine the next series of events. Williams (1961) has presented an elegant model of this sort in discussing the metamorphosis of insects. By experimental manipulation, the insect may have the "wrong" hormone produced and, instead of going ahead to the next phase of the development, it may play the preceding series of events over again. We have no clear cases in symbiotes where such replaying is known, but this lack may be due to the experimental work accomplished rather than to the nature of the organisms. Rogers has suggested that the parasitic nematodes may lack the "hormones" for the steps of development. These are furnished by the host in the form of chemical and physical conditions which trigger *new* reactions of the parasite, resulting in its molting. The present author would argue that this state is not at all peculiar to the nematodes, but is quite a general reaction of symbiotic organisms; and, though entailed by lack of an endocrine mechanism, it represents a block deletion of genetic information. This portion of information must be furnished by the host and the playout of information from the genetic material of the host must be such as to jump the block in the symbiote's coded message for development.

This interpretation puts the data on the nematodes in somewhat more general terms and allows us to extend our line of thought to other forms which may superficially appear to differ quite markedly. For example, in the case of the tapeworms, it has been recognized that the presence of bile salts may produce an "irritability" effect, causing a larval worm to become motile, or may be involved in the hatching of shelled cestode embryos (see p. 131). The same sort of effect may be produced on certain other cestode species by the presence of bicarbonate. In these cases, there is an obvious alteration in the observable behavior of the organisms. It is not known whether or not there may be production of chemical substances in the parasite in response to the host-furnished stimuli. The excystment of various protozoans requires specific conditions (information) which the host must furnish in order for development to proceed. This dependence on host information seems to be a common theme in the relation of symbiotes and hosts. In the case of forms that enter the host through the external surface, it is obvious that the continuation of development requires some sort of stimulus which is furnished by the host. None of these seem to have been studied with the specific purpose of trying to determine the nature of the stimulus although it is quite obvious that some stimulus exists. We are dealing, then, with a very general phenomenon which may be stated as a principle: The host must have genetic information and thus the capacity to furnish the necessary compounds and/or physical conditions to overcome a genetic block in the development of a given symbiote. This statement may be referred to as the principle of interrupted coding.

As will become apparent when other adaptations of parasites are considered, this may be a subprinciple to a more general concept: The basic element of integration in parasitism is the dependence of the parasite on those mechanisms which are concerned with the maintenance of the steady state in the host body (p. 121 et seq.). This type of general statement is hinted at by Smyth's concept of nutritional levels in development (see below). Smyth's concept, however, actually represents a different principle which is likewise characteristic of organisms in general: The physiological requirements of an organism differ at different stages of development. In the case of many animal symbiotes this principle is quite dramatically obvious. It is also implied in the observations of Hutner and his associates (1957) that the nutritional requirements differ in a given organism as a function of the temperature of the environment.

Smyth (1959) discussed what he termed "nutritional levels of development" in the life cycles of parasitic helminths, suggesting that the nutritional level of the environment plays a major role in determining the degree of maturation of an organism and that there is a minimal nutritional level of an environment below which maturation cannot take place. The data supporting this concept can also be used to argue that the course of development can be explained in terms of the principle of interrupted coding discussed above. Thus, the failure of a plerocercoid larva of a tapeworm to initiate maturation in the yolk sac of a chick may be due to the failure of the "host" to furnish the necessary conditions for jumping the

blocked information feedback. In none of the cases which Smyth has discussed has it been shown that it can be attributed to what can be called nutritional deficiency in the chemical sense rather than a lack of chemical "signals." This point needs further investigation; many of the foregoing remarks can be labeled as highly speculative.

GENERAL REMARKS

In this chapter, we have attempted to show that, following the exercise of those adaptations involved in reaching a host, new adaptive responses are involved in recognizing, entering, and reacting in such a fashion that establishment may ensue. For example, a symbiote entering through the host mouth that reacts too slowly may be out of the host before establishment can occur. Timing is thus critical. These adaptations of symbiotes must be considered as integrative in character, typically functioning over quite short periods of time.

SUGGESTED READING

DICKINSON, S. 1960.
DROPKIN, V. H. 1955. The relations between nematodes and plants. *Exptl. Parasitol.* 4: 282.
LEWERT, R. M. 1958.
READ, C. P. 1950.
ROGERS, W. P. 1962.
ROGERS, W. P. 1966b.

SMITH, H., and J. TAYLOR (eds.). 1964. *Microbial Behaviour "In Vivo" and "In Vitro."* Cambridge University Press, New York.
STIREWALT, M. A. 1966.
WOOD, R. K. S. 1960. Chemical ability to breach the host barriers. In *Plant Pathology* (eds., J. G. HORSFALL and A. E. DIMOND). Academic Press, New York.

7

Symbiote Nutrition

Whether we are speaking of symbiotic or non-symbiotic organisms, nutrition is an important factor, linking an organism to its food supply. In symbiotic organisms the *essence* of ecology is the nutritional relationship between the symbiote and its host. The factors of competition and natural selection press each species toward a specialized food supply. However, it may be emphasized again that the entire pattern of nutrition is genetically tied to the operation of the whole organism, including all of the specialized functions which lead to "identifying" the host by reacting to the environment offered, entering a host and the changes in activity concerned with establishment. These factors, discussed separately in this book, are tied to the purely chemical nutritional requirements of the symbiotic organism. In some cases, the synchronization of the life history may make the difference between life and death, regardless of the nutritional requirements. The first concern of a symbiote must be to get to a host in which it will be able to live.

It has been pointed out that the feeding of an animal in nature is often considerably more complex than simply furnishing it with a mixture of required substances (Beck, 1956). House (1959) suggested that the term *nutritional requirements* should be restricted to the chemical factors essential to the adequacy of the diet; the term *chemical feeding requirements* should be restricted to the chemical factors important to normal feeding behavior; and the term *physical feeding requirements* restricted to requirements in dietary texture, position, light intensity, and other physical factors that influence feeding behavior. In examining the information available, it is obvious that we know more about nutritional requirements than about chemical or physical feeding requirements.

FOOD-GETTING MECHANISMS

The primary concern of organisms in general is the obtaining of food in satisfactory quantity and of satisfactory quality for the maintenance of life and the reproduction of the species. Since many symbiotic organisms are literally living in a pool of food, it is of interest to examine the modes of feeding in some of them. It has already been mentioned that many symbiotes have adaptations for chewing or biting the tissues of the host, and it has been indicated that some of them appear to have enzymatic mechanisms for getting about through host tissues; the latter may also be involved in the obtaining of nutrients.

We may first be concerned with those organisms which bite or suck food from the host. This pattern of feeding is seen in several phyla. The trematodes, many nema-

145

todes, some arthropods, hirudinean annelids, and some others show adaptations of this sort. The hookworm nematodes have been studied in this respect and show extreme adaptation for a biting and sucking pattern of nutrition. A relatively large volume of blood is passed through the bodies of these parasites from their sucking activity on the intestinal mucosa. Much of the material is not digested and passes out of the anus of the worms as undigested blood. This may serve a respiratory function as well as a nutritional one.

In some groups, the sucking activity is not a specialization associated with parasitism. Among the muscoid flies, for example, sucking is a common mode of feeding. Those that have become suckers of blood have evolved mechanisms for penetrating the skin of hosts, but the sucking mechanism is quite similar to that in non-blood-sucking species which feed on liquid food. In the laboratory there are frequent difficulties in studying the feeding of parasites. For example, in the usual saline media used in studying metabolism, the nematode *Nippostrongylus* does not ingest the liquid medium. The physical and/or chemical feeding requirements are apparently not satisfied in such media (Roberts and Fairbairn, 1965). Hookworms do not appear to ingest liquid media in the absence of serum (Warren and Guevara, 1962; Fernando and Wong, 1964).

Food-Getting in Some Protistans

Among the parasitic protists there are forms which take in solid food by phagocytic mechanisms. Some of these show specializations for the ingestion of cells but may also live on other solid materials in the digestive tract of the host. *Entamoeba histolytica* is such a case. Shaffer and Iralu (1963) showed that there are distinct differences in the ability of different strains of *E. histolytica* to lyse human or ox red cells. It may be inferred that many of the forms which bite and suck food

from the host must have enzymatic mechanisms for the digestion of the materials. There is little information on the precise nature of such mechanisms. Some of the nematodes have been shown to have proteolytic and amylolytic enzymes in extracts of the digestive tract, but it has not been established that digestion occurs in the lumen of the gut in these animals. Some parasitic arthropods have been shown to possess digestive enzymes, although in one case there is evidence that a symbiotic bacterium of the genus *Pseudomonas* may be involved in the breakdown of protein, the arthropod then utilizing the digested material. Some forms may be capable of ingesting solid food under one set of circumstances but living entirely on liquid food under other circumstances. Interest may be attached to observations on the stimulation of phagotrophy in *Tetrahymena*. In chemically defined media this animal does not ingest significant amounts of food through the oral apparatus, but, in a proteose-peptone medium, ingestion through the oral apparatus is important.

Absorption Without Digestion

There are some forms which may rely entirely on the absorption of nutrients in solution and are actually incapable of digestion. The cestode and acanthocephalan worms lacking an intestinal tract may be in this category. It is reasonably certain that the tapeworms, at any rate, do not produce amylolytic or proteolytic enzymes which are used in digesting food in the environment. The vertebrate stages of hemoflagellate Protozoa may be in the same category. Search for digestive activity in these organisms has consistently failed. In this connection, the absorption mechanisms may therefore be of great importance in symbiosis. This will be discussed below.

Limited Digestive Capacities

Some symbiotes can ingest the liquid portion of the host juices and can carry out some digestion but are not capable of biting or breaking into host tissues to any significant extent. Some of the adult ascarid nematodes are in this category. It seems probable that these symbiotes can carry out some digestive function (how much is not known) but these functions may well be specialized. This subject is relatively uninvestigated. The presumed enzymes involved in the movements of migratory phases of certain symbiotes (p. 138) might also be construed as digestive in function. The growth which occurs during the migrations of some species implies that they feed during these movements, and some ingestion of liquefied host tissue must be presumed to occur.

Extracorporeal digestion occurs in at least some nematodes parasitizing plants. These are forms possessing a mouth stylet used in penetrating host substance (Fig. 2–6, p. 23). The dorsal gland is thought to produce a digestive secretion which flows out through the mouth. Liquefied food is then ingested (Linford, 1937). This mode of feeding requires further study.

Feeding of Malaria Parasites

The mechanisms by which malaria parasites utilize hemoglobin, or rather the protein portion of hemoglobin, have seemed quite mysterious. Knowledge of the properties of cell membranes in general made it seem rather unlikely that the molecule could penetrate the cell as an entity. Several workers hypothesized that the parasites could secrete digestive enzymes and hydrolyze hemoglobin as an initial step, and studies with extracts indeed showed that the parasites contain such enzymes (Moulder and Evans, 1946; Cook et al., 1961). One of the difficulties in this interpretation was the frequently observed fact that the malarial pigment is found inside the parasite rather than in the cytoplasm of the host. Light was shed on the problem by Rudzinska and Trager (1957, 1959) who studied the ultrastructure of *Plasmodium*

lophurae and *P. berghei*. Thin sections revealed the formation of vacuolar processes, which were interpreted as evidence of phagotrophy. Similar processes were reported in the related protozoan *Babesia rodhaini* (Rudzinska and Trager, 1962). More recently, Aikawa and his colleagues (1966) have described a cytostome in erythrocytic stages of eight species of *Plasmodium*. This cytostome appears to function in the ingestion of host-cell cytoplasm. Vacuoles containing ingested cytoplasm are pinched off from the filled cytostome (Figs. 7–1 and 7–2). Presum-

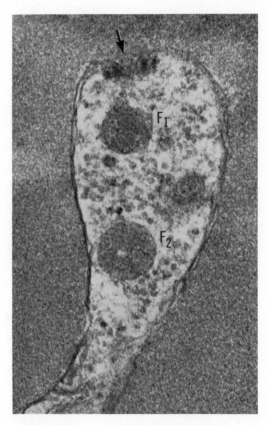

Fig. 7–1 A cytostome (*arrow*) in the trophozoite of the simian malaria organism, *Plasmodium knowlesi,* showing the pinching off process of food vacuole formation. One food vacuole (F_2) has completely formed while the other (F_1) is still connected with the cytostome wall. ×84,000. (Furnished through the courtesy of Dr. M. Aikawa and *Military Medicine.*)

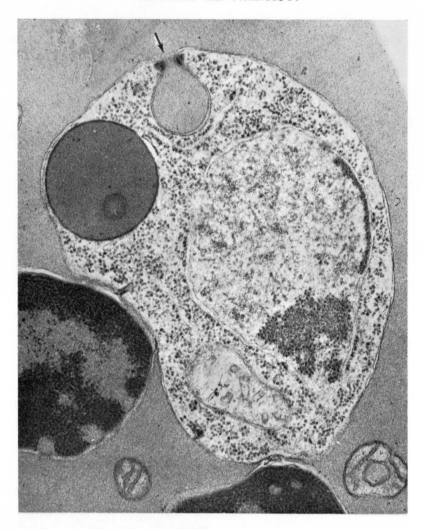

Fig. 7–2 A trophozoite of the avian malaria organism, *Plasmodium gallinaceum.* ×33,750. The cytostome which is ingesting host-cell cytoplasm is indicated by the arrow. (Furnished through the courtesy of Dr. M. Aikawa and *Military Medicine.*)

ably, digestive enzymes are secreted into the vacuole since the heme pigment granules have been observed to collect in these structures.

There are marked differences in the size of the cytostome among the species of *Plasmodium* investigated, the cytostomes of species living in birds having diameters about three times larger than those of species in mammals. According to Aikawa et al. (1966) such differences, as well as

differences in the chemical nature of the pigments, result in significant variation in the size of the pigment residues found in different species of *Plasmodium*. There is some evidence that other sporozoans, such as gregarines, have cytostomes which probably function in intracellular feeding (Fig. 7–3).

Rudzinska et al. (1965) examined several species of malaria parasites and reported that digestion of the content of the vacuole seems to follow two patterns—in *Plasmodium falciparum* digestion takes place within the food vacuole in which the pigmented residue of hemoglobin digestion accumulates; on the other hand, in *P. vivax* vesicles are pinched off from the food vacuoles and digestion takes place in the small vesicles. The residue does not therefore accumulate in a large food vacuole but accumulates in small vesicles.

DIGESTION IN HELMINTHS

In the following paragraphs some very specific examples of information on the feeding of symbiotic helminths will be reviewed. These have been selected to demonstrate the difficulties involved in arriving at firm conclusions from data available on the nutritional relationships of symbiotes and hosts.

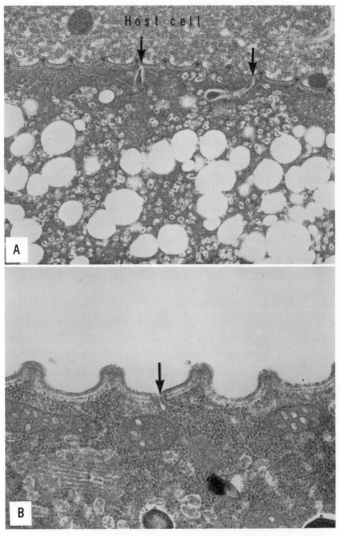

Fig. 7–3 Cytostomes in the surface structure of *Lankesteria,* a sporozoan symbiote of mosquitoes. Arrows indicate cytostome. *Upper,* ×10,600. *Lower,* ×38,700. (Electron micrographs were furnished by R. Walsh and C. Callaway.)

Digestion in Nematodes

Lee (1965) reviewed our knowledge of digestion in nematodes. A number of hydrolytic enzymes have been identified in extracts of the gut of nematodes and several have been identified in gut tissues by histochemical procedures. In a number of cases this constitutes good circumstantial evidence that digestion is carried out in the gut. However, there seem to be a limited number of instances in which more direct evidence is available.

Convincing evidence that an enzyme extracted from tissue of a parasite's digestive tract may actually function as a digestive enzyme was provided by Thorson (1956a), who studied a proteolytic enzyme extracted from the esophagus of the hookworm *Ancylostoma caninum*. The extracted enzyme was specifically inhibited by serum from a dog made immune to *Ancylostoma* by repeated infection. These data constituted direct evidence that the dog had been in contact with this antigen at the tissue level. Thorson (1956b) was also able to produce some immunity to *Ancylostoma* by injecting dogs with a worm esophageal extract containing the proteolytic activity.

Lee (1962) directly observed the secretion of an esterase in the gut of *Ascaris*. This is a merocrine secretion, in which droplets coalesce and pass through the boundary of intestinal cells into the lumen.

Digestion in Trematodes

Very little is known of specific digestive enzymes in intestinal trematodes. This has been discussed by Jennings (1968) in a comprehensive review of digestion in flatworms. Mention may be made of a protease extracted from schistosomes which has a very high specificity for hemoglobin and globin, as measured by the release of tyrosine residues (Timms and Bueding, 1959; Senft, 1965). Since a hemochromogen has been demonstrated in the schistosome gut (Rogers, 1940a) and the disappearance of hemoglobin from media in which schistosomes have been incubated *in vitro* was observed (Halawani et al., 1949), there is circumstantial evidence that these worms have a proteolytic digestive enzyme acting on hemoglobin. However, it is not known whether this enzyme is secreted into the lumen of the schistosome gut.

Erasmus and Öhman (1963) furnished direct evidence that the adhesive organ in strigeid trematodes secretes hydrolytic enzymes and is probably of significance in extracorporeal digestion. Thorsell and Björkman (1965) showed that *Fasciola* can carry out extracorporeal digestion of gelatin in contact with the flukes; saline in which flukes had been incubated caused some digestion of the protein.

Digestion in Tapeworms

There is no evidence that tapeworms can elaborate digestive enzymes, although intracellular hydrolytic enzymes most certainly occur in these worms. The present author has attempted to demonstrate hydrolytic digestive enzymes in intact *Hymenolepis diminuta* and all attempts have failed. The worms have been incubated for periods of up to four hours with glycogen, starch, serum albumin (both rat and ox), or casein. No measurable amount of these substrates enter the worm nor is there measurable hydrolysis. In addition, the worm has been incubated with ^{14}C-labeled algal protein or serum albumin which allowed a very sensitive determination of the liberation of acid-soluble or ethanol-soluble material. No hydrolysis was detected. It was reasoned that, since some vertebrate digestive enzymes act primarily on denatured rather than native protein, denaturation of the protein might be necessary for the action of worm enzymes. Serum albumin was denatured by several procedures, including urea treatment followed by dialysis, heat, and mild acid treatment. These preparations were then used to determine whether the intact worm could carry out proteolysis. No hydrolysis could be detected. There is recent evidence that some tapeworms have hydrolytic enzymes in the tegument surface which may act on organic phosphates in the ambient medium.

THE FOOD OF *FASCIOLA*

There remains broad disagreement as to whether the trematode *Fasciola hepatica* feeds primarily on blood or other tissues during its life in the bile ducts of the vertebrate host; it appears that, at times, workers have attributed to *Fasciola* a delicacy of food selection which may not exist. Dawes' recent studies of the early life stages of *Fasciola* in the vertebrate showed that the young worm, burrowing through the liver, feeds mainly on liver parenchyma. Even here, the breakdown of liver tissues inevitably results in local hemorrhages, and the fluke may ingest some blood (Dawes, 1961; 1963d).

Various workers have reported finding erythrocytes in the gut of *Fasciola* taken from the bile ducts (Sommer, 1880; Stephenson, 1947) and may have been overimpressed by this finding, since the "only recognizable elements in the gut of the fluke consisted of red and white blood corpuscles" (Stephenson, 1947). It should be pointed out that the finding of intact erythrocytes in the gut may indicate that erythrocytes are not as efficiently broken down into unrecognizable components of the caecal contents as some other cells, e.g., duct epithelium.

Other evidence that blood is a major food of *Fasciola* is as follows: In an heroic experiment, Railliet (1890) injected a mixture of 500 grams of plaster of Paris, 45 grams of a blue dye, and 1000 grams of water (not 100 grams as quoted by Stephenson) into the carotid artery of a sheep and later observed blue material in the caeca of *Fasciola* from this host. This cannot be considered a conclusive demonstration of the sanguinophilic nature of *Fasciola*. The worm has been observed to feed on clotted blood *in vitro* (Weinland and von Brand, 1926; Stephenson, 1947). However, this may have little similarity to life in a host, since Stephenson observed that the flukes will also feed on each other *in vitro*. Some workers, accepting the idea that *Fasciola* is a blood-sucking worm, have carried out radioactive tracer experiments to determine the amount of blood taken up by the flukes. These experiments, utilizing ^{32}P-labeled erythrocytes or ^{131}I-labeled protein (Jennings et al., 1956) and ^{51}Cr-labeled erythrocytes (Pearson, 1963), showed that *Fasciola* acquires small amounts of the radioactivity intravenously administered to rabbits or sheep. Unfortunately, none of these workers carried out a determination of whether the radioactivity was still in the labeled component in the blood at the end of the experiment. Such determination is a necessary precaution when using isotopes to study blood volume in healthy animals and most certainly should have been done in studies on animals with fascioliasis. Significant amounts of radioactivity were found in the duct bile from infected sheep, which adds to the ambiguity.

It has been assumed by some workers that the anemia frequently seen in fascioliasis is due to the simple fact that the worms remove blood from the host. However, it may be pointed out that Sinclair's study of the anemia in sheep with fascioliasis (1964) showed it to be a normocytic, normochromic anemia without reticulocytosis. This is not completely consistent with the view that the anemia is due solely to constant bleeding of the host.

Dawes (1963a, c, d) and Dawes and Hughes (1964) presented direct evidence that *Fasciola* feeds on the thickened bile duct epithelium. Dawes' photographs of sectioned feeding flukes seem convincing. Dawes (1963c) has made interesting observations on the changes in bile duct epithelium which he relates to the view that *Fasciola* browses on the epithelium. He showed that during the migration of *Fasciola*, but *before* it enters the bile duct, there is a marked hyperplasia of the bile duct epithelium. According to Dawes, the fluke begins to feed on this tissue shortly after entering the duct.

Mansour (1959) showed by direct experiment that *Fasciola* can absorb glucose through the external surface. Flukes, with the oral sucker ligated, metabolized glucose from the suspending medium at the same rate as unligated animals. Pearson (1963) erroneously stated that "Mansour (1959) claimed that neither absorption nor excretion of nutrients takes place in the gut. . . ." Study of Mansour's work does not indicate that he reached such a broad conclusion but was concerned with the absorption of a low-molecular-weight nutrient.

Since there is evidence that the worm can absorb sugar through the tegument, this must be taken into consideration as a probable feature of the nutrition of *Fasciola* in the host. Normal bile contains a number of low-molecular-weight compounds of potential nutritional significance (see Campbell, 1960, for example). If *Fasciola* is capable of absorbing these through the tegument and if these are present in the bile of hosts harboring *Fasciola*, we must alter our ideas of what and how *Fasciola* eats. The clinical features of fascioliasis even suggest that the nutritional interactions of *Fasciola* and its host are more complex than the simple devouring of blood by the worm. It is suggested on the basis of the evidence available that *Fasciola* has a mixed mode of nutrition. The worm devours cells which are available to it in the bile ducts (including mainly epithelial cells and such blood cells as may become available) which cells are digested in the gut and the soluble products taken into the body. In addition, it absorbs some or-ganic compounds through the tegument. It is plain that some careful physiological and chemical experimentation is needed to shed light on the relative importance of these elements in the nutrition of *Fasciola*.

THE FOOD OF HOOKWORMS

There is rather clear evidence that hookworms are bloodsucking organisms. This has been directly observed by various workers (Wells, 1931; Nishi, 1933; and others) and blood cells have been demonstrated in the worm's gut (Hsü, 1938a). Several investigators have pointed out that a considerable portion of the red cells ingested pass through the gut of *Ancylostoma caninum* in an apparently intact state. This passage of whole cells was also observed to be the case when *A. caninum* was allowed to suck blood through a rubber membrane *in vitro* (Roche and Martinez-Torres, 1960). Wells (1931) estimated blood loss by sucking into a calibrated pipette the blood ejected from the terminal gut of *A. caninum* feeding in an anaesthetized dog. Wells estimated that the worm could remove from the host as much as 0.8 ml of blood per day. Nishi (1933) used similar methods. Roche and Martinez-Torres (1960) used a tagged red cell method and estimated that this worm removed from 15 to 63 cu mm per day. The results obtained *in vitro* by Roche and Martinez-Torres agreed well with their observations on *in vivo* rates of bloodsucking. Clark et al. (1961), using isotopic labeling of red cells, estimated a mean loss of 0.07 ml/24 hours (maximum 0.12 ml) due to the feeding of individual *A. caninum* in dogs.

Using the ^{51}Cr-labeling technique, Roche et al. (1957) concluded that the human hookworm, *Ancylostoma duodenale*, produces a greater blood loss than *Necator*, removing about 0.2 ml/day/worm, whereas their data obtained with patients with pure *Necator* infections indicated a blood loss of about 0.01 to 0.06 ml/day/worm (average, 0.03). After estimating a correction for iron reabsorption (see below), the data of Foy et al. would indicate a loss of about 0.013 ml/day/worm in *Necator* infections.

Roche and Perez-Gimenez (1959) presented evidence that, in humans infected with *Necator,* nearly 50% of the iron entering the gut through hookworm feeding activity was reabsorbed. Erythrocytes were doubly labeled with ^{51}Cr and ^{59}Fe and, after introducing the labeled erythrocytes into the circulation, the appearance of the isotopes in the feces was followed for several four-day periods. Since ^{51}Cr was known to be poorly reabsorbed, the iron loss was calculated from the ^{51}Cr in the feces and compared with the iron loss directly determined by the quantity of the iron isotope in the feces of the same individuals. The difference in the two quantities was considered to represent iron reabsorbed. Further evidence for such reabsorption was obtained by Aparcedo et al. (1962). Evidence that this reabsorption is not a specific feature of hookworm disease was obtained by feeding blood tagged with ^{51}Cr and ^{59}Fe to anemic patients without hookworm infections (Layrisse et al., 1961). It should be mentioned however, that iron reabsorption may vary considerably as a function of the diet. It has been shown that iron chelates formed with certain sugars result in abnormally high iron absorption which may result in serious disease. Cytosiderosis of the African Bantu, a nutritional disease related to a high-carbohydrate, low-protein, high-iron diet, may be an example (Stitt et al., 1962).

In connection with the blood-feeding habit of the hookworms, it is of interest that the addition of serum is necessary for the utilization of glucose from the external medium when *Ancylostoma caninum* is incubated *in vitro.* If serum is not present, the worms apparently do not feed (Warren and Guevara, 1962).

THE FOOD OF *TRICHURIS*

Various workers have been interested in the food of the nematode *Trichuris.** Blood has been demonstrated in the gut of the worm by finding blood cells, or by finding iron, "blood" pigments, or occult blood by presumptive chemical reaction. Otto (1935) reported that blood occurred in the feces of 50 out of 54 humans with *Trichuris* infections. Most recently, Burrows and Lillis (1964) have referred to *Trichuris* as a bloodsucking worm.

As in the case of *Fasciola,* the finding of blood cells in the gut of *Trichuris* may lead to over-enthusiastic acceptance of the idea that this worm feeds primarily on blood. Some carefully executed studies of the gut, in trichuriasis, must not be overlooked. Christofferson (1914) described peculiar modifications of host cells about the anterior region of *Trichuris* in the host. Cell transformations in the infected host mucosa were also observed by Sagredo (1925) and Lewinson (1925), and Hoeppli (1927; 1933) described the tunnels of the worms in the intestine of humans and baboons, noting alterations of epithelial cells; Hoeppli believed that extracorporeal digestion was important in the nutrition of *Trichuris.* Smirnov (1936), after reviewing the literature and examining sectioned *Trichuris,* decided that evidence for the role of the worm as a blood feeder was inconclusive, and some workers, e.g., Jung and Jellife (1952), have been quite cautious in discussing the dietary habits of whipworms as this may relate to disease.

On the basis of the data available, the present author cannot accept the verdict of Burrows and Lillis (1964) that *Trichuris* has been shown to be a "bloodsucking"

* References to the older literature cited on the food and feeding of nematodes may be found in the review of Ackert and Whitlock (1940) and are not included in Literature Cited at the end of this book.

parasite nor that its blood-eating propensities explain the anemia sometimes associated with trichuriasis. It seems more likely that *Trichuris* feeds on living tissues and that blood is one of the tissues with which it comes in contact. It obviously does not reject blood, but its pattern of feeding appears to be quite different from that seen in, for example, the hookworms.

FEEDING IN VARIOUS NEMATODES

Evidence for the tissue-feeding of a number of nematode parasites of the digestive tract has been reviewed by Ackert and Whitlock (1940) and by Hobson (1948). Since these reviews, some additional work has shed further light on these problems. Rogers and Lazarus (1949) found that *Nippostrongylus* rapidly acquires inorganic ^{32}P-orthophosphate injected intramuscularly into the host, whereas *Ascaridia galli* fails to acquire significant amounts of phosphate given to the host intravenously. This difference is attributable to the very different feeding behavior of the two worms, *Nippostrongylus* being a feeder on host tissues and *Ascardia* feeding on the gut contents of the host. Esserman and Sambell (1951) carried out similar experiments with *Haemonchus, Trichostrongylus,* and *Oesophagostomum* in the sheep. The rates at which these three nematodes acquired intravenously administered radiophosphate clearly indicated that they feed on the tissues of the host. However, when labeled phosphate was given to the host by intra-abomasal injection, *Haemonchus* and *Trichostrongylus* acquired the label more rapidly than the tissues of the abomasum or small intestine. This may indicate that these worms also feed on the gut contents. This would bear further investigation.

Clark et al. (1962) measured the blood loss from sheep infected with *Haemonchus* by administering red cells tagged with ^{51}Cr or ^{59}Fe and estimated an average blood-feeding rate of 0.049 ml/day/worm (range,

0.005–0.173). These findings may be compared with an estimate of many years ago by Martin and Clunies Ross (1934). These workers determined the phosphorus content of eggs and the egg output of *Haemonchus.* From these data, they calculated the minimal amount of blood which would supply the phosphorus. Doubling their minimum estimate (to account for males and for waste), their data indicate a blood loss of 0.03 ml/day/worm.

Mention may be made of an ingenious approach used by Rogers (1940b). Rogers determined the zinc in the tissues of *Strongylus vulgaris* and *S. edentatus* and in the gut tissues of horses. To account for the amount of zinc in the worms, Rogers estimated that 100 *S. edentatus* would have to eat from 400 to 2,100 grams of mucosa per year. However, with the more recent appreciation of the rate at which epithelial cells of the mucosa are shed and thus available in the lumen of the gut (see p. 256), there is the possibility that *Strongylus* may derive some of its zinc from the contents of the host intestine. Rogers concluded that the amount of blood taken from the host was small. After determining the amount of hematin in the gut of *S. edentatus*, he calculated that 0.0009 to 0.0002 ml of host blood would yield an amount of pigment equivalent to that found. Of course, as Rogers recognized, such calculations are provisional since no time scale is available to judge the rate of hemoglobin acquisition and loss. It may be emphasized that a visible blood pigment in the gut of a parasite may represent a very tiny amount of blood and may be an unreliable criterion as to whether blood constitutes a significant portion of the diet.

ABSORPTION OF FOODS
BY HELMINTHS

In the nematodes, the absorption of organic food almost certainly involves the gut. Carbon-14-labeled amino acids fail to enter the body of *Ascaris* when the body is ligated at head and tail but rapidly appear in the pseudocoelomic fluid in unligated worms (see also discussion by Roberts and Fairbairn, 1965). Fisher has recently shown that the gut of *Ascaris* transports glucose against a concentration difference from the luminal phase to the pseudocoelomic phase. This transport is blocked by the anthelmintic drug, dithiazanine.

Among the worms which lack a gut (tapeworms and acanthocephalans), it is assumed, materials are absorbed through the external body surface. However, Mansour (1959) showed that the liver fluke *Fasciola* can also absorb glucose through the external surface. Ligaturing the oral opening of this worm had no effect on the rate at which glucose was taken up from the medium. Phifer (1960a, b, c) carried out a detailed study of the absorption of glucose by the tapeworm *Hymenolepis diminuta*. Using very short incubation periods and isotopically labeled sugar, Phifer showed that at least 94% of the absorbed glucose could be recovered in a chemically unaltered form. Absorption was nonlinear with respect to the concentration of the sugar and was accumulated against a concentration difference. Previous addition of inhibitors of metabolism or starvation of the worms resulted in a lowering of the rate of glucose absorption. All evidence points to a process of active transport in the absorption of sugar by this tapeworm.

A number of sugar analogues were tested by the present author and certain ones found to be competitive inhibitors. These observations are consistent with the interpretation that there is specificity of the absorption locus. Von Brand and his colleagues examined the absorption of sugar by the tapeworm *Taenia taeniaeformis* and showed that the process is dependent on the presence of sodium ions. This sodium-dependence is characteristic of active sugar transport in a variety of other animal tissues.

Taenia was also found to have a mechanism for the absorption of glycerol.

The absorption of amino acids by the tapeworms *Calliobothrium* and *Hymenolepis* has been studied systematically. In both worms amino acids are transported against a concentration difference. A number of amino acids were shown to act as inhibitors of the absorption of other amino acids and, in all cases tested, these inhibitions were shown to be competitive in nature. Further, it was shown that a mixture of amino acids acts as though it were a competitive inhibitor of the uptake of any single component of the mixture. However, careful study showed that the absorption of amino acids by *Hymenolepis* was considerably more complicated than appeared evident at first. Not all amino acids are taken in through the same membrane locus, and evidence was obtained that there are several different loci through which a given amino acid may be taken and the affinities of these separate loci for a given amino acid differ. When the worm was reared in two different kinds of hosts, differences in the relative absorption of different amino acids appeared. This was interpreted not as changes in the nature of the loci but rather as changes in the relative numbers of loci of the different types. A mathematical expression for the interactions of amino acids in a mixture was derived and tested. This showed that the effects of various mixtures of amino acids on the absorption of a single component is predictable. Studies were also made of the fluxes across the membrane of the amino acid methionine (Read, Rothman, and Simmons, 1963). Purines and pyrimidines are absorbed by this worm by mediated processes (MacInnis et al., 1965), although it should be mentioned that urea is taken up by the tapeworm *Calliobothrium* by what appears to be diffusion (Simmons et al., 1960).

Rothman and Fisher (1964) showed that the acanthocephalan *Moniliformis* has specific systems for the absorption of amino acids. The competitive interactions between different amino acids appear to conform to those of classical enzyme kinetics.

ENERGY SOURCES OF SYMBIOTES

Definitions of parasitism, mutualism, and commensalism are usually couched in nutritional terms. Therefore, it is important to examine the comparative nutrition of major groups of symbiotes, with some attention to its specific relation to symbiosis. However, as will be apparent, it is usually difficult to make any clear association of specific nutritional requirements and a symbiotic mode of life.

Except for some of the Protista, all animal organisms require an energy source in the form of oxidizable organic compounds. For the moment, it is of little importance whether these are aerobic or anaerobic oxidations. The commonest source of energy for animal organisms seems to be carbohydrate, a bulk product of plant photosynthesis. Examination of the information available on animal symbiotes indicates that all which have been examined have well-developed mechanisms for the oxidation of carbohydrate although they vary in the degree of specialization as to the spectrum of carbohydrates which can be utilized. There is a reasonable amount of evidence that carbohydrate is an absolute requirement as an energy source for many animal parasites. This may not be true of animals in general, since the proper balance of protein and fat will allow growth and reproduction of many nonparasitic organisms. Exceptions are mainly insects, such as certain lepidopterans, bees, and some flies and mosquitoes.

Among some of the protozoans, the requirement for a carbohydrate source is often quite apparent. The trypanosome stages of the African pathogenic trypanosomes die rather quickly *in vitro* if they are not supplied with carbohydrate in the suspending medium (von Brand, 1952). In general, trichomonad protozoans require the inclusion of carbohydrate in the medium to obtain significant growth; these organisms show considerable differences among the species in terms of what kinds of carbohydrates will support growth. *Trichomonas vaginalis*, for example, can only use glucose and its polymers, whereas *T. gallinae* can use a variety of other sugars (Read, 1958). The parasitic amebas grow in media containing sugars, and a specificity for carbohydrate quality has been demonstrated by Entner (1958). Parasitic ciliate protozoans may be able to use protein as an energy source as some of their free-living relatives do, but this does not seem to have been examined by satisfactory experimentation.

There is a considerable body of evidence that tapeworms require carbohydrate for growth and reproduction. This evidence has been reviewed in detail by Read (1959) and may be summarized as follows: Several species of tapeworms have been found to exhibit a dramatic reduction in the quantity of stored polysaccharide, a cessation of growth and egg production, and a loss of much of the strobila when carbohydrate is deleted from the host diet for relatively short periods of time. When small amounts of carbohydrate are added to the diet, the size and reproductive rate of *Hymenolepis diminuta* are found to bear an approximately linear relationship to the amount of carbohydrate in the host diet over a certain critical range. Of considerable interest is the finding that, of sixteen species of tapeworms examined, fourteen species are severely limited in the kinds of carbohydrate which can be metabolized (Read, 1959; Laurie, 1961). The fourteen species will only metabolize, to a significant extent, glucose and galactose of a variety of sugars tested. Since these worms do not have the external hydrolases to make these sugars available from the polymerized forms (maltose and higher sugars), this implies that they must depend on the host to make free monosaccharide sugars available and the rates of carbohydrate metabolism indicate that considerable quantities must be made available. This aspect of tapeworm nutrition may be sufficiently limiting to necessitate a parasitic mode of life for these organisms.

Acanthocephala may require carbohydrate for normal growth and reproduction, a requirement satisfied from host dietary sources. Growth of *Moniliformis dubius* is sharply arrested and the body weight and polysaccharide content decrease rapidly if the host is placed on a carbohydrate deficient diet (Read and Rothman, 1958). Data on other acanthocephalans are not available.

The evidence that trematodes require carbohydrate as energy source is not clear-cut but the data available suggest that this is the case. Addition of glucose to culture media prolongs the life of *Schistosoma* or *Fasciola* (Bueding, quoted in von Brand, 1952; Robinson, 1956; Stephenson, 1947; Rohrbacher, 1957). Experiments involving alteration of the host's diet would not seem to be meaningful with these animals since they probably satisfy energy source requirements from the host's tissues without being directly dependent on the ingesta. This is certainly true of the tissue-dwelling forms and may also be true of those inhabiting the gut.

There is only suggestive evidence that some nematodes living in the intestine require carbohydrate from the host diet. Reid (1945a, b) showed that if the avian host is starved for a short period of time, there is a loss of the parasitic nematode *Ascaridia galli*, as well as a marked decrease in the glycogen content of the worms. The loss in glycogen produced by host starvation closely paralleled the loss in worms incubated for similar periods in non-nutrient salt media. This is consistent with other evidence that *Ascaridia* feeds on the contents of the intestinal lumen (Rogers and Lazarus, 1949). In cultivation experiments, it has been shown that certain carbohydrates prolong the life of some nematodes, namely juvenile *Eustrongylides* and adult *Litomosoides* (references in von Brand, 1952).

There is little evidence that nitrogen compounds, e.g., amino acids, can serve as energy sources for parasitic animals. Various reactions of amino acids in parasites have been reported which would result in the formation of carbohydrate or closely related substances. However, as pointed out by Gordon (1959) the fact that a pathway can be demonstrated does not allow the conclusion that it can operate at a sufficiently high level to satisfy nutritional requirements.

Characteristically, parasitic animals do not seem to use fats as an important energy source. In view of the fatty materials which they often produce as end products of metabolism, this may not be surprising. An exception is the juvenile of *Trichinella*, which von Brand et al. (1952) found to use lipids as a major substrate for aerobic respiration. It was suggested by these workers that lipid oxidation might be an important source of the energy required for maintenance of motility.

NUTRITION OF BACTERIAL SYMBIOTES

The nutritional demands of various symbiotic microorganisms may be indicated in the nature of host-symbiote associations shown in Table 7–1. Generally, those bacteria which may live as facultative symbiotes live even more commonly in decaying organic matter. Many of the bacteria which live as obligate extracellular symbiotes do not seem to have highly specialized nutritional requirements and should be capable of living outside of hosts. As a matter of fact, many of them survive and may even multiply as free-living organisms but are apparently not capable of prolonged persistence outside hosts. Others of this

Table 7–1

Relation Between Some Symbiote Habits and Nutritional Requirements [a]

Probable Nutritional Requirements During Symbiosis	Symbiote Habit			
		Obligate		
	Facultative	Obligately Extracellular	Facultatively Intracellular	Obligately Intracellular
Simple carbon and energy source, inorganic nitrogen	*Pseudomonas* *Escherichia*	Typhoid bacillus Cholera vibrio		
B vitamins, amino acids, nitrogen bases, etc.	*Clostridium* *Proteus*	*Micrococcus* Dysentery bacillus Anthrax bacillus		
Complex natural materials —blood, serum, etc.		Streptococcus Pneumococcus Diphtheria bacillus *Leptospira*	Gonococcus Meningococcus *Brucella* Tubercle bacillus	Pleuropneumonia-like organisms *Bartonella*
Unknown requirements satisfied only within living cells or organisms		Syphilis spirochaete		Viruses Psittacosis organisms Rickettsiae Leprosy bacillus

[a] Modified from Moulder, 1962.

type, such as *Streptococcus,* have somewhat more exacting nutritional needs and are correspondingly less capable of survival outside the bodies of hosts, as are facultatively intracellular organisms, such as the gonococcus. The obligately intracellular parasites tend to have highly complex nutritional requirements and, in general, are of smaller body size than organisms in the other groups. Some organisms, such as *Bartonella,* which appear to be obligately intracellular in hosts can be grown in complex laboratory media. In such instances, there is no obvious indication that the nutritional requirements impose a necessity for intracellular life. Some of the obligately intracellular parasites show evidences of nutritional peculiarities which may preclude life outside a living host cell. For example, rickettsiae seem to be incapable of retaining essential cofactors when sus-

pended in salt solutions. Coenzyme A and pyridine nucleotides apparently leak out of the organisms. Further, to obtain minimal incorporation of a labeled amino acid into rickettsial protein, it was necessary to add all of the amino acids, four ribonucleotides, high potassium–low sodium, ATP, coenzyme A, and DPN (Bovarnick and Schneider, 1960). The permeability of the organisms to highly polar compounds which do not readily penetrate other cells and the ready leakage of these substances from the rickettsiae suggest that a major determinant for intracellular life may be a general incapacity to regulate the flow of nutrients into and out of the symbiote cell. This dependence of the symbiote on the host to perform regulatory function will be mentioned again since dependence on host homeostatic mechanisms may be the single common denominator of symbiosis.

It should be stated categorically that the nutritional requirements shown to pertain for a microorganism grown in culture in the laboratory may have little resemblance to the subsistence of that microorganism when it is inhabiting a host. Synthesis mechanisms may be "turned off" in a host as the symbiote feeds on host substance. This problem has been examined in some detail by Smith and Taylor (1964). Attention may be directed to the "disappearance" of a number of enzyme systems found in the culture forms of hemoflagellate protozoans after development in a vertebrate host (see p. 171).

COMPARATIVE NUTRITION OF SYMBIOTIC PROTOZOANS

Nutrition of Hemoflagellates

The hemoflagellate protozoan *Crithidia fasciculata*, a symbiote of mosquitoes, was cultivated in a defined medium in 1953 (Cowperthwaite et al.). It was the second animal organism to be cultured in a completely defined medium, the first being the free-living ciliate *Tetrahymena pyriformis*. Hemin was found to be required and eleven amino acids were found to be essential. A number of B vitamins were found to be required at relatively high concentrations. Of these, it was found that folic acid could be deleted if a polysubstituted pterdine compound was substituted for it. This investigation led to a fairly complex series of studies which has shed light on the mechanisms involved in the metabolic utilization of folic acid (see Guttman, 1963).

During the past few years considerable progress has been made in defining the nutritional requirement of other hemoflagellate protozoans. Citri and Grossowicz succeeded in growing species of *Trypanosoma*, *Schizotrypanum*, *Leishmania*, and *Herpetomonas* in partially defined media. Hematin is required by these forms, and it may

be anticipated that the requirements of these forms will soon be known. The simplest nutritional requirements reported for a hemoflagellate are those of *Crithidia oncopelti*, isolated many years ago by Noguchi from the milkweed bug *Oncopeltus*. Newton (1956) found that this species did not require hematin and could be grown in a medium containing a single amino acid (methionine), three water-soluble vitamins, glucose, and inorganic salts. The present writer verified Newton's results with his strain of the organism. However, there is evidence that some strains of *C. oncopelti* contain an endosymbiotic bacterium. Thus, a reevaluation of the nutritional requirements of this organism is in order (see Guttman and Wallace, 1964).

Trager (1957) has grown *Leishmania tarentolae*, a hemoflagellate from reptiles, in a chemically defined medium. This species was found to require purines and pyrimidines, fifteen to seventeen amino acids, and several B vitamins. Like *Crithidia*, this form required unusually high concentrations of folic acid. One of the most interesting findings was that pyridoxal and choline could interchangeably satisfy a requirement of *Leishmania*. Trager also reported that, in media with suboptimal concentrations of choline, the flagellates became rounded, lost their free flagella, and resembled the leishmania stage of this hemoflagellate. A parallel instance of the effect of a nutrient in the induction of morphological change in the hemoflagellates is the report that a serum protein is responsible for the appearance of the trypanosome stage of *Trypanosoma mega* from frogs (Steinert and Bonné, 1956).

Guttman and Wallace (1964) have furnished a comprehensive review of the nutrition of this group of symbiotic flagellates, and Guttman (1966) has cultured three species of *Leptomonas* in a defined medium. The data available indicate strong nutritional similarity among the genera of hemoflagellates. The very high folic- or folinic-acid requirement masks a requirement for an unconjugated pteridine, which has been called the "*Crithidia* factor." Protozoans other than hemoflagellates do not respond to the *Crithidia* factor; the significance of this apparent nutritional specialization in the hemoflagellates is not plain at this time.

Nutrition of Trichomonads

The requirements of the trichomonad protozoans are incompletely known. However, some of them have been shown to require C14–C18 saturated fatty acids, C18–C20 unsaturated fatty acids, tocopherol (or related compounds), and cholesterol (Shorb and Lund, 1959; Lund and Shorb, 1962; Shorb, 1964). They show some resemblance to the free-living ciliate Protozoa in these requirements. Some of the trichomonads appear unable to utilize purine and pyrimidine bases but require nucleotides, as well as various water-soluble vitamins and at least 13 amino acids. The nutrition of trichomonads has been reviewed in detail by Shorb (1964).

Nutrition of Amebas

Until quite recently, the symbiotic amebas had resisted all attempts to grow them axenically. The amount of effort devoted to such work with the dysentery ameba, *Entamoeba histolytica,* was enormous and the returns were most discouraging. Eventually it was possible to grow the organism in the presence of bacteria whose metabolism had been arrested with antibiotics, but this did not allow the gathering of information on the nutritional requirements. The first ameba to be grown in pure culture was *Entamoeba invadens* from reptiles. Stoll (1957) had considerable success in growing this form in a liquid medium, and it may be anticipated that some definition of its nutritional requirements will soon be available. Diamond (1961) cultivated *E. histolytica* under axenic conditions.

Nutrition of Malaria Symbiotes

During World War II, interest in malaria in the armed forces stimulated a considerable amount of research on the physiology of malaria parasites. A number of studies on the cultivation of various species within host erythrocytes maintained outside the host body yielded a limited definition of the food requirements of the parasites (see McKee, 1951). Trager (1941, 1943) showed that the addition of glutathione and pantothenic acid favored the growth of *Plasmodium lophurae* in duck red cells. Anfinsen and his colleagues (1946) found that *p*-aminobenzoic acid, a precursor of folic acid, was required for the growth of *Plasmodium knowlesi* in monkey red cells. Further, it was found that the inhibition of plasmodial growth produced by sulfonamide drugs could be reversed by *p*-aminobenzoic acid, which further supported the idea that malaria parasites synthesize folic acid from *p*-aminobenzoic acid and other simple compounds (Rollo, 1955).

In the same type of red cell–parasite culture, it was found that the multiplication of *P. knowlesi* was markedly enhanced by the addition of methionine, but requirements for other amino acids were not readily demonstrable in such cultures (McKee, 1951).

In the past few years, Trager has attempted the cultivation of *P. lophurae* outside host cells. Addition of a number of substances to cell-free complex media greatly prolonged life of the parasites and permitted some multiplication. Such substances included ATP, diphosphopyridine nucleotide, pyruvic acid, malic acid, and coenzyme A (the coenzyme form of pantothenic acid). Of great interest is the fact that the malaria parasite is apparently permeable to these compounds, some of which are highly polar in nature. Cells in general are not permeable to such substances. This point was referred to in the case of rickettsiae (p. 158). Trager noted that in red-cell-free cultures, the addition of pantothenic acid was without effect, suggesting that the malaria organism depends on the host cell for the synthesis of coenzyme A. This has been reinforced by the recent finding that the enzyme catalyzing the initial reaction in the pathway of coenzyme A synthesis (pantothenic acid → phosphopantothenic acid) is present in host erythrocytes but not in *Plasmodium* (Bennett and Trager, 1967). The only other organisms which seem to require coenzyme A are a strain of *Treponema pallidum* (the syphilis spirochaete) and the rickettsiae. These organisms are also obligate parasites. The beneficial effects of ATP on the survival of *Plasmodium* outside host cells is not explainable by the lack of the enzymes involved in the synthesis of this compound from adenosine diphosphate. Trager (1967) found that *P. lophurae* contains the appropriate kinases. However, host cells infected with *P. lophurae* show a decreased ATP content, and Brewer and Powell (1965) reported that the human parasite *P. falciparum* developed more rapidly in individuals whose red cells had a relatively higher ATP content.

It has already been mentioned that the malaria organisms, like rickettsiae, have peculiar permeability characteristics. Highly polar compounds such as ATP and coenzyme A penetrate the cell, and these organisms appear to be incapable, or only partially capable, of maintaining the internal pools of low-molecular-weight metabolites when removed from the host cell. It may be suspected that, since they live in low sodium–high potassium environments, these organisms may lack the ion-gradient-coupled systems now thought to operate in the cellular accumulation of a wide variety of organic compounds.

Nutritional Variation in Protozoans

There are interesting nutritional variations in some symbiotic protozoans. The strain of the hemoflagellate *Crithidia fasciculata* which lives in anopheline mosqui-

toes requires hematin but the strain which lives in culicine mosquitoes does not. It has been suggested that this is correlated with the fact that *Anopheles* feeds more frequently on blood than *Culex*, which may reproduce without blood meals, and it may be noted that the hemoflagellate only lives in adult mosquitoes (Lwoff, 1951). On the other hand, the hemoflagellate *Leptomonas pyrrhocoris*, which parasitizes a plant-feeding insect, has been reported to require hematin in culture. However, this flagellate is not an inhabitant of the digestive tract but lives in the tissues of the insect where hematin or heme-containing proteins are available.

Some additional remarks should be made concerning changes in nutritional requirements which may occur with changes in environmental temperature. Such changes may be of considerable significance in the life cycles of many symbiotes living in warm-blooded vertebrate hosts. It was shown that the free-living flagellate *Ochromonas* shows changes in nutritional requirements when grown at elevated temperatures (Hutner et al., 1957). The symbiote *Crithidia fasciculata* shows rather dramatic changes with temperature elevation (Table 7–2). Guttman (1963) has pointed out that these "temperature factors" appear at rather close intervals. A medium may need supplementation for each 0.2° C temperature increase. Compounds which may stimulate growth at one temperature become absolute requirements at a slightly higher temperature. It may readily be seen that this kind of interaction between temperature and nutritional requirements may have interesting implications in determining whether or not a given vertebrate is a suitable host. Also, it may have significance in assessing the biological significance of fever.

NUTRITION OF METAZOANS

Nematode Nutrition

There has been much interest in the past few years in the cultivation of parasitic

Table 7–2

Changes in Factors Required by Hemoflagellate Protozoan *Crithidia fasciculata* with Increases in Temperature of Cultivation [a]

Temperature	Requirement
22–27°C	Minimal defined medium (Cowperthwaite et al., 1953) supports good growth. Stimulation by increased amounts of leucine, isoleucine, phenylalanine and tyrosine.
28–30°	Factors stimulatory at 22–27° are now essential. The following are stimulatory: glutamate, succinate, lactate, and additional Ca^{++}, Fe^{++}, and Cu^{++}.
32°	Factors stimulatory at lower temperatures are now essential.
32.4°	Additional substrate carbohydrate is required.
33–33.5°	1.5 × concentration of whole medium, sufficient at last temperature interval, is stimulatory.
33.6–34°	Addition of lecithin, choline, and possibly vitamin B_{12} and inositol are stimulatory. An extract of dried egg yolk is more stimulatory than the defined compounds.

[a] After Guttman, 1963.

nematodes. A number of species have been cultivated axenically through most of the life cycle. Beginning in 1940, Glaser was the first worker to obtain a definite axenic cultivation with the successful culture of *Neoaplectana glaseri,* a parasite of the Japanese beetle. Stoll has extended these studies and defined many of the physical requirements of this species, carrying them in culture continuously for many generations (Stoll, 1959); Jackson (1962) grew *N. glaseri* in a defined medium containing about 60 components, and a requirement for folic acid was subsequently demonstrated.

Weinstein and collaborators made very important contributions by cultivating *in vitro* various strongyline nematodes of vertebrates. The rodent nematode *Nippostrongylus* was cultivated through all stages in the life cycle. Media used were quite complex, containing such materials as a chick embryo extract (Weinstein and Jones, 1959). Leland (1963), using similar media, successfully grew all stages of *Cooperia punctata* from egg to adult. However, in few of these studies has reproduction been accomplished. In some instances the worms failed to mate; in others mating and fertilization occurred but the eggs failed to develop. These findings are reminiscent of results obtained in studies on growth of insects receiving diets of borderline adequacy. Many other attempts have been made to cultivate symbiotic helminths *in vitro.* These have been reviewed in detail by Silverman (1965).

Although none of the parasitic worms has been cultured in a medium which is chemically defined, mention must be made of studies on the nutritional requirements of the free-living rhabditoid nematode *Caenorhabditis briggsae,* which has been studied for several years by Dougherty and his associates. The ten amino acids which are required by the rat are also essential for this worm. Requirements for at least six of the water-soluble vitamins have also been demonstrated. In addition, the worm requires an as yet undescribed factor which is associated with protein and has some most peculiar biological properties (see Dougherty, 1959, for review of earlier work; and Sayre et al., 1963).

Parenthetically, it may be said that considerably more success has been attained in the cultivation of parasitic nematodes than is apparent from the scientific literature. Much of this work has been carried out under essentially secret conditions under the sponsorship of commercial firms, with the aim of developing methods which may be applicable in the development of vaccines against worms of veterinary significance. The writer deplores this practice of secrecy, mainly because it may have delayed the development of vaccines against hookworm and perhaps other serious helminth pathogens of human populations.

Tapeworm Nutrition

In the case of the tapeworms, there are a number of recent successes in growing them outside of hosts. Many of the earlier attempts represent records of survival rather than cultivation (see von Brand, 1952). In an extensive series of studies, Smyth has reported the cultivation of the plerocercoid larvae of several pseudophyllidean tapeworms, obtaining differentiation of the reproductive systems and production of eggs. Mueller (1959) reported the growth and differentiation of a pseudophyllidean, *Spirometra*, with the worm developing from the procercoid to the plerocercoid stage. In this case, Mueller has carried the worm through the development which it would ordinarily undergo in a cold-blooded intermediate host. Berntzen and Mueller (1964) have reported the successful cultivation of *Spirometra* from the plerocercoid to the young adult, and it may be anticipated that this worm will soon be cultivated through its entire life history outside a host.

Hymenolepis diminuta and *H. nana* were cultivated outside the vertebrate hosts in a flow-culture system (Berntzen, 1961; 1962). One interesting point in this work was the demonstration that the worm requires carbon dioxide for growth. Schiller (1965) grew *H. diminuta* in a stationary diphasic culture system, and Hopkins (1967) reported the successful culture of *H. nana* in a liquid medium under rather simple physical conditions. It may be expected that some definition of the chemical nutritional requirements of hymenolepid tapeworms will soon be forthcoming. These animals grow extremely rapidly and may furnish an important research material for the study of differentiation.

Smyth (1967) has contributed new and exciting observations on the cultivation of the taeniid cestode *Echinococcus granulosus*. This worm normally grows and reproduces asexually as a cystic larval form (hydatid cyst) in the extraintestinal tissues of warm-blooded herbivorous animals. The adult worm develops in the small intestine of warm-blooded carnivores, most commonly canines. Smyth examined the *in vitro* growth of *Echinococcus* larvae in media containing a complex mixture of known constituents (Parker's 199 tissue culture mixture), hydatid fluid, and bovine serum. When the culture medium was monophasic, the larval protoscolex underwent differentiation toward a cystic form (larval). On the other hand, when the medium was diphasic, with a coagulated bovine serum base, the worms differentiated as adult worms. This work is of great interest since it may allow analysis of factors involved in initiation of growth and differentiation. Smyth's observations lend great weight to the importance of recognizing the feeding requirements discussed on page 145.

Nutrition of Trematodes

Attempts to cultivate trematodes *in vitro* have on the whole been less successful than the cultivation of tapeworms. Ferguson (1940) obtained maturation of the progenetic larva of the strigeid trematode *Posthodiplostomum*, and growth and differentiation of the related form *Diplostomum phoxini* has been obtained (reviewed by Clegg and Smyth, 1968). Because of the medical importance of the blood flukes, there have been a number of attempts to culture *Schistosoma in vitro*. These have been moderately successful, the most impressive results being those of Clegg (1965) who was able to obtain rapid initial growth of young worms in a complex medium; later however, growth slowed and was essentially abnormal in character. Similar results were obtained with the lung fluke *Paragonimus* by Yokogawa and his colleagues (see Yokagawa, 1965).

For more detailed discussions of the cultivation of helminths the reviews of Silverman (1965) and Clegg and Smyth (1968) should be consulted.

NUTRITION OF PARASITIC INSECTS

Outstanding success has been attained in ascertaining the nutritional requirements of a number of parasitic insects. Among them are the following: the Asiatic rice borer (*Chilo*), the onion maggot (*Hylemya*), and the pink bollworm (*Pectinophora*), whose larvae parasitize specific plants; *Phormia regina* and *Calliphora vicina*, flies whose larvae cause myiasis in vertebrates; and *Pseudosarcophaga affinis* and *Kellymyia kellyi*, dipteran endoparasites of insects. These studies have shown that insects which feed on higher plants and animals have nutritional requirements which are qualitatively very similar to those of other kinds of insects (House, 1958a).

However, there is good evidence that the relative quantities of dietary constituents may be extremely important in determining whether a diet is near an optimum rather than merely adequate. Thus it has been shown that about ten amino acids are required by insects, including parasitic ones. However, when the relative quantities of amino acids are varied, it is found that species differ in relative response to diets. The data of Table 7–3 show the amino acid composition of four experimental diets. Growth of houseflies was better on mixtures 3 and 4 than on 1 and 2; mixture 3 gave lowest mortality. On the other hand, mixture 1 was highly satisfactory for *Pseudosarcophaga*, and mixture 2 was the best developed for the onion maggot *Hylemya*. Plainly, definition of nutritional requirements must take into consideration the relative proportions

Table 7–3

Composition of Four Amino Acid Mixtures Used in Studying Insect Nutrition [a]

L-Amino Acid	Mixture (grams per 100 ml of diet)			
	1	2	3	4
Alanine	0.102	0.100	0.100	0.106
Arginine	0.084	0.070	0.122	0.092
Aspartic acid	0.122	0.044	0.128	0.046
Cysteine	0.028	0.044	0.026	0.024
Glutamic acid	0.218	0.396	0.210	0.212
Glycine	0.030	0.156	0.156	0.170
Histidine	0.028	0.044	0.048	0.060
Hydroxyproline	0.038	0.034	0.034	0.042
Isoleucine	0.122	0.112	0.104	0.128
Leucine	0.224	0.210	0.154	0.156
Lysine	0.140	0.120	0.116	0.160
Methionine	0.076	0.030	0.060	0.064
Phenylalanine	0.112	0.090	0.134	0.088
Proline	0.160	0.150	0.150	0.160
Serine	0.140	0.078	0.134	0.148
Threonine	0.076	0.034	0.108	0.116
Tryptophan	0.038	0.110	0.028	0.028
Tyrosine	0.130	0.056	0.070	0.088
Valine	0.132	0.122	0.118	0.112
TOTAL	2.000	2.000	2.000	2.000

[a] After House, 1959.

of dietary components, as well as the grosser question of whether or not a given substance is required. These observations lend considerable support to Lewis' balance hypothesis of parasitism (see p. 166).

NUTRITION AND ESTABLISHMENT IN HOSTS

In some cases, it has been shown that nutritionally deficient mutants of symbiotes exhibit marked alterations in their relationships with hosts. For example, a purine-requiring mutant of the pneumococcus was found to be avirulent for mice. If a mixture of four purines was injected into mice with the mutant, the virulence of the bacterium was completely restored (Garber et al., 1952). The appearance of avirulence, along with a requirement for purines or other metabolites, has been reported in several other symbiotic bacteria, including *Salmonella* and *Pasteurella* (Table 7–4). Hawking

Table 7–4

Effects of Injecting Metabolites (4 mg in 0.25 ml Arachis Oil) Intraperitoneally with PABA-less or Purine-less Mutants of the Bacterium *Salmonella typhi* [a]

	Deaths in 20 Mice Receiving		
Organism	Hypoxanthine	PABA	Arachis oil
[b] PABA-less	0	11	0
Purine-less	18	0	0
Wild type	16	16	13

[a] After Bacon, Burrows, and Yates, 1951.
[b] *para*-aminobenzoic acid.

and his co-workers (1954) showed that *Plasmodium berghei*, a protozoan parasite of rodents, fails to produce a progressive symbiosis in suckling rats or in rats on a milk diet. This failure is apparently due to a tissue deficiency of *p*-aminobenzoic acid, which is required by *Plasmodium*, since the infection progresses if the milk is supplemented with *p*-aminobenzoic acid (or with folic acid, for which *p*-aminobenzoic acid is a precursor). With suckling rats, the symbiote proliferates in the host if the nipples of the mother are smeared with *p*-aminobenzoic acid.

The absolute concentration of metabolites in host tissues may also determine the course of a symbiosis. Dubos (1954) described the action of a number of organic compounds on the tubercle bacillus. Some of these compounds stimulate growth at low concentrations but inhibit growth at higher concentrations.

The microbial symbiote *Brucella abortus* produces acute localized disease in the placenta and foetus of pregnant cows, commonly with subsequent abortion. In male cattle, sheep, goats, and pigs, the disease tends to be localized in the seminal vesicles. Keppie (1964) described investigations showing that this apparent tissue specificity is attributable to the presence of erythritol, a sugar:

$$
\begin{array}{c}
CH_2OH \\
| \\
H\text{-}C\text{-}OH \\
| \\
H\text{-}C\text{-}OH \\
| \\
CH_2OH
\end{array}
$$

The growth of *Brucella* is preferentially stimulated by erythritol. Fetal, placental, and seminal vesicle tissues from cattle were found to be rich in the this sugar, whereas other organs, such as kidney, liver, spleen, lymph glands or serum, were found to have very low concentrations of erythritol. Tissues from other species in which localized acute brucellosis occurs were found to contain the sugar, while tissues from host species in which such acute disease does not occur did not contain significant amounts (Table 7–5). Finally, it was shown that the injection of erythritol into guinea pigs, a relatively insusceptible host, markedly increased the infection rate with *Brucella melitensis* or *B. suis*, which also produce serious lesions in placental and seminal vesicle tissues of susceptible hosts (Table 7–6).

A parallel case may be the stimulatory effect of urea on the intracellular growth of the symbiote *Proteus mirabilis*. This organism is commonly associated with pyelonephritis, a destructive kidney disease of man. The growth of *Proteus* is markedly stimulated by concentrations of urea corresponding to those found in kidney homogenates ($0.03\ M$ urea).

There are also data suggesting that the satisfaction of a requirement for some single compound may be modified by the presence of other metabolites. For example, histi-

Table 7–5

Erythritol Content (μg/ml Extract) of Tissues from Hosts Susceptible or Non-susceptible to Acute Localized Brucellosis [a]

Tissue	Susceptible				Non-susceptible			
	Ox	Sheep	Goat	Pig	Man	Rabbit	Guinea Pig	Rat
Maternal serum	<2	<2	<2	<2	—	—	—	—
Placenta (fetal)	60	45	25	20	<2	<2	<2	<2
Seminal vesicle	35	15	60	8	—	—	—	—
Testis	3	5	8	3	—	—	—	—

[a] From Keppie, 1964.

Table 7–6

Increased Infection Rate of *Brucella melitensis* or *B. suis* in Guinea Pigs Induced by Injection of Erythritol [a]

Number of Symbiotes Injected	Erythritol Dose (g)		% Infected After 1 week
	1st Day	Daily	
500 *B. melitensis*	1	0.2	83
	0	0	5
100 *B. suis*	0.04	0.008	60
	0	0	8

[a] Modified from Keppie, 1964.

dine-requiring mutants of the bacterium *Erwinia aroideae,* a symbiote of plants, showed quite variable capacities for growth in turnip tissues which were shown by chemical analysis to contain adequate amounts of histidine for the symbiote. On the other hand, if the bacteria were inoculated with nutrient broth, the bacteria proliferated in the host tissues (Garber et al., 1956). In another case, it was shown that tryptophan-requiring mutants of the bacterial symbiote of plants *Pseudomonas tabaci* could utilize tryptophan only in the presence of other non-required amino acids. Other examples are described in consider-

ing the genetics of symbiosis (pp. 200 and 217). These findings will be of significance in examining symbiote evolution.

Mention should be made of the balance hypothesis of parasitism (Lewis, 1953) and the related hypothesis of Garber (1956). In both cases, the establishment and maintenance of parastism is considered to be determined by the balance of stimulatory and inhibitory metabolites in the tissues of potential hosts. Much of the data described in preceding paragraphs is consistent with the general hypothesis, but the original papers should be consulted for a more elaborate discussion.

NUTRITIONAL LEVELS IN DEVELOPMENT

It has been pointed out that quantitative nutritional requirements of certain metazoan parasites may change as development proceeds. In the case of forms which live in different places at different times in the life cycle, we would also expect that changes in chemical and physical feeding requirements would occur. However, one set of nutrient concentrations may be quite adequate for bringing a parasitic flatworm to the stage of organ development whereas an increase in some or all nutrients may be required for gamete formation (Smyth, 1959). Further, failure to supply a sufficiency of nutrient during the larval development of an insect may not interfere with the development of the larva; the effect may appear in the failure of the adults to reproduce normally (House, 1959).

It is pertinent to ask whether the nutritional requirements of parasites may be involved in determining whether a given host and parasite can live together, in other words, whether the nutritional requirements can be implicated in determining whether a given host is a satisfactory one for a parasite. There is essentially no evidence from which to argue an answer to this question. In those few instances in which the parasite has been grown in a defined medium outside a host, the requirements shown in the test tube cannot be directly related to conditions in a host: the nutrition has been taken out of context. The tacit assumption that there is *a* requirement for a given substance is of little significance in the case of organisms which live outside of cells. The quantity of the requirement is also of obvious importance, but of even more importance is the necessity for definition of the remaining factors impinging on the physiology of the organism in its habitat.

In the test tube, the organism is living under conditions which are even more sheltered than those which it endures when living in the interior of another organism. The main changes in the environment are those wrought by its own physiological activity. The regulatory processes of the host do not come into play. Resistance responses which may represent action against a nutritional activity are absent. Even more importantly, the functional activity required of the parasite has been altered. For example, since there is no necessity for hanging on to a host, the simplest form of adaptation for parasitism is not called into play. The actual energy requirements may thus be altered. These points are well illustrated when we examine the knowledge of the nutritional requirements of bacterial parasites. We have much knowledge of the nutritional requirements of the bacteria *in vitro*. However, this information has told us essentially nothing about the nutritional requirements or, perhaps more importantly, the nutritional relationships of bacteria living in a host. The presence of antimetabolites or other substances which modify the nutrition of symbiotes in different hosts has not even begun to be evaluated. The exact relationships will not be understood until nutritional studies on symbiotes are integrated with ecology.

The foregoing remarks should not be construed as a defeatist's attitude toward the general problem of determining the nutritional requirements of parasitic organisms. It is obvious that it will be necessary to obtain much information on the requirements of organisms grown *in vitro* before the nutrition in hosts can completely be understood. However, we emphasize the point that there is much information on the environment of parasites which must be obtained before the nutritional data can be related to the parasitic phenomenon. We have already indicated that our knowledge of the environment of parasites of the digestive tract is very deficient (p. 140). Even such commonly recognized events in the digestive tract as secretion, digestion, and absorption of protein, carbohydrate, and fat are poorly understood. Many of the new techniques of biochemistry have not been utilized adequately to study them.

GENERAL REMARKS

In only a few cases, involving intracellular parasites, do the nutritional requirements appear to be so qualitatively specialized that they can be construed as specializations associated with the symbiotic mode of life. On the other hand, the data on chemical and physical feeding requirements of symbiotic organisms are so poorly known that no such conclusion is possible. In some cases, e.g., the tapeworms, the lack of digestive capacities, coupled with the apparent requirements for low-molecular-weight organic compounds, suggests that

nutrition of the worms could only be satisfied under very specialized conditions such as those obtaining in a digestive tract, although the substances required may not be very unusual.

The demonstrated importance of the molar ratios of required amino acids among the insects emphasizes that the term "nutritional requirement" should also specify the context in which requirement for a particular substance is shown. While it is now tacitly recognized that "balanced diets" allow organisms to prosper, our understanding of why a particular diet is better than another containing different relative amounts of the same substances is poorly developed. Further, nutritional requirements of a symbiote must eventually be restored to the framework of symbiosis. The difficulties of such an analysis in the case of many microbial symbiotes have been explored by Smith and Taylor (1964).

SUGGESTED READING

ACKERT, J. E., and J. H. WHITLOCK. 1940.

ALLEN, P. J. 1965.

ARTHUR, D. R. 1965. Feeding in ectoparasitic Acari with special reference to ticks. *Adv. Parasitol.* 3:249.

BERNTZEN, A. K. 1966.

CLEGG, J. A., and J. D. SMYTH. 1968.

DOUGHERTY, E. C. 1959.

GARBER, E. D. 1956.

GUTTMAN, H. N., and F. G. WALLACE. 1964.

HONIGBERG, B. M. 1967.

HOUSE, H. L. 1962. Insect nutrition. *Ann. Rev. Biochem.* 31:653.

JENNINGS, J. B. 1968. Nutrition and digestion. (Platyhelminthes). In *Chemical Zoology*, Vol.

2 (eds., M. FLORKIN and B. T. SCHEER). Academic Press, New York.

KEPPIE, J. 1964.

LEWIS, R. W. 1953.

READ, C. P. 1966.

READ, C. P., A. H. ROTHMAN, and J. E. SIMMONS, JR. 1963.

SHORB, M. S. 1964.

SILVERMAN, P. H. 1965.

TAYLOR, A. E. R. (ed.). 1967. *Problems of In Vitro Culture.* Blackwell Scientific Publications. Oxford and Edinburgh.

TAYLOR, A. E. R., and J. R. BAKER. 1968. *The Cultivation of Parasites In Vitro.* Blackwell Scientific Publications. Oxford and Edinburgh.

WEITZ, B. 1960.

8

Metabolism of Selected Symbiotes

It has become almost trite to speak of symbiotic organisms, particularly parasites, as degenerate or highly specialized from the physiological standpoint. In this chapter we shall attempt to examine, in a highly abridged fashion, some additional ways in which symbiotic phases of symbiotes may be physiologically specialized. It should be noted that many of the specializations mentioned in other chapters and not specifically mentioned in this one have an underlying physiological basis. The separation of chapters is a purely arbitrary matter dependent on the prejudices of writers.

COMPARATIVE BIOCHEMISTRY AND SYMBIOTE METABOLISM

A given symbiotic organism will have adaptations which represent modifications of a basic pattern peculiar to the group from which it evolved. For example, a flatworm symbiote will have as the raw material for evolution a certain background of organization which is common to all flatworms. Since it seems to be a fairly safe assumption that the symbiotic forms evolved from free-living ones, the most

profitable comparisons on the extent of physiological alteration associated with the assumption of symbiosis would be comparisons of the symbiotic forms with their free-living relatives. It is indeed unfortunate that in many cases such comparisons cannot be made. The information available is quite out of balance, in that, with some groups, there is a fair body of information available on symbiotic forms and practically none on related free-living forms. It may be remarked that comparative studies within smaller taxonomic categories are relatively inadequate.

Since a main purpose of comparative physiology and biochemistry is that of discerning the pattern of physiological evolution, and thus adaptation, the most significant studies may be those on closely related forms. For example, physiological studies on several members of the same genus might give us considerable more insight into the "physiological values" associated with speciation among symbiotic forms. Such studies are quite limited. A beginning is indicated in the studies of von Brand and others on trypanosomes, of Sherman and Jackson (1963) on enzymes in species of the nematode genus *Neoaplec-tana,* and of nutrition among hemoflagel-lates (Guttman and Wallace, 1964).

In some parts of this chapter the author has freely speculated on the significance of certain physiological properties, and the student should recognize such specula-tions for what they are. As in previous chapters, the method of approach is com-parative. Parenthetically, it may be pointed out that there are two extant meanings for the term "comparative biochemistry." The original use of this term was predicated on the idea that investigation of many dif-ferent living things would show that the basic chemistry is the same. More recently, the term has been applied to biochemical research aimed at finding differences among species.

The metabolic characteristics of sym-biotes are of great importance since they may shed light on operational aspects of the relationships and most certainly yield clues as to the specialization of the sym-biote for the type of life it leads.

Among the bacterial and fungal sym-biotes of plants and animals it has been most difficult to examine metabolism in terms of how it may proceed in hosts. The cultivation of these forms *in vitro* leads very quickly to alterations in metabolic pat-tern and, as a matter of fact, we know little more about metabolism of parasitic bacteria living in hosts than we knew in Pasteur's day. The mountainous literature on bacterial and fungal metabolism utilizing forms grown in culture will not be reviewed here.

On the other hand, a number of parasitic protozoans and helminths can be and have been studied after harvesting them from hosts. The "phenotypic commitment" to a particular pattern of metabolism has been made in a host under such circumstances, and it may be anticipated that a closer ap-proximation of metabolism, as it occurs in hosts, may be obtained. It is obvious that very important contributions now can be made by comparing the metabolism of, for example, tapeworms which have been cul-tured outside a host with that of worms harvested from a host.

Much more information is available on dissimilatory energy metabolism than on the synthetic aspects of metabolism in symbiotic organisms. In part this is at-tributable to the well-developed technology for studying energy metabolism.

CARBOHYDRATE METABOLISM— PARASITIC PROTOZOA

Almost all parasitic protozoans studied metabolize carbohydrate avidly. The non-reproducing trypanosome stage of *Schizo-trypanum cruzi* may be an exception. The sequence of reactions in the degradation, glucose → pyruvic acid, seems to be com-mon to all forms studied, but the enzyme for the reduction of pyruvic acid to lactic acid does not occur in some of the hemo-flagellates. The hemoflagellates also seem to lack the enzyme phosphorylase, a lack which is correlated with their general in-capacity to store sugars as polysaccharides. This failure to store an energy reserve is most dramatically evident in some of the African trypanosomes, which die quite rapidly *in vitro* if not furnished with an ex-ternal supply of carbohydrate. Malaria parasites also seem to lack the capacity for storing complex sugar reserves, although their close relatives, the coccidians and the gregarines, have been shown to contain glycogen. Quantitative studies on the utili-zation of the stored sugar in the two latter groups of organisms have not been made. Other symbiotic protozoans examined, in-cluding the trichomonads, the amebas, and the ciliates, contain stored polysaccharide materials, although in most of these cases little can be said concerning the functional mobilization of these materials for purposes of metabolism.

Cycloposthium, a ciliate from the cecum of horses (Fig. 8–1), and various ciliates

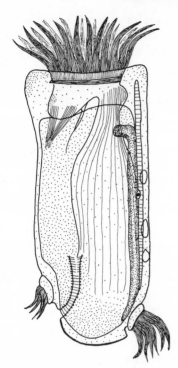

Fig. 8–1 *Cycloposthium*, a ciliate protozoan symbiote from the cecum of horses.

from the rumen of sheep contain the complex sugar amylopectin, but nothing is known of the synthesis or degradation of this polysaccharide in these organisms. Characterization of glycogens from trichomonads unfortunately was carried out on material isolated after treatment with strong alkali, a procedure which has been shown to result in markedly lowering the apparent molecular weights of these polysaccharides.

Extracts of the flagellate *Trichomonas foetus* degrade starch or glycogen, in the presence of inorganic phosphate, to a mixture of hexose phosphates, and Gompertz and Watkins (1963) demonstrated uridine diphosphoglucose pyrophosphorylase in this organism catalyzing the reaction:

uridine triphosphate + α-glucose-1-phosphate

⇌ uridine diphosphoglucose

+ inorganic phosphate

Synthesis of polysaccharide by transglucosylation has been reported to occur in *Trichomonas gallinae* and in some ciliates from the rumen of sheep.

Ryley (1955) showed that, under starvation conditions, *Trichomonas foetus* ferments stored glycogen to acid products, but there are few similar data to show that protozoan polysaccharides are utilized to satisfy energy requirements.

Extremes in the Hemoflagellates

In the presence of oxygen, the carbohydrate metabolism of protozoans ranges from complete oxidation of substrate, in the ciliates, to the very incomplete oxidations seen in certain hemoflagellate groups. Most of the symbiotic Protozoa seem to fall between these extremes and, as with the worms, carry out a mixed metabolism with some carbon being incompletely oxidized. Some extreme modifications, demonstrated in symbiotes living outside host cells, are seen in the trypanosomes of the *brucei-evansi* group (p. 174) taken from the vertebrate host. These trypanosomes degrade a negligible portion of carbohydrate carbon to the stage of carbon dioxide. Glucose is degraded almost quantitatively to pyruvic acid and a lesser amount of glycerol. This process is an aerobic one, oxygen being reduced to water in formation of pyruvate.

Grant and his colleagues have investigated the mechanisms by which the *brucei* group trypanosomes, including *Trypanosoma rhodesiense* and *T. gambiense,* reoxidize the reduced pyridine nucleotides arising in the aerobic oxidation of glucose to pyruvic acid. It was found that, in the presence of catalytic amounts of α-glycerophosphate or dihydroxyacetone phosphate, two enzymes could maintain an oxidation-reduction cycle as follows:

$$\text{DPNH} \diagdown \quad \substack{\text{dihydroxyacetone} \\ \text{phosphate}} \quad \diagup \text{H}_2\text{O}$$
$$\text{DPN} \diagup \quad \text{α-glycerophosphate} \quad \diagdown \tfrac{1}{2}\text{O}_2$$

Under anaerobic conditions, the reoxidation of glycerophosphate does not occur and, through phosphatase action, glycerol is produced. As might be expected from the above, the blood stream trypanosomes of this group seem to lack the enzymes of a tricarboxylic acid cycle. This dearth implies not only that they do not require the cycle for energy production, but that they do not require intermediate compounds from the cycle for purposes of synthesis. Of course, they could obtain such intermediates from hosts. As described on page 109, trypanosomes undergo marked changes in morphology during the life cycle. It might be expected that physiological changes also occur. Still, the changes in the pattern of energy metabolism in *Trypanosoma rhodesiense* and *T. gambiense* are quite remarkable. The culture forms, which seem to correspond to the forms found in the proventriculus of the tsetse fly host, have a respiratory quotient of 0.97, compared with 0.09 for the trypanosomes from the vertebrate host. Further, succinic and acetic acids are produced by the culture forms (von Brand et al., 1955). Studies on enzymes present suggest that the tricarboxylic acid cycle functions in the aerobic metabolism of *T. rhodesiense* culture forms.

There has been considerable interest in the "switching" of metabolism occurring in trypanosomes, and it has been assumed that the changes were triggered by changing the environment from blood to invertebrate gut or the reverse. However, in studying the vertebrate blood forms of a polymorphic strain of *Trypanosoma brucei*, Balis found that the short stumpy blood forms responded to α-ketoglutaric acid. Vickerman (1965) verified this and furnished additional evidence that the switching on of the apparently more elaborate energy metabolism, seen in the insect phase of the flagellate life cycle, actually takes place in the blood stream of the vertebrate.

In the transforming of *Leishmania donovani* from the leishmania to the leptomonad form, there is mitochondrial proliferation from the compact kinetoplast (Rudzinska et al., 1964) with an accompanying increase in cytochrome components and a decrease in lactic dehydrogenase (Krassner, 1966). Presumably, derepressions of genetic components occur, but further study of these systems is required.

In contrast to the above, the trypanosomes of the *lewisi* group from the vertebrate host and the related flagellates, *Crithidia oncopelti* and *C. fasciculata*, have mixed fermentations, converting glucose into various mixtures of lactic, pyruvic, acetic, and succinic acids and glycerol or ethyl alcohol. These forms have all or at least the major enzyme components of the tricarboxylic acid cycle. It is important to note that glucose carbon is not assimilated by hemoflagellates. Glucose, for example, serves as an energy source but not as a carbon source. Studies with a number of species have shown that less than 1% of glucose carbon is incorporated into cell substance, but essentially all glucose carbon appears in the end products of catabolism. Since carbohydrate metabolism seems to serve only as energy metabolism, it might be inferred that cell synthesis would require preformed metabolites from the host. The complex nutritional requirements of hemoflagellates are consistent with this separation of energy metabolism and synthetic metabolism.

Trichomonad Metabolism

The trichomonad flagellates appear to be anaerobic organisms. The anaerobic fermentations of the trichomonads are interesting in that fatty acids, including lactic and succinic acids, as well as carbon dioxide and molecular hydrogen are produced. The mechanism for hydrogen formation needs clarification. Addition of formic acid stimulates hydrogen evolution in *Trichomonas foetus* and both formic dehydrogenase and hydrogenase activity have been demonstrated. This may suggest a net reaction:

$$HCOOH \rightarrow CO_2 + H_2$$

There is some evidence that the nature of the products may vary to some extent with the kind of medium in which the organisms are grown *in vitro*. The species seem to vary in the possession of the enzymes of the tricarboxylic acid cycle. *Trichomonas gallinae* appears to have a full complement of the enzymes associated with the cycle, but *T. vaginalis* has an incomplete cycle and may only be capable of oxidizing certain dicarboxylic acids. Unlike the hemoflagellates, the trichomonads assimilate carbohydrate carbon. But it does not follow that the nutrition of trichomonads is simplified by a high order of synthetic capacities.

Special mention may be made of *Trichomonas termopsidis*, a symbiote from the intestine of termites. This species metabolizes cellulose, but its growth is not supported by starch or glycogen as energy sources.

Metabolism of Amebas

Strains of *Entamoeba histolytica* seem to differ in the end products of carbohydrate metabolism. Entner and Anderson (1954), working with an unspecified strain, identified lactic and succinic acids as major products. On the other hand, Bragg and Reeves (1962) found carbon dioxide, hydrogen, acetic acid, and ethyl alcohol to be the major fermentation products of the Laredo strain of *E. histolytica*. In other strains, the formation of H_2S as a concomitant of carbohydrate metabolism has been reported (Kun et al., 1956).

Metabolism of Sporozoans

The ability of malaria organisms (the genus *Plasmodium*) to completely oxidize carbohydrate seems to vary considerably. *Plasmodium gallinaceum* oxidizes a considerable portion of glucose metabolized to carbon dioxide, whereas, in *P. berghei*, less than 2% of the glucose metabolized can be accounted for as carbon dioxide. In all species studied, *Plasmodium* produces lactic acid, even under aerobic conditions. It almost seems that they are not "geared up" to carry all the carbohydrate through the pathways of complete oxidation. *P. gallinaceum* clearly has the components of a tricarboxylic acid cycle which seems to function in carbohydrate oxidation (Speck et al., 1946). In *P. berghei*, on the other hand, the tricarboxylic acid cycle plays a negligible role in metabolism (Bowman et al., 1961). Further, the apparently impaired ability of malaria parasites to synthesize such critical cofactors for metabolism as coenzyme A (see p. 160) and the suggestion that they may utilize adenosine triphosphate of host-cell origin indicate that metabolism in these symbiotes differs from host metabolism in fundamental respects.

In *Toxoplasma*, a relative of *Plasmodium*, about half of the glucose metabolized is accounted for as carbon dioxide. Lactic acid is a major product of aerobic metabolism; small amounts of acetic, propionic, butyric, and valeric acids are also produced. This organism appears to possess at least a portion of the tricarboxylic acid cycle (Fulton and Spooner, 1960). It should be mentioned that significant changes in energy metabolism seem to occur during development of the oocysts of the sporozoan *Eimeria* (see p. 94). Wilson and Fairbairn (1961) found that carbohydrate was oxidized during the early stages but, after about 10 hours, the organism changed to a pattern of lipid oxidation.

Electron Transport in Protozoans

The mechanisms for the terminal transport of electrons in the energy metabolism of parasitic Protozoa have been the subject of considerable attention in the past and have been reviewed by Baernstein (1963). Since the overall pattern of metabolism is so highly variable, even with some forms which are clearly anaerobic by necessity, a great deal of work has been done on the sensitivity of protozoan metabolism to chemical inhibitors which are thought to act on electron transport mechanisms. Cyanide sensitivity has been a favorite subject of study because heavy metal components of respiratory systems are sensitive to this agent. It has sometimes been assumed that sensitivity to this inhibitor showed the involvement of a cytochrome system, but it seems doubtful that the inhibitions are sufficiently specific to justify such a conclusion. Anaerobic gas production of the obligately anaerobic trichomonads, for example, is sensitive to cyanide. However, it has been shown that one of the enzymes in the sequence, glucose → pyruvate, is a heavy metal cyanide-sensitive system and an additional enzyme step below pyruvate is also cyanide-sensitive. Neither of these appears to be a cytochrome component.

There are many data showing that the hemoflagellate protozoans vary considerably in the terminal oxidation mechanisms. The respiration of trypanosomes in the *lewisi* group (see Table 8–1 for grouping of trypanosomes) is markedly inhibited by cyanide but relatively insensitive to inhibitors of sulfhydryl enzymes. Some data of Fulton and Spooner (1959) suggest that cytochrome components may play a role in terminal oxidation in *T. cruzi*, but such a role has not been unequivocally demonstrated. *T. lewisi*, on the other hand, clearly appears to have a cytochrome system: The bands of cytochrome components have been demonstrated spectroscopically, light-reversible carbon monoxide inhibition of respiration has been demonstrated, and succinate oxidation is sensitive to Antimycin A. The glycerophosphate oxidase system

Table 8–1

Classification of Mammalian Trypanosomes [a]

Section A
  Group I (*lewisi*)
    T. theileri
    T. lewisi
    T. cruzi

Section B
  Group II (*vivax*)
    T. vivax
    T. uniforme
  Group III (*congolense*)
    T. congolense
    T. dimorphon
    T. simiae
  Group IV (*brucei*)
    Subgroup 1. (*suis*)
      T. suis
    Subgroup 2. (*brucei*)
      T. brucei
      T. rhodesiense
      T. gambiense
    Subgroup 3. (*evansi*)
      T. evansi
      T. equinum
      T. equiperdum

[a] According to Hoare, 1957.

seen in some trypanosomes (p. 171) does not seem to function as a major part of terminal electron transfer in the *lewisi* group.

In the trichomonad flagellates, cyanide has no influence on oxygen uptake. However, most of these organisms are anaerobes and the significance of oxygen uptake in the life of the organism can only be regarded as dubious. Of more import is the fact that heavy metal systems seem to be involved in the anaerobic oxidations of trichomonads and, as previously mentioned, there is evidence for the participation of heavy metal systems in their metabolism. A detailed study of these systems is not available.

Of the forms studied in groups II, III, and IV (Table 8–1), the bloodstream forms (trypanosomes) are insensitive to cyanide, and cytochrome components are not detectable spectroscopically. However, the culture forms of *T. congolense*, *T. rhodesiense*, and *T. gambiense* have a cyanide-sensitive respiration and some cytochrome components have been demonstrated, suggesting that a cytochrome system is involved in terminal oxidation. The change in electron transport mechanisms in the differentiation of blood stream forms to culture forms, and the reverse, is consistent with other changes in energy metabolism already mentioned (p. 172). It should be noted that the patterns of respiratory metabolism exhibited by the mammalian trypanosomes shows a striking parallel with the groups of Table 8–1, which were based on morphological and other biological criteria.

The respiration of several species of malaria organisms (*Plasmodium*) is cyanide-sensitive, suggesting a role of heavy metal systems, but definitive information is not available. On the other hand, the related organism *Toxoplasma* was studied by Fulton and Spooner (1960) and found to contain at least three cytochrome components, as well as a cyanide-sensitive respiration.

From observations on the dysentery ameba, *Entamoeba histolytica*, it may be inferred that unusual pathways of electron transport occur. The coupling of carbon dioxide production from glucose with the production of hydrogen sulfide from sulfhydryl compounds suggests peculiarly specialized electron transport (Kun et al., 1956). Cytochrome components could not be detected in *E. histolytica*.

For very thorough reviews of respiratory metabolism of Protozoa, the monographs of Danforth (1967) and Ryley (1967) should be consulted.

METABOLISM OF SOME INTRACELLULAR SYMBIOTES

In addition to the kinds of symbiotes examined in preceding paragraphs, there are a large number of organisms that live in intimate association with the host as intracellular parasites. These include many of the small bacteria and organisms ranging on down in size to viruses. A considerable amount of work has been done on the metabolism of rickettsiae. These organisms, little understood for a very long time, are now regarded as small bacteria. Considerable difficulty was met in early studies due to the necessity for removing the parasite from residual host material. It was necessary for investigators to separate host and rickettsial enzymes from one another and to successfully isolate the somewhat delicate rickettsiae from host materials. This was done by careful use of differential centrifugation and has been described in detail by Bovarnick and co-workers in a series of papers (1949–1960).

Rickettsiae have a somewhat unique respiratory metabolism; they do not metabolize glucose nor any of the phosphate esters studied. They do not oxidize amino acids, with the exception of glutamic acid which is apparently a major energy source. The oxidation of this compound was the first metabolic activity discovered in rickettsiae, the major products being ammonia, carbon dioxide, and aspartic acid. This, of course, suggests that glutamic acid may be transaminated to aspartic acid or may be oxidized. There is some evidence that the oxidation of glutamic acid occurs by way of a Krebs cycle or by some modification of this cycle—although it must be said that the existence of a cycle has not been strictly proven. Activation of several rickettsial enzymes by DPN suggests pyridine enzymes. Further, the cells contain large concentrations of riboflavin. On the other hand, the inhibition of glutamic acid oxidation by cyanide suggests the functioning of a heavy metal system of some type. Hayes et al. (1957) obtained some evidence for the presence of cytochromes and flavoproteins which is suggestive for the functioning of these systems in the transport of electrons from glutamic acid to molecular oxygen. Interestingly enough, the concentration of these electron acceptors was several times lower than is found in corresponding concentrations of other common bacteria. Bovarnick showed that oxidative phosphorylation occurs during the oxidation of glutamic acid with a P:O ratio in the range typically encountered in the oxidative phosphorylation of intact cells. Evidences for other co-factor requirements in the enzymology of these organisms are discussed in Chapter 7 in connection with their nutrition.

We may pass from the rickettsiae to the psittacosis organisms, which have traditionally been regarded as viruses but more recently have been regarded by some as derived from bacteria. The psittacosis organisms appear to be even more limited in their energy metabolism than rickettsiae. When these agents were purified by methods resembling those used with the rickettsiae, they failed to metabolize any of the amino acids, pyruvic acid, or the components of the Krebs cycle. No oxidation occurs when molecular oxygen, DPN, or TPN are added to the organisms. Glucose is not phosphorylated nor has glycolysis been observed. The only oxidation observed is the oxidation of DPNH with added cytochrome c, a reaction catalyzed by a flavoprotein in other organisms. Since this activity is proportional to the infectiousness of the preparations and is destroyed by agents which inactivate the organism, it may be suspected that this is a true biochemical property of the particles being studied.

Moulder (1962) has argued cogently that the psittacosis group of microorganisms are energy parasites; being dependent on their host cells for supplies of high-energy metabolites, such as ATP and other nucleotide triphosphates, as well as such compounds as acetyl-CoA and the like. This type of dependency would, of course, furnish a rather complete explanation for the obligate parasitism of these organisms, since such nutritional requirements could scarcely be met in the outside world.

Studies on the pox viruses have yielded similar information with respect to independent energy-yielding enzyme systems. None have been found, although particles isolated from cells do have significant concentrations of copper and of flavin adenine dinucleotide. These substances are firmly bound to the particles and are not dissociated by mild treatment; however, all attempts to show that they might act as cofactors for electron transport enzymes have been unsuccessful. As with the psittacosis agents there is no evidence, although it has been sought, that the pox viruses have any independent energy metabolism. They also appear to be energy parasites. Similar findings are available with the bacterial viruses and with several plant viruses. It may truly be said that with such organisms there is no basis for a separate study of energy metabolism and nutrition, in the sense that these features of an organism may be separated as when examining the physiology of an organism such as a tapeworm.

CARBOHYDRATE METABOLISM—WORMS

Many symbiotic animals seem to require carbohydrate for growth and reproduction (see p. 156). It is thus not surprising to find that symbiotic worms characteristically metabolize carbohydrate at high rates and that many species examined have a very high content of stored polysaccharide in the tissues. At the extreme, some tapeworms have glycogen comprising as much as 60% of the dry weight. Attempts to correlate high glycogen content with oxygen-poor habitats have not been particularly profitable.

Glycogen seems to be the commonest polysaccharide of worms, but the structure of these glycogens is not well known. Bueding and his colleagues have studied the molecular-weight distribution of gly-

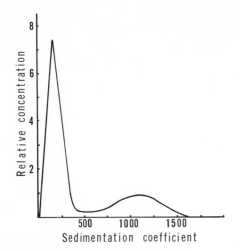

Fig. 8–2 Centrifugal fractionation of glycogens from the tapeworm *Hymenolepis diminuta*. (From data of Orrell et al., 1964.)

cogens isolated from the nematode *Ascaris*, the trematode *Fasciola*, and the tapeworm *Hymenolepis*. Two major fractions with very high molecular weights were found; in the case of *Hymenolepis*, the major glycogen fractions have molecular weights of 60 to 900 million (Fig. 8–2). Agosin et al. (1957) reported that the tapeworm *Echinococcus* has polysaccharides containing galactose and glucosamine, in addition to glycogen.

In parasitic worms living in the lumen of the intestine of the host and not feeding on tissues to a significant extent, the polysaccharide content seems to fluctuate as a function of the ingestion of carbohydrate by the host. Such fluctuations have been observed in tapeworms, nematodes, and acanthocephalans. In such worms, glycogenesis is readily observed when starved worms are incubated *in vitro* with glucose (see Read, 1961, for references).

In 1957, Fairbairn and Passey isolated the non-reducing disaccharide trehalose from *Ascaris* tissues, and, subsequently, Fairbairn (1958) found this sugar in the tissues of a variety of invertebrates. Fisher (1964) demonstrated the synthesis of trehalose from glucose in preparations of the acanthocephalan *Moniliformis,* and synthesis of trehalose from glucose in several tissues of *Ascaris* has been demonstrated. Reproductive tissues were most active in the synthesis (Feist et al., 1965).

Size and Metabolic Rate

Parasitic worms metabolize carbohydrate at phenomenal rates. The blood fluke *Schistosoma* metabolizes in an hour an amount of glucose equivalent to as much as a fifth of its dry weight. A number of species metabolize carbohydrate at rates above 5 grams per 100 grams of body weight per hour (see von Brand, 1952, 1966; Read, 1961). The relative size of worms is not a reliable criterion for predicting probable rates at which carbohydrate will be metabolized. The physiological state of worms is of at least equal importance, and the rate of growth of a particular species may prove to be of importance. Starvation markedly depresses the rate of metabolism of stored carbohydrate but may markedly increase the rate at which externally supplied carbohydrate will be metabolized (Glocklin and Fairbairn, 1952; Read, 1956; Mansour, 1959; Read and Rothman, 1957; Fairbairn et al., 1961). Another important factor in determining rate of carbohydrate metabolism is the pattern of chemical degradation. As will be discussed below, the mixed fermentations seen in helminths suggest that there is variation among species in the amount of energy obtained from a molecule of sugar.

Products of Metabolism

The end products of carbohydrate metabolism observed with worms studied *in vitro* have been examined rather intensively in the last few years. Most parasitic worms seem to excrete incompletely oxidized derivatives of carbohydrate although certain ones may oxidize a proportion of the carbo-

Table 8–2

Products of Carbohydrate Metabolism Excreted into Suspending Medium *in vitro* by Various Symbiotic Worms

Phylum and Class	Species	Site in Host	Products of Metabolism
Aschelminthes (Nematoda)	*Dracunculus insignis*	Subcutaneous tissues	Lactic acid.
	Litomosoides carinii	Thoracic cavity	Lactic acid, small amounts of acetic acid.
	Dirofilaria uniformis	Subcutaneous	Lactic acid.
	Trichinella spiralis (juveniles)	Muscle fibers	2-, 3-, 4- and 6-carbon volatile acids, traces of lactic acid.
	Trichuris vulpis	Cecum	Formic, acetic, propionic, butyric, *n*-valeric, 6-carbon, and lactic acids
	Heterakis gallinae	Cecum	Acetic, propionic, lactic, pyruvic, and succinic acids
	Ascaris lumbricoides	Intestine	Acetic, propionic, alphamethyl-butyric, *cis*-alphamethylcrotonic, *n*-valeric, and 4- and 6-carbon acids; lactic acid; acetylmethylcarbinol
Platyhelminthes (Trematoda)	*Schistosoma mansoni*	Vascular system	Lactic acid
	Fasciola hepatica	Bile ducts	Acetic, propionic, and lactic acids
	Clonorchis sinensis	Bile ducts	Lactic acid +?
Platyhelminthes (Cestoda)	*Moniezia expansa*	Intestine	Lactic, succinic, and higher fatty acids
	Hymenolepis diminuta	Intestine	Lactic, succinic, acetic acids
	Echinococcus granulosus (juvenile)	Liver or lung cysts	Acetic, lactic, pyruvic, succinic acids; ethyl alcohol
	Oochoristica symmetrica	Intestine	Lactic acid
	Phyllobothrium foliatum	Intestine	Lactic acid
Acanthocephala	*Moniliformis dubius*	Intestine	Formic, acetic, lactic acids

hydrate to carbon dioxide and water. As will be seen in Table 8–2, they show considerable variation. It may be emphasized that incomplete oxidation occurs even in the presence of oxygen, although the pattern may be somewhat different in the presence of oxygen than in its absence. This point will be discussed further in connection with the question of whether the capacity to live under relatively anaerobic conditions is an adaptation for parasitism.

In Table 8–2, identified products from the fermentations of a number of parasitic worms have been listed. It may be seen that there is considerable variation even within the same taxonomic group. In some cases, we cannot say that the data are representative of the taxonomic group. For example, the trematodes which have been studied are relatively aberrant forms, with respect both to their body form and their location in hosts. Even so, it may be seen from these limited data that the metabolic products of this group may prove to be highly variable. Bueding (1950) found that racemic lactic acid is the major end product of metabolism of the blood fluke *Schistosoma,* accounting for 80 to 90% of the glucose used by the worms *in vitro* in the presence or absence of oxygen. On the other hand, Mansour found that the major end product of the liver fluke *Fasciola hepatica* was propionic acid, with considerably lesser quantities of lactic and acetic acid produced. The author (unpublished) found that about 50% of the acid produced by the Chinese liver fluke, *Clonorchis,* is lactic acid.

Among the tapeworms studied, *Moniezia* and *Hymenolepis* may produce considerable quantities of succinic acid under certain conditions. Lactic acid may be produced as the major fermentation acid by *Oochoristica, Echinococcus,* and *Phyllobothrium foliatum* but is a minor product of metabolism in six other species studied by Laurie (1961). Carbohydrate metabolism in these worms has been reviewed by Read and Simmons (1963).

Great variation in fermentation pattern is seen among the parasitic nematodes. Juvenile *Trichinella* produce *n*-valeric acid as the main end product of carbohydrate metabolism. Small amounts of 2-, 3-, 4-, and 6-carbon volatile fatty acids are also produced but lactic acid is only produced in trace quantities (von Brand et al., 1952). On the other hand, the nematode *Litomosoides* which lives in the thoracic cavity of cotton rats converts 80% of the total carbohydrate utilized to L-(+)-lactic acid along with a small amount of acetic acid when it is studied in the absence of oxygen. In air, *Litomosoides* converts 30 to 45% of the metabolized carbohydrate to lactic acid and larger quantities of acetic acid and acetylmethylcarbinol are produced. Another tissue nematode from racoons, *Dracunculus insignis,* forms lactic acid as the major product of metabolism whether oxygen is present or not. Thus, these forms which live in the tissues outside the digestive tract show great variation in their fermentation patterns. However, it must be pointed out that these forms are not closely related nematodes and all have probably evolved from nematodes which were originally parasites of the digestive tract.

Examination of the data available on the nematodes living in the digestive tract shows that there is also considerable variation in the products of carbohydrate metabolism. *Ascaris lumbricoides* produces a mixture of fermentation acids including acetic acid (20 to 25%), propionic acid (10%), 4-carbon acids (2 to 5%), 5-carbon acids (40%), and 6-carbon acids (20 to 30%). The 5-carbon acids consist of alphamethylbutyric, *cis*-alphamethylcrotonic (tiglic), and *n*-valeric acids in the approximate ratio of 5:3:2. Of the fermentation acids produced by the fowl nematode *Heterakis gallinae,* 70% are volatile acids, consisting almost entirely of acetic and propionic acids. Lactic, pyruvic, and succinic acids are also produced. *Trichuris vulpis* from the cecum of the dog also produces an array of fermentation acids. The products of this latter species may profitably be compared with those of *Trichinella* to which it is closely related. The general pattern of the fermentations are not greatly different. However, considerably more data with other species are needed before any conclusions can be drawn. It would be of great interest to study other species of *Trichuris* and of *Capillaria,* another closely related form.

Laurie (1959) studied the acids produced *in vitro* by the acanthocephalan *Moniliformis dubius* and found that the greatest part was made up of almost equal proportions of acetic and formic acids, when the worm was metabolizing endogenous carbohydrate. When glucose was added to the medium, lactic acid production increased from about 3% of the acid to about 20% of the excreted acid. Products of the metabolism of other acanthocephalans do not seem to have been identified.

Table 8–3

Occurrence of Glycolytic Enzymes in Helminth Symbiotes

Symbiote	Phosphorylase	Phosphoglucomutase	Hexokinase	Phosphohexose Isomerase	Phosphohexokinase	Phosphotriose Isomerase	Aldolase	Phosphotriose Dehydrogenase	Enolase	Lactic Dehydrogenase
Trematodes										
Fasciola hepatica					X					
Schistosoma mansoni	X	X	X	X	X	X		X		X
Cestodes										
Echinococcus granulosus		X	X	X		X	X	X		X
Hymenolepis diminuta	X	X	X	X		X	X	X		X
Taenia crassiceps							X			
Taenia taeniaeformis	X	X	X	X	X	X		X		X
Nematodes										
Ascaris lumbricoides	X	X	X	X		X			X	X
Ditylenchus dipsaci		X	X							X
Trichinella spiralis			X	X	X	X			X	X
Acanthocephala										
Moniliformis dubius						X		X		X
Neoechinorhynchus emydis						X				X

Enzymes of Carbohydrate Metabolism

There is a reasonable amount of evidence that the so-called Meyerhof-Embden sequence of reactions is involved in the primary catabolism of carbohydrate. This evidence consists of the identification of enzymatic steps in the sequence and identification of compounds in the sequence. Data on the occurrence of specific glycolytic enzymes are listed in Table 8–3. There are some differences in the details of operation of some systems. For example, Bueding and Yale (1951) found that diphosphopyridine nucleotide could not be removed from the lactic dehydrogenase of *Ascaris* by ordinary dialysis. However, as has been pointed out by Agosin and Aravena (1959), the demonstration of a particular enzyme may bear no relation to its relative activity in the intact animal or tissue. As cases in point, *Trichinella* and *Ascaris* have lactic dehydrogenases and fortified homogenates of these worms produce considerable quantities of lactic acid. However, only very small quantities of lactic acid are produced by intact individuals of either species.

During the past few years, there has been enhanced interest in the detailed characterization of enzymes of energy metabolism. Fractionation of extracts of *Schistosoma mansoni* showed that the worm has four distinct hexokinases which react specifically with glucose, fructose, mannose, and hexosamine (Bueding and MacKinnon, 1955b). Glucosamine was found to inhibit the glycolysis of intact schistosomes; it was shown that the powerful glucosamine kinase results in the formation of glucosamine-6-phosphate which is the actual inhibitor of glucokinase. This results in an inhibition of glycolysis (Bueding, Ruppender, and MacKinnon, 1954). This is of some interest since mammalian hexokinase is not inhibited by glucosamine-6-phosphate and would indicate a fundamental difference between the glucokinase of the worm and that of its host. The fructokinase of schistosomes differs from mammalian fructokinase in two important aspects; the worm enzyme catalyzes phosphorylation of fructose in the 6-position, whereas the mammalian enzyme phosphorylates in the 1-position. Further, the worm enzyme is inhibited by glucose and does not catalyze phosphorylation of sorbose, whereas the converse is true of the mammalian enzyme (Bueding and MacKinnon, 1955b).

The juvenile of the tapeworm *Echinococcus* also has 4 hexokinases catalyzing phosphorylation of glucose, fructose, mannose, and glucosamine. There seem to be some kinetic differences between the enzymes from *Schistosoma* and *Echinococcus*, but these have not been investigated in detail (Agosin and Aravena, 1959). *Trichinella* also has the capacity to phosphorylate these sugars but it is not known whether this worm has specific kinases. It would be of interest to determine the physiological significance of a specific mannose kinase in worms.

Bueding and his colleagues have carried out a most instructive series of studies on the chemical nature of glycolytic enzymes of schistosome trematodes and their hosts (see Read, 1961, for references). Certain differences in the kinetics of lactic dehydrogenase (LDH) from *Schistosoma mansoni* and mammalian muscle were observed. Injection of purified mammalian muscle LDH into roosters yielded sera which would inhibit enzyme activity of mammalian muscle but had no effect on LDH from *S. mansoni*, *S. haematobium*, or *S. japonicum*. Further, when chickens were immunized with LDH from *S. mansoni* the antiserum inhibited the LDH from *S. mansoni* or *S. japonicum* but had no effect on mammalian LDH. Preincubation of worm enzyme with its co-factor, diphosphopyridine nucleotide, prevented the inhibition by the anti-schistosome sera; this suggests that the antibody reacts in the vicinity of the site of interaction of the enzyme and the co-factor.

Bueding and MacKinnon (1955) also made an immunological comparison of phosphoglucose isomerases from *S. mansoni* and rabbit muscle, these enzymes being quite similar in kinetic characteristics. A specific antiserum, prepared by injecting chickens with the schistosome isomerase, inhibited the activity of the worm isomerase but was without effect on the mammalian enzyme. Previous incubation of the worm enzyme with its substrate, fructose-6-phosphate, partially protected the enzyme from the inhibitory action of the antiserum, supporting the conclusion that the sites of immunochemical and catalytic activity are closely associated on the enzyme molecule. These very elegant studies offer a powerful model for comparative studies of the enzyme makeup of symbiotes.

Detailed study of another enzyme from schistosomes shed light on the mechanism of action of trivalent antimony compounds which are used in therapy of schistosome infections. These substances were shown to inhibit phosphofructokinase activity of the worms (Mansour and Bueding, 1954). Addition of mammalian phosphofructokinase to worm homogenates which had been poisoned with trivalent antimonials gave a reversal of the inhibition and it was shown that the mammalian enzyme is relatively insensitive to trivalent antimony. It was also possible in this case to demonstrate kinetic differences between the worm and mammalian enzymes (Bueding and Mansour, 1957).

These studies have shown quite conclusively that the glycolytic enzymes of parasites and their hosts may differ in kinetic properties (such as affinity for substrates, pH optima, etc.), in substrate specificity, in immunochemical properties, and in reaction with chemical agents (e.g., trivalent antimonials). These are strong arguments for those who would use chemical tools to examine the differences between different species of organisms. Again, it may be said that careful studies of this sort on closely related species may be of great significance in examining problems of evolution.

In addition to the Meyerhof-Embden sequence of reactions, there is evidence for the occurrence of the hexose monophosphate shunt reactions in about sixteen species of parasitic worms belonging to several phyla. However, at least in *Ascaris* muscle and in the tapeworm *Hymenolepis,* the Meyerhof-Embden sequence seems to be the major pathway in the production of the volatile fatty acid products (Entner and Gonzalez, 1959; Saz and Vidrine, 1959; Scheibel and Saz, 1966).

The Central Role of Pyruvic Acid

Many of the chemical reactions resulting in the variety of end products observed in parasitic worms seem to involve pyruvic acid as a starting point. The enzyme which reduces pyruvate to lactate, lactic dehydrogenase, is widely distributed in parasitic worms although, as remarked above, lactic acid is not always a prominent product of worm metabolism. Under anaerobic conditions the nematode *Litomosoides* carries out a dismutation of pyruvic acid as follows:

$$2 \text{ pyruvic acid} \rightarrow 1 \text{ lactic acid} + \text{acetic acid} + 1 \text{ CO}_2$$

Acetylmethylcarbinol is also an important product of pyruvic acid metabolism in this worm. The same compound is formed by *Ascaris* muscle; the synthesis seems to involve condensation of "active" acetaldehyde with free acetaldehyde as has been reported for other tissues (Saz et al., 1958).

There is considerable evidence that the volatile fatty acids produced by various worms have their origin in pyruvic acid. Fairbairn (1954), studying the formation of propionic acid by *Heterakis,* concluded that pyruvate was an intermediate. Agosin and Aravena (1959) showed that the formation of acetic, valeric, and caproic acids in homogenates of *Trichinella* was stimulated by the addition of pyruvic acid. Saz and Vidrine (1959) studied the formation of propionic acid by *Ascaris* muscle and concluded that the reactions shown below occur. These reactions explain the formation of both succinate and propionate as products of *Ascaris.* Saz and Weil (1960) showed that the branched-chain fatty acids produced by *Ascaris* also involve this pathway, with a condensation of acetate with the second carbon of propionate. This is followed by reductions that lead to tiglic acid and to alpha-methylbutyric acid, which are fermentation products of this worm (see top of page 183).

The Tricarboxylic Acid Cycle

The foregoing reactions suggest that there may be a tricarboxylic acid cycle or some form of it in parasitic worms. Since many textbooks in biochemistry imply that the cycle is a cosmopolitan affair in living matter, it is worthwhile to examine this conclusion. In 1950, Massey and Rogers showed that malonic acid, a classical inhibitor of succinic dehydrogenase, inhibits the respiration of the nematodes *Nematodirus, Ascaridia,* and *Neoaplectana.* This

$$
\begin{array}{ccccc}
\text{CO}_2 & & \text{COOH} & & \text{COOH} & & \text{COOH} & & \text{CO}_2 \\
+ & & | & & | & & | & & + \\
\text{CH}_3 & \xrightarrow{\text{2 DPNH}} & \text{CH}_2 & & \text{CH} & \xrightarrow{\text{2 DPNH}} & \text{CH}_2 & & \text{CH}_3 \\
| & & | & & \| & & | & & | \\
\text{CO} & \longrightarrow & \text{CHOH} & \longrightarrow & \text{CH} & \longrightarrow & \text{CH}_2 & \longrightarrow & \text{CH}_2 \\
| & & | & & | & & | & & | \\
\text{COOH} & & \text{COOH} & & \text{COOH} & & \text{COOH} & & \text{COOH} \\
\text{pyruvic} & & \text{malic} & & \text{fumaric} & & \text{succinic} & & \text{propionic} \\
\text{acid} & & \text{acid} & & \text{acid} & & \text{acid} & & \text{acid}
\end{array}
$$

$$
\begin{array}{ccccc}
\text{CH}_3 & \text{CH}_3 & \text{CH}_3 & \text{CH}_3 & \text{CH}_3 \\
| & | & | & | & | \\
\text{COOH} \longrightarrow & \text{C} = \text{O} \longrightarrow & \text{CHOH} \longrightarrow & \text{CH} \longrightarrow & \text{CH}_2 \\
+ & & & \| & | \\
\text{CH}_3-\text{CH}_2 & \text{CH}_3-\text{CH} & \text{CH}_3-\text{CH} & \text{CH}_3-\text{C} & \text{CH}_3-\text{CH} \\
| & | & | & | & | \\
\text{COOH} & \text{COOH} & \text{COOH} & \text{COOH} & \text{COOH}
\end{array}
$$

acetic acid + propionic acid   methylaceto-acetic acid   beta-hydroxy-alpha-methyl butyric acid   tiglic acid   alpha-methyl butyric acid

inhibition was decreased by the addition of intermediate compounds of the Krebs cycle and the accumulation of succinate in malonate-poisoned preparations was increased by the addition of fumarate, fumarate plus pyruvate, or citrate. In 1951, these same workers showed that respiration of *Ascaridia* and *Nematodirus* was inhibited by fluoroacetate and that this inhibition could be relieved by the addition of certain intermediate compounds of the tricarboxylic acid cycle. Further, when fluoroacetate was added, along with oxaloacetate and acetate, accumulation of citrate was observed.

In 1957, Goldberg showed that juvenile *Trichinella* will oxidize all of the compounds of the cycle and showed that citrate is synthesized when acetate and oxaloacetate are added to homogenates of the organism. These constitute rather strong proofs of the same sort used by Krebs in erecting his hypothesis of the cycle, and it seems valid to conclude that these worms have a tricarboxylic cycle through which pyruvate is oxidized. On the other hand, attempts to demonstrate the oxidation of tricarboxylic acids in flatworm parasites have been uniformly negative although, in all cases tested, oxidation of succinate, fumarate, and malate has been demonstrable. There is reason to suspect that, in these instances, the cycle is not an important pathway for the oxidation of pyruvate. This is also the case in some nematodes. In the distantly related nematodes *Ascaris* and *Litomosoides,* there is doubt that a tri-

carboxylic acid cycle is of any significance. As a matter of fact, though *Ascaris* has a succinic oxidase system, the enzyme has proven to be very different in character from the enzyme in mammalian tissues. The *Ascaris* succinoxidase contains neither cytochrome c nor cytochrome oxidase, both of which are a necessary part of the mammalian system. This terminal oxidation system of *Ascaris* appears to be a flavoprotein containing flavin adenine dinucleotide as its prosthetic group and is involved in the production of succinate rather than its oxidation (Bueding, 1962a). It should be mentioned that there is evidence that phosphoenolpyruvic carboxykinase is involved in carbon dioxide fixation leading to succinate formation in *Hymenolepis diminuta* (Prescott and Campbell, 1965). Bueding and Saz (1968) have reported that there is a correlation between the relative amounts of this enzyme in the tissues of *Ascaris, Hymenolepis,* and *Schistosoma* and the relative proportions of succinate produced by the three worms.

Terminal Oxidations

There is evidence that the terminal oxidation mechanisms of worms have undergone profound changes. Such a concept has already been implied in the foregoing paragraphs. For some years, it was more or less assumed that in animal tissues the final steps of oxidation involved the cytochrome-cytochrome oxidase system. However, studies on worms have shown that this is not the case. In the nematodes *Ascaris, Litomosoides, Trichuris,* and *Trypanoxyuris,* no activity attributable to cytochrome c or cytochrome oxidase could be detected (Bueding and Charms, 1952; Rathbone, 1955; Read, 1960). On the other hand, there is evidence for cytochrome oxidase, and in some instances, cytochrome c reductase in the nematodes *Trichinella, Rictularia, Nematodirus,* and *Ascaridia;* in the tapeworms *Hymenolepis, Dibothriocephalus, Triaenophorus,* and *Moniezia;* and to a very slight extent, in the trematode *Schistosoma mansoni* (references in Read, 1961). In the case of *Schistosoma,* it is of interest that the amount of cytochrome system activity would account for no more than 10% of the respiration of the organism (Bueding and Charms, 1952), whereas, in *Trichuris,* the cytochrome system is sufficient to account for total oxygen consumption (Bueding et al., 1961).

Since some of the forms discussed above seem to have mechanisms for the complete oxidation of carbohydrate, how can we then explain the fact that even in the presence of oxygen they seem almost uniformly to excrete partially oxidized products of carbohydrate metabolism? As in the case of some of the parasitic protozoans, metabolism seems to be a leaky affair in which compounds pass out of the organism before they can be further metabolized.

It may be remarked that our information on the patterns of oxidation in the free-living stages of parasitic worms is very scanty. There is now evidence that there is a cytochrome system in operation in the egg of *Ascaris* during its period of development outside the host and during its early phase in a host. The situation in *Ascaris* may be compared with the differences in electron transport mechanisms in different stages of hemoflagellate protozoans (p. 174) or with the changes in the oxidation patterns seen in the development of some insects.

THE ROLE OF OXYGEN IN METABOLISM

Some years ago a controversy developed concerning the question of whether animal parasites required oxygen to sustain life. The controversy has dissipated itself with the development of a better understanding of the significance of oxygen in metabolism and with the elucidation of patterns of metabolism in a number of species of parasitic organisms. It may be pointed out that oxygen simply serves as an electron acceptor in metabolism and is reduced to water. Other compounds may serve as electron acceptors but the energy released when an organic compound serves as electron acceptor is considerably less than when oxygen functions in this same capacity.

Generally speaking, parasitic organisms will take up oxygen when it is available. However, examination of the habitat of parasitic organisms yields some indication of whether or not it may be available. In the intestine of warm-blooded vertebrates, the oxygen tension is extremely low in the center of the lumen although it may be relatively high very close to the mucosa. If inflammation occurs in a tissue, there is a lowering of oxygen tension (Dubos, 1954). On the other hand, in the absence of inflammation the oxygen tensions in tissues or in the blood may resemble those of many other shallow aquatic habitats.

Some symbiotes can be shown to be injured by oxygen. Such truly anaerobic organisms include the ciliate protozoans from ruminants, the termite flagellates, and some of the trichomonads. Adult *Ascaris* is deleteriously affected by oxygen tensions prevailing in air. In many other instances, it would appear that parasites are facultative anaerobes, capable of living under anaerobic conditions but utilizing oxygen when it is available. The question of whether oxygen has any significance in energy terms has not been clearly determined. Bueding showed that some helminths take up more glucose in the absence of oxygen than in its presence (Pasteur effect) but that glucose metabolism of some other species was not affected by the presence or absence of oxygen. It may seem peculiar that the schistosomes, for example, apparently derive no benefit from the presence of oxygen since they live in the vascular system of the host and oxygen is available. However, it may be borne in mind that the schistosomes probably evolved from a strigeid-like trematode which lived in the gut. The data available suggest that the presence of oxygen in the habitat is not a reliable criterion for determining that a parasite has a requirement for oxygen.

It is perhaps more pertinent to ask whether an organism may utilize oxygen at the oxygen tensions which actually prevail in its habitat. Unfortunately, much of the experimental data available has been obtained by studying organisms in air which is considerably higher in oxygen than any of the sites in a host. Most parasites have no structural mechanisms for obtaining oxygen but rely on diffusion through the surface. Diffusion is of course more favored when the surface/volume ratio is high in a small parasite than when it is relatively low in a large one. Thus, oxygen uptake would tend to be dependent on oxygen tension and surface/volume ratio. In some small worm parasites such as *Nippostrongylus muris* of rodents, the oxygen uptake under tensions resembling those of the habitat may reach values which are 80% of those observed in air (Rogers, 1949). Similarly, a study of the oxygen tensions in cysts of the tapeworm *Echinococcus* and of the rate of oxygen uptake by larvae indicates that the larva of this worm probably has an aerobic metabolism in the host (Fig. 8–3). On the other hand, in some forms which take up oxygen, the amount taken up would not

suffice for the oxidation of a significant amount of an energy source. In the tapeworm *Hymenolepis diminuta*, the oxygen taken up would account for complete oxidation of no more than 5% of the glucose taken up by the worm (Read, 1956). The significance of oxygen to parasites has been discussed in considerable detail by von Brand (1952, 1960a).

A further remark must be made concerning changes in metabolic pattern during the life cycle. *Ascaris*, which seems to have an anaerobic metabolism as an adult, clearly requires oxygen for development of the embryo. Change in the electron transport system has been mentioned. In addition, the developing embryo of *Ascaris* utilizes lipid in energy metabolism and lipid is also converted to carbohydrate (Fairbairn, 1955). Similarly, the symbiotic larval phase of the arthropod *Gasterophilus* does not appear to utilize fatty acids, although stored lipids may be metabolized in the pupa and adult phases of the fly (Van de Vijver, 1964). These are very profound modifications of metabolism and should be examined as repression-derepression phenomena.

INTERLOCKING OF ENERGY METABOLISMS

From what has been said it will be clear that some intracellular symbiotes, certainly the viruses, repress or derepress information in the host-cell genome, resulting in modifications in metabolism. The gross changes in metabolism in malignant mammalian cells, with a shift from an oxidative to a glycolytic pattern, is well known and may represent this type of phenomenon. Increase in respiration is a general responsive reaction of plant tissues infected with fungal, bacterial, or viral symbiotes. This enhancement is not due to the simple addition of symbiote respiration to that of the host. Further, it was shown some years ago that, in wheat leaves infected with rust

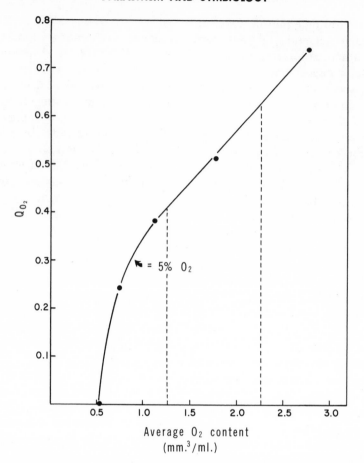

Fig. 8–3 The oxygen consumption of *Echinococcus granulosus* larval forms in cyst fluid as a function of the oxygen content of the fluid. The broken lines represent the extremes of oxygen tension in liver cysts within the host. (From Read and Simmons, 1963, after Farhan et al., 1959.)

fungus *Puccinia*, the Pasteur effect [*] is abolished (Sempio, 1950; Allen, 1953).

It has also been shown that there is an increase in the degree of glucose dissimilation via the pentose phosphate shunt (Shaw, 1963). Some authors have pointed out that such a change may involve increased synthesis of aromatic substances, including polyphenols, which appear in increased concentrations in infected plants.

Further, an increase in protein synthesis accompanies the respiratory increase in several fungal-host associations (Uritani, 1963; Staples and Stahmann, 1964; Andreev and Shaw, 1965). In studying the early stages of the establishment of the obligate parasitic rust fungus *Puccinia* on its host, Shaw (1967) has furnished evidence that parasite information may derepress host genetic information leading to synthesis of new protein. This synthesis may in turn serve as stimulus to initiate the development of nucleoli and subsequently of ribosomal RNA and protein in the parasite.

[*] The Pasteur effect is defined as the inhibition of fermentation in living organisms under aerobic conditions, including a decrease in rate of carbohydrate degradation.

These events would imply a high order of integration of metabolisms of host and parasite and might explain the complex host relations of *Puccinia* (see p. 107).

Interlocking of metabolisms is suggested in some other instances. For example, the enhanced metabolic rate and modification of carbohydrate metabolism seen in snails infected with trematodes is a case in point (von Brand and Files, 1947; Cheng and Snyder, 1962; Hacker, 1968). Similarly, there appear to be modifications of carbohydrate metabolism in mammalian hosts parasitized by the protistans *Plasmodium*, *Trypanosoma*, and *Hemobartonella* (Mercado and von Brand, 1967) and in arthropod hosts harboring arthropod symbiotes (Smith, 1913; Hughes, 1940).

"LOSS" OF FUNCTION

A word may be said concerning the apparent simplifications of metabolism in symbiotes which may occur with the assumption of this mode of life. In some cases, these appear to be repressions of systems in one stage of the life history (e.g., cytochromes in *Ascaris* or oxidation mechanisms in hemoflagellates). In other instances, genetic deletions may have occurred. Since these modifications appear to be widespread and profound, they must be of special significance in considering the evolution of symbiosis, and are discussed in this context on page 243.

THE HEMOGLOBINS OF SYMBIOTES

Since hemoglobins are typically associated with terminal oxidations in many familiar animals, something may be said of their distribution in some symbiotes. Hemoglobins do not seem to have been found in symbiotic protozoans, cestodes, or acanthocephalans, but are known from several species of trematodes, nematodes, and symbiotic arthropods. The occurrence of hemoglobin in a bacterial-legume symbiosis has been mentioned (p. 198). In this latter case, it is characteristic of the symbiosis rather than of the symbiote.

The hemoglobins of symbiotic nematodes are best known and differ somewhat from the hemoglobins of their hosts in absorption spectra. The symbiote hemoglobins differ sharply from the host proteins in the extremely high affinity for oxygen at very low partial pressures. As a result of this latter property, no dissociation of oxyhemoglobin occurs except at very low concentrations in the tissues. Such observations have led some workers to conclude that these hemoglobins probably do not function in an oxygen-transporting capacity. However, Lee and Smith (1965) pointed out that oxygen tensions of low values, appropriate to respiratory function of these symbiote hemoglobins, seem to prevail throughout the vertebrate gut. Further, the hemoglobin of *Ascaris* functions differently under high CO_2–low O_2 than under low CO_2–low O_2 and shows a negative Bohr effect. That is, dissociation does not increase with acidification as occurs with mammalian hemoglobin and, according to Smith (1963), dissociation of *Ascaris* hemoglobin is maximal at pH 7.0. These observations may call for conservatism in assessing the possible role of nematode hemoglobins in respiration (see Okazaki et al., 1965a, b).

LIPIDS OF SOME SYMBIOTES

Until rather recently, information on lipid metabolism of symbiotes was mainly restricted to static analyses of lipid content and the nutritional requirements for specific lipids. Advances in methodology in the past few years have promoted much new investigation of lipid biochemistry, in general, and have resulted in some new information on lipid metabolism in symbiotes.

The total amount of fatty material found in various symbiotes is highly variable and shows no particular correlation with their location in hosts. Of the forms studied, lipid content is highest in two quite dissimilar forms, a malaria parasite, *Plasmodium knowlesi,* and the tapeworm, *Moniezia expansa,* in both of which about 30% of the dry weight is lipid. When fractionated, phospholipids and unsaponifiable fats are often found to constitute a considerable proportion of the total. Examination of phospholipids shows differences between protozoan and helminth groups, but these differences are probably not related to adaptation for symbiosis. For example, cerebrosides have been found in tapeworms but have not been found in any protozoan. On the other hand, flagellate symbiotic protozoans do not contain sphingomyelin, although sphingomyelin occurs in ciliates. Further cardiolipin is found in three hemoflagellates of the genus *Crithidia* but not in the related forms, *Trypanosoma cruzi* or *Leishmania donovani* (Hack et al., 1962). An unusual phospholipid component was discovered in rumen ciliates—a phosphonic amino acid, 2-amino-ethylphosphonic acid or ciliatine, which is now also known to occur in free-living ciliates and several marine invertebrates. Ciliatine apparently does not occur in flagellates. Von Brand (1966) has tabulated the fatty acids of various animal symbiotes.

The major sterol found in hemoflagellates seems to be ergosterol, although cholesterol was reported earlier as the major sterol in *Trypanosoma cruzi* and *Leishmania donovani.* Cholesterol appears to be the major sterol in the sporozoans (*Plasmodium* and *Goussia*) examined. Cholesterol appears to be the major sterol, as well as the major unsaponifiable lipid, in tapeworms (Thompson et al., 1960; Fairbairn et al., 1961). Data on the trematodes do not allow conclusions on this point. In contrast with the tapeworms, very little of the unsaponifiable lipid of the nematodes *Ascaris* and *Parascaris* is sterol. A significant portion is made up of glycosides in which the carbohydrate component is a 3,6-dideoxyhexose named ascarylose. The aglycones are 22- to 37-

carbon alcohols (Fouquey, 1961; Jezyk and Fairbairn, 1967a). These glycosides also occur as esters containing acetic, propionic, α-methylbutyric, and α-methylvaleric acids, previously mentioned as products of carbohydrate metabolism in *Ascaris.*

A significant difference between hemoflagellates and various free-living flagellates is the occurrence of γ-linolenic acid in the symbiotic forms and α-linolenic acid in dinoflagellates, phytomonads, and euglenoids. It is of interest that both γ-linolenic and α-linolenic acids occur in the free-living chrysomonads. Dewey (1967) has reviewed the lipid composition of Protozoa.

Lipid Requirements

It will be clear that nutritional requirements for specific lipids (discussed in Chapter 7) imply that (1) the organisms require such lipids as energy sources or as body constituents and (2) the organisms are not capable of synthesizing adequate amounts of required lipids from other compounds available. Thus, nutritional requirements *may* yield circumstantial evidence for the presence or absence of metabolic pathways for the synthesis of a given compound. However, such studies must be used with care. For example, *Trypanosoma cruzi* may show an apparent requirement for stearic acid, but this requirement disappears if the organism is furnished with carbon dioxide (Boné and Parent, 1963).

Degradation of Lipids

Most symbiotic hemoflagellates and trichomonads do not seem to utilize lower fatty acids as energy sources, although many free-living flagellates readily metabolize them. The hemoflagellate, *Leishmania brasiliensis* seems to be exceptional in its capacity to oxidize acetate. Free-living ciliates and the rumen ciliates seem to utilize lower fatty acids as energy sources. However, the processes involved are clearly different; the rumen ciliates metabolize fatty acids anaerobically, producing hydrogen and carbon dioxide whereas fatty acid oxidation in free-living ciliates seems to be aerobic in character. The metabolism of lipids by *Eimeria* oocysts has been mentioned above but data on their sporozoan relatives, the malaria parasites, do not seem to be available.

No adult forms of helminth symbiotes have been shown to utilize lipid as an energy source, although embryonic stages of some nematodes developing outside hosts most certainly metabolize fatty components.

Lipid Biosynthesis—Protista

Isotopically labeled acetate is incorporated into lipids at a very low rate in rickettsiae (Bovarnick and Schneider, 1960), but nothing seems to be known concerning possible conversions of acetate to other fatty acids. Although the psittacosis organisms have a very high lipid content, nothing is known of biosynthesis. The myxoviruses, arboviruses, and herpes viruses all contain lipid in the outer envelopes. In these forms the lipid is of host origin (Kates et al., 1962; Pfefferkorn and Clifford, 1964).

While the free-living ciliate protozoan *Tetrahymena* carries out dehydrogenation of higher fatty acids, e.g., stearate → oleate (Erwin and Bloch, 1963), the rumen ciliates of the genus *Isotricha* mainly carry out hydrogenation reactions (Gutierrez et al., 1962; Williams et al., 1963). Free-living phytomonad flagellates do not seem to desaturate palmitic and stearic acids (Erwin et al., 1964), although several hemoflagellates can synthesize oleic acid by desaturation of stearic acid (Korn et al., 1965). These latter workers showed that various hemoflagellates differ in their capacity to desaturate higher fatty acids, as well as in ability to produce carbon chain elongation. Studies on the amebas *Acanthamoeba* and *Hartmanella* have shown that the pathway for biosynthesis of unsaturated fatty acids differs from that in higher animals. Acetate serves as a precursor for all fatty acids, both saturated and unsaturated (Korn, 1964; Erwin et al., 1964): [*]

$$\text{acetate} \rightarrow \text{stearate} \rightarrow \text{oleate} \rightarrow \text{linoleate}$$
$$\rightarrow \text{linolenate} - - -$$
$$\rightleftharpoons \text{11,14-eicosadienoate} \rightarrow$$
$$\text{8,11,14-eicosatrienoate} \rightarrow \text{arachidonate}$$

It would be of great interest to determine whether the obligately symbiotic amebas show such capacities for fatty acid synthesis. It might be inferred that their capacity to synthesize lipids is more restricted since the growth of *Entamoeba invadens* is inhibited by steroids, whereas that of free-living amebas is not (Lesser, 1953), and cholesterol appears to be a nutritional requirement of *Entamoeba* spp. (Griffen and McCarten, 1949). The primitive ameba *Labyrinthula* can convert cholestenone to a sterol, probably cholesterol (Vishniac and Nielsen, 1956). However, such speculation may be premature. In the case of the symbiotic flagellate *Trichomonas foetus*, labeled acetate is incorporated into phospholipid, triglycerides, and sterol esters (Halevy, 1963). Negligible amounts of acetate are incorporated in sterols which is consistent with the fact that *T. foetus* requires sterols for growth. It would be of considerable interest to examine more precisely the products of lipid biosynthesis from acetate in amebas and trichomonads. Virtually nothing is known of lipid synthesis in sporozoans. The fatty acids produced from carbohydrate metabolism of parasitic Protozoa must contribute to lipid constituents of some of these organisms, but studies have not been directed to this point.

Lipid Biosynthesis—Worms

Some attention has been directed to lipid metabolism in tapeworms. It has been

---

[*] Pathway in mammals is indicated by broken arrows.

found that *Hymenolepis* appears to have separate transport mechanisms for the absorption of lower (1 to 8 carbons) and higher (16 to 22 carbons) fatty acids from the environment (Arme and Read, 1968). Fairbairn and his colleagues have found that this worm cannot carry out *de novo* synthesis of higher fatty acids, has some capacity for increasing the chain length of higher fatty acids, and is evidently incapable of desaturating higher fatty acids. Further, the fatty acid composition of the worm's lipid seems to be determined by what is available in the host intestine (Ginger and Fairbairn, 1966b; Harrington, 1965; Jacobsen and Fairbairn, 1967).

Although some analytical data are available on the component fatty acids of acanthocephalans, no information on biosynthesis or incorporation of exogenous fatty acids seems to be available (Beames and Fisher, 1964).

Beames et al. (1967) showed that *Ascaris* incorporates large amounts of isotopically labeled acetate into ascaroside esters while small amounts of acetate are incorporated into triglycerides and phospholipids. Although considerable amounts of acetate label were found in 16-carbon and 18-carbon fatty acids, higher fatty acids (up to 28 carbons) were also labeled. Jezyk and Fairbairn (1967b) showed that labeled acetate, myristate, palmitate, or stearate are incorporated into the aglycone portion of ovarian ascarosides (glycosides) of *Ascaris,* the data suggesting mechanisms for *de novo* synthesis and for chain lengthening of higher fatty acids. The general pattern of lipid metabolism thus discerned in nematodes appears to be quite different from that in tapeworms, but more information on other species is required for a well-based conclusion.

NITROGEN METABOLISM

As might be expected, analyses of symbiote proteins have yielded no surprises in terms of qualitative amino acid constitution. Differences are very general in character. It might be expected that differences among symbiotes or between symbiotes and closely related non-symbiotes would be found in the metabolism of low-molecular-weight nitrogen compounds.

Reductive amination of keto acids has been described in tapeworms (Daugherty, 1954) and in ovary tissue of the nematode *Ascaris* (Pollak, 1957) but has not been described in Protozoa, although it clearly occurs in those phytoflagellates requiring no dietary amino acids.

Synthesis of amino acids by transamination has been studied in a few symbiotes. Rickettsiae can carry out the reaction,

$$\text{glutamate} + \text{oxaloacetate} \rightarrow \text{aspartate} + \alpha\text{-ketoglutarate}$$

Other transaminases have not been found in rickettsiae. The only protozoan symbiotes examined for transaminases seem to be hemoflagellates. In those studied, a number of amino acids will serve as amino group donors in the reactions, pyruvic acid → alanine and α-ketoglutaric acid → glutamic acid (Zeledon, 1960). On the other hand, of the limited number of helminth symbiotes studied, the schistosome trematodes, the tapeworms of the genus *Hymenolepis*, and the nematode *Ascaris* seem to be quite limited in the ability to synthesize amino acids through transamination reactions (Pollak and Fairbairn, 1955; Wertheim et al., 1960). These forms are compared in Table 8–4. The limited interconversion of amino acids in tapeworms has been verified by studies on the fate of labeled amino acids in intact worms. On the other hand, the liver fluke *Fasciola hepatica* can utilize at least ten amino acids as amino donors in the formation of glutamic acid (Daugherty, 1952). It should be mentioned that antimony compounds used in treating schistosomiasis have been reported to inhibit transaminases of *Schistosoma,* although these drugs do

Table 8-4

Number of Amino Acids Serving or Not Serving in Some Animal Symbiotes as Amino Donors in Transamination Reactions, Pyruvate → Alanine or α-Ketoglutarate → Glutamate

Symbiote	Number of Amino Acids Reacting in Pyruvate → Alanine	Number Not Reacting	Number of Amino Acids Reacting in α-Ketoglutarate → Glutamate	Number Not Reacting
Endotrypanum	10	3	8	5
Leishmania donovani	11	—	9	—
L. enrietti	3	10	8	5
Trypanosoma cruzi	14	—	12	1
T. vespertilionis	13	—	12	1
Schistosoma japonicum			3	19
Hymenolepis citelli	1	15	3	12
H. diminuta	3	13	3	11
H. nana	1	15	2	12
Ascaris	4	14	4	14

not affect the counterpart enzymes from mammalian host tissues.

Some animal symbiotes may incorporate carbon from glucose or acetate into amino acids, showing limited ability for amino acid synthesis. For example, the dysentery ameba, *Entamoeba histolytica,* produces labeled aspartic acid, glutamic acid, and alanine from labeled carbohydrate (Becker and Geiman, 1955). Generally, the data available on symbiotic protozoans is quite scanty. Tapeworms also produce a limited number of amino acids from labeled glucose (Prescott and Campbell, 1965). Reliable data for nematode symbiotes do not seem to be available. Investigations of amino acid synthesis in animal symbiotes are so limited that no general conclusions are possible. This is clearly a subject on which information is needed.

Protein Synthesis

The high rates of reproduction observed in many species of symbiotes imply high rates of protein synthesis. It might be expected that rates of symbiote protein synthesis might differ at different times in symbiosis. In *Trypanosoma lewisi,* for example, Pizzi and Taliaferro (1960) observed that the rates of incorporation of labeled amino acids into protein were highest in trypanosomes freshly injected into new hosts, next highest in rapidly dividing forms from the blood, and lowest in "adult" (slowly dividing) forms from the blood. These forms correspond to some of the stages of development in this symbiosis (see Fig. 5–15, p. 109).

Environmental factors affecting energy metabolism may also affect protein synthesis in symbiotes. For example, the incorporation of amino acids into protein is sharply reduced in the tapeworm *Hymenolepis* if carbon dioxide is not present. In this organism, protein synthesis (and growth) is sharply reduced if the symbiote's tissue glycogen is reduced by starving the host for 24 hours.

Studies by Agosin and Repetto (1967) suggest that protein synthesis in some symbiotes may have specialized characteristics.

These workers found that, unlike other cell-free systems studied, polyuridylic acid did not stimulate the incorporation of amino acids into protein of microsomes or ribosomes from the tapeworm *Echinococcus*. Protein synthesis was also insensitive to chloramphenicol and there was evidence of unusual specificity in the s-RNA. These observations justify further careful study of this and other protein-synthesizing systems in symbiotes.

End Products of Nitrogen Metabolism

Most protistan symbiotes seem to produce ammonia as a major end product. Apparent excretion of amino acids by the malaria parasite–red blood cell system has been reported. This seems to be due to hydrolysis of host-cell protein, followed by selective incorporation of the liberated amino acids; the unincorporated amino acids then efflux into the suspending medium. The rumen ciliate *Entodinium caudatum* leaks amino acids into nonnutrient media after removal from the host; the quantities involved suggest that hydrolysis of cell protein is occurring in this case.

Several helminth symbiotes have been reported to excrete amino acids into the suspending medium *in vitro*. In some cases, it is not clear whether these compounds originate in the tissues or from the digestive tract of the symbiote.

Protozoans have not been found to produce urea, whereas several helminths synthesize this compound. Campbell and Ehrlich et al. presented strong evidence for a Krebs-Henseleit urea cycle in the tapeworm *Hymenolepis* and the trematode *Fasciola*. Arginase, a terminal enzyme in the sequence of reactions leading to urea,

has been reported from nematodes, trematodes, and cestodes. The nematode *Ascaris* lessens ammonia production and increases urea formation when the worm is confined to a small volume of medium *in vitro*. Several trypanorhynchid tapeworms metabolize urea, forming carbon dioxide and ammonia. This observation is of particular interest since these worms live in the spiral intestine of elasmobranchs where the normal urea concentration in the environment is 0.3 to 0.5 M.

The excretion of a variety of amines has been reported to occur in nematodes (*Ascaris, Trichinella, Nippostrongylus*) and larval cestodes (*Taenia*). These compounds probably arise from the decarboxylation of amino acids. *Ascaris* has been shown to form histamine, cadaverine, and putrescine from the corresponding amino acids. There is a possibility that amines formed by symbiotes might have toxic effects on hosts, but this has not been demonstrated to occur.

GENERAL REMARKS

Symbiotic organisms show two major features in metabolism: First, there is a tendency to excrete partially oxidized carbon compounds, even when the symbiote appears to have the necessary enzymes for further oxidation. Second, profound modifications of metabolic pathways seem to occur during the life cycles of forms showing metamorphosis.

It may be suggested that there is a general correlation between the degree of physiological integration of host and symbiote and the loss of biosynthetic capacities in the symbiote. In many symbiotes, this results in a metabolism in which catabolic and anabolic processes may be linked mainly at the level of energy transformation rather than through carbon flow.

SUGGESTED READING

ALLEN, P. J. 1953.

BAERNSTEIN, H. D. 1963.

BRAND, T. VON. 1952.

BRAND, T. VON. 1966.

BUEDING, E. 1949. Metabolism of parasitic helminths. *Physiol. Rev.* 29:195.

BUEDING, E. 1962. Comparative aspects of carbohydrate metabolism. *Fed. Proc.* 21:1039.

DANFORTH, W. F. 1967.

FAIRBAIRN, D. 1957.

GOODMAN, R. N., Z. KIRÁLY, and M. ZAITLIN. 1967. *The Biochemistry and Physiology of Infectious Plant Disease.* D. Van Nostrand & Co., Princeton, N.J.

GRANT, P. T., J. R. SARGENT, and J. F. RYLEY. 1961.

GUTTMAN, H. N., and F. G. WALLACE. 1964.

HONIGBERG, B. M. 1967.

MANSOUR, T. E. 1967.

MOULDER, J. W. 1962.

READ, C. P. 1961.

READ, C. P. 1968.

READ, C. P., and J. E. SIMMONS, JR. 1963.

RYLEY, J. F. 1967

SASSER, J. N., and W. R. JENKINS (eds.). 1960. *Nematology.* University of North Carolina Press, Chapel Hill, N.C.

SAZ, H. J., and E. BUEDING. 1966.

SHAW, M. 1963.

SHAW, M. 1967.

URITANI, I. 1963.

9

Genetics of Symbiosis

We have seen that symbiosis ranges from the extremely intimate interaction of host and symbiote in virus-cell relationships to very loose associations of hosts and symbiotes of the barnacle-on-the-whale type. There is some parallelism in the extent to which the genomes and phenotypes of host and symbiote interact and the level of integration in a given symbiosis. There is considerable variation in our understanding of interactions of host and symbiote genetics, and it may seem surprising that we have more understanding of virus-cell interactions than we have of interactions between extracellular symbiotes and their hosts. One reason for this lies in the attention directed by geneticists and biochemists to certain virus-cell systems which have been unusually valuable in shedding light on genetic mechanisms. While it is of value to examine the genetics of symbiotes in terms of understanding underlying mechanisms, the main purpose must be directed to understanding the genetics of the host-symbiote combination.

VARIATION IN BACTERIAL POPULATIONS

Since the days of Pasteur and Koch, bacteriologists have recorded changes in populations of bacteria. However, the present century was well under way before serious study was made of the nature and basis of these variations. So much interest was generated in the use of bacteria for the study of heredity that there is now a well-established field of bacterial genetics, and some recent recipients of the Nobel Prize received it in recognition of work with these organisms.

We may choose certain examples of well-studied bacterial variation, as related to parasitism, to show the ways in which populations of these organisms may vary. In the early 1920's Arkwright described variants of the coli-typhoid-dysentery group of bacteria. These variants were most easily characterized by the fact that they yielded rough granular colonies when cultivated in the laboratory on solid media. It was soon noted that this roughness, along with some other changes to be dealt with presently, was accompanied by a loss in the virulence of the organism when it was injected into a host. These variants have been designated R strains whereas the usual, virulent forms, which form smooth colonies, have been called S forms. In these organisms, the S $\rightarrow$ R variation is associated with the loss of a polysaccharide-containing material which characterizes the surface of the S forms, and there is a relative increase in the lipid components in the cell surface of the R forms. Similar sorts of variation were observed by Avery and his colleagues in the pneumococcus, and in this case the change from S to R is associated with the loss of the characteristic capsule and the capsular polysaccharide that seems to determine virulence. It may be briefly pointed out that the S-to-R variation is not the only one which may be associated with a loss in virulence; others are known.

In all of the earlier work, the appearance of variants was observed in organisms grown in culture but not given any special treatment to enhance the rate at which variation occurred. We now know that the appearance of these variants can be induced at an increased rate by treating cells with mutagenic agents, such as ultraviolet light, X-ray, or nitrogen mustard compounds. It may be reiterated here that treatment with these agents does not appear to change the kinds of variations which appear, but merely changes the *rate* at which variations appear.

The R variations undoubtedly appear in populations of organisms living in hosts. However, there is evidence that they do not prosper in hosts. Zelle (1942) studied the fate of mixtures of strains of *Salmonella typhi-murium* and obtained evidence of the selection of S and R forms in the host. Small numbers of stable virulent variants were mixed with large numbers of less virulent variants and the mixtures injected into mice. At death, the organs of the mice yielded cultures with an increased proportion of virulent organisms. In other experiments, virulent and avirulent strains were injected into inbred strains of susceptible and highly insusceptible mice. It was hoped that a differential effect of the two kinds of hosts on the bacteria would be demonstrated; however, such was not the case. There was an enhancement of virulence in both groups of mice, indicating that regardless of the susceptibility of the host, any less virulent variants were more readily destroyed than the strains from

which they arose, whereas more virulent variants tended to replace the parent strain in the selective medium furnished by a host.

On the other hand, Lincoln (1940) studied host effects on the composition of artificially mixed cultures of virulent and avirulent forms of the bacterium *Phytomonas stewarti*. Mixtures were inoculated into susceptible or relatively insusceptible hosts and the proportion of virulent or avirulent bacteria measured as a function of time. In these experiments, the kind of host inoculated was of significance. In highly susceptible hosts, the proportion of avirulent bacteria increased while in relatively insusceptible hosts there was a marked selection favoring the virulent symbiote strain (Fig. 9–1). Obviously, in artificial culture media the differential factors which destroy virulent and avirulent forms may not be present. While studies on organisms in culture may tell us much about the kind of variations which an organism is capable of producing, it tells us little about the relative numbers or success of such variants as components of a population in a host.

Another type of bacterial variation which has captured considerable public attention

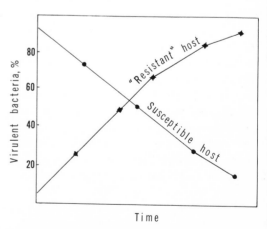

Fig. 9–1 The effect of successive host passage on proportion of virulent to avirulent bacteria in infections of *Phytomonas stewarti* on maize. (From data of Lincoln, 1940.)

in the past few years is the development of resistance to antibiotics. It is now known that, in a population of microorganisms, there is an occasional variant which is relatively insusceptible to a given antibiotic although the normal population may be largely susceptible. On a purely rational basis, it is not difficult to see how selection of those organisms which are resistant would occur in a host receiving antibiotics. However, the full story of the development of drug resistance in microorganisms has not yet been elucidated. Drug resistance is discussed further on page 215.

THE STEM RUST-WHEAT SYSTEM

As an example of genetic complexity in a plant host-symbiote system we may use wheat and its stem rust fungus *Puccinia graminis*. The plant pathologists have long recognized that in *P. graminis* there is a subspecies *tritici* which is capable of parasitizing wheat, whereas the variety *avenae* parasitizes oats and certain wild grasses but not wheat. Within the subspecies *tritici* there are numerous races, which differ in their ability to attack certain varieties of wheat. These races can in turn be subdivided into subdivisions or biotypes, a biotype being a population of individuals which are genotypically identical.

As a matter of fact, at least six varieties of *Puccinia graminis* are now known in North America, differing from each other chiefly in the genera of grass hosts parasitized. There are also minor differences in spores which specialists can recognize. Within the variety *tritici*, over 297 physiological races have been identified. These are identified by their capacities to produce disease in genetically standard types of wheat, under standardized conditions. Interestingly, as the number of new wheat strains increases by selection and hybridization, revision of some of the parasite races into other divisions has been necessary. Also, the pathogen is normally undergoing

mutation and hybridization, and new races are periodically discovered.

Rhizobium and Root Nodules

As mentioned on page 53, the so-called root nodule bacteria of the genus *Rhizobium* live in symbiosis with leguminous plants (Fig. 9–2). Some of these relationships have been investigated in considerable detail and will serve as examples of the way in which symbiosis may be affected by the genotype of the participants.

Various strains of *Rhizobium* show considerable specificity in regard to the host plants which they can infect, and this characteristic has been used in their classification. However, such specificity is not always absolute, differing in degree from one strain to another, and is not well correlated with other characteristics. Nodule bacteria are normal constituents of the soil and may exist for many years in the absence of host plants. However, the presence of host plants elicits an increase in the number of bacteria around the root hairs and there is evidence that this is due to secretion of stimulatory substances by the plants. Various strains of *Rhizobium* differ considerably in the rates at which they multiply under the influence of these root exudates.

Microscopic examination of clover roots growing in agar with *Rhizobium* shows masses of bacteria among the root hairs through which infection usually takes place. There is deformation of the root hairs, as evidenced by curling of the distal ends, in the presence of the bacteria, and there is some evidence that this is due to the production of the plant growth hormone, indole–acetic acid, by the microorganisms. This deformation seems to be a necessary prelude to infection, although strains not capable of infecting a host may still produce this root hair deformation. After entering the root parenchyma, the bacteria induce host-cell division by secretion of a

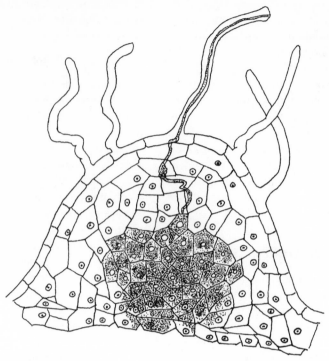

Fig. 9–2 Cross-section through a pea nodule with a bacterial infection "thread" which has entered through a root hair. *Rhizobium* is multiplying in the inner cortex. ×300. (Redrawn from Frank.)

substance which can diffuse from cell to cell in host tissue. However, the number of nodules produced is a characteristic of a given bacterial strain, different strains showing large differences in their capacities to induce nodule production. Individual strains of the bacteria differ not only in the characteristics of infection but also in their effectiveness in fixing nitrogen in the nodules produced on the same type of host. The nodules usually formed are one of two types: (1) *Effective nodules* that fix quantities of nitrogen quite adequate for the needs of the host. Such nodules are usually on main roots, few in number, and large in size. (2) *Ineffective nodules* that fix little or no nitrogen. These occur all over the root system and are numerous and very small in size.

Effective and ineffective nodules are similar in the early stages of development. However, as development proceeds the two types differ more and more. In effective nodules further growth occurs and there is a considerable mass of central bacterial tissue. Most of the bacteria are within host cells and the microorganisms frequently are branched, swollen, or otherwise deformed in appearance. The host cells are greatly enlarged, cell division ceases, and the nuclei show degenerative changes. These infected cells contain hemoglobin, which is not produced by the plant without the bacteria nor by the bacteria without the plant. The hypertrophied cells, containing non-dividing bacteria and hemoglobin, are features of the symbiosis and are correlated with nitrogen fixation. The duration of the existence of the individual nodule varies considerably but is frequently several months.

In the ineffective nodule, growth ceases rather early and necrosis of host tissue occurs. Internal necrosis is actually complete when the nodule is about two weeks old. Such nodules do not contain hemoglobin and, as indicated, do not fix nitrogen. Ineffective strains are not uncommon and, like other bacteria, *Rhizobium* is liable to the production of variant forms differing in one or more characters.

Some variants show complete change in the effectiveness of nodules produced. Culture in the cold and infection with phage have produced ineffective variants from effective strains and, reciprocally, ineffective ones have been induced to be effective by phage infection (see p. 209). Variations may also be observed in the number of nodules produced in the root system, and strains may completely lose the ability to infect root hairs. Further, strains which are effective on one plant species may be ineffective on another.

Recognizing that inherent bacterial strain differences will affect the outcome of the *Rhizobium*–host plant interaction, we may consider the hereditary factors of host plants which may be involved. Red clover is a well-studied example. Complete insusceptibility of clover to infection with *Rhizobium* is unusual but has been shown to be inherited as a simple recessive factor associated with a maternally transmitted factor. A significant connection between insusceptibility and other characters has not been observed. The age at which nodules appear on plants has been shown to be inherited but the genetics is complex, obviously involving more than one gene locus.

The number of nodules which form on the root of an individual plant is an hereditary plant characteristic. In some cases this character behaves as a simple recessive and is specific as a response to a single strain of *Rhizobium*. Homozygous recessives of this type form large numbers of nodules with a specific strain of bacterium but produce only a few nodules with other effective bacterial strains. In another case, it has been shown that nodule number is deter-

mined by relative insusceptibility to infection. In this instance, the character is determined in a complex genetic fashion and is independent of the bacterial strain.

Response to effective strains of *Rhizobium* is also inhibited in more than one pattern. One of these appeared to be a simple recessive. Of some interest was Nutman's observation (1956) that, over a period of years, the bacterial strain, to which the homozygous recessive gave an ineffective response, gave rise to stable mutant bacteria which were capable of eliciting an effective response in the recessive plants. Some of the host hereditary factors associated with the symbiosis are shown in Table 9–1.

Table 9–1

Hereditary Factors in Red Clover Related to *Rhizobium*-Clover Symbiosis [a]

Symbiotic Character	Mode of Inheritance	Bacterial Strain Relationships
Insusceptibility	Simple recessive and maternal component	Independent of strain
Infection time	Complex	Independent of strain
Nodule number	Simple recessive	Strain specific
	Complex	Independent of strain
Ineffectiveness	Simple recessive	Strain specific
	Simple recessive	Independent of strain
	Complex	Independent of strain

[a] After Nutman, 1963.

From the information available on the *Rhizobium*-clover symbiosis, it is obvious that the genetics of these systems is complex and, in most cases, does not seem to be associated with characteristics which can be readily observed in either member of the association when they are studied singly.

The Apple Scab Symbiosis

As another example of the type of genetic study which may be carried out on a host-parasite system, we may consider the symbiosis of the apple plant and the scab fungus *Venturia inaequalis*. The parasite is an ascomycete in which the dikaryotic phase of the life cycle is transient. The true diploid phase is limited to a brief premeiotic period in the young ascus and the parasitic phase is haploid. Since there is only one of each pair of homologous chromosomes during parasitism, any mutation is immediately expressed, unless its expression is suppressed by genic interaction.

Because of this haploidy, another ascomycetous fungus, *Neurospora*, has been used by Beadle and Tatum and numerous other geneticists as favorable material for studies in general genetics. Keitt and Langford (1941) recognized the value of this in the study of host-parasite genetics of *Venturia*. Of considerable importance is the fact that all the products of meiosis are present in the ascus and may thus be isolated for study, and Keitt and Langford devised techniques for isolating, in serial order, the eight ascospores from an ascus. They found that single-spore isolates were self-sterile haplonts and belonged to one of two mating-type groups. Intragroup matings were sterile whereas intergroup matings were fertile. They developed methods for culturing and mating *in vitro* and for testing the pathogenicity under greenhouse conditions on specific host varieties. Two types of host reaction, "lesion" and "fleck," proved to be stable characters for study. When wild-type lines producing "lesion" were crossed, all the resulting ascospores produced the same reaction. Similarly, "lesion" × "fleck" produced a 1:1 ratio of cultures with lesion and fleck symptoms (Keitt et al., 1943).

The foregoing results were obtained with a single host variety. When a study was made of lesion and fleck reactions in a cross

of a line producing lesions on the apple varieties Haralson and Wealthy but flecks on Yellow Transparent and McIntosh apples with a line producing *converse* reactions, the progeny showed only lesion and fleck reactions in a 1:1 ratio (Table 9–2). Both parental types, as well as recombinants, occurred in the progeny, and analysis led to the conclusion that lesion reaction on Haralson and Wealthy was determined at one genetic locus and fleck reaction on Yellow Transparent and McIntosh varieties at another locus (Keitt et al., 1948). Additional studies revealed that twelve or more loci were involved in the lesion or fleck characteristics of different fungus lines. Alleles conditioning the fleck response were epistatic to those conditioning the lesion response. Studies on host genes which conditioned the response indicated single locus control.

Biochemical mutants of *Venturia* were isolated by treating the fungus with nitrogen mustard or ultraviolet radiation to increase the mutation rate. Genetic recombination experiments showed that characters fell into three linkage groups. Mutants showing a variety of growth deficiencies were isolated, including types requiring single vitamins, nitrogen bases, amino acids, and in one case, reduced sulfur. In relating these results to parasitism, it was necessary to determine whether a particular nutritional deficiency influenced the pathogenicity on a host. Also, if a particular deficiency was associated with a loss of pathogenicity, it was necessary to determine whether pathogenicity was restored by supplying the substance which the symbiote could not synthesize. It was also recognized that the amount of the required substance present in host tissues would probably be of significance. It was found that mutants requiring choline, riboflavin, purines, pyrimidines, arginine, histidine, methionine, or proline showed a loss of pathogenicity.

It was believed that the losses of pathogenicity were actually due to the defi-

Table 9–2

Inheritance of Pathogenicity in Progeny of 35 Asci Derived from Crosses Between Lesion-producing (L) and Fleck-producing (F) Strains of Apple Scab Fungus, *Venturia inaequalis*, Tested on Apple Varieties Haralson (H), Wealthy (W), Yellow Transparent (Y), and McIntosh (M) [a]

PATHOGENICITY OF PROGENY OF THE CROSS

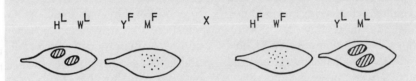

H^L W^L Y^F M^F X H^F W^F Y^L M^L

Type of ascus		Symptoms		No. of asci
No. of spores	Pathogenicity	HW	YM	
4	H^L W^L Y^F M^F			5
4	H^F W^F Y^L M^L			
2	H^L W^L Y^F M^F			
2	H^F W^F Y^L M^L			18
2	H^F W^F Y^F M^F			
2	H^L W^L Y^L M^L			
4	H^L W^L Y^L M^L			12
4	H^F W^F Y^F M^F			

[a] From Keitt et al., 1948, after Johnson, 1960, with permission of Academic Press.

ciencies because (1) the mutants were auxotrophic, (2) mutants with like deficiencies showed some loss of pathogenicity, (3) mutant progeny from crosses of non-pathogenic mutants with wild type were always non-pathogenic while the wild-type progeny from the same crosses were pathogenic.

In direct tests it was found that pathogenicity could be restored to six of eight mutants if the required nutrient was applied to the plant host each day. Mutants recovering pathogenicity were those deficient for choline, riboflavin, pyrimidines, arginine, histidine, or methionine. Examination of the chemical composition of host tissues showed that the substances required by the mutants were present but, at the infection site, they were at concentrations below those required for growth of the fungus (Kline et al., 1957).

SOME ANIMAL SYMBIOSES

Malaria

Some evidence for variation in animal symbiotes undoubtedly has a genetic background. It has become widely recognized that the human malaria parasites vary from one geographical location to another. The variation is complex in that it sometimes involves changes in the reaction of parasite and vertebrate host and sometimes in reaction of parasite and the invertebrate host. These variations are probably independent, but there seems to be no valid evidence that this is indeed so. The differences between strains of malaria parasites is seen in humans who live in hyperendemic areas and have considerable immunity to the parasites which are locally prevalent. When such a person moves to another malarious area, he may come down with clinical malaria due to exposure to strains of the parasite to which he has little or no resistance (see p. 81).

In the case of the invertebrate host, there are numerous examples in the literature

showing that strains of malaria from one locality may fail to infect, or infect at a low rate, anopheline mosquitoes from a different geographical area which are known to be efficient transmitters of malaria. There are even such differences in the susceptibility of mosquitoes of the same species from different geographical localities. Ward (1963) studied the genetic aspects of the susceptibility of the mosquito *Aedes aegypti* to the avian malaria parasite *P. gallinaceum*. Starting with a mosquito strain with high susceptibility, he reduced susceptibility by 98% in 26 generations of selection and attributed the genetic variation to a single genetic factor. The whole problem of susceptibility of mosquitoes to malaria parasites has been discussed by Huff (1965).

Huff (1941) reported that the susceptibility of the mosquito *Culex pipiens* to the bird malaria parasite *Plasmodium cathemerium* is a recessive character due to a single pair of genes and is inherited in a simple Mendelian fashion. Trager (1942) developed by laboratory selection a strain of *Aedes aegypti* mosquitoes which was more susceptible to the avian malaria parasite *Plasmodium lophurae* than the original colony but Trager's data suggested that, in this case, inheritance was not as simple as the example studied by Huff. Micks (1949) carried out similar experiments with *Culex pipiens* and *Plasmodium elongatum*.

In a series of papers, Greenberg and his associates attempted to study the genetics of the avian malaria parasite *Plasmodium gallinaceum*. A number of genetic markers were developed, mainly with a view to understanding the basis for resistance to antimalarial drugs. Hybridization among some variant strains was accomplished but a precise genetic analysis was not completed. As Huff (1963) remarked, it was a great loss when Greenberg found it necessary to abandon this work and the parasite strains so carefully developed.

One of the most interesting examples of the role of the genome in determining host susceptibility to a parasite is that of sickle cell hemoglobin (S) in human populations. Erythrocytes containing hemoglobin S become distorted when the hemoglobin is partially deoxygenated, assuming a sickle shape (hence the name of this factor). In individuals who are homozygous for S, the resulting sickle cell anemia causes death in early life; heterozygous individuals, on the other hand, survive. But cells containing hemoglobin S are not suitable for the development of malaria parasites. In highly malarious areas of Africa, individuals who do not carry sickle trait are likely to die in childhood from malaria infections. Thus, in such regions there is natural selection for hemoglobin S since it has survival value when malaria is present. As malaria control is extended in Africa, it may be anticipated that this otherwise deleterious genetic trait of man will no longer be of survival value (see p. 269). There is also evidence that a genetic deficiency for glucose-6-phosphate dehydrogenase may confer insusceptibility to malaria (Allison and Clyde, 1961).

Variation in Amebiasis

In studies on the protozoan *Entamoeba histolytica* by Entner and his associates (1962, 1965), a total of ten strains of *Entamoeba* have been analyzed with respect to eighteen genetic markers under standardized conditions. All of these strains were derived from human hosts. In all cases there was found to be a remarkable stability in the pattern of the characteristics for each strain. Some were tested within a few weeks after being isolated from the host, others years later.

The amebas could be separated into two distinct groups, one group of which Entner and his associates referred to as "true" *histolytica*. Some of these were from cases of amebic disease while others were from individuals without symptoms. The second group of three species differed sharply in at least six characteristics. In five of the characteristics the differences were so clear-cut that the investigators could, in selective media, kill off all the population in any strain of one group leaving the other group surviving and growing. The characters tested included resistance to drugs, temperature resistance or capacity to grow at room temperature, and the ability of eleven sugars to support growth. Immunological studies by Goldman et al. (1962) generally supported the recognition of two genetic groups of this species as indicated by the studies described above. Genetic analysis of this kind may shed more light on the problem of speciation in the parasitic amebas.

Variations in Mosquito Vectors

There is evidence for the importance of the genome in determining the susceptibility of mosquitoes to infection by filarial nematodes. Studying this experimentally, Kartman (1953) carried out selective breeding experiments with *Aedes aegypti* and established mosquito strains which were susceptible or refractory to infection with the nematode *Dirofilaria immitis;* MacDonald (1962) has shown that there is a genetic basis for the susceptibility of *Aedes aegypti* to the human filaria, *Brugia malayi;* and MacDonald and Ramachandran (1965) found that, in *Aedes,* a sex-linked recessive gene controlled development of the filarial nematode *Wuchereria,* as well as *Brugia.*

Schistosome Variation

The schistosome trematodes show evidence of variation and isolation of populations which probably differ in genotype. Hsü and Hsü (1958) and others have shown that *Schistosoma japonicum* has at least four recognizably different strains occurring in China, Japan, Formosa, and the Philippines. The Formosan strain does not develop in primates but is a parasite of various small mammals. The snail intermediate hosts in these four localities belong to four different species of the genus *Oncomelania*. Strains of *S. japonicum* from Japan will not infect the intermediate hosts of the Formosan strains. It has been shown by Wagner and Chi that four Oriental strains of *Oncomelania* will interbreed in the laboratory. Thus, studies of the genetic interactions of this host-parasite system are undoubtedly feasible. Newton (1953) showed that susceptibility of strains of the snail *Australorbis* (*Taphius*) *glabratus* to the blood fluke *Schistosoma mansoni* is a heritable character and that several genetic factors may be involved.

A Sex-Linked Infection

A most curious symbiosis is that involving a spirochaete bacterium of the genus *Treponema* and the fruit fly *Drosophila*. The symbiote has been called the sex-ratio agent and is maternally inherited. Infected male zygotes are killed at an early stage of development, but the daughters of infected female flies develop normally and contain the symbiote. Infected females thus produce almost exclusively female offspring. Genetic studies indicate that the symbiote is not associated with host chromosomes and is transmissible by injecting uninfected flies with infectious material. However, a genetic interaction is suggested by the differential effect on males and females and by experiments showing that, in all cases in which flies have but a single X chromosome, the infection is lethal (Sakaguchi and Poulson, 1963).

PARAMECIUM AND SYMBIOTES

A most interesting example of the genetics of a host-symbiote ensemble has been

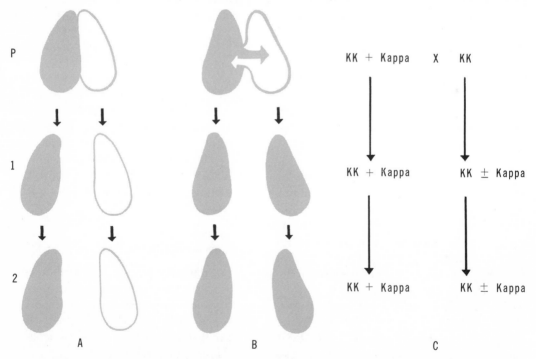

Fig. 9–3 The inheritance of killer and sensitive traits in *Paramecium*. Gray cells are killers and white cells are sensitives. Column A indicates results when no cytoplasm is exchanged between parents (*P*) and Column B results when parents exchange cytoplasm. Column C represents the genes and cytoplasmic condition (presence or absence of kappa) in the various animals. (After Sonneborn.)

studied by Sonneborn and others (Sonneborn, 1959). It was found that certain strains of the ciliate protozoan *Paramecium aurelia* liberate into the environmental fluid a substance called *paramecin,* or P, which is poisonous for individuals belonging to certain other strains. Strains which are so affected were called *sensitives* and strains producing the toxic substance were termed *killers.* When sensitives are exposed to P, very obvious changes in morphology occur; the sensitive animal seems to literally waste away. Killers are immune to the effects of P. Fortunately, from our standpoint, sensitives can be mated to killers if the two types are brought together for conjugation and then separated to fresh culture fluid.

The production of P and sensitivity to it are inherited in *Paramecium aurelia.* This is shown by mating killers to sensitives known to be genetically identical with respect to nuclear makeup (Fig. 9–3). It may be seen that the inheritance of killer capacity seems to be associated with the cytoplasm rather than the nucleus and, indeed, Sonneborn for a time referred to it as a plasmagene. The conjugant which receives cytoplasm from a killer gives rise to killers whereas the one which has only the sensitive type of cytoplasm gives rise to sensitives. The amount of cytoplasm exchanged in conjunction is essentially proportional to the length of time during which a cytoplasmic bridge connects the conjugating protozoans. When a killer is mated to a sensitive the effects of conjugation time may be rather precisely studied (Fig. 9–4). It was eventually recognized that the killer phenomenon was attributable to a symbiote, which was named *kappa.*

Properties of kappa which eventually led to the recognition that it has the attributes

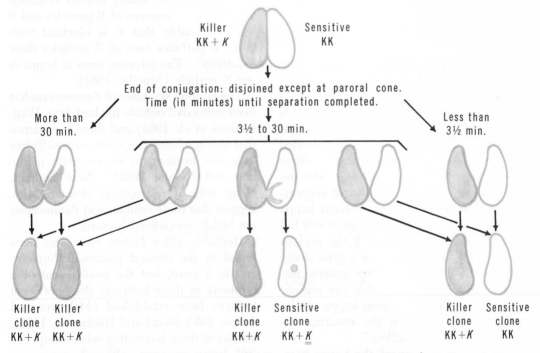

Fig. 9–4 The effects of transfers of different amounts of cytoplasm between mates in crosses of KK + kappa killers (K) with KK sensitives. The amount of cytoplasm exchanged is roughly proportional to the time the paroral bridge persists after the conjugants have otherwise separated. (After Sonneborn.)

of a symbiote are these: (1) kappa undergoes mutation; (2) the rates at which kappa multiplies have been determined—certain types of kappa multiply more rapidly than others; (3) when a killer paramecium undergoes division, kappa is distributed randomly between the daughter cells; (4) kappa can be destroyed by exposing killer paramecia to high temperature or X-rays; (5) a killer paramecium contains 200 to 1,000 particles of kappa (Fig. 3–15); (6) the killer power of the protozoans depends not only on whether they contain kappa but also on how much kappa is present; (7) a protozoan only needs to possess a single kappa particle to form more and become a killer; (8) kappa particles are 0.2 micron or more in length and can be seen with the light microscope (studies with the electron microscope have suggested a resemblance to the bacterial cell); (9) kappa particles contain deoxyribonucleic acid; and (10) sensitive animals can be "infected" with kappa and become killers by suspending them in high concentrations of kappa particles.

When considered in detail, these characteristics lead to the conclusion that kappa is a symbiote, although it seems to have unusual effects in producing disease in cells in which it is *not* living. Detailed study of the kappa-*Paramecium* system has yielded much interesting information on the nuclear inheritance of characters which render the individual paramecium capable of supporting the growth of kappa. Though kappa may be present in the cytoplasm, it will fail to grow and will disappear if the nucleus of the host does not contain a gene designated as K. By appropriate genetic manipulation it was shown that the nuclear capacity of killers to support kappa can be further enhanced, with the resulting development of "super-killers."

Further examination of the kappa-*Paramecium* system revealed that it has other ramifications. Additional types of particles have been recognized and designated pi, mu, lambda, nu, and sigma. These appear to be related to kappa but have different properties. Infection with pi, regarded as a mutant of kappa, does not result in the liberation of P nor are infected cells immune to the effects of P. Mu results in the death of sensitive animals during conjugation and mu-infected cells are termed mate-killers. Kappa itself was found to involve two very different types of particles: One type, designated the B particle (bright), contains refractile bodies (R bodies) and the other was termed N particle (nonbright). Chemically, the B and N particles appear to be similar, containing DNA, RNA, protein, carbohydrate, and phospholipid (Smith-Sonneborn and van Wagtendonk, 1964). However, the B particles do not appear to undergo reproduction, whereas N particles are capable of fission. B particles arise from N particles with the appearance of R bodies, but the process does not seem to be reversible. Killing activity is associated with the presence of B particles and it seems probable that P is identical with intact B particles (not all B particles show P activity). The infective form of kappa is the N particle (Mueller, 1963).

The lambda symbiote of *Paramecium* has been cultivated outside the host (van Wagtendonk et al., 1963) and there is evidence that the symbiote can synthesize sufficient folic acid to meet the requirements of the host cell (Soldo, 1963). These findings, along with ultrastructural characteristics, suggest that these symbiotes of *Paramecium* are highly specialized bacteria.

Heritable killer factors have also been found in the ciliated protozoan *Euplotes* and in a yeast, but the involvement of a symbiote in these instances does not seem to have been established (Makower and Bevan, 1963; Siegel and Heckmann, 1966). Studies of these interesting relationships are still being pursued, although some geneticists tended to lose interest in them as soon as it became plain that kappa was not a plasmagene.

Mutualistic relationships between certain algae and various animals were described in Chapter 2. Experiments on some of these associations have furnished information on genetic interactions. The ciliate protozoan *Paramecium bursaria* was freed of symbiotic algae and then experimentally infected with algae from the same host strain (homologous) or from other host strains or species (heterologous). In all cases tested, stable hereditary associations were formed. However, there were differences in the rate of infection, the rate of algal multiplication, and the degree to which growth of the host was promoted by the presence of the algae. These differences were found to be functions of specificities of both host and symbiote. On the other hand, algae from *Stentor*, another protozoan genus, formed stable associations with *Paramecium* in some instances but not in others. In one case, Karakashian (1963) found that infection of a *Paramecium bursaria* strain with algae from a hydra resulted in more growth promotion than was obtained with algae from *Paramecium*. Karakashian and Siegel (1965) drew the following conclusions: (1) There are specific differences in growth and reproduction of various associations and that these differences pertain among strains of host and symbiote of the same, as well as different, species. (2) The success or failure of interspecific infections depends on the particular combination tested and is not predictable on the basis of present knowledge. (3) The characteristics of a particular combination are functions of specificities of host and symbiote.

BACTERIA AND BACTERIOPHAGES

As already mentioned, many strains of bacteria produce and liberate virus particles, known as bacteriophages, without showing evidence of disease in the bacterial population (p. 54). Basically, the association of these bacteriophages with bacteria consists of the addition of phage genetic material to the bacterial genetic apparatus. This united phage and bacterial genetic structure multiplies at the rate of bacterial reproduction. Such phages are termed *lysogenic* to differentiate them from *lytic* phages. In the lytic association the deoxyribonucleic acid (DNA) of the phage replicates faster than the bacterial host DNA. New phage protein is produced and, in 15 to 60 minutes, the bacterium bursts and a number of new infective phage particles are liberated. In the lysogenic association, known as lysogeny, massive multiplication of phage DNA is not demonstrable. In lysogeny, the phage genome is replicated in a non-infectious form called prophage, and production of infective particles only occurs occasionally. A large body of experimental data has shown that the prophage carries the information for the production of bacteriophage particles; that there is only a single prophage per bacterial chromosome; and that the prophage is attached to a specific locus on the bacterial chromosome. The general features of the lytic and lysogenic cycles of bacteriophage are shown in Figure 9–5.

Phages developing a lysogenic relationship are called *temperate*, whereas those showing the lytic pattern are termed *virulent*. Temperate phages may mutate to virulent or vice versa. Study of temperate phages has yielded much important information in genetics, and such phages are known to live in association with bacteria of the common genera *Escherichia, Shigella, Salmonella, Pseudomonas, Corynebacterium, Rhizobium, Xanthomonas, Micrococcus*, and others. In some cases, the definition of a phage as temperate depends on a careful definition of the conditions under which a bacterium is infected. Phage lambda, which lives in association with *Escherichia coli* (strain K12), has been shown to behave differently under different conditions of bacterial growth, age, temperature, etc. Lysogeny is established almost 100% of the time if old bacteria, which

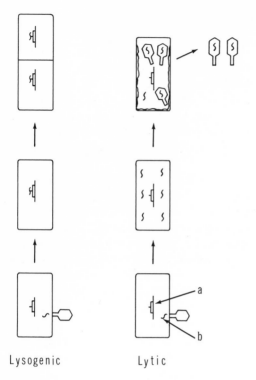

Lysogenic   Lytic

Fig. 9–5 The lysogenic and lytic development of a bacterial virus. Prophage (*b*) becomes attached to the bacterial chromosome at a receptor site (*a*) in the lysogenic cycle and prophage is replicated in synchrony with the bacterial genome. In the lytic cycle, prophage replicates without attachment and whole bacteriophage is produced, resulting in host cell lysis and liberation of new virus. See also Fig. 3–12. (Adapted from various authors.)

low a lysogenic or lytic pattern. Generally speaking, the decision can be most readily influenced by the variation of external conditions shortly after infection and is more difficult to alter after growth has proceeded.

It is amazing that a given prophage reaches, recognizes, and is attached to a specific site on the bacterial chromosome. There is some correspondence of structure of the bacterial and viral nucleic acids. Of great significance is the control of the reproduction of prophage in the lysogenized bacterium. The prophage is replicated in synchrony with the genetic material of the host cell and behaves as though it were part of the host genome. This has been used to argue that the genetic material of the phage had its evolutionary origin in the bacterial chromosome. On the other hand, the vegetative growth of a lytic phage is not synchronized with the replication of host genetic material, the virus nucleic acid increasing at about tenfold the normal rate of bacterial replication. After lysogenization of the host cell has occurred, genetic characters of the prophage are thought to produce a repressor which, if formed in sufficient amount, prevents the synthesis of virus protein. In this manner, the vegetative growth seen in the lytic cycle is blocked. If the repressor falls below a certain level, virus protein is produced and induction of the lytic cycle occurs. Other genetic characters, of both phage and bacterial genomes, allow the attachment or insertion of prophage into the bacterial chromosome. It is not known if the same genetic characters, or additional ones, control the replication of prophage in synchrony with bacterial DNA.

Phage genomes frequently carry genetic information which enables them to perform functions that have no obvious relation to phage reproduction. This may be due to the incorporation of information which was originally bacterial DNA into phage DNA.

have been washed and suspended in .01 *M* magnesium sulfate, are exposed to 5 or more phage particles per cell at 37° C, followed by incubation in tryptone broth at 37° C (Fry, 1959). If the bacterial cells are exposed to a dilution of 1 phage particle per cell about half of the infected cells show a lytic response. Exposure of young bacterial cells or a temperature shock at 42° C just after infection also favors the lytic pattern. This exemplifies the labile nature of the decision as to whether the phage will fol-

A case in point is illustrated in the phenomenon of transduction, discovered by Zinder and Lederberg (1952). The transduction of bacterial markers determining the fermentation of galactose by phage lambda is of particular interest. A portion of the chromosome receptor for the prophage involves the gene carrying the information for galactokinase, the enzyme phosphorylating galactose. The gene is readily exchanged with part of the prophage and, when phage lambda multiplies in a lytic cycle, the galactokinase gene is replicated as part of the virus. If such a phage is now used to lysogenize a bacterial cell lacking the galactokinase gene, the bacterium acquires the capacity to phosphorylate galactose. Thus, we have viral control of cellular function which is a converse of cellular control of viral function (reproduction) observed in the lysogenic phenomenon. Other cases of transduction are known; in *Micrococcus aureus*, genes for antibiotic resistance have been transduced (Morse, 1959) and transduction in a phage-*Rhizobium* symbiosis may change the nature of a *Rhizobium*-clover symbiosis (see p. 199).

One of the most astonishing examples of a phage-bacterium relationship is that between a phage and *Corynebacterium diphtheriae,* which is considered to be the agent causing the disease diphtheria. In this case, infection of the bacterium with a temperate phage results in the production of diphtheria toxin. In culture media outside a host, the nature of the medium also becomes important. The toxin is only produced in iron-deficient media (see p. 27). The relationships of bacteriophages have been treated in detail by Adams (1959), Arber (1963), Barksdale (1959), Hayes (1964), Stent (1963), and others. The historical role of phage in the development of molecular biology has been described in interesting personal terms by Cairns et al. (1966).

Phage-Bacteria vs. Kappa-Paramecium

The lysogenic phage-bacteria systems may be compared with the kappa-*Paramecium* system (discussed on p. 204). Lysogenic phages and kappa are transmitted by heredity, may confer immunity on host cells against the lethal effects of other external particles, and have effects on the metabolism of host cells. However, phage is attached to the host chromosome while kappa resides in the cytoplasm. The transduction phenomenon observed with phages has never been observed with kappa. Nothing comparable to the lytic vegetative phase is known in the kappa relationships. Thus, while the systems show some similarities, they also exhibit significant differences.

VIRUS INFECTIONS OF HIGHER ORGANISMS

Induction of Disease in Insect-Virus Symbioses

There is some evidence that the genetic control of basic physiological functions in insects has a relation to the induction of virus disease by changing the status of occult virus (see p. 56). Most of the information available has been obtained by Japanese investigators working with *Bombyx mori*, the silkworm. Almost all silkworm strains reared in Japan contain occult nuclear polyhedrosis virus and the viral disease can be induced by cold treatment of silkworm larvae. There are clear strain differences in the rate of cold induction, and the cold induction rate in resistant, inbred silkworm strain lines is not necessarily higher or lower than in susceptible strains. That is, the rate of cold induction appears to be independent of the degree of resistance normally exhibited by a given silkworm strain. An interesting observation is that the F_1 hybrids, exhibiting heterosis and resistance to virus diseases under natural

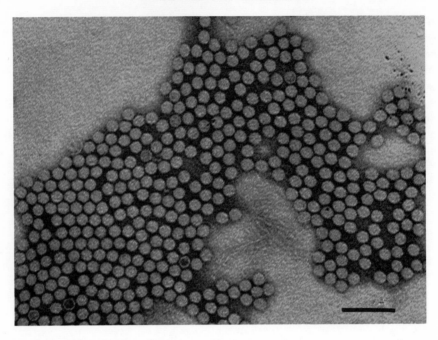

Fig. 9–6 Poliomyelitis virus, L.Sc. strain. Line is 0.1 μ. (Courtesy of Drs. H. D. Mayor and S. McGregor and the *Journal of Virology*.)

conditions, show a higher induction rate than their parents. Detailed genetic analyses of these and other induction phenomena in insect-virus associations have not yet been performed (Aruga, 1963). The induction of these viruses shows some resemblance to the induction of lysogenic bacterial viruses and genetic studies would be highly desirable.

ANIMAL AND PLANT VIRUSES

While the viruses of bacteria have been investigated in great detail as a material for molecular genetics, there is not yet a systematic genetics for the viruses of animal or plant hosts. However, some attempt can be made to briefly review what is known.

Among the RNA-containing viruses, polio virus (Fig. 9–6) has several distinguishable mutants. When host cells are infected with two types of polio virus, the progeny may have coat protein of both types but only one type of RNA, indicating

a ready exchange of coat proteins. Genetic recombination of polio strains has also been demonstrated, although the frequency is less than 1% (Ledinko, 1963). The myxoviruses, such as influenza and Newcastle disease virus, have lent themselves to genetic study. Recombination, with the appearance of new combinations of genetic markers from the two parental types, was readily demonstrated with a very high frequency of recombinant types (Hirst, 1962). Simpson and Hirst observed another type of genetic interaction. When cells are simultaneously infected with a strain of influenza A virus which does not produce cell pathology and with ultraviolet-killed particles of a strain which can produce cell pathology, stable recombinants appear at a low frequency.

Recombination and reactivation of the large DNA viruses, belonging to the pox group, have been demonstrated. The vaccinia virus conveniently has mutants which form lesions of different colors on the chorioallantoic membrane. When mutants were systematically crossed, they fell into two groups. Members of the same group would not cross with each other, but would cross with members of the other group (Gemmel and Fenner, 1960).

An interesting phenomenon in vaccinia virus is the appearance of what have been termed conditional lethal mutations. Thus, a mutant may grow in chick cells but not in pig cells, presumably because some of its genetic information cannot be translated into functional products by the translation mechanism in pig cells (Fenner, 1965). This is of course simply an additional demonstration that the host genome is of significance in the culmination of a symbiosis. Other cases of this are known. The Aleutian disease virus of mink, for example,

kills the host in 3 to 6 months after inoculation if the host is homozygous for the Aleutian gene (Sapphire mink), whereas host animals which are not homozygous (Pastel) do not die for about 2 years.

Among the viruses living in plant hosts, many naturally occurring variant forms are known. They differ in the types of lesions produced in plant hosts and in some instances even show differences in crystal pattern on purification. Tobacco mosaic virus mutants have been produced by treating the purified virus with mutagenic agents. Some of these are defective in their capacity to form a normal coat protein. This virus has offered excellent material for analysis of the genetic code since the protein monomer is one of the few whose amino acid sequence is completely known (Fig. 9–7).

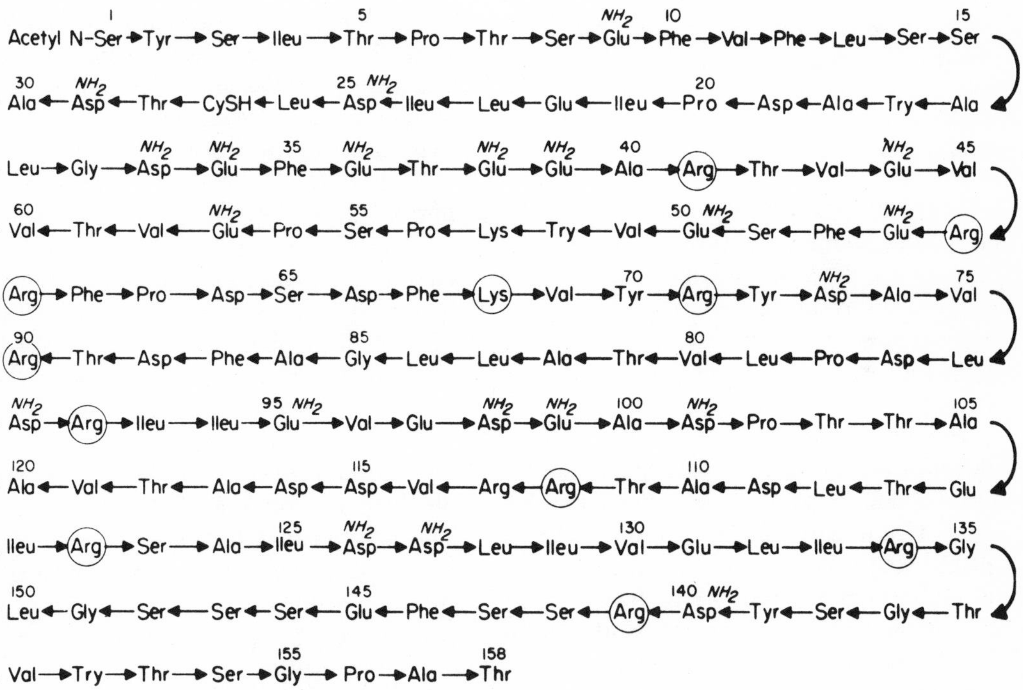

Fig. 9–7 Tobacco mosaic virus. This is the sequence of 158 amino acid residues in the protein subunit of the common strain of tobacco mosaic virus. The basic amino acid residues which are sites of attack by trypsin are circled. They subdivide the protein into 12 peptides, all but one of which terminate in arginine or lysine. See Fig. 9–8. (From Fraenkel-Conrat, 1962, *Design and Function at the Threshold of Life: The Viruses*, with permission of Academic Press.)

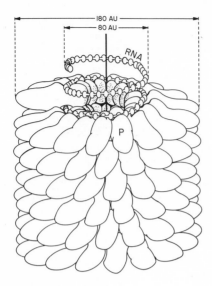

Fig. 9–8 The structure of the tobacco mosaic virus, based mainly on the X-ray diffraction studies of Rosalind Franklin. About a twentieth of the rod-shaped virus particle is shown. The complete virus contains 2,200 protein subunits (P) and the RNA chain is coiled between them. (From Klug and Caspar, *Advances in Virus Research*, VII, 1960.)

The fully known coat protein, whose corresponding RNA is available in pure form, allowed study of the effect of mutagenic agents and correlation of base changes produced with changes in the amino acids specified (Fig. 9–8).

Numerous attempts have been made to demonstrate genetic recombination in viruses living in plant hosts. When two related viruses are present in the same host plant, strains having what appear to be hybrid characteristics have been found (Thompson, 1961). The data available are highly suggestive but insufficient to prove conclusively the occurrence of recombination.

A special kind of symbiosis between viruses may be mentioned. Certain strains of tobacco necrosis virus (TNV) are accompanied by a satellite virus which is much smaller and has a different protein coat than TNV. Alone, the satellite virus cannot initiate infection nor can it replicate. When TNV is present, both viruses grow. Reichman (1964) showed that the RNA of the satellite contains 1,200 nucleotides, which is just enough to code for the protein coat containing 372 amino acids. There is thus no genetic information to code for functions required to initiate infection or for replication (RNA replicase). The satellite apparently depends on TNV to supply these functions. Other examples of satellite viruses continue to be discovered (Fig. 9–9).

TRANSFORMATIONS

In transformation, first recorded for the pneumococcus by Griffith (1928) and studied intensively by Avery and his colleagues, a clone of organisms acquires some characteristic of a second clone after exposure to the deoxyribonucleic acid of the second clone. The change is heritable and may involve drug resistance, pathogenicity, or other characteristics. Transformation also is known to occur in the bacterial symbiotes of plants. In the bacterial species *Xanthomonas phaseoli*, four types of culture colonies are recognizable. All four grow well in plant hosts but differ in the capacity to produce lesions. The amount of polysaccharide in the bacteria and the degree of pathogenicity increase in a parallel fashion and appear to be dependent on three genetic loci, designated A, B, C. The non-functional alleles a, b, c, occur in the least pathogenic strains. In this instance, transformation may occur from very pathogenic to less pathogenic or in the opposite direction.

Transformations have been effected between *Agrobacterium tumefaciens* (the agent producing crown gall in plants) and some related bacteria. Tumor-inducing ability can be transmitted from virulent crown gall bacteria to avirulent strains and to other species, including *A. rubi, A. radio-*

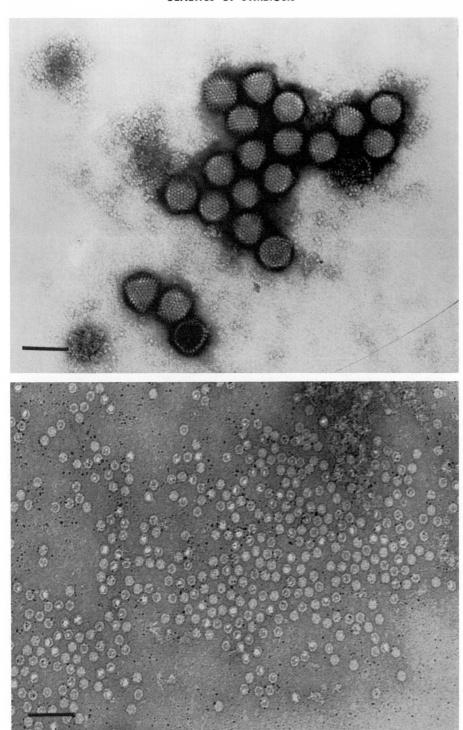

Fig. 9–9 Adeno virus (*top*) and adeno-associated satellite virus (*bottom*). Both are DNA-containing viruses. Line length is 1 μ. (Courtesy of Drs. H. D. Mayor and L. E. Jordan.)

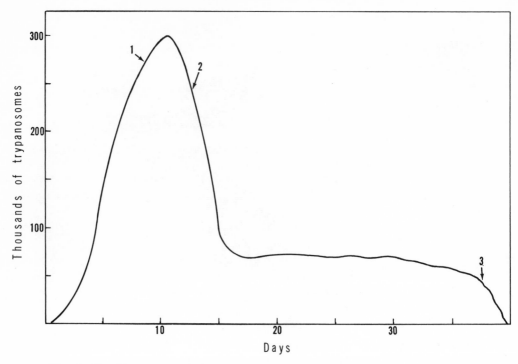

Fig. 9–10 The pattern of development of a *Trypanosoma lewisi* population in the rat. At *1*, ablastic immunity slows the rate of reproduction. At *2* and *3*, lytic antibodies cause death of the protozoan. (From pooled data accumulated in the author's laboratory.)

bacter, and *Rhizobium leguminosarum* (Klein and Klein, 1956). Since transformation of the rhizobia symbiotic in leguminous plants is now known, further genetic analysis of bacterial specificity in these relationships would now be feasible (see page 197 and review by Balassa, 1963).

Reported transformations in parasitic Protozoa include a virulence transformation in *Trichomonas* (Honigberg and Read, 1960) and drug resistance in *Trypanosoma* (Inoki and Matsushiro, 1960).

RAPID CHANGES IN SYMBIOTE POPULATIONS

The changes occurring in the composition of populations of reproducing animal symbiotes have been examined in a few cases. One of the best-known is that of the flagellate protozoan *Trypanosoma lewisi* in the rat, studied by Taliaferro and Taliaferro (1922). The course of an infection proceeds as follows: After an incubation period in which no trypanosomes are found in the blood, the organisms increase rapidly in numbers, sometimes attaining several hundred thousand per cubic millimeter of blood. A crisis then occurs and most of the symbiotes are destroyed. Some of them, however, remain in the blood for a further period of several weeks to several months. A second crisis then occurs and all trypanosomes disappear from the blood. The rat is now immune to a second infection. These events are shown in Figure 9–10. There are several events during this cycle of development for which the Taliaferros (1922) furnished explanation. During the initial rise in trypanosome number there is an increasing inhibition of reproduction of the symbiotes due to the formation by the host of a reproduction-inhibiting antibody. The crisis with the rapid decrease in numbers coincides with the production by the host of a lytic antibody which kills a large proportion of the population. The residual population is not killed by this lytic antibody. However, the second crisis with the disappearance of trypanosomes coincides with the formation of another lytic antibody to which the residual population is susceptible. It may be noted that, although there is a difference in the composition of the population before and after the first crisis of numbers, there is negligible reproduction after about the tenth day.

A somewhat different pattern is observed in some pathogenic trypanosome infections. In Figure 9–11 are shown the changes in numbers in a population of *Trypanosoma rhodesiense* in a guinea pig. It may be noted that there are two number crises in this infection. However, unlike *T. lewisi* infections, there is reproduction between the two crises. The trypanosomes comprising the population after day 30 are dif-

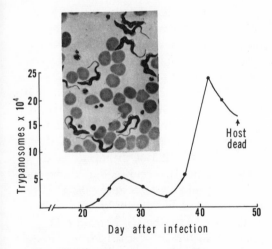

Fig. 9–11 The course of a *Trypanosoma rhodesiense* infection in the guinea pig. No ablastic immunity develops during the infection. The two crises in numbers are due to lytic antibodies. (Photo of *T. rhodesiense* by courtesy of CCM: General Biological, Inc., Chicago.)

ferent from the original strain in being resistant to the lytic antibody responsible for the first crisis. Further, after the second crisis the trypanosome population is composed of cells which are different in being resistant to the lytic antibodies responsible for both the first and second crisis.

In addition to consideration of the long-term genetic changes which have led to symbiosis or to changes in symbiosis (dealt with in Chapter 10), we may direct some attention to certain other changes which may occur in relatively short periods of time and, in some cases with considerable frequency.

DRUG RESISTANCE

The general idea that microorganisms may become resistant to a chemotherapeutic agent after a host has been treated has become widely publicized. The broad use of antibiotics has made the public, as well as the physician, aware that the bacteria are quite capable of "learning" to live with such substances. This awareness has been further reinforced by a similar phenomenon, the development of resistance to insecticides by a variety of insects of medical, veterinary, and agricultural significance. In actuality, the development of drug resistance by microorganisms has been known for quite a long time. The first demonstration that a disease agent could become resistant to drugs in the course of treatment of the host was made in Paul Ehrlich's laboratory with the protozoan *Trypanosoma brucei*, which causes the disease *nagana* in domestic animals in Africa. When mice, experimentally infected with *T. brucei*, were treated with the dye parafuchsin, some animals were cured of the infection. In others, the trypanosomes disappeared for a time but subsequently reappeared. Treatment of these recurrent infections resulted in a loss of parafuchsin effect and some of the mice died with overwhelming trypanosome infections. When these parafuchsin-treated trypanosomes were inoculated into fresh mice the infections were unaffected by treatment of the host with parafuchsin; the trypanosomes were parafuchsin-resistant.

Most of the early work was confined to trypanosomes until the period in which specific synthetic agents began to be widely used against the infectious agents. Thus, when sulfa drugs appeared, so did sulfa-resistant microorganisms. When synthetic antimalarial drugs came into wide use during World War II, the species of *Plasmodium* began showing drug resistance. As noted above, the use of antibiotics multiplied the instances manyfold.

Among the pathogenic trypanosomes, resistance to a wide variety of compounds has been observed. In addition to para-fuchsin, trypanosomes have been found to become resistant to trypan blue, acriflavin, a number of organic arsenical compounds, derivatives of phenylstibonic acid, aliphatic and aromatic diamidines, and antrycide, a compound with quaternized quinaldine and pyrimidine rings. The development of full resistance requires weeks or months of treatment, but some enhancement of resistance has been observed with single treatments of the host with certain of these agents. Full resistance may be a relatively stable character. In 1955, Fulton and Grant reported that a strain of *T. rhodesiense* had maintained its resistance to the arsenical, atoxyl, for twenty-four years after its last exposure to the drug. In other cases, resistance has been reported to diminish in a few months after removal of the drug. There is evidence that drug resistance can develop rather rapidly in trypanosomes parasitizing human populations. In one area of the Congo, the first tryparsamide-resistant cases of sleeping sickness were reported in 1929, but by 1932 resistance was observed in 50% of the cases treated.

The basic mechanism of drug resistance in trypanosomes is rather poorly understood. Several workers feel that the permeability of the cell is involved, but the evidence available does not permit a definite conclusion. It has sometimes been assumed that the development of resistance simply involves the selection of drug-resistant mutants from the trypanosome population. Unfortunately, this has not been demonstrated.

Clear-cut resistance of malaria parasites to chemotherapeutic agents was not observed until the 1940's, when several new antimalarial compounds came into use in treating human cases. Development of high resistance to proguanil (paludrine) was observed in laboratory infections. It had previously been shown that drug resistance in trypanosomes is retained after the flagellates have been transmitted to the arthropod vector, the tsetse fly, but malaria parasites differ in that *Plasmodium* undergoes a sexual cycle of development in the arthropod (see p. 104). Studies of drug resistance after passage through mosquitoes showed that there was no loss of drug resistance by *Plasmodium* after five successive sexual cycles. Resistance was maintained for over a year. However, it should be mentioned that Trager and colleagues (1967) have shown that *P. berghei* loses its previously developed resistance to the drug chloroquine when it is transferred from the mouse to the hamster host.

Resistance of malaria parasites to pyrimethamine was also observed, and cross-resistance between this drug, certain sulfonamides, and proguanil suggested that the mode of action of the drugs might be related. Study has shown that these compounds probably interfere in the metabolism of the vitamin, *p*-aminobenzoic acid (PABA), in the synthesis of folic acid, which is in turn concerned in nucleic acid synthesis. Resistance may thus be related to enhanced capacity to carry out PABA and folic acid synthesis. The genetics of drug resistance in malaria parasites has not been comprehensively studied, undoubtedly because of the technical difficulties.

Resistance to chemotherapeutic agents has been observed in several other protozoan parasites, including coccidia and the flagellate *Trichomonas,* and it seems certain that others will be discovered at about the same rate that new chemotherapeutic agents are discovered. Bishop (1959) reviewed, in a comprehensive manner, the entire problem of drug resistance in protozoans.

HETEROGENEOUS SYMBIOTE POPULATIONS

It is extremely important to point up a special significance of variation in populations of symbiotes. Not only does variation provide the means by which organisms are available for selection in a host, but the entire pattern of the symbiosis, *as it occurs in nature,* is made up of populations containing variants. Schneider (1956) presented an elegant experiment showing the effects of having mixed types of organisms on the outcome of an infection of *Salmonella typhimurium* in the mouse. Using selected inbred insusceptible and susceptible strains of mice, as well as randomly bred, non-selected mice as hosts, Schneider infected the animals with "pure" virulent, "pure" avirulent, and mixed virulent and avirulent organisms. The results are summarized in Table 9–3. It is obvious that

the definition of the host as susceptible or insusceptible is markedly dependent on the structure of the symbiote population introduced. The uniformly virulent strain killed *all* mice which were tested, whereas the uniformly avirulent microorganisms resulted in survival of all the mouse genotypes tested. It was only when a mixed population of bacteria was administered that the insusceptible mice were actually insusceptible as compared with the observed susceptibility of the susceptible mice. Parenthetically, these results show quite nicely that the definition of susceptible or insusceptible is definable only in terms of the combination of host and symbiote genotypes.

Similarly, Schneider was able to show the effects of nutritional factors, as related to the composition of host and symbiote genotypes in the same symbiosis. Mice and bacteria similar to those used in the experiments described above were used. Some mice were given a diet composed of natural food materials and others were fed a chemically defined so-called synthetic diet. The results of the interaction of genotypes and the nutritional factors is shown in Table 9–4. The effects of diets are shown in the random-bred mice infected with mixed virulent and avirulent organisms. Obviously then, increased survivorship of mice infected with S. *typhimurium* can be achieved by manipulating the composition of genotypes in the host or symbiote population as well as by altering the physiological parameters within the host by diet. Such experiments show the difficulty in analyzing many "natural" situations in terms of host-symbiote interaction. In viral populations, heterogeneity may assume a different significance, as in the action of a helper virus (p. 220).

Table 9–3

Effect of Pathogen Population Composition on Host Survivorship [a]

	Host Genotype		
	Inbred, Selected, Resistant	Random-bred (Outbred) Nonselected	Inbred, Selected, Susceptible
Clonal virulent	Died!	Died	Died
Mixed virulent and avirulent	Survived	?	Died
Clonal avirulent	Survived	Survived	Survived

[a] From Schneider, 1956, *Ann. N.Y. Acad. Sci.* 66:337.

OBSERVED CHANGES IN HOST-SYMBIOTE ENSEMBLES

There are a few instances in which a parasitic organism has been introduced

Table 9–4

Effect of Natural (N) and Synthetic (S) Diet on Survivorship Following Infection in Nine Different Genetic Circumstances [a]

	Host Genotype		
Pathogen Genotype	Inbred, Selected, Resistant	Random-bred (Outbred) Nonselected	Inbred, Selected, Susceptible
Uniformly virulent	N—Died S—Died	N—Died S—Died	N—Died S—Died
Mixed virulent and avirulent	N—Survived S—Survived	N—Survived ↑ Dietary Effect ↓ S—Died	N—Died S—Died
Uniformly avirulent	N—Survived S—Survived	N—Survived S—Survived	N—Survived S—Survived

[a] From Schneider, 1956.

into a host population in nature and the resulting interaction has produced an obvious epidemic, followed by changes in population composition such that after several generations a significant alteration of the interaction has occurred.

In discussing self-regulation in natural communities, Pimentel et al. (1962) cite the case in which a parasite was introduced in the oyster population off Prince Edward Island, Canada. The oyster population was sharply reduced and remained under severe selection pressure from the effects of parasitism. Gradually sufficient changes occurred in the oyster-parasite population so that the oysters regained their population numbers. Parasitism continued but the prevalence of disease was reduced.

A beautiful example of the genetic evolution of a symbiote-host combination is seen in the relationship between the myxomatosis virus and the rabbit population in Australia. In Brazil, myxomatosis virus is a very mild disease of local rabbits—the only manifestation of infection being the production of some thickened skin lesions. The virus is transmitted by two species of

mosquitoes which, after feeding on the infected skin, transfer the virus mechanically to new hosts. The disease was first described in South America when European laboratory rabbits became infected.

On the other hand, when the European rabbit, which belongs to a different genus than those of South America, becomes infected, a disease appears which produces almost 100% mortality. There is a generalized spread of the virus, especially to the lungs and skin. Myxomatosis was liberated in the Australian continent in 1950, and, since the rabbits of Australia are of an introduced European species, an active spread of the disease was observed in the warm season of 1950. Very high mortality rates among these rabbits were observed within a few miles of the point at which the virus was introduced and shortly thereafter as far as 200 miles away. The distribution and biting behavior of the transmitting mosquitoes seemed to determine the pattern by which myxomatosis spread in Australia. During the succeeding warm seasons of subsequent years, there were widespread epizootics in those areas where high populations of rabbits existed, and where mosquitoes were available. During this period the rabbit population dropped to perhaps 10% of what it had been in the years before 1950. This had obvious benefit for sheep and cattle raisers.

By 1958, some changes had taken place both in the rabbits and in the virus. The virus began to show a real diminution in virulence, and after two more years a new strain of virus was clearly recognizable. It differed from the laboratory strain in having a lowered virulence and a prolonged survival time. It may be thought that this new Australian strain had advantages in the relatively long period of survival during which the virus was available to infect new mosquito vectors. Changes in the host were also observable—by 1956 the mortality had dropped in the rabbits themselves when they were tested with the original laboratory strain of the virus. Necessarily, changes in the host to a more insusceptible condition on a population basis was a much slower process because of the reproductive rate, but it was clearly evident in rabbits whose ancestors had been the survivors of five successive epidemics. When young wild rabbits, from areas which had experienced these repeated episodes, were kept in the laboratory until they had lost their natural antibodies and tested with the field Australian virus, there was a marked difference in their reaction. Normal laboratory rabbits showed a 90% mortality, whereas the young wild rabbits showed a 50% mortality. A year or so later the mortality of the Australian rabbits had dropped to 25%. There was clear evidence for a genetically based change in susceptibility to the virus and a change in the virus itself. The total population of rabbits in Australia has increased, although it is still somewhat lower than in the pre-1950 period (Fenner, 1959).

A similar pattern of evolution of virus and host has been observed in the myxomatosis-rabbit relationship in England. Following the introduction of the virus, there was a sharp decrease in the rabbit population. This drop produced some rather astonishing side effects in England. With changes in the flora, plants appeared which had not been seen for many years, and a new luxuriance was clearly observed in the hedgerows of England. During succeeding years, there has been a parallel alteration of the virus and the rabbit, and the rabbit population of Britain is again on the increase. It seems likely that these alterations of host and symbiote in Australia and in England will eventually result in symbiote-host associations similar to those previously seen in South America.

Pimentel et al. (1962) have furnished a model of the sequence of events leading to the development of homeostasis in a parasite-host system (Fig. 9–12). Clearly, the events function as a feedback system. How-

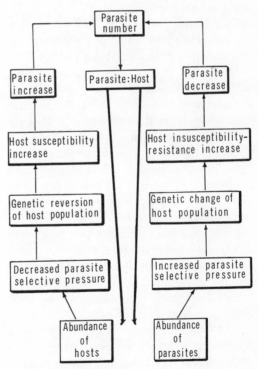

Fig. 9–12 A model of parasite-host ecology which would tend toward development of homeostasis. (Modified from Pimentel et al., 1962.)

ever, the model of Figure 9–12 is a genetic feedback system for host populations and does not take changes in the parasite into consideration.

VIRUS GENETICS AND CANCER

As indicated on page 29, there is convincing evidence that a number of cancers in various animals are induced by viruses. However, we need to know whether all cancers, and specifically those of humans, are induced by viruses. The appreciation that new genetic information may be introduced into bacterial cells by lysogenic phages has furnished new concepts for examining the cancer problem. Since some animal cancers are caused by DNA-containing viruses and some by RNA-containing viruses, there is reason to believe that tumor viruses may produce cancer by more than one mechanism.

One of the best known DNA viruses is the polyoma virus, which multiplies in various rodents. It is a small virus containing a DNA of molecular weight about 3×10^6, which is sufficient to code approximately five proteins. In the host cell, polyoma virus may multiply in the cell nucleus, and the host cell is killed by the lytic infection. Occasionally, however, the virus does not multiply, but the infected cell is changed into a cancer cell, a sequence resembling lysogeny. Both types of polyoma-virus–host-cell interaction have been observed in tissue culture. No infectious polyoma virus can be detected in the cancerous cell, which also resembles the lysogenic phage-bacterium relationship. However, it has thus far not been possible to induce a lytic virus cycle in polyoma cancer cells. If this is indeed a lysogenic relationship with polyoma provirus inserted in a host's chromosome, we are left with another interesting puzzle: What selection factors have operated to favor evolution of this developmental pattern?

The Rous sarcoma virus is probably the best-known RNA tumor virus. It belongs to the virus group known as myxoviruses, which are structurally more complex than the polyoma virus (other well-known myxoviruses are the influenza and mumps viruses). Rous sarcoma contains RNA of about 10^7 molecular weight, sufficient to code more than 20 proteins. Unlike many other viruses, Rous virus, as well as other myxoviruses, reproduces and is extruded from the host cell without cell death. When a normal chicken cell is infected by a *single* Rous virus particle, it is rapidly converted to a cancer cell. Such a cell does not release any new virus. On the other hand, if a chicken cell is infected with several particles, it becomes cancerous and new Rous virus particles are produced.

When first discovered, the finding that single-particle infections did not result in virus reproduction although infection with several particles yielded virus reproduction seemed peculiar. However, it was found that when infected cells which were not producing virus were superinfected with a closely related virus (Rous-associated virus), the cells began to produce Rous virus. Only in cells infected with this helper virus is complete Rous virus replicated.

Rous virus was thus termed a defective virus, and it was shown that the helper virus is necessary for the formation of the outer coat. More than one kind of helper virus is known and the Rous virus produced by infected cells always has a coat protein characteristic of the particular helper virus involved. It is important to note that cells infected with Rous virus without helper virus are converted to malignant cells although no new virus is produced. It is thus possible that other malignant tumors may be caused by defective viruses like Rous virus. Examinations of such tumor cells by electron microscopy would be of little use in detecting viruses. There is the possibility that helper viruses may be discovered which would result in the release of cancer viruses from human malignant cells.

GENERAL REMARKS

The basis for integration in symbiosis is clearly in the genetic systems of the interactants. Although it is perhaps simpler to demonstrate the direct interaction of symbiote and host genomes in the case of virus-cell relationships, the furnishing of information from the symbiote genome to the host genome is implied in the action → reaction phenomena which characterize symbiosis, even those which we termed simple in nature (Chapter 3). Phenotype modification of the interactants in symbiosis requires an exchange of information between the genotypes.

SUGGESTED READING

ALLISON, A. C. 1957.

BARKSDALE, L. W. 1959.

CAIRNS, J., G. S. STENT, and J. D. WATSON. 1966.

DULBECCO, R. 1963.

FENNER, F., and F. N. RATCLIFFE. 1965.

JOHNSON, T. 1960.

KARAKASHIAN, S. J., and R. W. SIEGEL. 1965.

NUTMAN, P. S. 1963.

RAPP, F., and J. L. MELNICK. 1966.

RUBIN, H. 1964b.

SONNEBORN, T. M. 1959.

STENT, G. S. 1963.

TREMBLEY, H. L., and J. GREENBERG. 1954.

WARD, R. A. 1963. Genetic aspects of the susceptibility of mosquitoes to malarial infection. *Exptl. Parasitol.* 13:328.

WRIGHT, J. W., and R. PAL (eds.). 1967. *Genetics of Insect Vectors of Disease.* Elsevier Publishing Co., New York.

10

Evolution

The circumstantial evidence for organic evolution may now be considered to be overwhelming in cogency. No competent scientist now seriously doubts its reality, although there may be differences of opinion on the details of mechanism. To treat the evolution of symbiosis is a very difficult task. The symbiote and its host have undergone evolution, the former with varying degrees of linkage to host evolution. In some cases, much of the evolution of the host may have been influenced to only a minor extent by its role in symbiosis. In some cases we may suspect that evolution has been affected by past symbioses of which we have no record. Any discussion of the evolution must be highly speculative. The degree to which symbiote evolution has been affected by changes in the host will be expected to differ in facultative and obligate symbiosis. It will also depend on the number of species serving as hosts and, hence, on the degree of isolation. It may also be kept in mind that many symbiotes spend part of their lives outside of hosts and that a set of selection factors may operate which are, in a sense, independent of those operating in the host.

GENERAL PATTERNS

In examining symbiotic organisms with respect to their origins, it becomes apparent that symbiosis has appeared many, many times in the evolution of living things. The distribution of the symbiotic habit through the phyla would argue that these events have been independent ones. Further, it seems evident that in some phyla the adoption of symbiotic life has occurred independently within the group. This is obviously so in the Arthropoda, Aschelminthes, Platyhelminthes, and the Protista.

It may legitimately be asked whether a particular mode of living seems to lead to symbiosis. As far as known, parasites seem to be heterotrophic. As is generally the case, so bald a generalization must have exceptions. There are a few euglenoid (chlorophyll-bearing) flagellates living in the posterior digestive tracts of amphibians. Examining the heterotrophic organisms, we find that parasitism occurs in groups that are either saprozoic or predaceous. This restriction may be true even within a phylum. It is difficult to postulate any particular characteristic which predisposes to parasitism. The mechanisms actually involved probably varied from one case to another. In the arthropods, for example, the development of the skin-invading habit by the jigger flea *Tunga* undoubtedly arose from the more superficial parasitism of other fleas, which in turn probably developed as an alteration of a predaceous habit. On the other hand, the invasion of living tissues by the larvae of certain flies probably arose as a further elaboration of the capacity for developing in decaying carcasses or necrotic wounds in a living animal.

However, there is a recurrent theme in the life histories of animal parasites. With great frequency, parasites enter a host by being eaten. This may imply that opportunity for parasitism and the adopting of this mode of life quite frequently involved the potential parasite in a role as the intended victim of a predator. If so, the tables were turned on numerous occasions and the predator became the "victim." As indicated in Chapter 3, this may also be an important mechanism in the establishment of mutualism.

It does not seem necessary to postulate any elaborate preadaptations for symbiosis. Even in those groups having a large number of symbiotic species the actual number of forms which primitively adopted symbiotic life were probably few. In the flatworms, for example, three or perhaps four primitive forms may have given rise to a large number of symbiotic species. The tapeworms probably had a single primitive parasitic ancestor and the trematodes may have had no more than two. These symbiotic forms have undergone a very great radiative evolution as symbiotes. The extant symbiotic turbellarians had perhaps another ancestor and have not undergone great radiative evolution. The same arguments are pertinent in considering the nematodes. Only a few forms independently adopted symbiosis. Each has undergone a more or less elaborate evolution after entering symbiosis. It may be postulated that symbiosis was adopted by certain relatively generalized, rather than specialized, members of various phyla and that the specializations have occurred after assumption of the habit of living in a host.

EVOLUTION OF "TOLERANCE"?

Parasite and host species which have lived together for long periods are often said to have developed mutual tolerance. Thus, when parasitism with little or no pathology is observed it has sometimes been taken as an indication that the association is an old one (cf. Chandler and Read, 1961; Cameron, 1956; and others). Ball (1943) questioned this generalization, citing instances in which parasites have been introduced into new hosts without the subsequent appearance of gross disease. Examples may be cited which show the converse. As a matter of fact it seems nigh impossible to predict how a parasite may behave in a new host. As Ball pointed out, three species of malaria parasites produce little disease in their usual monkey host, *Macacus irus*. However, when these parasites are introduced into a strange but closely related host, *Macacus rhesus*, one species produces very severe disease in the new host while another causes very mild symptoms. The species producing violent disease in the rhesus monkey yields a mild disease in another new host, man (see also Bray, 1963, for discussion of malaria organisms).

An interesting example is found in comparing the relative pathogenicity of rickettsiae in man. The species causing typhus have parasitized man for many centuries and are still highly pathogenic. On the other hand, the species causing rickettsial pox is thought to have initiated its relationship with man about 1945 and had a low pathogenicity at the outset.

Stauber (1958) studied the effects of the hemoflagellate protist *Leishmania donovani* on several species of unusual hosts. Some of Stauber's data are presented in Figure 10–1. It is obvious that these animals show great variability in capacity to support the parasite. The outcome of the infections ranged from death in hamsters and cotton rats to essentially no disease in rats and rabbits. None of these animals can be said to have had extensive evolutionary experience with this parasite.

On the other hand, it seems plain that high pathogenicity of a parasite might be

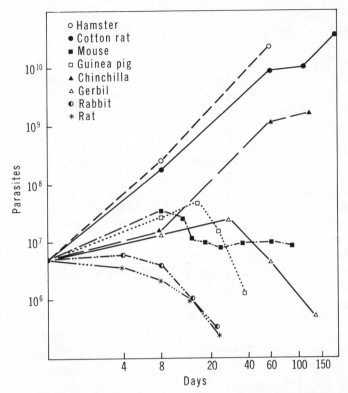

Fig. 10–1 The course of *Leishmania donovani* infections in eight species of small mammals, as determined from parasite counts in the liver on various days after inoculation. (From Stauber, 1958.)

selected against in situations where transmission to a high proportion of the host population can occur. Recognition of more than one evolutionary route to a host-parasite relationship with little disease seems to be the most sensible view. A lack of pathogenic effect in a new host may argue for a lack of adaptation of the parasite for the new host. Low pathogenicity might thus indicate a recent association without much evolutionary adaptation or it might indicate an extended period of mutual evolution toward tolerance.

As Allee et al. (1949) pointed out, pathogenicity of a parasite in its individual host might become greater during its evolutionary history without disoperation, if the proportion of infection in the total population of hosts was relatively low, the evolution of balance in such cases being between populations and not necessarily between individuals. If pathogenicity is high and disease rate is high in the population, it may set up a selection pressure which results in changes in the host with little evolution of the parasite. The adjustments may include (1) the development of enhanced resistance or insusceptibility mechanisms (cf. malaria and sickle trait; see below), (2) an increased reproduction to offset mortality, or (3) changes in behavior which reduce the rate of transmission. Medical parasitology furnishes some well-documented examples.

The Case of Sickle Trait

It has sometimes been assumed that inborn insusceptibility to a disease-producing parasite can be taken as evidence of a general soundness and fitness of the host organism. However, an example among humans indicates that such a conclusion cannot be reached without rather severe qualification. It is now known that humans may enjoy a considerable insusceptibility to malaria if their red blood cells contain something between 30 and 40% of an unusual form of hemoglobin, known as hemoglobin S, instead of the usual hemoglobin A. However, as a result of containing hemoglobin S, the red cells of such individuals tend to collapse when the hemoglobin is deoxygenated and the cells become sickle-shaped rather than round. Persons having such red cells are said to show sickle cell trait. Sickle cell trait is found in persons in some Mediterranean areas, Africa, and India. These are areas in which malaria is or has been prevalent in the recent past. Such people are not particularly incommoded by having the sickle cell trait and, as noted above, have some degree of insusceptibility to malaria. This would seem to be a case in which selection for a trait has resulted in enhanced fitness for living in malarious areas. However, there is a joker in the deck.

The formation of hemoglobin S is governed by a relatively simple genetic mechanism. Persons who have sickle cell trait are heterozygous in having one gene for hemoglobin S and one for hemoglobin A. They have derived the sickle trait from only one of their parents. When two persons having sickle cell trait marry and have children, one-quarter of their children will be homozygous for hemoglobin S, inheriting the gene from each of the parents. When an individual is homozygous all of the hemoglobin is of the S type. As a result the individual suffers from a disease known as sickle cell anemia and the chances of living past childhood are very poor. Thus, along with the insusceptibility to malaria such a population pays the price that one-quarter of its children are genetically marked for an early death. In heavily

malarious areas, the price is not too much to pay for the survival of half the children who will be heterozygous for hemoglobin S and will be relatively insusceptible to malaria. On the other hand, the significance of sickle trait sharply changes when man reduces or eradicates malaria in such a population. The presence of the sickle trait now renders the population less fit than a population not carrying this gene. The conclusion is inescapable that the possession of an insusceptibility must not be considered a desirable (or undesirable) trait except within the framework of the totality of the organism and its relations to its environment. This was discussed in a thought-provoking manner by Medawar (1960).

Advantages of Disease

It might be expected that the production of disease by a parasite would tend to be eliminated by natural selection. A parasite which causes decrease in the number of hosts is also eliminating its food supply, and disoperation would be most acute when only a single or very few host species are parasitized. However, it must not be concluded that pathogenic effects are always harmful. From the standpoint of population dynamics of hosts, the occurrence of disease may be an important factor in limiting population numbers. Without endorsing pathogenicity, it may be noted that disease has been an effective check on human populations for many centuries. There has been a high birth rate in many parts of the world to partially counterbalance the effects. We now seem to be in the dilemma produced by continuation of the high birth rate with the curtailment of the mortality due to the effects of parasites. Disease may be important in controlling the density of many animal populations, although the data available do not allow a broad, rigorous analysis. There are delicate involvements of behavior, endocrine responses, and resistance mechanisms.

Ball (1943) has pointed out that, if one accepts the view that parasitism may arise from a free-living pattern, evolving into commensalism and thence to parasitism, it is probable that there are at least two stages at which an evolving symbiote-host system would not exhibit gross pathology: In the early stages, the symbiote behaves as a commensal; and later, following the selective effects of extreme pathogenicity, the pathology might be minimal. Thus, it is virtually impossible to distinguish the evolutionary history of a symbiosis from the apparent pathology exhibited. This problem is discussed further on page 224.

A detailed examination of the evolution of all groups of symbiotes is not feasible. It is obvious that the symbiotic habit has developed independently in many cases, sometimes within a single phylum. A few examples may show some of the evolutionary patterns which have led to varying degrees and modifications of symbioses.

MALARIA

This term is used to denote parasitisms involving certain sporozoans and their hosts (see p. 104). The parasites are members of the subphylum Sporozoa, all of which live in symbiosis with animal hosts. A well-balanced general discussion of the evolution of the Sporozoa has been presented by Baker (1965). There seems to be general acceptance of the view that the malaria parasites (*Plasmodium*) and related members of the suborder Haemosporina evolved from a primitive form which invaded and reproduced in the liver parenchyma of mammals. This primitive form in turn arose from a coccidian parasite of vertebrates (see p. 94).

From the primitive liver parasite, there seems to have been a progressive evolutionary emancipation from fixed tissue cells. In the most primitive of the true malaria organisms, such as *Haemoproteus* (Fig. 10–2), only gametocytes are found in the circulating blood cells. Subsequently, in most of the genus *Plasmodium*, dividing forms are found in both the blood and fixed tissue cells. Finally, in *Plasmodium falciparum,* all stages in the vertebrate are passed in the circulating cells except for a single initial generation of schizonts (Bray, 1963). Baker (1965) remarked that future evolution may result in a mammalian species of *Plasmodium* with no exoerythrocytic development at all. There is some reason to believe that the plasmodiids of birds and of mammals are products of two separate evolutionary lines. This hypothesis is consistent with the restriction of the mammalian malaria organisms to development in anopheline mosquitoes and the avian forms to development in culicine mosquitoes.

TRYPANOSOMIASES

In considering the symbioses involving hemoflagellate protozoans of the genus *Trypanosoma*, it is necessary to briefly consider evolution of the group to which they belong. Related genera are symbiotes of

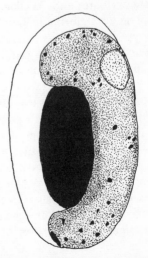

Fig. 10–2 The protozoan *Haemoproteus* in a red blood cell of the Baltimore oriole. Black body is host-cell nucleus. (Redrawn from Coatney and West, 1940.)

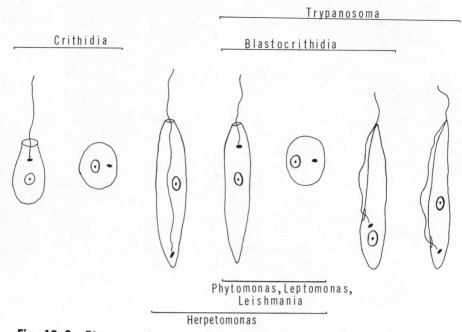

Fig. 10–3 Diagrammatic representation of morphological forms found in various genera of hemoflagellate protozoans. (Modified from Hoare, 1967.)

insects or of insects and plants. Only recently has new progress been made in clearly defining the morphology of the various life stages characterizing the various genera (Hoare and Wallace, 1966). The morphology of forms in the life cycle and the types of host associations (Fig. 10–3) have been important criteria in attempting the construction of evolutionary hypotheses for the group. Two quite different views of hemoflagellate evolution were posed in the early part of this century and have persisted. Minchin proposed that the trypanosomes arose as parasites of vertebrates and subsequently parasitized bloodsucking invertebrate hosts. Wallace (1966) has discussed this hypothesis. On the other hand, Leger postulated that the ancestors of trypanosomes were parasites of insects. As some insects developed bloodsucking habits, their parasites adapted to life in vertebrate hosts. Hoare (1967) and a number of other authors support the latter hypothesis. In the present author's opinion

the latter view seems most acceptable. A number of hemoflagellates occur in non-bloodsucking arthropods. Further, the transmission mechanisms of the hemoflagellates show increasing specialization, which is consistent with the concept of a hemoflagellate-invertebrate origin. Among those forms living only in insects, the cystic forms escape from the host in the feces and are scattered in the environment, depending on chance to reach a new host. Additional specialization is apparent in those species which depend on direct contamination of the mucous membranes of the vertebrate host. Further specialization is represented among those forms, parasitizing insects and vertebrates, and transmitted to the vertebrate host when the insect is eaten by the vertebrate. There is increased specialization in those forms directly transmitted to the vertebrate through injection by a bloodsucking insect. In this latter case, little is left to chance.

The species of *Trypanosoma*, unlike the

malaria protozoans, are not limited to a particular order of insect hosts but live in association with flies, fleas, and hemipteran bugs; one species, *T. equiperdum,* has completely eliminated the arthropod host and is transmitted venereally among horses. To further complicate the relationships, at least one species lives in alternate associations with leeches and fishes or amphibians. Further, some hemoflagellates have been described from marine mollusks and nematodes. There is considerable need for study of the hemoflagellates in lower vertebrate hosts since much of our speculation on evolution is bounded by the emphasis on hemoflagellate-mammal associations. The generic group *Trypanosoma* may represent convergent evolution of forms having quite different origins in invertebrate hosts. This

possibility has been discussed by Baker (1963, 1965), who suggested two main lines of trypanosome evolution from primitive leptomonad symbiotes of annelids, one line leading to a crithidial stock and one line to a leptomonad stock. The pattern is summarized in Figure 10–4. Wallace (1966) has presented a detailed summary of the taxonomy of the hemoflagellates from insect hosts.

In examining evolutionary trends in mammal-trypanosome symbioses, Hoare (1967) furnished convincing evidence that the evolution of many of these associations has occurred in the recent past. For example, the *T. evansi*-like trypanosomes, living in domestic ungulates of South America, appear to be species which are less than a hundred years old.

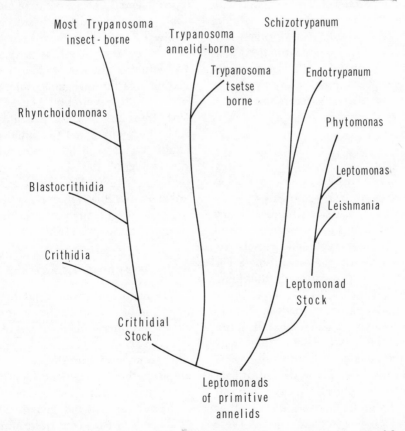

Fig. 10–4 A postulated evolution of hemoflagellate protozoans. (Modified from Baker, 1965.)

An important difference between the parasitic flagellates and sporozoans would bear mentioning at this point. The evolution of these groups is difficult to compare since they differ in a very important respect bearing on mechanism, and perhaps rate, of evolution. The sporozoans undergo sexual reproduction, which allows recombination to occur, whereas the flagellates do not, so far as is known, have mechanisms for sexual reproduction. This means that, in the flagellates, isolation of mutant individuals can occur in a single generation. It should be mentioned that transformations (p. 212) have been described in trypanosomes by Inoki and Matsushiro (1960). Genetic transformation of the flagellate *Trichomonas gallinae* was reported by Honigberg and Read (1960). Treatment of an avirulent strain of *Trichomonas* with a cell-free preparation from a virulent strain resulted in enhanced virulence of treated cells. The transformation was blocked by treatment with deoxyribonuclease. Such transformations may be of significance in allowing recombination in flagellates.

AMEBIASIS

The symbioses involving various amebas and their hosts have in some cases clearly evolved independently of each other. Many of the amebas living in vertebrates are of the so-called *limax* type and closely related to well-known soil organisms. The relationships are generally of the commensal type (Fantham, 1936). Some of the normally free-living *limax* amebas, *Acanthamoeba*, can live in mammals. If introduced into the nasal cavity, they may penetrate the mucosa and live in the brain, lungs, or other sites. These do not appear to be laboratory curiosities since "natural" infections occur (Culbertson, 1961). It is not yet completely clear as to whether these are facultative parasites.

The amebas of the genus *Entamoeba* (see p. 93) seem to have an origin other than the *limax* line. *Entamoeba* includes a species complex ranging from *E. moshkovskii*, which lives in sewage, to *E. coli*, a commensal in the gut of vertebrates, to *E. histolytica* and *E. invadens*, which are clearly parasitic, feeding on host tissues.

OXYURIASIS

The parasitisms involving the oxyurid nematodes, or pinworms, are confined to primates, rabbits, rodents, American opossums, reptiles, and amphibians (except for a single peculiar form in horses). Unlike the associations of protozoans discussed above, there is no alternate invertebrate host in the life of these parasites. However, members of a closely related family, the thelastomatids, live in association with millipedes and insects and it seems probable that the oxyurid-vertebrate associations evolved from thelastomatid-arthropod associations. It is tempting to speculate that the eating of the nematode-arthropod association was the mechanism of introduction of oxyurids to vertebrate hosts. However, since transmission of the parasites from host to host is contaminative, initial association could just as well have occurred through the eating of the shelled embryos along with vegetation. The initial parasitism involving amphibians may have been an evolutionary event from which the oxyurid-mammal associations did *not* arise.

RHABDITID NEMATODIASES

The nematode genus *Rhabditis* seems to be in the process of evolution toward parasitism, or rather some members of the group have evolved toward such relationships. The group also furnishes an excellent example of the independent adoption of symbiosis by various species, and it may be seen that the original generic relationship of these forms may be quite obscure after a few more millions of years. Some species of *Rhabditis* are free-living animals, some must be termed facultative parasites, and some may have what amounts to an obligate parasitic portion of the life cycle. *Rhabditis coarctata* lives in dung and may pass a portion of its life encysted on the outside of dung beetles, thus serving the function of dispersing the nematodes to fresh food supplies. *Rhabditis pellio* passes a portion of its life in the nephridia of earthworms; when an infected earthworm dies the young nematodes devour the decomposing carcass and come to sexual maturity. *Rhabditis strongyloides* breeds in soiled animal bedding and in soiled hair about the anus of mammals, and has been observed living in diseased skin of mammals. It is not difficult to visualize a future evolution of a parasitism of annelids, in one case, and of vertebrates in another.

The rhabditid nematodes of the genus *Strongyloides* may have evolved from a form with the habits of *Rhabditis strongyloides*. The adults of *Strongyloides* may be found in feces-contaminated soil, where they reproduce. The larval worms produced may be of either of two types, a so-called rhabditiform larva having a bipartite esophagus with a posterior bulb (Fig. 10–5B) or a strongyliform larva with a long tubular

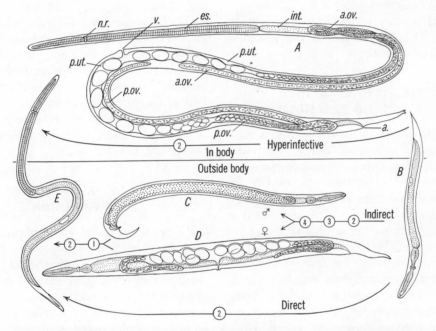

Fig. 10–5 The life pattern of *Strongyloides stercoralis*. The worm may reproduce within the vertebrate host (*top*) or outside the host (*bottom*) and has two alternative patterns when development occurs outside the host. The parasitic female (A) deposits eggs in the intestinal mucosa of the host. These hatch as rhabditiform larvae (B) which may rapidly metamorphose into infective filariform larvae (E) inside the host. On the other hand, the rhabditiform larvae (B) may leave the host in the feces. The circles enclosing numbers represent rhabditiform larval stages, not drawn in the diagram but similar in appearance to B. Thus, the direct cycle includes first and second rhabditiform larval stages and a filariform larval stage outside the host; the indirect cycle includes four rhabditiform larval stages which become free-living adult males (C) and females (D), then two rhabditiform stages (offspring of C and D), and finally a filariform stage which reenters the body of a host. Abbreviations: *a.*, anus; *a.ov.*, anterior ovary; *es.*, esophagus; *int.*, intestine; *n.r.*, nerve ring; *p.ov.*, posterior ovary; *p.ut.*, posterior uterus; *v.*, vulva. (From Chandler and Read, 1961, with permission of John Wiley & Sons, Inc.)

esophagus (Fig. 10–5E). The rhabditiform larvae continue development to the adult form in the soil. However, the strongyliform larva must become parasitic for development to continue. This infective larva penetrates the skin of a vertebrate and is carried in the blood stream through the heart and to the lungs. Here the young worm enters the alveoli and is ultimately transported to the pharynx. If it now is swallowed by the host, maturation of the worm is completed in the small intestine. There is considerable evidence that the worm in the vertebrate gives rise to new worms by parthenogenesis, a phenomenon observed in strictly free-living rhabditids as well. The life histories of *Strongyloides* are illustrated in Figure 10–5.

PECULIARITIES OF THE
ASCARIS–PIG PARASITISM

The life history of *Ascaris* with its seemingly bizarre migration in the vertebrate host has long seemed puzzling (see p. 95). Various suggestions to explain it have been made. In 1920, Fulleborn suggested that the ancestors of *Ascaris* entered the host by penetrating the skin. Later Fulleborn and also Cameron suggested that the larvae migrated because they were descended from ancestors which utilized an intermediate host. It had long been known that nematodes belonging to genera closely related to *Ascaris* do indeed parasitize intermediate hosts. However, this was not fully appreciated until 1949, when Tiner showed that the *Ascaris columnaris*–skunk parasitism is effected by the ingestion of mice harboring encysted larvae of the worm. *A. columnaris* normally migrates in the tissues of rodents and remains viable in an encysted state. This relationship with rodents was also demonstrated to occur in the *Ascaris devosi*–ferret parasitism. Sprent (1954) has reviewed the body of evidence supporting the view that the *Ascaris lumbricoides* migration is related to the migrations of ancestral forms in an intermediate host. A further elaboration of the migratory habit in ascarids is seen in *Toxocara canis*, in which the larvae migrate to the foetus in a pregnant dog host.

In surveying the life history patterns of ascarid nematodes, Sprent (1962) concluded that the use of intermediate hosts is a very primitive characteristic. He further suggested that the Ascaridae originated as parasites of marine arthropods and that evolutionary radiation occurred among marine animals. The spread to terrestrial hosts may have occurred through the eating of eggs by littoral coprophagous animals (or arthropod-eating animals), such as rodents. By harboring encysted larvae in their tissues, rodents may have become intermediate hosts for the ascarids of terrestrial carnivores. In extending their host range to non-carnivores, the ascarids have dispensed with the intermediate host but have not been able to completely dispense with larval migration.

PARASITES AS INDICES OF
HOST EVOLUTION

We have suggested by implication that there is some general sort of relationship between the evolution of hosts and of parasites, that in effect there may be evolution of parasitisms. It may be appropriate to consider the possibility that a careful examination of the parasites of various hosts might give us information concerning the phylogenetic relationships of the hosts themselves. Various specialists have applied themselves to such problems and we may examine certain examples.

Fleas as Indicators

Most of the fleas seem to be highly specific with respect to types of hosts on which they are found. In most of these cases it seems certain that the factors leading to isolation are not concerned with the phylogeny of the host but rather with the ecological place of the host, although obviously phylogeny and ecology frequently go together. Hopkins (1957) has pointed out that the host habit of living in isolated colonies is clearly a factor which is conducive to specificity in the fleas. One explanation offered for this observation is that it is relatively difficult for fleas, emerging from the larval stage in the nests of hosts which live an ecologically isolated colonial life, to find themselves on a host belonging to some other species. It is obvious that the colonial mode of life in the host will facilitate the adoption of specificity by a flea, since the random hopping of the animal (what Waterston has called speculative jumping) is far more likely to bring it to a host of the same species than if the host were solitary. Since the correlation of fleas with the host seems to be more concerned with ecology than with phylogeny, transfer to new host groups must have taken place in many cases. There seems to be good reason to believe that fleas are primarily parasites of mammals.

Yet, in at least sixteen cases according to Hopkins, one or more members of a mammal-infesting group have made the rather fundamental change from mammal to bird. Similarly, in many genera there are species infesting rodents and insectivores, and there are even species which seem to be able to live as true parasites on members of both of these orders. The fleas of marsupials seem to be readily transferred to rodents. There are instances in which a member of an insectivore-infesting genus has transferred to a mustelid and one case in which there has been a similar transfer from a bird. There are a few instances in which a flea family or subfamily is restricted to one order of hosts. Thus, it seems that flea incidence will probably not provide any useful hints about host phylogeny except perhaps at the specific level.

In the same way, it is difficult to use fleas in making any estimate of the chronology of the relationships between fleas and their hosts. The presence in Australia and South America (where marsupials still persist in numbers) of the essentially marsupial-infesting family Stephanocircidae suggests the possibility that this family existed when marsupials were the highest mammals and certainly before the link between South America and Australia by way of Antarctica was broken, assuming there was such a link. The presence of a special family on bats might suggest the probability that this infestation dates to the origin of the Chiroptera.

The fact that the fleas have a free-living part of the life cycle and, during the free-living portion of the life, are influenced by factors which have nothing to do with the phylogeny of the host has probably resulted in relatively easy transfer from one host group to another. This set of habits has probably caused such obscuring of the original patterns of host association that the present patterns of associations are practically useless as a guide to the phylogeny of the host.

Fish–Trematode Relationships

Of the more than one hundred families of trematodes which have been named, it seems likely that that number will probably be generally accepted as valid. Almost half are families from fishes. Classification of this very large number of species is still somewhat unsettled, owing not so much to the nature of the organisms as to the failure of zoologists to study them. As has been pointed out, the trematodes require at least one and most often two intermediate hosts (see p. 103). It is apparent that a thorough discussion of specificity in these animals would have to take the intermediate hosts into consideration. Unfortunately, very few life cycles are now known. It is probable that host specificity would vary to some extent at any level of the life cycle.

At any rate, we are in no position to consider in any detail the host specificity of any part of the life cycle except that of the adult. Although the data available do not allow us to say very much about the particular portion of the intestinal tract inhabited by trematodes from fishes, it is safe to say that most of them are restricted to the intestine. Some genera are known, or at least recognized, to inhabit typically certain areas of the intestine. However, this is rarely recorded in any detail.

The rather conspicuous problem encountered by students of the fish trematodes involves the feature of convergent evolution, which seems to have occurred in many cases. Manter (1966) has pointed out that the independent evolution of certain conspicuous features is so common among the digenetic trematodes that it is almost impossible to make a satisfactory key to the families. For example, the loss of the ventral sucker has occurred in some members of various unrelated families. The posterior location of the ventral sucker is not limited to the amphistomes but occurs in at least three other families found in fishes. These families are not thought to be related to amphistomes at all. The absence of a cirrus sac is a character in a number of very different groups of trematodes, as is also the lack of a pharynx. Thus great care must be exercised in utilizing various morphological characters and neglecting other considerations. Manter points out that the correct evaluation of a trematode would require a consideration of all the details of its morphology, its life cycle, and its biology, meaning the types of hosts. Host specificity is not marked in all the families of digenetic trematodes but prevails to a sufficient extent to make it frequently an aid in correct classification of a given trematode. Manter has reviewed several instances in which the value of host relationships were important in understanding the taxonomic position of a particular trematode. The collection data available suggest that the digenetic trematodes of marine fishes show considerable host specificity. A few species are known to infect fishes belonging to different families, but the majority of species have been collected from a single species of hosts or from hosts of the same or closely related genera.

There are of course exceptions to this general rule, primarily in the families of Hemiuroidea. As a matter of fact (in figures presented by Manter), approximately 50% or more of the digenetic trematodes collected in such diverse places as Japan, the Tortugas, the Mediterranean, and Britain were found on a single species of hosts. It is of interest that the forms collected around the British Isles showed the least host specificity. This would support the expectation that increased specificity should accompany greater speciation. Speciation of trematodes in warmer seas probably accompanies high speciation of hosts, both definitive and intermediate.

Certain specialized families of digenetic trematodes seem to be associated with particular types of fishes, within which they have undergone speciation. In some cases there seems to have been a more or less parallel evolution of trematodes and fishes, but sometimes the speciation has actually involved the trematodes to a greater degree than the host. This possibility is best exemplified by the numerous species of the family Accacoeliidae (Fig. 10–6) in the intestine of *Mola*, the oceanic sunfish. In this single host, whose digestive tract would seem to offer a rather uniform environment, there are no less than five genera and ten species belonging to this single trematode family, and all of them are host-specific. The present author's experiences with *Mola* and the nature of its digestive tract suggest that there may be very real biochemical differences between *Mola* and many other fishes. This may be due to the very large quantity of coelenterates eaten by *Mola*.

Sharks and rays are hosts to a very limited number of digenetic trematodes. Manter

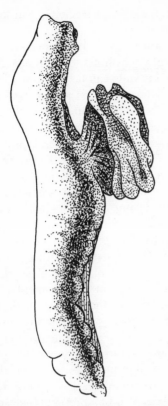

Fig. 10–6 An accacoelid trematode, Ac-
cacladocoelium, from the sunfish Mola. (Redrawn from Dollfus, 1935.)

indicates that about thirty-one species are
known to mature in these fishes. The
trematodes of the elasmobranchs show a
marked host specificity at the generic level.
No genus of trematodes, which is clearly
parasitic in elasmobranchs, is also known
from bony fishes, with perhaps one exception. However, no family of digenetic
trematodes is limited to elasmobranchs.
Oddly, not a single species of trematode is
known certainly to inhabit the spiral valve
of elasmobranch fishes. This absence of
trematodes from the spiral valve may be
related to the high concentration of urea in
the lumen (see p. 74). However, our
knowledge of the biochemistry of the gut
of fishes in general is quite deficient; there
may be other physiological barriers.

The trematodes of elasmobranchs are
not primitive. Their relatives are much
more richly represented in bony fishes.
Considering their very small numbers and
the absence of primitive species, it seems
probable that most or perhaps all of them
were derived from the trematodes of bony
fishes. Since the bony fishes first appeared
in the Jurassic, which is about 130 million
to 165 million years ago, we can conclude
that the earliest infections in elasmobranchs
and the evolution to generic but not family
levels occurred much later than that time.
The evolution of trematodes within the
bony fishes has been much more extensive,
as it has also been in land animals.

The trematodes of freshwater fishes are,
in general, different from those of marine
fishes. Some forms which migrate, such as
the eel and salmon, may acquire parasites
from either region, and brackish-water
fishes also sometimes contain trematodes
that are characteristic of marine fishes.
Certain families of Digenea are represented
in both freshwater and marine habitats but
no species is certainly known to occur in
both. Some families—the Plagiorchidae and
the Opisthorchidae—are not uncommon in
freshwater fishes but are not known from
marine fishes. Both families are common
in land animals.

A few genera occur in both marine and
freshwater fishes. There are relatively large
genera with a very broad geographical
distribution; these are predominantly marine, except for *Phyllodistomum*, which
not only occurs in freshwater fishes but also
in amphibians. The Digenea of fishes do
not show high host specificity, such as is
found in the Monogenea, which may be of
more ancient origin. The Digenea of marine fishes are extremely numerous and
diverse, perhaps as much so as their hosts.
Some of them have enough host specificity
at the level of species, genus, and, occasionally, family to make a knowledge of the
host relationship highly useful in the correct classification of the trematode and, to

a somewhat lesser extent, in revealing relationships among the host groups. The difficulty again is to untangle those relationships due to ecological causes and those arising from phylogeny. Actually the status of the parasite in each case has to be appraised on its own merits. The very large number of species of Digenea helps in recognizing the exceptions, and eventually the knowledge of life cycles will probably clarify the picture. The vast unexplored marine territory of the South Pacific will probably furnish material. Here speciation of the hosts is probably maximal and here as well our information is minimal.

It is recognized that the host is an important attribute of the parasite. The host-parasite ensemble is determined partly by phylogenetic factors. Understanding host relationships is an aid in understanding the parasites and, conversely, the parasites which are present constitute an attribute of the host animal.

EVOLUTIONARY ASPECTS OF HOST SPECIFICITY

Before discussing host specificity, an obvious point must be made. It is unrewarding to consider the problems of host specificity unless the conclusions can be based on sound identification of the hosts and the parasites. There is absolute necessity for adequate morphological study and extreme care in making identifications.

One approach to the problem of host specificity is from the negative standpoint, asking, with Mayr (1957), "Where does host specificity break down and under what circumstances?" In some cases we have reason to believe that a similar ecology favors transfer; we find that birds, such as sandmartins, and mammals, such as ground squirrels, which have in common the attribute that they live in holes in the ground, have related fleas. Whenever birds and mammals live alike, they may also share their fleas. It is evident in these cases that the physiological specificity of at least some fleas is low.

In other cases, host specificity is undoubtedly governed by physiological factors. This view can be confirmed by failure in the laboratory to establish certain forms in new hosts. Even in these cases there are sometimes very specific factors operating, in addition to more general physiological ones. Feather structure seems to be one of these specific factors, at least as far as bird lice are concerned. There are groups of birds having similar feathers and harboring related species of Mallophaga, even though the bird groups are not at all closely related. One wonders whether the relationship between the bird lice of rheas and ostriches is not merely a manifestation of the similarity of the feathers of these birds. This speculation is based on the observation that bird lice show feather preference.

A more confusing factor, perhaps, is the effect of intermediate hosts in the food chain. All organisms that feed on the same intermediate hosts present themselves as candidates for infection. For example, cephalopods are presumed to be the intermediate hosts for tapeworms of the family Tetrabothriidae (Baer, 1954). Thus, we find that the adult worms of this family occur in all kinds of mammals and birds that feed on cephalopods. They are found in whales, penguins, gulls, gouramis, and so forth. Animals that do not feed on cephalopods are not infected.

Secondary Transfers of Symbiotes

We have mentioned the frequency of secondary transfers of parasites from one host group to another, but it might be well to cite some examples. One well-known hawk louse is also found on owls and one species from cuckoos occurs on hawks. Pigeons share genera with the falliform birds; one genus of lice which is characteristic of African mouse birds has a very close relative on an Oriental genus of falcons.

Another genus of biting lice, originally on marsupials, has evolved genera on the hystricomorph rodents and on lagomorphs (rabbits). Another family originally on hystricomorphs has secondarily colonized South African monkeys, cricetid rodents, parakeets, and lagomorphs. Most of the genera of Trichodectidae are highly host-specific on carnivores, more specifically canids. Yet one genus is found on lemurs, one on South American monkeys, and one on ungulates and one on tree sloths. The fact that ostrichs and rheas have sclerostome nematodes has been cited as evidence for a relationship of these birds; however, this conclusion ignores the fact that sclerostomes occur in all sorts of grass-eating animals. Another instance of this sort occurs on the Andean plateau: a tapeworm of the genus *Monoecocestus*, normally occurring in rodents, is found in a grazing, burrowing bird belonging to the Tinamidae. There is evidence that host transfers are so frequent as to sometimes weaken the case for using the parasitic fauna as an unveiling indicator of relationships. Evidence obtained from the parasites may be suggestive, but it can rarely be considered absolute proof without other evidence. An instance of its value was the finding that individual octopi on the Pacific Coast harbor one of two kinds of mesozoans in the kidneys. A careful study showed that two species of *Octopus* were present.

DISPERSAL AND EVOLUTION

The role and means of dispersal are highly important in considerations of the evolution and speciation of symbiotes. There is a tendency among recent authors to consider the local interbreeding population as a basic unit in evolution. The size of this population depends largely on a means of dispersal of the individuals. A local population may be highly restricted in some sedentary species or it may be nearly worldwide in an inhabitant of temporary pools whose eggs are blown around by the wind. The definition of "population" for symbiotes may cause difficulties. If the entire life cycle occurs on a single host, all the inhabitants of a single host are a population.

In a wider sense, all the individuals of a host population form an interbreeding population. When their intermediate hosts have some greater dispersal facilities than the vertebrate, it is the dispersal radius of the intermediate which represents the interbreeding population in a genetic sense. Speciation is the division of a single interbreeding population into two reproductively isolated ones. The development of internal isolating mechanisms is preceded in symbiotes by some period of spatial isolation exactly as in free-living animals (Clay, 1949). The problems of spatial isolation between symbiote populations thus become exceedingly important. Clay has indicated some potential barriers and suggested the importance of geographical differences in distribution of symbiotes on the same vertebrate host. The shift of the symbiote from one host to another is probably easiest where there is an empty ecological niche on the new host. This transfer occurs more often in peripherally isolated portions of the range of a host or where there is some shift in the ecology of the host. There are cases of geographic variation in host specificity or apparent host specificity (symbiote incidence).

The isolation of different symbiote populations on different hosts seems to be somewhat comparable to the isolation of free-living animals on islands. It has become customary to designate slightly different host races as subspecies, each designation corresponding to the equivalent of geographic races in free-living animals. There are certain difficulties here. As long as the life cycle of the symbiote takes place on the host, there is very effective isolation between populations on different hosts. When, however, part of the life cycle is outside of the vertebrate host, some special difficulties are raised. When, for example, the cercariae of the strigeid trematode *Apatemon* occur in freshwater snails and the later stages in fishes and leeches, it is difficult to see why there is not an apparently common pool of cercariae and metacercariae. Yet ten subspecies of this trematode have been described from various ducks. One possibility here, of course, is that the differences in different vertebrate host species are non-genetic modifications. This hypothesis has not been tested by experiment. Beaver's (1937) classical study on the variation of the trematode *Echinostoma revolutum* in different hosts showed conclusively that non-genetic modifications may readily occur in some species. Beaver readily synonymized several species during the course of his study.

INVASION AND COMPETITION

The evolutionists speak of multiple invasion if the same island is repeatedly colonized. According to Mayr (1957), there are two prerequisites for the success of a later invasion. The first wave of immigrants must have become full species; that is, it must have acquired isolating mechanisms before a second colonization takes place. There must be sufficient ecological divergence between the successive colonists to eliminate competition, since it is recognized that two closely related species cannot coexist in the same area if their demands on the environment are identical. One or the other is superior under these circumstances and will replace the less fit species.

Except for work by Schad, this generalization, known as *Gause's rule*, has not received much attention among parasitologists. There are many records in the literature of the existence of two or more congeneric species in the same host. The most outstanding examples probably occur in the tapeworm family *Hymenolepididae*.

A shrew, for example, may harbor three, four, or five species of the genus *Hymenolepis*. There are many instances of this. Veterinary parasitologists have long recognized that a number of species belonging to the family Trichostrongylidae may occur in the same individual host species of ruminant animal. Unfortunately, we have little information on how much these parasites may segregate in different parts of the intestinal tract. In view of the importance of competition as an evolutionary factor, it would seem extremely important to record such facts of distribution with precision.

There is in fact laboratory evidence that different species of parasites may show evidence of competitive effects. The acanthocephalan *Moniliformis* is affected by the presence of the tapeworm *Hymenolepis* in the small intestine of the rodent. Interactions between the nematode *Nippostrongylus* and *Hymenolepis* and between two species of *Hymenolepis* have also been recorded. In the literature of medical parasitology, the statement is frequently made, in discoursing upon some parasitic infection, that the unfortunate host may succumb to secondary bacterial infection. These are clearly cases in which there has been a secondary invasion of the habitat by organisms belonging to a completely different taxonomic group. Although in this case the evidence for competition is not apparent, it would seem that the first colonizing wave of parasites has altered the environment in such a way as to make it more readily colonized by some other group. This leads to the well known vicious cycle relationships sometimes seen in parasitism (see p. 70).

Host Specificity

The term *host specificity* is one which has been used many times and actually has meant different things to different people.

In its broadest terms, it simply means the restriction of a symbiote to one, or some definitely limited number of, host species, without implication as to mechanism for this limitation on distribution. In these terms, there is no question that host specificity is a valid concept. All organisms have some restriction on their distribution; otherwise we should be knee-deep in algae, jellyfishes, or what have you. However, when we examine the term *host specificity* as it has been used in more restricted senses, we have certain difficulties. We may see that in the biology of a given symbiote, there will be certain limiting factors on its distribution which are directly related to the manner in which it gets from one host to another. The mechanisms for reaching hosts described in Chapter 5 would indicate that these specializations will apply some restriction to the kinds of hosts in which a symbiote will be found. Many instances can be cited of what is usually referred to as aberrant parasitism, in which a given symbiote may on some rare occasion find itself in a host in which it does not usually develop. In some cases, the symbiote finds this unusual environment quite satisfactory from the standpoint of its development and reproduction and may settle down to its usual type of life. On the other hand, the environment may not be wholly satisfactory for the fulfillment of the life needs of the symbiote. It may fail to establish itself or to grow after it has infected the host. Or, stimulated by unusual physico-chemical factors, it may wander in the host to locations in which it is not usually found. It may even do more than one of these things. For example, the larva of the dog ascarid *Toxocara canis* is stimulated to considerable wandering when it finds itself in the body of man; in addition, the worm is not able to fulfill the requirements for growth and reproduction in the human host and does not develop into an adult.

It is important to differentiate host speci-ficity that has its origin in the failure of opportunity to infect a variety of hosts from host specificity that has its origin in physiological compatibility with a restricted group of hosts. In those cases in which failure of opportunity is the basis, there is always a moderate possibility that conditions or habits of potential hosts will change and the symbiote may then find itself inhabiting new host species quite regularly. Or, the symbiote may be transferred to a new geographical location in which the opportunity for inhabiting new hosts is regularly present. When host specificity has its basis in opportunity we may expect to find varying degrees of distributional radiation.

On the other hand, when there are physiological factors involved in determining the distribution of a given symbiote, this imposes somewhat more drastic limitations. It must be pointed out, however, that a symbiote can always live in more species of hosts than the number in which it is found in nature. Even from the standpoint of its physiological capacities and specializations, the symbiote is not a frozen entity. It can vary both in genotype and in phenotype, and there is thus some plasticity in its physiological capacities. Symbiotes have been "trained" to live in hosts with which there initially appeared to be considerable physiological incompatibility. We may cite as an example the studies of Desowitz and Watson on *Trypanosoma vivax*, normally a parasite of ruminants. These workers found, as others had before them, that this protistan did not develop in the rat. However, if the rat was given an injection of sheep serum, along with the trypanosomes, the trypanosome succeeded in establishing itself in this host. After several transfers from rat to rat with accompanying sheep serum, it was found that the sheep serum could be deleted and that the trypanosome was now capable of parasitizing the rat without any chemical help from the investigators. The chemical basis of this phenomenon is not yet well understood, but it most certainly demonstrates that a parasite can "learn" to live in a host with which it initially appears to be physiologically incompatible (Desowitz, 1963).

Physiological vs. Ecological Specificity

We may thus differentiate, in theory, host specificity having what may be called an opportunistic basis from that having physiological compatibility as a basis. It is pointless to argue that one is more important than the other, since both are always present. One or the other may be more strongly involved in a given instance, but the two are not commonly distinguishable with certainty except by careful laboratory analysis. Even in the laboratory, there are certain pitfalls. For example, Schiller (1959) studied the capacity of the mouse tapeworm *Hymenolepis nana* to infect a variety of mammals, many of which it has never been found to inhabit in nature. Some of these animals were susceptible, indicating that the failure to parasitize these hosts in nature was probably due to failure of opportunity.

On the other hand, some hosts could not be infected with *Hymenolepis nana*, and it is attractive to postulate that there is physiological incompatibility with these hosts. However, careful study of one of these hosts revealed another type of complication. The grey squirrel was readily infected with *H. nana* in the laboratory, as long as the animals were fed dog biscuits, a distinctly unnatural diet for squirrels. When they were fed natural foods, such as acorns or mushrooms, they were completely refractory to infection. This would seem to be a case in which the usual behavior of the host in its selection of food would render it physiologically incompatible with *H. nana*, even if the opportunity for infection were excellent. As a similar example, the coccidian protozoan *Eimeria mohavensis* shows considerable host specificity in na-

ture. The kangaroo rat *Dipodomys panamintimus* is normally found to be infected, whereas *D. merriami* is not. On the other hand, either species of kangaroo rat is a quite satisfactory host in the laboratory (Doran, 1953). A similar situation exists in the distribution of the tapeworm *Oochoristica deserti* in kangaroo rats. The "natural" and "unnatural" hosts are equally susceptible in the laboratory (Millemann, 1955).

Experimental study of physiological incompatibility may be of value in giving us the approximate range of physiological compatibilities, but as the foregoing will indicate, these determined limits may be imprecise. Another difficulty in the definition of physiological incompatibility is our almost complete lack of information on what these incompatibilities may be. We have been blithely speaking of them as though they were single entities when in reality they probably are not. In the case of a given symbiote, there may be three or four points of physiological incompatibility in one kind of potential host but only a single point of incompatibility in another potential host. These have not been defined experimentally, but they must be, before there can be any real understanding of the physicochemical limits on parasite distribution.

BACTERIAL EVOLUTION

There seems to be substantial evidence that bacteria have evolved along five major lines with the development of symbiotic relationships occurring independently on numerous occasions (Stanier and van Niel, 1941). These include (1) cocci; (2) the photosynthetic bacteria; (3) polar-flagellated forms; (4) the non-motile gram-positive rods; and (5) the peritrichously flagellated rods, developing spores. The general line as visualized by Stanier and van Niel is shown in Figure 10–7.

When the base compositions of the

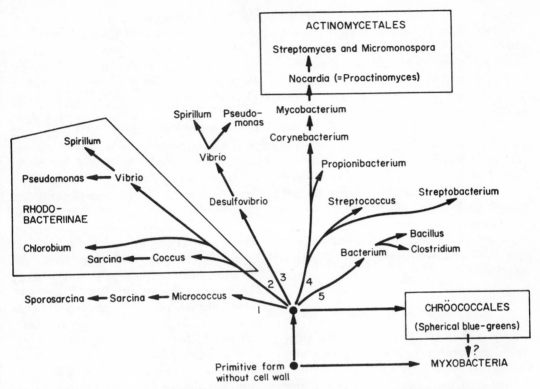

Fig. 10–7 A postulated evolution of the principal groups of bacteria and their near relatives. (From K. V. Thimann, © 1963, *The Life of Bacteria,* with permission of The Macmillan Company.)

nucleic acids of bacteria are compared with respect to the percentages of guanine and cytosine combined, there is a relationship to the taxonomy. Some selected examples of these percentages are shown in Table 10–1. It is clear from this type of evidence that symbiosis has developed independently in a number of cases. In many of these groups it is also quite easy to find a gradation from a free-living life to a facultative symbiotic life to an existence totally committed to symbiosis.

An example of the variation within a single bacterial genus showing a sequence from free-living to symbiotic organisms is observed in the acid-fast bacteria *Mycobacterium.* The first member of this group to be discovered was the leprosy bacillus, which has never clearly been cultivated outside of a host organism. Next came the

Table 10–1

Data on Base Composition of Deoxyribonucleic Acids Isolated from Various Bacteria[a]

Organism		Percentage: Guanine + Cytosine
Streptomyces	(3 species)	74
Micromonospora		72
Pseudomonas	(3 species)	63–67
Azotobacter	(3 species)	55–57.5
Aerobacter	(6 strains)	55–59
Erwinia	(7 species)	52–54
Salmonella	(7 species)	49–54
E. coli	(10 strains)	50–53
Bacillus	(3 species)	34–46
Streptococcus	(3 species)	34–39
Clostridium	(4 species)	27–32

[a] From Marmur et al., 1963.

discovery of the tuberculosis bacillus, an organism which is difficult to cultivate but which can be cultivated outside the host. Later, other organisms such as Johne's bacillus, responsible for a chronic enteritis in cattle, and various saprophytic acid-fast organisms were found. Among the latter are the butter bacillus *M. butyricum*, the Timothy grass bacillus *M. phlei*, and various forms found in manure and soil. Although detailed data on precise nutritional requirements of all of these forms do not appear to be available, there seems to be a clear evolutionary pattern toward a more and more rigorous and definitive obligate symbiotic relationship with another organism.

THE ORIGINS OF VIRUSES

Since the 1930's, there has been widespread support for the theory that most animal viruses evolved by degenerative evolution from larger parasitic microorganisms. The main support for the hypothesis of a degenerative evolution seems to come from the evolutionary history that seems to obtain with microorganisms, bacteria living in symbiotic relationships certainly tending to have less synthetic ability than related free-living forms. Perhaps the most convincing arguments that have been brought to bear are those described by Moulder (1962) in his discussion of the biochemistry of intracellular parasitism. The knowledge that myxomatosis and related agents, as well as the rickettsiae, have properties that clearly relate them to the bacteria, furnishes somewhat more convincing evidence of intermediate forms between the bacteria and the viruses. One of the striking differences between the bacteria and the viruses is the absence of a limiting unit membrane in the latter, and as Burnet pointed out several years ago, after the organism has freed itself from a continuing spatial differentiation from its hosts, new opportunities for "simplifying" evolution open up. Protein synthetic mechanisms of the host become more and more indistinguishable from those of the symbiote.

There are, however, alternative theories concerning virus evolution. In the main, these hold that viruses arose as subcellular elements related to cellular constituents. The similarity of DNA-containing bacteriophages and other DNA-containing plasmids in bacteria is highly suggestive. The latter include fertility (F) factors which determine mating in certain bacteria, resistance (R) factors determining transmissible resistance to specific toxic agents and some other factors. Like phages, these plasmids may be attached to the bacterial chromosome and may leave the chromosomal attachment with fragments of the bacterial genome attached. Phages and these bacterial plasmids may replicate autonomously in the host cell. It has been suggested that phages may have been derived from plasmids which could have undergone evolution in new host cells. However, the converse might also have occurred; that is, plasmids may have evolved from bacteriophages.

There are clearly differences between the bacteriophages and the DNA viruses of plants or animals, as there are fundamental differences between the procaryotic bacterial cell and eucaryotic cells. As indicated in Chapter 3 (p. 68), many organelles in eucaryotic cells contain DNA. The DNA of mitochondria, chloroplasts, and kinetoplasts of flagellate protozoans is quite different from the nuclear DNA of the parental cell. Further, there is evidence that the DNA of these organelles is functional, coding the synthesis of messenger RNA and, hence, protein. The amount of DNA present is comparable to the amounts in viruses.

However, organelles such as chloroplasts and mitochondria do not resemble viruses in their organization. Rather, they show greater resemblances to more complex unicellular organisms, and their origin from endosymbiotic microorganisms has been suggested (Lederberg, 1952; Sagen, 1967). It is quite suggestive, in this respect, that protein synthesis in chloroplasts and mitochondria is inhibited by chloramphenicol, as is protein synthesis in bacteria. On the other hand, most of the protein synthesis in eucaryotic cells is not affected by chloramphenicol (Sissakian et al., 1965; Kroon, 1965). Viruses could be derived from one or more of the genetically specific cell organelles. It may be seen that theories concerning the evolutionary origins of DNA viruses are not mutually exclusive. Luria and Darnell (1967) have discussed this in some detail.

The origins of the RNA viruses offer difficult problems. They might represent some unique line of completely independent genetic evolution. This does not appear probable since the RNA viruses act as messenger RNA, being integrated with the cellular mechanisms for synthesis and translation. On the other hand, the RNA viruses may have evolved from DNA viruses whose messenger RNA has attained capacity for replication. There is also the possibility that messenger RNA of host-cell origin acquired a replication mechanism.

LOSSES OF SYNTHETIC FUNCTION

Some years ago Lwoff (1944) pointed out that, on adequate media, auxotrophic mutants of microorganisms could have a selective advantage over their prototrophic parents because of the energetic economy effected by deletion of a biosynthetic pathway.* This was of course based on the assumption that the prototroph would continue to perform the biosynthesis under all circumstances. Later work on feedback inhibition and gene repression has shown that the presence of the end product in the medium often tends to suppress the biosynthesis of that end product. Thus, Lwoff's original idea seemed questionable.

Zamenhof and Eichorn (1967) examined

---

* It may be recalled that the term *auxotrophic* refers to a mutant having a nutritional requirement not seen in the wild type, which is referred to as *prototrophic*.

the question experimentally. These workers studied the growth of each of several auxotrophic mutants in competition with the prototrophic strain of a bacterium, *Bacillus subtilis*, in media which were adequate for the auxotrophs. The data showed that the mutants requiring histidine, indole, or tryptophan have a distinct selective advantage over the parental strain when grown in media containing the nutrient required by the mutant. Further, it was shown that a mutant with a block early in the pathway for tryptophan synthesis had a selective advantage over a mutant blocked further along in the pathway. Zamenhof and Eichorn pointed out that the cases studied by them were gene inactivations resulting from point mutations. Thus, the economy effected in metabolism did not include the synthesis of the structural gene, messenger RNA, and perhaps the inactive enzyme itself. They postulated that, if mutations were deletions resulting in loss of a DNA segment, the additional advantage in a suitable medium may include faster replication of the chromosome and saving on sugars, bases, amino acids, and ATP required by the prototroph to synthesize this portion of the DNA, messenger RNA, and protein.

From the foregoing it may be seen that, in a suitable host furnishing a variety of prefabricated metabolites, mutants having deletions may have a selective advantage over parental types. A positive selection pressure for loss of synthetic capacity would result.

"Losses" in Energy Pathways

A somewhat related hypothesis concerning the selective advantages of a "simplified" energy metabolism was presented several years ago (Read, 1961). As pointed out in Chapter 8, symbiotic animals usually carry out incomplete oxidations of energy-yielding substrates. Carbohydrates may be metabolized to the fatty acid state rather than to carbon dioxide and water, leaving a considerable amount of potential energy in the end product. For this reason, symbiotic organisms have been termed "wasteful" and "inefficient." It has often been implied that symbiotes are inefficient since there is no requirement to be other than prodigal in the utilization of energy sources.

However, this last teleological statement obfuscates the fact that, for symbiotes, the selection pressure for maintenance of food-hunting mechanisms has essentially been removed. Free-living organisms have selection pressures for the solution of the physiological problems of food getting and for maximum utilization of food. Maintenance of food-getting mechanisms requires energy, and maintaining a metabolic system, which is not completely efficient but which allows extraction of the largest possible amount of energy per food molecule, also has an energy cost for the free-living organism. It must be concluded that the maintenance of the complex metabolic system must confer selective advantage rather than the hyperelaboration of food-getting mechanisms, in free-living forms.

Since selection for maintaining food-getting mechanisms has been markedly reduced in symbiotes, it might be concluded that simplification of catabolic reactions could occur without being selected against. As a matter of fact, it may be argued that deletion of catabolic reactions might have positive selection value because of the reduction in energy utilization effected by such deletions.

In addition to the above, there may be an additional positive selection pressure for simplification of energy metabolism with the assumption of symbiotic life. It may be suggested that a critical selection pressure, opposed by selection pressure for food-getting mechanisms, is the ratio

$$\frac{\Delta F - \Delta H}{\Delta F}$$

where ΔF is the free-energy change for overall catabolism and ΔH is the energy not available for metabolic coupling. This relationship, the energy utilization ratio, does not involve specific differences in the free energy changes of different pathways of metabolism, but expresses the metabolic efficiency of a given set of processes. A change in this ratio may be expected with a reduction in the number of processes involved. Process thermodynamics would predict that an increase in the ratio would occur with a decrease in the number of steps. This increase would follow from the principle of process waste, which simply states that, as the number of processes increases, the ratio of real work output per unit of theoretical work output decreases. When the energy metabolism of symbiotes is examined in terms of this concept, the appearance of incomplete oxidation may be an expected result of the selective advantages accruing from an increase in the energy-utilization ratio. In these terms, the application of the terms "wasteful" or "inefficient" to symbiote metabolism is a form of scientific Puritanism.

IMMUNOLOGICAL FACTORS IN SYMBIOTE EVOLUTION

It will be clear that selection factors which may act in the evolution of symbiotes must include immune mechanisms of the host. Symbiote variants which elicit a rapid immune response from the host may be deleteriously affected and selected against in a population of symbiotes. The immunological environment in a partially immune host population producing a very intense selection for antigenic variants of bacteria and viruses has been suggested by a number of investigators. Burnet termed this "immunological drift." As an example, the selection of antigenic variants of influenza virus in partially immune mice has been well described (Edney, 1957). The changes in the myxomatosis virus in Australian rabbits can be partially attributed to such selection (see p. 218). The rapid spread of bacterial and virus infections may occur to levels allowing transmission before individuals can manifest an effective immune response. However, when a significant part of the population has developed immunity, this may limit growth and spread of the symbiote, favoring antigenic variants.

Dineen (1963) pointed out that, in the case of metazoan endoparasites, it is necessary for the organism to remain in contact with the host until it attains the reproductive phase. This period may very much exceed the time required for an effective immune response. Under such circumstances, the selection pressure of the host's immune response is likely to be more specific and to favor the survival *to reproductive age* of only those variants having sufficiently reduced antigenic differences from the host. The process of selection of variants showing reduced antigenic disparity with the host may result from deletion of genes for antigenic character, or an acquisition by mutation of an antigenic character of the host, or both. This sharing of antigens by host and parasite has been termed molecular mimicry by Damian (1964), who referred to antigenic determinants of parasites, resembling those of the host to such an extent that they do not elicit the formation of antibodies, as eclipsed antigens. Damian developed a model relating the distribution of human blood group antigens to the distribution of infectious agents.

It is clear that molecular mimicry could arise by change of the host or symbiote genotype. However, the briefer life and shorter generation time of the symbiote would seem to make it likely that the major changes attributable to selection would occur in the symbiote genotype. Under exceptional circumstances there might indeed be selective effects on host population components (see the case of myxomatosis, p. 218).

The view that there is a threshold level of antigenic "information" from a symbiote required for an immune response from a host is compatible with what is known of immunity (see Chapter 4). The determinants of this threshold level in a host-symbiote combination are the extent of antigenic difference between the host and symbiote and the rate of antigenic information flow. If threshold for an effective immunity response does not significantly drift during evolution of the relationship, antigenic differences and flow rate should be related inversely. Since the flow rate of antigenic information will be a function of the number of symbiotes in a host, it may be seen that reduction of antigenic differences between host and symbiote will result in a subliminal tolerance of an increased symbiote population.

If the evolution of the host-symbiote combination shows increasing tolerance of larger symbiote populations, it seems likely that there should also be selection for decreased pathogenicity. However, there may be a lower limit on pathogenicity, in the case of parasites, if the pathogenic effects on the host are related to a satisfaction of a nutritional requirement. As long as a symbiote produces some pathogenic effect, survival of the symbiote-host relationship may be favored by some degree of antigenic difference of host and symbiote. The effect of antigenic difference will be to limit the pathogenicity to tolerable levels by regulating the size of the symbiote population. It may well be that, as concluded by Dineen, the *control* of parasite population may be more meaningful than complete elimination. Dineen and his colleagues have produced a considerable amount of experimental evidence to support the general hypothesis (Dineen et al., 1965; Donald et al., 1964).

Selection by Co-responses

In a number of symbioses, the host responds to the presence of the symbiote by producing a number of antibodies which do not adversely affect the survival of the symbiote. As long as only a single symbiote species is involved, such "immune" responses would have no obvious effect in selection. However, Schad (1966) has pointed out that such antigenic stimulation of an immune response may have significance when two or more symbiote species are present in a host. The apparent lack of correlation between humoral antibodies and immunity to a specific symbiote may be attributable to the natural selection of symbiote antigens which stimulate host responses acting against competitor symbiotes. If two symbiotes, A and B, are in competition in a host and if the host response elicited by an antigen of A has no effect on A but has an effect on B, natural selection should favor genotypes of A which allow the expression of this antigenicity. Hunter et al. (1961) reported what may be an example of this phenomenon. These workers found that previous infection of mice with the blood fluke *Schistosoma mansoni* resulted in some immunity to another trematode, *Schistosomatium douthitti.* In reciprocal experiments, *S. mansoni* was not affected by previous *Schistosomatium* infection nor was any resistance shown when the immunizing and challenging species were the same.

It seems clear that the evolution of symbioses has indeed been affected by immune selection factors, but much more work is required to elucidate the relative significance of such factors.

GENERAL REMARKS

Although it is clear that there is no common pathway of evolution leading to symbiosis, it is apparent that such pathways have been followed on many independent occasions. The subsequent evolutionary flowering which has occurred in many symbiote groups suggests that the assumption of a symbiotic life may promote speciation; perhaps there is an analogy in the speciation which is apparent in tropical rainforests. Certainly there is selection pressure for specialization, as we observe when we examine the locking-in of specific symbiote-specific host combinations. The powerful tools of systems analysis might allow us to examine boundary conditions in ecological terms which would, in turn, allow assessments of evolutionary change in contemporary host-symbiote populations.

SUGGESTED READING

BAER, J. (ed.). 1957. *First Symposium on Host Specificity Among Parasites of Vertebrates.* Institute of Zoology, University of Neuchâtel, Switzerland.

BALL, G. H. 1943.

CAMERON, T. W. M. 1964.

CLAY, T. 1949.

CONWAY, D. P., and J. H. WHITLOCK. 1965.

DARLINGTON, C. D., P. F. MATTINGLY, and C. G. SMITH. 1960. Symposium on the evolution of arboviruses. Trans. Roy. Soc. Trop. Med. Hyg. 54:90.

DOUGHERTY, E. C. 1951.

HOARE, C. A. 1967.

KARAKASHIAN, S. J., and M. W. KARAKASHIAN. 1965. Evolution and symbiosis in the genus *Chlorella* and related algae. *Evolution* 19:368.

LWOFF, A. 1944.

MANTER, H. W. 1966.

PARKER, C. A. 1957. Evolution of nitrogen-fixing symbiosis in higher plants. *Nature* 173:780.

SAGEN, L. 1967.

SCHAD, G. A. 1966.

SONNEBORN, T. M. 1967. The evolutionary integration of the genetic material into genetic systems. In *Heritage from Mendel* (ed., R. A. BRINK). University of Wisconsin Press, Madison, Wis.

SPRENT, J. F. A. 1959. Parasitism, immunity and evolution. In *The Evolution of Living Organisms* (ed., J. N. LEEPER). Melbourne University Press, Melbourne, Australia.

TAYLOR, A. E. R. (ed.). 1965. *Evolution of Parasites.* Blackwell, Oxford.

VANZOLINI, P. E., and L. R. GUIMARAĒS. 1955. Lice and the history of South American land mammals. *Rev. Brasil. Entomol.* 3:13.

WEBB, J. E. 1946. Phylogenetic relationships of the Anoplura. *Proc. Zool. Soc. London.* 116:49.

ZAMENHOF, S., and H. H. EICHORN. 1967.

11

Epidemiology and Ecology

To this point we have been concerned mainly with relationships between individual hosts and their symbiotes. However, as implied at several points, symbiosis may be examined in terms of populations of hosts. When infectious disease is examined in such terms it is generally referred to as *epidemiology*. With the large body of knowledge available on the biology of human diseases, the term has most frequently been applied to the dynamics of human diseases, but there is no good reason for not extending it to cover hosts of both plant and animal kingdoms. The terms *epizootic* and *epiphytic* have been used to describe the level of prevalence of disease in animals or plants, respectively. However, the term *epidemic*, literally translated from the Greek as "upon the population," can be applied in the general sense to populations of any kind of organism.

EPIDEMIOLOGY AND ITS RATIONALE

One of the most universally impressive biological phenomena is the passing of an epidemic of serious infectious disease through a population. Epidemics have taken a greater toll of human life than wars, and man's history has been much affected by periodic waves of parasitism with ensuing disease. However, not all epidemics produce high mortality rates. As we might conclude from preceding chapters, many symbioses may appear in populations and reach epidemic proportions without producing serious manifestations of disease. It might be well before we proceed further to indicate what we mean by *epidemic*. An epidemic may be defined as a sudden sharp increase in the occurrence of parasitism in a population of nonresistant hosts.

Epidemiology deals not only with populations of host organisms and the occurrence of disease but also must be concerned with what might be called the setting in which events occur. In the case of humans and their diseases, this setting must involve the characteristics of the social community, the climate, and a variety of other factors which may be lumped under the term environment.

Long before men knew the real basis of infectious disease, the concept of contagion had developed, and in some instances this recognition led to some control. The brilliant deductions of John Snow, often called the father of the science of epidemiology, showed that contaminated drinking water was the mode of transmission in the London cholera epidemics of 1850 and 1860. The development of the germ theory of disease and the elucidation of transmission mechanisms led to the full development of epidemiology as a discipline. Medical epidemiology concerns itself with the ecology of man as it relates to disease. For many years epidemiology was mainly concerned with infectious disease and parasitism, and the foci of interest were human populations treated in a specialized fashion. In the past few years, the epidemiologists, who are for the most part medically trained, have become aware of that area of biology known as ecology. This awareness has not as yet been unusually fruitful since, unknown to themselves, most epidemiologists were already population ecologists of a special type.

The working epidemiologists must often deal largely with information which is available *after* an epidemic has occurred. He ordinarily cannot plan a set of experimental conditions and his methods of examining information are largely statistical. There are exceptions to this constraint; the experimental method was used with some success in determining the effectiveness of the vaccine for poliomyelitis. Epidemiologists, on the basis of the previous history of this disease, could make certain predictions as to the probable occurrence of poliomyelitis in the population in the future. This predictive ability allowed the planning of intelligent experiments in which the vaccine was administered to a very large group of individuals and not administered to a second large group. The subsequent occurrence of the disease in the two samples was then followed.

The Epidemiologists' Ecology

The epidemiologist frequently can analyze data on the occurrence of a particular disease and come to some conclusion as to what it seems to be associated with in the transmission. Snow (1855), for example, obtained evidence that the bacterial disease, cholera, was associated with water in London. Snow noticed that, in an area

south of the Thames River, two-thirds of the population was served by either the Southwark and Vauxhall or the Lambeth water companies. The Southwark and Vauxhall company obtained its water from a grossly polluted portion of the Thames, while the Lambeth water intake was from a relatively clean section of the river. Each company had laid water mains through this London area, some houses in a single street obtaining water from one while other houses received water from the other company. Snow carried out a house-to-house investigation, determining the source of water and carefully tabulating the occurrence of cholera deaths. After finding the total houses served by each company, Snow tabulated the rates (Table 11–1). Thus, Snow

Table 11–1

Deaths from Cholera per 10,000 Houses, as Related to London Water Supply in 1854[a]

Water Supply	Number of Houses	Deaths from Cholera	Deaths per 10,000 Houses
Southwark and Vauxhall Company	40,046	1,263	315
Lambeth Company	26,107	98	37
Other London districts	256,423	1,422	59

[a] Data from Snow, 1855.

showed that the same kinds of people, living in similar circumstances, had nine times as many cholera deaths when the water came from a highly polluted source. Snow's observations were not widely accepted at the time since they did not seem to be consistent with the prevalent view that cholera was caused by a miasma.

It is important to realize, however, that Snow's analysis told him nothing about the causative agent. This limitation is the difficulty in the recent furor over the question of whether or not the smoking of cigarettes causes cancer in humans. The epidemiologists have shown rather conclusively that there is a correlation between the smoking of cigarettes and the occurrence of lung cancer. However, this does not *prove* that smoking cigarettes causes cancer, just as Snow's analysis did not show that the cholera vibrio has a causal relationship to cholera. The author is willing to take sides in the cigarette controversy, since he is convinced that there is a relation between cigarette smoking and cancer. It is plain that the epidemiologists have furnished sufficient circumstantial evidence for a relationship to justify a very thorough study of the possible causal relationship between cigarettes and lung cancer. It would have been foolish to drink from London water wells in 1855 after Snow's analysis of cholera epidemiology, even though Snow did not identify the parasitic agent, a bacterium. This digression may aid the student in understanding both the value and limitations of epidemiology.

The first systematic studies of epidemics in which the movements of the parasitic agent were actually followed involved studies on bacteria. Koch, who contributed so much to the concept that bacteria can produce disease, studied the distribution of cholera organisms in humans during epidemics in Germany. He was astonished to find that the organism could be isolated from some individuals who were not suffering from cholera. This led to the realization that healthy carriers of an infectious agent may be most important in the epidemiology. Study of the distribution of a parasitism in a population must therefore include information on the extent to which such hidden infections occur. It is perhaps not surprising that this is so, since we have already made the point that hosts vary in their reactions to parasites and that parasites vary in their reactions to hosts (p. 217).

The Carrier and Endemic Disease

The existence of carriers is of obvious importance in those instances in which parasitism has a lethal outcome in certain hosts. If no carriers existed, infection with an agent would rapidly reduce its population of hosts to the vanishing point and the causal agent would disappear. In understanding the ecology of a disease and a disease-producing agent, the importance of the role of the carrier host cannot be overemphasized. Further, it has come to be recognized that the duration of infection in carriers may vary. Some individuals may become immune. Such changes will influence the proportion of susceptibles in a given population as well as the number of carriers or potential carriers of the agent.

In addition to the appearance of immune individuals who have had inapparent infections, some individuals showing overt disease may survive the parasitism and become immune. The duration of this immunity is also of some importance in the ensuing history of the population in determining whether an epidemic may repeat itself at some future time or whether the infection may linger in the population for a protracted period after the epidemic of disease has essentially come to a close. In this latter case, when a disease lingers on in a population and a more or less constant proportion of the individuals in the population are experiencing infection, we speak of the disease as *endemic* rather than epidemic. The so-called childhood diseases are of this type. A disease which is completely absent from a population is of course called *non-endemic.*

EPIDEMIOLOGY AND CHANGING DISEASE

It will be obvious at this point that most of the attributes of symbiotes and their hosts which have been considered in the preceding chapters will have a great deal to do with the ecology of a particular parasitism. The multitude of adaptive capacities of the symbiote, including its mechanisms for getting from host to host and for maintaining itself in hosts, will be primary considerations. The reaction of the host to the parasite and the capacity of the ensemble to exist without marked dysfunction will determine to some extent the effect of the symbiosis on the population and, thus, the ultimate history of the infectious agent in the host population.

Changes in Epidemiology

Since the definition of disease itself includes the host, we may dispense with the use of the phrase "hosts and their diseases" and simply speak of disease. The information available at this point would lead us to expect that the characteristics of certain diseases would differ with geography and within different segments of a given population. The implications of genetics and of natural selection would also lead us to expect that the features of disease would change with time.

This is indeed the case. In our own country, the epidemiology of infectious disease has undergone dramatic alterations with time for a great variety of reasons, not the least of which is control through the knowledge furnished by epidemiologists. Although infectious diseases were four of the top eight leading causes of death in the United States at the turn of the century, by 1950 they had been essentially displaced by other types of diseases such as heart disease, cancer, and arteriosclerosis (although the latter are not infectious, they may involve symbiotic relationships).

It is virtually impossible to rationalize a complete explanation for these changes. Along with dramatic development of methods of treating infectious diseases, such as the application of antibiotics, we have begun to refrigerate our food, use central heating and air conditioning, apply insecticides, alter our sanitary procedures, and spend a large number of waking hours in automobiles. Collectively, these alterations of life patterns have resulted in an increase in the average life span, mainly because fewer children die from the so-called diseases of childhood. This change in turn has created the opportunity for many of the diseases of older people to occupy positions of greater prominence. The age composition of our population has changed. These altered circumstances, of course, create seemingly never-ending sets of new problems for the epidemiologist. A change at present in progress in the United States will in a few years result in a large relative increase of individuals who are less than thirty years of age.

CONCEPTS OF ETIOLOGY

study of causes; as in causes of disease

The underlying concepts for what is termed *etiology* are basically those referred to by Paul (1958) as the seed, the soil, and the climate. There is always a temptation to overemphasize the first of these. The seed, or etiological agent, is easy to grasp. It is a tangible entity, a worm, a protozoan, or a bacterium, and, as indicated in Chapter 1, whole fields of study have focused on etiological agents. It is our purpose, and that of epidemiologists, to show that the etiological agent is only a single factor in a complex of causality.

For purposes of understanding, it is often best to limit discussion to the etiology of a single disease and to consider one etiological agent at a time. We have already pointed up the fact that there is a distinct difference between infection and disease, a matter of great importance in considering the role of the carrier, an infected individual who is not obviously diseased.

The second category in etiology, the soil, is of course the host plus its condition, when it contacts the etiological agent. The factors involved here will include susceptibility and capacity for development of resistance.

This category has been much more difficult to measure and to analyze. The advent of immunological tools has helped, but even here the measurement of, for example, antibody level in the blood is of limited value in assessing the true functional resistance of a host to a given etiological agent.

The third factor, climate, is the environment in which contact of seed and soil occurs. This factor is indeed difficult to measure because climate, as here used, is much broader than, say, the weather. We can subdivide, of course, into the *macroclimate*, which will include meteorological factors such as temperature, humidity, rainfall, and so on, and *microclimate*, which will include details of the living conditions of the members of a population or population segment. The latter would include such things as kind of food eaten, sanitary conditions, working hours, and such. Classical examples of the effects of climate are seen in the changes in specific diseases observed in time of war.

EXPERIMENTAL EPIDEMIOLOGY

Since the early part of this century, a few men have attempted to study epidemics under laboratory conditions. Topley (1942) in England and Webster (1946) in the United States were pioneers in such investigations and were mainly concerned with certain primary questions: What factors initiate epidemics of infectious disease? What factors determine the duration of epidemics? How do infectious agents maintain themselves in populations? It is profitable to examine the methods by which answers to these questions have been sought.

In experimental epidemiology, it may be presumed that the etiological agent and the mechanism for transmission from one host to another are known. However, before we progress to an experimental approach it is necessary to make a few remarks about what kinds of natural epidemics are recognizable. The immune state of the population is very important in this regard, and recognition of this factor allows us to discern the general basis for two types of epidemic. Type 1 epidemics occur in what have been termed virgin populations which are exposed for the first time to a virulent infectious agent. Type 2 epidemics occur in populations in which the virulent infectious agent has been established previously. An example of a Type 1 epidemic is the introduction of measles into a population of Eskimos who have had no previous exposure to the disease. A Type 2 epidemic is seen in the seasonal outbreak of measles in juveniles in the United States involving a population which has harbored the infectious agent for many generations. In the latter case it is presumed that a large enough crop of non-resistant individuals is born and grows up between epidemic episodes. It is of course important to know whether the immunity of the population fluctuates and to know where the infective agents are between epidemics.

One explanation for the genesis of epidemics is that genetic variation in the etiological agent occurs during the interepidemic period and increased virulence appears. The occurrence of disease increases and an epidemic appears. An alternative explanation is that an epidemic begins because population immunity declines, giving rise to the possibility of sharp change with increased infection and disease rates. A third possibility is that a change in microclimate, such as an impairment of sanitation, leads to a sudden increase in the dosage of the infectious agent. In some cases, changes in microclimate might affect resistance and change the dosage of an infectious agent as well.

The possibilities indicated above are perfectly sound working hypotheses and can be partially tested by experimentation. Attempts were first made to examine the relation of fluctuations in virulence of bacterial parasites to the course of an epidemic. It had been known for quite a long time that the virulence of bacteria decreased when the microorganisms were cultured repeatedly under axenic conditions. It was also known that repeated culture in hosts frequently increased the virulence.

In the first experiments carried out, a microbial parasite, *Salmonella*, was introduced into a group of mice of standard age and size kept in a standardized amount of space. The progression of the consequent epidemic was carefully followed. In other experiments, various factors such as diet or space were altered. It was found that, after a given interval, if a single strain of parasite was used, a certain number of infected mice succumbed to the infection, a certain number became sick and recovered, and a certain number became infected but showed no evidence of disease. The response of individual mice was not uniform but, if batches of twenty or more mice were used, the results for the group were regular and predictable. Using this reproducible pattern, Webster compared the virulence of *Salmonella* from dying host individuals with the same strain isolated from the feces of healthy surviving animals. No differences in virulence could be detected.

Similar results have been obtained by various workers with other microbial parasites and with viruses. There is evidence that different strains of the same bacterial parasites will produce different results when allowed to spread in a susceptible herd of mice. There is also some evidence that a given bacterial parasite may vary in its capacity to infect during an experimental epidemic, but it has not been shown that this influences the progress of the epidemic. On the other hand, analysis of natural epidemics suggests that variation in virulence and in infectivity do occur. It seems probable that change in these characteristics is only an occasional event rather than a usual feature determining fluctuations in disease and death in an extended epidemic (see papers by Webster, 1946; Topley, 1942; Greenwood et al., 1936).

Experiments in Manipulating Epidemics

There is good experimental evidence that such things as the degree of dispersal, distribution, or duration of contact influence the course of an epidemic. The studies of Greenwood and his colleagues (1936) are good examples. In one experiment the effect of discontinuous contact was examined. Twenty-five mice were infected with *Salmonella*. These and 100 uninfected mice were individually kept in separate cages. Three times a week all the mice were herded into a single large cage and 2 new normal infected mice were added at the same time. An epidemic began among the normal mice but soon regressed and after 70 days there were no deaths from mouse typhoid. After 149 days, the population had increased to 180 and there had been no deaths for 80 days. The population was then brought together in one cage. An epidemic appeared and, although addition of 6 new mice per week was continued, the population fell to 44 mice by the 298th day. When discontinuous contact was again imposed, the death rate sank at once and the population rapidly rose to 100. This pattern was maintained up to 15 months, at which time bringing the animals together in one cage again produced an epidemic, reducing the population to 20.

These and various other experiments of this general type have been of aid in interpreting some natural epidemics and have shown quite elegantly that aggregation or dispersal are sufficient to induce major changes in epidemics of some infectious diseases. The role of the diet and of the genetic constitution of host and of parasite are obviously also amenable to experimental study and have been previously mentioned (p. 217).

A valuable contribution to epidemiology has been the observing of the spread and course of infection in populations of mice containing both resistant and non-resistant hosts. This situation would correspond to the Type 2 epidemic. One way in which this has been studied has involved daily addition of a constant number of mice to an infected population over an extended period of time. The addition of non-resistant animals to infected herds containing infected carriers of *Salmonella* tends to prolong the epidemic, whereas the addition of resistant mice has the opposite effect. When the number of non-resistant mice added was small, the death rate in the population varied widely but regularly. However, not until the number of non-resistant individuals reached a certain level did the death rate reach a level which could be termed an epidemic.

Related Studies with Insects

Park (1948) carried out an interesting study on the effects of parasitism and of competition between populations of two closely related species of beetles, *Tribolium confusum* and *T. castaneum*. Park was concerned with the quantitative changes in populations of these flour beetles in the presence and absence of the sporozoan protistan *Adelina tribolii*, which produces a more serious disease in *Tribolium castaneum* than in *T. confusum*. Studies of single-species control cultures of the beetles showed that the population developed, and eventually established, a steady-state number characteristic for each. *Adelina* had a dramatic effect when introduced into populations of *T. castaneum*. The host population dropped in number and established a new and much lower steady state population. *Adelina* had a negligible effect on *T. confusum* populations. When uninfected *T. confusum* and *T. castaneum* were placed together, intense competition ensued, and one of the two species always became extinct; sometimes one species emerged as the viable population and some-

times the other. With *Adelina* present in mixed populations of the two beetles, *T. castaneum*, because of its higher reproductive capacity, increased during the early stages while *T. confusum* declined somewhat. Subsequently, *T. castaneum* showed a marked decline due to heightened mortality as a consequence of epidemic transmission of *Adelina*. At this time, *T. confusum* gradually began to multiply. *T. castaneum* continued to decline until a critically low density was reached and *T. castaneum* finally became extinct. Thus, the combined effects of competition and an epidemic of an infectious agent produced an effect which neither regularly produced alone.

Similarly, Utida (1953) showed that when the bean weevil, *Callosobruchus chinensis*, and the cowpea weevil, *C. quadrimaculatus*, were reared together, the cowpea weevil became extinct. However, if a parasitic wasp was added to such mixed weevil populations, both species of weevils persisted indefinitely. The parasite showed no preference between the two weevil species and brought about increased stability.

Competition and Mutualism

The role of symbiotes in affecting competition between related host species is well illustrated in Slobodkin's (1961) study on the competition between the brown hydra, *Hydra littoralis*, and the green hydra, *Chlorohydra viridissima*. The latter is infected with algal symbiotes. In the light, with brine shrimp available as food, both species increase in number. However, as population density increases, the individual hydras become smaller and smaller. *Chlorohydra*, with its photosynthesizing algal symbiotes, does not become smaller as rapidly as *Hydra*, and the brown form is finally shut off from food by the overwhelming green population and dies out. On the other hand, when mixed populations of hydras were reared in the dark, the two populations were stabilized and both species persisted for an extended period. Slobodkin (1961) discussed the possibility of developing first-order models for systems such as these.

DYNAMIC ASPECTS OF NON-CONTAGIOUS INFECTIONS

We have discussed various parameters in the epidemiology of infectious disease, but up to this point we have treated only those instances in which a parasite spreads by contact of one host with another. However, as we know, many parasitisms involve parasites which leave and/or enter the definitive host body through the offices of an intermediate host. A great deal of information is available on such diseases in man and his domestic animals. The epidemiology of such diseases is frequently complicated by the fact that man may be only one of a number of species of vertebrate hosts. If only man (or some other single vertebrate species) and an arthropod are involved in the biology of the parasitic species, the relationships are less complex than would be the case if several different vertebrates are concerned. In the case of malaria parasites, for example, the biology of the particular vector *Anopheles*, with special regard to breeding places, sites for resting, blood preferences, and climate, must all be taken into consideration. Malaria furnishes an excellent example because the special epidemiology in various localities has been worked out.

It is considerably more difficult to work out a clear epidemiological picture when a parasite is gregarious in its host relationships. An extreme example is *Dermocentroxenus*, the rickettsia involved in the etiology of Rocky Mountain spotted fever. This parasite not only lives in a great variety of vertebrates to which it is transmitted by the bites of ticks, but it is also transmitted from one generation to another among the tick hosts. The epidemiology of Rocky Mountain spotted fever encompasses a large portion of regional ecology. Similarly, epidemiology of a disease transmitted by more than one arthropod will involve broad ecological parameters. An example of this kind is seen in tularemia, the etiological agent being a bacterium of the genus *Pasteurella*. This organism may be transmitted by ticks, flies, or by contact with rabbits. The seasonal changes observed in transmission modes are indicated in Figure 11–1 and are a very gross indication of a complex epidemiology.

It is surprising that little meaningful experimental epidemiology has been pursued with parasitisms in which vector organisms are concerned. However, it is instructive to examine the development of information which has led to understanding of epidemiology and to control of given diseases.

ECOLOGY OF SYMBIOSIS

We are less concerned with the ecology of disease than we are with the ecology of symbiosis. As we have already seen, these concepts are not identical, and we are forced to work with them in quite different ways. One of the difficulties involved is that our thinking on the subject tends to be clouded by medical or veterinary considerations on the one hand or by the thinking of the "pure" zoologist on the other. It is imperative to remove these particular forms of bias if we are to consider them in a general manner.

As pointed out in Chapter 1, the study of symbiosis may be viewed as ecology with a special emphasis. In preceding pages, an attempt has been made to emphasize the symbiotic relationship rather than the symbiotes as organisms. When we therefore arrive at the point of coming right out and talking of ecology, much of what might be said has already been presented. How-

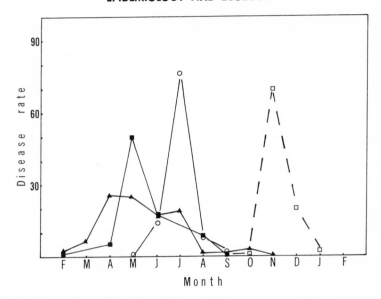

Fig. 11–1   The seasonal prevalence of tularemia transmitted by the ticks, *Dermacentor andersoni* (▲) and *D. variabilis* (■), by the biting fly, *Chrysops discalis* (O), and by contact with rabbits (□). (From data in *Public Health Reports* 52:107, 1937).

ever, certain principles and features may be underscored.

Neither parasites nor hosts nor host-parasites live in a vacuum. They are in an environment which is larger in context than the confines of the digestive tract or of the host body, in the case of the symbiotes themselves. The host-symbiote system may be visualized as existing in general in an environment resembling that of the uninfected host, but, as we have already seen, the responses of the host-symbiote system may differ from that of the uninfected host. Further, although we tend to think that symbiotes differ from free-living animals in the stability of the environment in which they exist, we must bear in mind that the totality of the organism includes its life history. In many cases, there are marked changes in the environment of a symbiotic organism during its life history. The symbiote must obviously have the necessary adaptations for survival during these ecological shifts.

The Ecological Niche of Symbiotes

It will be plain that a symbiotic organism will have a natural habitat in a somewhat delimited ecosystem. The ecosystem may include vectors and definitive hosts; or, in simpler form, it will include the biological complex in which the symbiotic organism lives out its entire life history and produces a new generation. Such an ecosystem is not a static affair and is constantly undergoing shifts and changes of one sort or another. The Russian Pavlovskii has pointed out that such ecosystems or *nidi* may be stumbled upon by man or by man's domestic animals. Man or his animals may then become a part of the ecosystem of the symbiote in a local sense.

Excellent examples of this are seen in rickettsial infections transmitted by ticks. These parasitisms do not require man as a part of the ecosystem for their survival. They have existed and will continue to exist in the absence of man. However, when man enters the ecosystem and is fed upon by infected ticks, he may become a host for the rickettsiae. In the past few years, we have become increasingly aware that many of the diseases of man exist in nature in ecosystems in which man plays a negligible part. Man's involvement is a secondary ecological event resulting from his literally wandering into the ecosystem.

The modern ecologist concerns himself with a community of organisms; in its most sophisticated areas, ecology is no longer concerned with what the organisms are but simply describes the overall energy exchanges of the community in terms of productivity through the agency of the absorption of radiant energy. By examination of energy relationships, it is possible to quantitatively evaluate the control of population size. However, this tells us only that control occurs and that organisms do not disobey the laws of thermodynamics. We must ultimately be interested in mechanisms of control in the finer sense.

The very basic role of symbiosis and of symbiotes in these mechanisms has been implied in the recognition that populations are affected by epidemics of disease. However, our information on the role of symbioses in the biology of communities is rather meager, if we examine those instances in which overt disease is not an impressive part of the parasitism pattern. It would be of great interest to determine the degree to which symbioses affect natural populations. Accurate determinations of the amount of symbiote tissue produced in an ecosystem would be desirable and necessary to an understanding of the relationship of symbiosis to the ecosystem. Such studies have not been carried out, except for certain captive host-parasite systems which are decidedly artificial. Scrimshaw has made a start in this direction by pointing out the necessity for studying the effects of parasitism on nutrition, as well as the effects of nutrition on parasitism (Scrimshaw et al., 1959).

Problems with Ecological Niches

When we come to consider the ecological niche of the symbiote itself, we have to be careful in defining our terms. As indicated above, many symbiotes occupy more than one niche during the course of a life history; it is essential that we study each niche separately but not be led into the trap of generalizing from information on only one of the niches. With this in mind, we may consider the problem of defining the ecological niche of a symbiotic organism (Fig. 11–2). In the case of an organism living in the digestive tract of a vertebrate host, it is not enough to say that it lives in the small intestine. It has become quite plain that there are various kinds of niches in the small intestine and that more rigorous definition is at least possible, although our real information on this subject is somewhat scanty. It is recognized that there are linear gradients in the small intestine as well as in the gut as a whole (see p. 140). In addition, there are gradients from the center of the lumen to the wall of the gut. As a matter of fact, the author has designated the region near the mucosa as the paramucosal lumen and indicated certain properties of this region which would roughly differentiate it on chemical and physical grounds from the lumen proper (Read, 1950). In addition to these features of the environment, the type of food utilized by a parasite in its niche must be considered a part of the definition of the niche. Two ameba species, for example, living in the same portion of the gut, may actually occupy different niches if they feed on different material. *Entamoeba histolytica* and *E. coli* may occasionally show such a relationship.

We may now consider a fundamental question regarding the ecological niches of symbiotes. In 1934, Gause proposed the hypothesis that no two species can share the same ecological niche indefinitely. Our question simply is whether or not symbiotes

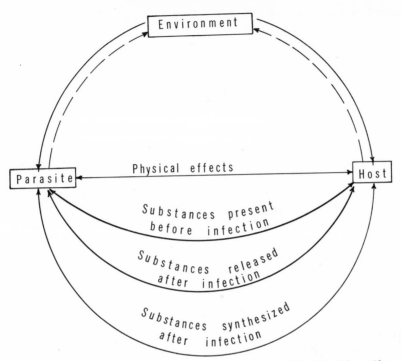

Fig. 11–2 A summary of host and symbiote interactions. (Modified from Shaw, 1967.)

conform to Gause's hypothesis. Studies on trichostrongyle nematode parasites of domestic animals have shown that, although the positions occupied by several given species in a host overlapped to some extent, they differ in their linear distribution in the host gut.

Holmes (1961) has shown that the distributions of two unrelated worms, *Hymenolepis* and *Moniliformis*, overlap considerably when each of those symbiotes is studied in the absence of the other. However, when they are both present in the same host individual, there is a contraction of linear distribution so that there is a considerably reduced tendency for linear overlapping in the host small intestine. Schad (1963) studied the distribution of some closely related oxyuroid worms in the large intestine of the tortoise *Testudo* and found that there is some overlapping in terms of linear distribution. Of great interest was Schad's observation of differences in the

distribution with respect to proximity to the mucosa and the suggestion that there may be real differences in the food habitats of the pinworms involved. The interference phenomena in viral infections of cells may be interpreted as supporting Gause's hypothesis. The available evidence suggests that Gause's hypothesis is valid in the case of symbiotes, but many more data are required before a strong statement on this score is appropriate.

Limiting Factors

It is always tempting to attempt definition of single factors which may limit the distribution of a species. For example, there is a considerable literature relating the distribution of animals to temperature limits of the organism and the prevailing extremes of temperature of the environment. Unfortunately, such studies frequently have been measurements of temperature rather than the great array of other environmental features which vary and may or may not be directly related to temperature. One gets the impression that temperature has often been measured because it is easy to measure rather than because of its fundamental action as a limiting factor of the environment. In some cases, we may see suggestions of complex interactions which may serve as limiting factors for parasitic organisms. Rothman's (1959) delineation of the interaction of pH and bile salt concentration in the inhibition of carbohydrate metabolism in tapeworms may be a case in point, since there are gradients of pH and bile salt concentration in the intestinal environment of these worms. Carbon dioxide gradients may also be important. The competitions between amino acids in their absorption by these same parasites can also be visualized as possible limiting factors in the broad sense, assuming that amino acids are required foods (see p. 155).

It would be of great interest to study possible relationships between temperature and nutritional requirements. The studies of Hutner, Guttman, and their associates have shown that, in free-living and symbiotic Protozoa, the nutritional requirements may undergo rather dramatic changes when the temperature is elevated. Other examples of probable complex limiting factors could be mentioned. However, it should be kept in mind that we are basically dealing with the limitations of organisms themselves. They have limits of variation and can undergo a certain amount of adaptation to the environment in which they find themselves, but there are definite limits to this variation, even on the genetic level.

Environment and Plant Disease

Plant pathologists have devoted an enormous amount of study to those factors of the environment that determine whether a particular organism will live in or on a host plant and produce disease. Since plants are affected much more markedly than

many animals by alterations of the physical nature of the environment, it is not surprising to find that a symbiosis in which a plant is host may be sharply affected by temperature, humidity, oxygenation, hydrogen ion concentration of the soil, and similar factors. We may consider certain such examples of the alteration the host-symbiote relationship.

Study of the geographical distribution of certain diseases of common food plants strongly suggests the importance of temperature. The fungal diseases known as wilts generally occur in more southern areas and are most severe in warm weather. Experimental study has shown that, when host plants are exposed to various soil and air temperatures, the soil temperature is very important in determining the rate and degree of disease development. Further, the amount of growth of the fungi at different temperatures in culture is proportional to the quantity of disease observed at similar soil temperatures. Such a relationship is shown in Figure 11–3. However, the relationship is frequently not so apparently simple. In the case of seedling blight, an-

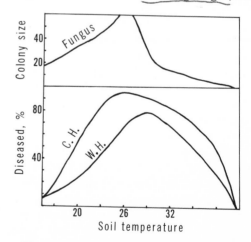

Fig. 11–3 The relation of temperature to the growth in culture of the cabbage yellows fungus, *Fusarium oxysporum,* and to the development of cabbage yellows disease in cabbage seedlings of two varieties, Commercial Hollander (C.H.) and Wisconsin Hollander (W.H.). (Redrawn from data of W. B. Tisdale.)

other fungus disease, the parasite may produce disease in either wheat or corn seedlings. In wheat seedlings the development of disease is greatest at temperatures between 24° and 28°C, which corresponds with the maximum growth rate of the fungus in culture. In corn, however, maximum disease appears in plants maintained at soil temperatures between 8° and 16°C and no disease appears at 28°C. In both cases the fungus is least pathogenic at the temperature which is optimum for growth of the host. There are other examples which show the complexities of the effects of soil temperature.

It may be emphasized that measurement of disease occurrence is not necessarily a measure of the occurrence of symbiosis. To illustrate: It was observed repeatedly that seed potatoes from apparently healthy fields in the northern United States yielded plants with marked symptoms of crinkle mosaic virus disease when grown in southern states. In this instance the northern growing season is during the hot summer months, whereas, in the southern parts of the country, the relatively mild but cool winter months are the main growing season. Under the warmer conditions of the northern summer, disease did not occur although the plants were commonly infected.

The course of symbiosis may be affected by soil moisture, although in some associations this seems to be of little consequence. Soil moisture may influence the infection of plants by potentially pathogenic agents through direct effects upon the pathogen or by effects on the length of the period during which the host is susceptible. The effects of moisture on the fungus causing flag smut disease of wheat (*Urocystis*) furnishes an example. If wheat is sown under very dry conditions and this is followed by rain, spores of the fungus and the wheat seed germinate at the same time and a large number of young wheat plants become infected. On the other hand, if the wheat is sown under wet conditions, subsequent infections of wheat are low in number, ap-

parently because most of the fungus spores germinate before the wheat seed.

Rainfall may be important in another connection. The fungus disease of beans known as anthracnose is hardly known west of the Rocky Mountains. The dissemination of the spores of this parasite is effected by spattering rain. Since beans are nearly always grown in the low-rainfall periods in the western United States, establishment and spread of this disease is prevented.

Hydrogen ion concentration of soil may have an effect on the course or extent of infections of plants although the effects are frequently not very pronounced. One of the most pronounced is seen in the course of infection of potatoes by the scab fungus *Streptomyces*. There is little disease in potatoes grown in soils with a pH of 5.0 or below. The severity of disease increases with pH up to about 7.5.

In many host-parasite combinations the nutrition of the host has an effect on the outcome of the association (see p. 218). The many experimental studies carried out show that generalizations cannot be made. Increasing the concentration of a nutrient or group of nutrients may cause the appearance of pronounced disease in one case and depress the appearance of disease in another. This variation may in effect be a function of either host species or parasite species. Figure 11–4 shows the difference in effect of nutrients observed with two parasites of tomato plants. From the data available, it would seem that the effects of host nutrition on the course of virus diseases of plants may be the only ones showing consistency. As in virus diseases of animals, improved nutrition of the host seems to promote the growth of the infectious agent.

Natural Barriers

A number of different kinds of barriers may act to prevent the coming together of potential associates. The most obvious is a simple geographical one: that is, the

Fig. 11–4 The differential effects of mineral nutrients on the development of *Fusarium* wilt (*top*) and bacterial canker (*bottom*) in tomato plants. The plants on the left were grown in sand containing very limited mineral nutrients. Those on the right were grown with thirty times greater concentration of mineral nutrients. It may be seen that wilt symptoms are increased in plants with weaker nutrient whereas canker symptoms are increased in plants with higher nutrient.

potential host and symbiote are geographically separated from one another and do not come together. It is a common experience to find that some hosts, not found in symbiosis with a particular symbiote in nature, may readily become associated in the laboratory. The golden hamster is a good example. In the laboratory, this animal readily harbors a variety of helminths and protozoans which it never encounters in its natural environment. Historically, our plant quarantine laws came into being because of human transport of pathogenic organisms into areas where susceptible hosts were present but from which the parasites had been geographically isolated.

Another type of barrier has been called *disease escape* by the plant pathologists. In these cases the potential host is not geographically separated but is separated by environmental influences. The potential host may be isolated by temporal factors. For example, the bacterial blight disease of walnut trees is of little consequence in California; new leaves, the susceptible tissues, do not appear until after the rainy season which is essential for infection. On the other hand, in Oregon rain continues for a longer period, extending beyond the period in which leaf tissues are exposed.

Host Density Effects

It will be obvious that an increased density of hosts may increase the probability that an infectious agent will pass from one host to another. When infection occurs directly, without involvement of vector populations, there may be a direct effect of host population density. Ensuing events will of course be modified by age composition of the host population, resistance mechanisms, and rates of genetic change in the population of infectious agents.

In addition to the effects above, physiological stress in vertebrate host populations is thought by some workers to be density-dependent and to be of importance in determining the effectiveness of resistance mechanisms. It is known that crowding of animals, with the ensuing competition for position in a social hierarchy, sometimes, but not always, accompanied by fighting, produces adrenal-cortical changes. These are thought to be mediated through the pituitary, with increased secretion of adrenocorticotrophic hormone (ACTH) and a resulting enhancement of adrenal cortex activity. It is known that the injection of adrenal corticoid substances depresses inflammatory reactions and other resistance responses to a variety of infectious agents. It has been shown that, in laboratory populations of mice, fighting reduces resistance to the nematode *Trichinella* and the tapeworm *Hymenolepis nana,* with parallel changes in the adrenal glands. Further, the higher the position of the individual in the social hierarchy, the less are the effects of fighting on apparent resistance (Davis and Read, 1958; Weinmann and Rothman, 1967).

Other Aspects of Stress

Although stress was related above to host density, it must be emphasized that stress is a major parameter in disease. Selye noted some years ago that in all diseases of humans there are elements of similarity in the first symptoms to appear. These symptoms are non-specific. Selye (1950) related them to changes in adrenal physiology and from his observations developed his concept of the "general adaptation syndrome." The three stages which Selye recognized follow: (1) the alarm reaction, in which the organism has a generalized reaction having many characteristics of inflammation; (2) the resistance stage, in which the response of the adrenal cortex results in some diminution of inflammatory reaction (this can be interpreted as a feedback mechanism operating to maintain homeostasis); and (3) the exhaustion stage in which the demands on the adrenals cannot be met by these organs and the organism, failing in its responses, may die. It is known that a great variety of stimuli are capable of initiating stress in vertebrate animals. In addition to crowding, these include insufficient or inadequate food, abnormal temperatures, electric shock, bright lights, loud noises, and intercurrent infections. Pasteur showed many years ago that non-specific stress could sharply alter the outcome of a symbiotic relationship between chickens and anthrax bacilli. Dubos (1954) discussed this at some length with regard to bacterial symbiotes. Similar effects have been observed in protozoan and helminth infections (Josephine, 1958; Kretschmar, 1965; Robinson, 1961; Sheppe and Adams, 1957; Welter, 1960).

POPULATION EXPLOSION AS EPIDEMIC

Our world is presently concerned in a dilatory fashion with a problem which is potentially at least as dangerous as nuclear war. This is the phenomenon of human population increase which is a most interesting and extremely complicated enigma since its analysis really involves consideration of the social and genetic history of man. The rate of cultural evolution has increased progressively whereas the limited number of genetic characters in the human genetic system may increasingly limit the absolute number of possible mutations. Thus, human genetic evolution should progressively decrease in rate. One of the most dramatic manifestations of the accelerating cultural evolution is the population explosion. The growth of world population is not a recent phenomenon, but the curve of this growth has many characteristics in common with the curve of cultural evolution.

At least two major factors seem to be involved in the population explosion, and these are factors which should have been predictable. Cultural evolution has re-

sulted in the capacity of man to prolong life and to produce more food. Unfortunately, this evolution has not included a marked capacity to control, on a worldwide basis, the rate of reproduction. We might compare this cultural evolution to an epidemic or, as the author referred to it several years ago, examine it as the epidemiology of improved health. If we analogize the transmission of technical information, in this case related to health, to the transmission of an infectious agent, a number of interesting analogies emerge (see p. 284).

SYSTEMS ANALYSIS AND HOST-PARASITE

We have earlier remarked that the application of systems analysis to host-parasite systems may hold the key to development of a science of symbiology. Special attention must be directed to a paper which appeared in the scientific literature in 1969. Ratcliffe et al. (1969) have applied a systems analysis approach to the *Haemonchus*-sheep system (see p. 92). The model developed provides a concise summary of ideas about the relationship known as haemonchosis.

The major lesion in this infection is anemia, which is measured by determining the volume of red cells per unit of blood (the hematocrit value). There is variation in the disease suffered by individual sheep; Fig. 11–5 depicts the variation in hematocrit changes occurring in different individual sheep. We also know that there is an inverse relationship between hematocrit value and parasite egg production (Whitlock, 1966). We are immediately faced with a significant ecological problem: Some sheep differ from others. However, for purposes of analysis, the problem may be generalized.

To account for this variability it is necessary to postulate threshold values for individual animals in a model of parasitic

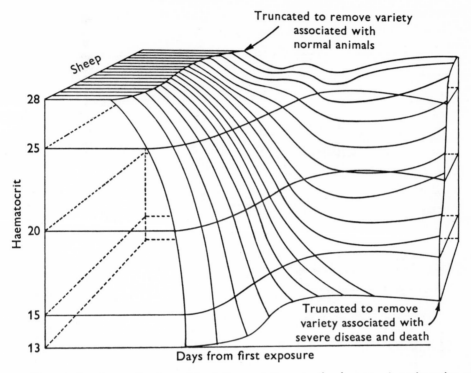

Fig. 11–5 Generalized model of the variations in the hematocrit trajectories of different sheep infected with *Haemonchus contortus*. (After Ratcliffe et al., 1969, with permission of the authors and *Parasitology*.)

mechanisms, as depicted in Fig. 11–6. The model takes into consideration the factors involved in the life cycle of this nematode (pp. 92 and 129) but also recognizes that there are gaps in specific knowledge of the host-symbiote relationship. The continuous lines in Fig. 11–6 represent flows of real quantities; the dashed lines represent flows of information. The variables which must be specified in the actual input for a computer program are enclosed in dashed boxes. The S-shaped symbols denote instances in which provision has been made for some sort of function relating two variables. In programming, all such relationships are simulated by a single subroutine which can compute a great variety of potentially S-shaped functions. The exact

form of the function must be specified for each such relationship. It should be noted that, in a particular relationship, unless the variable exceeds a certain trigger value, the relationship becomes void. The sum of influences is recognized by the single abstract "inhibitor," which is quite satisfactory for analysis of the system.

A postulated model for the regulation of hematocrit in haemonchosis is presented in Fig. 11–7. The symbols used in Fig. 11–7 are similar to those used in Fig. 11–6. In actual computing, the "total erythrocyte volume" is given an initial value. Thereafter, it is updated according to the amounts of erythrocyte loss (which is known to be proportional to the egg production of the worms) and of erythrocyte

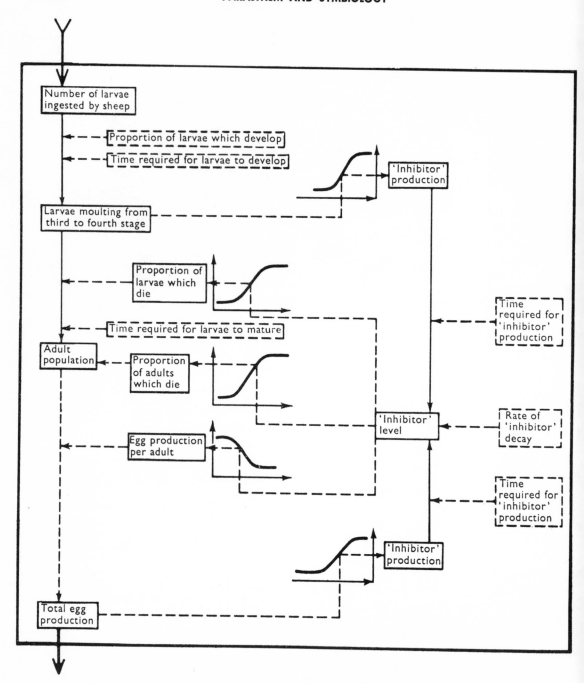

Fig. 11–6 A postulated model of the parasite control mechanism in haemonchosis. See text for discussion. (From Ratcliffe et al., 1969, with permission of the authors and *Parasitology*.)

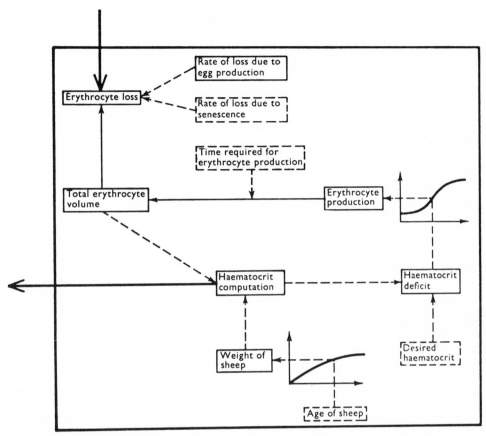

Fig. 11–7 A postulated model of hematocrit regulation. See text for discussion. (From Ratcliffe et al., 1969, with permission of the authors and *Parasitology*.)

production. The hematocrit level is computed by an empirical equation derived from historical data. The subroutine for generating S-shaped curves is again used, at this point for describing weight as a function of time. Although there is probably some feedback relation between the weight of the sheep and other components in the system, no allowance is made for this in the model.

A serious problem in this analysis is that the ratio of erythrocyte loss to symbiote egg production tends to be constant with a given sheep, but varies among sheep. However, by examining the relevant components, Ratcliffe et al. obtained a greatly simplified model of the *H. contortus*-sheep interaction; the model obtained could be used to calculate the trajectories of its variables. Comparison of the model with "live" sheep allowed a realistic explanation of the life-death expectancy of a given individual sheep based on ① the maximum capacity for erythrocyte production in an individual sheep and ② the relationship between erythrocyte production and erythrocyte deficiency in an individual sheep. The authors showed how a simulation model can provide the basis for selecting the specific variables which should be studied and for estimating the quantitative nature of these variables. For details, the original paper should be consulted (Ratcliffe et al., 1969).

GENERAL REMARKS

Some purists, particularly in veterinary science, have argued that it is fruitless to examine symbiosis in laboratory animals and that "understanding" can only come from study under "field" conditions. Unfortunately, such a view makes certain assumptions concerning the area of investigation. "Field conditions" have most often been fenced plots containing domestic animals and seem to be essentially outdoor cages. From the standpoint of epidemiology, they are natural populations of domesticated animals but may be quite different from natural populations of undomesticated animals. Scientifically, there is as much point in studying one system as another, depending on the aims and interests of the investigator, unless the study is constrained to answering a specific question about a specific system. In this case, substitutions are dangerous. Answers to specific questions concerning the diseases of cattle should be sought through the study of cattle rather than of rats. However, studies on diseases of rats may yield information that will be of significance in symbiology, including infectious diseases of cattle.

SUGGESTED READING

ALLEE, W. C., et al. 1949.

AUDY, J. R. 1958. The localization of disease with special reference to the zoonoses. *Trans. Roy. Soc., Trop. Med. Hyg.* 52:308.

BATES, M. 1950. Population as a unit of study. *Cold Spring Harbor Symp. Quant. Biol.* 15:36.

CHRISTIAN, J. J., and D. E. DAVIS. 1964.

DUBOS, R. J. (ed.). 1958. *Bacterial and Mycotic Infections of Man* (3rd ed.). J. B. Lippincott Co., Philadelphia. Especially Chapter 2, The evolution and ecology of microbial diseases. and Chapter 35, Principles of epidemiology.

DUBOS, R. 1964. Environmental biology. *Bioscience.* 14:11.

NOBLE, E. R. 1960. Fishes and their parasite-mix as objects for ecological studies. *Ecology.* 41:593.

PAUL, J. R. 1958.

READ, C. P. 1950.

SCHAD, G. A. 1963.

SMITH, T. 1934. *Parasitism and Disease.* Princeton University Press, Princeton, N.J.

TOPLEY, W. W. C. 1942.

WEBSTER, L. T. 1946.

WHITLOCK, J. H. 1961. Parasitology, biometry, and ecology. *Brit. Vet. J.* 117:337.

WHITLOCK, J. H., J. R. GEORGI, D. S. ROBSON, and W. T. FEDERER. 1966. Haemonchosis: An orderly disease. *Cornell Vet.* 56:544.

WILSON, D. E., E. C. BOVEE, G. J. BOVEE, and S. R. TELFORD, JR. 1967. Induction of amebiasis in tissues of white mice and rats by subcutaneous inoculation of small free-living, inquilinic, and parasitic amebas with associated coliform bacteria. *Exptl. Parasitol.* 21:277.

12

Symbiology and Human Affairs

It seems appropriate to explore quite briefly some aspects of symbiology as they relate directly to the affairs of men. Although many such aspects will have been suggested by preceding chapters, the past and future relations of symbiosis to man's social and economic history merit some special attention. Again, although it will be apparent that the treatment is spotty and anecdotal, references at the end of the chapter will introduce the interested student to additional reading material on some of the subjects mentioned.

A PERSPECTIVE

Although humans often tend to consider themselves outside the struggle for existence in the biological sense, we have not yet been able to liberate ourselves from two aspects of the struggle—the combative competition between ourselves which we call war and our struggles with the symbiotes which cause disease in ourselves, our crops, and our domestic animals. Although we have made enormous progress in our struggles with the agents of disease, and this century may see us escape the burdens of the great epidemics of the past,

our inventive capacities now threaten the destruction of the world because we have not been able to rid ourselves of the physical competition between men nor of our compulsions to despoil the environment. No single epidemic or group of epidemics has ever posed the threat presented by our ingenious machines of war and our reckless pollutions of water, earth, and air.

During the past few years the statement has sometimes been made that man is at the threshold of the complete conquest of infectious disease, and it is indeed true that we now know much of the organisms that are involved in human infectious disease. We know many of the limitations of such symbiotes and have developed a number of methods for controlling them. We seem to be able to evolve some methods almost as rapidly as the symbiotes can evolve; however, even here we have our limitations. The invention of powerful chemotherapeutic drugs, pesticides, and insecticides was followed by the development of symbiote tolerances for these substances, the phenomena of drug resistance. Thus, we have found it necessary to continue to invent new chemical agents, though the symbiotes often seem to work slightly faster than the chemists. Also, it should be pointed out that we have had very limited success in developing chemical agents which will act against viruses.

Human Disease and Social State

Comfortable Europeans and Americans living in the temperate zone frequently fail to recognize that there are millions of people living under almost the same conditions as they lived three thousand years ago. As we have already pointed out, some of our paramedical work has already affected these backward peoples—only, however, when they have not necessitated important social changes. That is to say, if a control measure can be instituted without making people learn to read or to wash their feet every day or to change some social custom, the control measure can be readily applied. However, application of such a control measure may generate an array of new social problems. We have mentioned the effects of malaria control on primitive populations—similar examples could be cited. In spite of our spectacular successes, we still have very far to go in meeting the necessity for improvements in the social and economic conditions of great masses of people, and we have limited mechanisms for bringing about these improvements. These critical needs seem to boil down to two main problems, those of malnutrition and education. We also have not come to grips with the paradoxes introduced when a backward people undergoes cultural change without repeating the histories of advanced nations. The social problems appearing when a people moves from communications by drum to television in a short period are not readily comprehended by the nations whose evolution has been less "instantaneous."

Human Disease and Geography

In these times a disease of a people in the tropics cannot be ignored in other parts of the world. International travel is now more common than interstate travel was only a few years ago. In previous times it took months or even years for a symbiote inhabiting humans to move from continent to continent. Even so, it occurred. Parasites can now move by air from Brazil to New Orleans, or from Dakar to New York in a few hours. Our hygienic isolation of a previous day is gone, and it makes no difference whether we like it or not. The world has become some kind of economic unit, and diseases which affect the production of a food crop in China or of domestic animals in Africa will ultimately affect us economically, since we are tied to the welfare of the underdeveloped countries of the world. We have less than 10% of the world's population on the North American continent and less than 10% of its area. Although we are using something approaching 50% of the products of the free world, we depend on foreign sources for many raw materials. It is obvious that diseases which affect the health and productivity of these areas are of direct economic concern, let alone of humane concern.

In spite of our advances, we are still plagued with perhaps the greatest difficulty of all: ignorance. We expect ignorance to be deep in some of the still primitive people who live in underdeveloped countries, but, unfortunately, we still have many vestiges of it in our own country. We can still find people who feel that vaccination should be abolished or that animal experimentation is completely unjustified. There seems to be a widespread acceptance of what must be termed pseudo-scientific mythology.

It is quite obvious that man's history is intimately related to his understanding of infectious disease, its underlying causation, and its control by the application of scientifically grounded principles of prevention and of specific chemotherapy. This understanding is an important example of a most obvious characteristic of human evolution, an increasing capacity to exert control over the environment. A few examples may illustrate that infectious diseases of man, his domestic animals, and his crops frequently appear to have been decisive in influencing the development of cultures and in altering human history and economic development. Later, we will examine the question of whether or not the conquest of disease is imminent.

LEPROSY

Even today, the word "leprosy" strikes a note of dread. A parasitism involving a bacterium of the genus *Mycobacterium,* human leprosy has been known from ancient times. It is referred to in ancient medical books of Japan, China, and India and is mentioned in several contexts in the Bible. It apparently occurred among the Israelites during their three hundred years of serfdom in Egypt and clearly created difficulties during the Exodus. Measures for quarantine and diagnosis are included in Mosaic law and described in Chapter 13 of the Book of Leviticus. According to the Egyptian historian Manetho, writing in 270 B.C., the Egyptians drove the Israelites from their country because they were lepers, and the plagues described in Exodus lend some credence to the idea. At any rate, the frequency with which leprosy is mentioned in the Bible indicates its prevalence and suggests its effects on the society of the times.

The leprosy bacillus was carried from Egypt to Greece and Italy; the Roman legions carried it to Europe. During the Middle Ages the returning Crusaders brought it into Europe, probably repeatedly, and into Britain. The Church and the Crown took steps in the thirteenth century to fight the disease by elaborate social prohibitions. Lepers were isolated and the Church declared them officially dead. By the end of the fifteenth century, the disease had abated in Europe, although it had spread to the New World and to the islands of the Pacific.

MALARIA

Although healthy Americans of the 1970's are much concerned with being overweight and with the diseases of high living and old age, malaria is still the most important human disease in the world. Our national experience in Viet Nam has shown that we cannot afford to consider malaria only as something of historical interest. How it has affected human populations in the past is difficult to evaluate. In India, for example, a million deaths per year are directly attributed to malaria. However, this does not tell the story of the effects of chronic fevers and illness through the childhood of millions of Indians whose physical and intellectual capacities are debilitated over long periods of time. The peoples of the earth who live between the latitudes of 45 degrees N. and 30 degrees S. have, through the symbiosis known as malaria, operated at a distinct disadvantage in competing economically with humans who live in temperate climates. Malaria, then, may have been a critical determining factor in the continuing cultural development of humans in some areas of the earth and the retardation of cultural development in other areas. However, the effects of malaria can be looked at in different terms. A few years ago, some African leaders pointed out that malaria was desirable from the standpoint of Africans, since it made much of Africa quite unsuitable as a habitat for Europeans.

We now possess powerful new weapons, including understanding of malaria biology, antimalarial drugs, and powerful insecticides, which can be used to markedly reduce, and in some cases eradicate, parasitism of humans by the protozoans of the genus *Plasmodium.* This control of malaria has had and is having marked effects on social, political, and economic developments in the tropical countries of the world. It must be understood that, in those areas having high death rates of infants and children who do not attain reproductive age, there have also been very high birth rates. Some stability of population numbers was formerly maintained by the opposing effects of these rates. Whenever malaria has been brought under partial control, there has been a dramatic increase in numbers of humans, the birth rate remaining virtually uncontrolled. In Ceylon, for example, malaria control is credited with reducing the death rate by three-fourths in a single decade. This reduction was accompanied by an increase in population of 35% in the same ten-year period. Increases of this magnitude result in great difficulties in economic planning, education, and attainment of political stability. In short, the problem of malaria and its control is responsible for many of the global social problems of our day and most certainly is deeply involved in the international antagonisms between the white and non-white people on earth. On the other side of the coin, malaria-causing organisms continue to demonstrate evolutionary ingenuity. United States troops in Viet Nam have had problems with strains of *Plasmodium falciparum* which are resistant to many of the synthetic antimalarial drugs. Malaria thus remains of concern to every human today.

AFRICAN TRYPANOSOMIASES

This group of diseases, involving flagellate protozoans, has had startling and widespread effects on modern African history. Between 1901 and 1905 more than 200,000 people from a population of about 300,000 are believed to have died in eastern Africa, in what was then Uganda. This area included the beautiful country around the Lakes Victoria, Albert, Edward, and George. There is circumstantial evidence that the infection was introduced into Uganda from the west coast of Africa by one of the porters accompanying the explorer Stanley in 1887.

Unlike human trypanosomiasis, the animal disease "nagana" had been recognized for many years in cattle and wild animals. It was mentioned by Livingstone in 1857 and in 1865. The species of trypanosome involved is associated with fatal disease in pigs, goats, sheep, horses, and cattle, although in wild animals the disease is much less severe. Over considerable areas in Africa, domestic animals have not been able to survive for a very long time. However, during the last fifty years the animal disease spread into areas whose native populations were very dependent upon cattle. It was estimated that, by 1946, at least one-half of the area of Uganda Protectorate was uninhabitable by cattle. In one district, Buruli, the cattle dropped in numbers from 13,500 to 150 during the years 1940–1945. The spread of these diseases of domestic animals has intensified the problems of overcrowding of uninfected areas, overuse of arable land, and human nutrition. These problems have contributed to social instability in the region between Kenya and Congo. Political and social stability can be attained in this region of Africa *only* if trypanosomiases are controlled. The European nations, particularly Britain, have poured enormous resources into attempted solutions of this problem during the past fifty years but with little avail. It should be regarded as a world problem, since it seems improbable that the Central African countries can control trypanosomiases on their own.

YELLOW FEVER

A mosquito-transmitted virus in its association with man causes yellow fever, or "yellow jack." It has had dramatic impact on human history, particularly in the Americas. For example, an epidemic of yellow fever is credited with the defeat of the French in Haiti by Toussaint L'Ouverture in 1893. The expensive failure of the French attempt to build a Panama Canal in the 1880's was to a considerable extent due to the terrible toll taken by yellow fever among the Europeans working on the project. When the Americans undertook construction of the Canal twenty-five years later, they devoted the first three years to preparation, including the control of *Aedes aegypti*, the mosquito vector of yellow fever. During the Spanish-American War, more soldiers died from yellow jack than from Spanish marksmanship. The Yellow Fever Commission under the leadership of Walter Reed discovered the mode of transmission in Cuba during this war. This discovery ultimately allowed control of the disease in many densely inhabited parts of the world.

TYPHUS

Epidemic typhus of humans involves a louse-transmitted rickettsial bacterium. As might be expected from the mode of transmission, typhus is associated with filth and poor hygiene and has played a significant role in human history when the human condition was at its ebb. These periods have most often been times of war and famine, but the disease, in earlier times, was common in jails, aboard ships, and in the crowded poor districts of European cities. Because prisoners in English jails were usually infested with lice, typhus was an occupational hazard for medieval judges. It was thought that carrying flowers furnished protection against typhus; hence, the present custom of flowers being carried by judges at the English Assizes.

Typhus in Spain has been considered to have affected the siege of Granada, in 1492, which resulted in driving the Moors from Spain. The disease played a significant role in the Thirty Years' War, and Napoleon's troops were greatly decimated by it during the Russian campaign of 1812. In World War II, typhus is said to have caused more deaths in concentration camps than did mass executions and starvation.

The ways in which the course of European history has been repeatedly altered by typhus has been described in considerable detail by Zinsser in his book *Rats, Lice and History*.

PLAGUE

Often referred to as the "black death," this disease is the result of the interaction of man and a bacterium, *Pasteurella pestis*. Epidemics of plague have affected the course of human history in varied ways. In the Christian Bible (I Samuel, Chapters 5 and 6), a plague outbreak is clearly described. The Philistines had seized the Ark of the Covenant and were visited with an epidemic. This disaster resulted in the return of the Ark to the Israelites because of the belief that the plague was a sign of divine displeasure. The mention of mice in connection with the plague suggests recognition of a relation between plague in man and in rodents (see p. 100).

Plague seems to have been involved in the waning of the Roman Empire. In a great epidemic between A.D. 542 and 594, it is estimated that about half of the population of the empire died. During the following thousand years, epidemics of varying severity occurred in Europe. In the fourteenth century, a devastating epidemic swept over Europe and killed about one-fourth of the population. It is estimated that half the population of England died in this epidemic. The disease smoldered through the fifteenth and sixteenth century and, in the Great Plague of London in 1664–1665, 70,000 of a population of 500,000 succumbed to the disease. An imaginative description of this epidemic is given by Defoe in *A Journal of the Plague Year*. Plague is also referred to many times in Pepys' *Diary*. It has been said that Newton's self-imposed quarantine, while avoiding the danger of plague infection, furnished the solitude needed for the writing of the *Principia Mathematica*.

The pandemic of the late nineteenth and early twentieth centuries was the most widespread in history, since it was carried over the entire world by trade and by travel. Initiated in China, it reached India, where 4.5 million people died from plague between 1903 and 1908. It spread over Asia, to parts of Europe, and to the Americas. Almost every country in the world was affected.

SCHISTOSOMIASIS

This parasitism, involving a trematode, is the most important human disease today attributed to a metazoan symbiote. As a matter of fact, with increased land irrigation during the last few years, schistosomiasis seems to be on the upgrade. In spite of very extensive research attempts, there has been no straightforward and easy cure. Some recent new drugs which can be administered by mouth are reported to have quite dramatic effects, and the pattern of schistosomiasis might change if this proves to be the case. There has been no easy means of controlling this human disease at the population level. In 1947, Stoll estimated that there were 114 million people affected with schistosomes in the world, and Maegraith (1958) considered schistosomiasis as the most serious parasitic disease on the mainland of China and estimated that there were in excess of 11 million infected people in that country. As a matter of fact, the reports coming from Red China have indicated that the Chinese consider this to be one of the most important of their endemic diseases. In the Middle East, schistosomiasis has been blamed as a major factor in the retarded development of such countries as Egypt, where there may be as many as 10 million individuals having chronic infections with this blood fluke. It is difficult to estimate the economic losses produced in those instances for which comparisons have been made, but they are considerable. During the recapture of Leyte in 1944, the infection of American troops caused a loss of over 300,000 working days and direct medical costs of $3 million.

There have been interesting geopolitical effects of schistosomiasis. After the conquest of the Chinese mainland by the Communist forces, the Nationalist Chinese withdrew to the island of Formosa. Formosa then became an important military target for the mainland Chinese government, and direct steps were taken to carry out a military assault on that island in 1950. Troops were moved in large numbers to southern areas of China for training in amphibious warfare. These were Chinese soldiers who had experienced no previous exposure to schistosomiasis. An estimated thirty to fifty thousand military cases of acute schistosomiasis were suffered by the Chinese forces in training and delayed the attack on the island of Formosa by at least six months—the attack originally planned for early 1950. During the delay period, President Truman of the United States ordered the Seventh Naval Fleet into the Formosa Straits to preserve neutrality between the mainland government and that existing on the island of Formosa. If the attack had not been delayed by schistosomiasis, President Truman might well not have made this decision, or would have made it at a time when the assault was actually occurring. This happenstance might have led to war between the United States and China (and perhaps Russia). The six-month delay was too long—the assault on Formosa did not occur and, to the present, no new opportunities for an attack against Formosa have arisen.

HOOKWORMS

Until a few years ago, hookworm was the most important metazoan infection of humans, during this century it has been brought under control in many countries to such an extent that, in many areas where the infection is endemic, it is not a serious public health problem. The effects of hookworm have never been as spectacular as those of some other infectious agents. It is an organism which causes insidious changes in the host. It tends to sap the vitality of the host, undermining the health and general efficiency, and may affect whole communities. Stoll remarked that at one time the Southern United States could well have been termed the "land of hookworm and honeysuckle," and for many years the so-called "poor white trash" in the rural areas of the Southern United States were regarded as lazy and irresponsible people. Plays were written about their poverty and ignorance, and they were regarded as the backward people of the nation. It was discovered that whole communities of these unfortunates were suffering from chronic hookworm disease. This stunted them physically and mentally and grossly interfered with their effectiveness. From this, we are today still reaping a harvest of social and economic backwardness, although hookworm disease has been largely conquered in the Southern United States. Its effects, along with those of malaria, were debilitating of a culture and it may be anticipated that, with the removal of these two factors, the South will develop a cultural level consistent with that of the remainder of the nation. It should be pointed out that we are talking about decreases in disease which have occurred since 1920.

It is fascinating to speculate that some of the interracial tensions existing in the United States have come to the stage of social expression because of the conquest of hookworm disease and malaria in the southern states. This change led to better general health, allowing a rise in the level of social aspirations, along with migration from rural to urban areas. Social revolutions cannot be mounted by men who are seriously debilitated by hookworm disease and malaria, these infections often being accompanied by malnutrition.

HUMAN DISEASE AND "EMPIRE"

Examination of the distribution and redistribution of people during the past hundred years shows that people with advanced technology (mainly firearms) were able to penetrate, conquer, and permanently colonize only those parts of the world in which they could bring infectious human disease under some control, or at least not be stricken with an array of new agents of disease. Thus, we find that Europeans conquered southern Africa, New Zealand, Australia, and parts of South America, while Europeans and Africans invaded and colonized North America. In the tropical regions of the world, Europeans were forced mainly to restrict their activities to financing and supervising the activities of native populations. Tropical Africa and India, for example, essentially remained in the hands of indigenous populations. Europeans could not cope with malaria, cholera, yellow fever, and a great multiplicity of other infectious diseases. Central Africa was a graveyard for adventurous Europeans, and there is no denying the central role of infectious agents in determining the history of African nations.

HUMAN LOSSES INVOLVING PLANTS

From the purely monetary standpoint, diseases of plants have caused losses of great magnitude. Before the twentieth century, forests of chesnut trees extended from New England to the southern Appalachians. About 1904, it was recognized that a new disease had appeared among these trees. It was found that the disease was attributable to infection with a previously unknown fungus, *Endothia parasitica*. Within a few years, the mortality of American chestnut trees had resulted in the virtual total loss of the eastern chestnut forests. There is some evidence that the fungus originally entered the United States on nursery stock from the Orient, where the host trees apparently have a low mortality as a result of the infection. The monetary loss of our chestnut forests and the prevention of their future establishment probably far exceeds the costs of all plant quarantine measures which might have been instituted to prevent such disasters.

The Fate of Elm Trees

The American elm tree has been described as the most beautiful of native trees. In American history, this tree has assumed a certain symbolism. William Penn, in 1682, negotiated his "treaty of purchase and amity," giving him title to Pennsylvania, under an elm tree. In 1765, the Sons of Liberty voiced their opposition to the Stamp Act in the shade of American elms. In 1775, Washington assumed command of the Continental Army beneath an elm tree on Cambridge Common. Daniel Boone convened the first government of Kentucky under an elm at Boonesboro. It has been a venerated plant in America. The American elm is subject to a number of diseases, involving fungi and viruses. However, until 1930, none of these diseases were epidemic in character and there was little reason to believe that this tree might become extinct.

In the summer of 1930, five dying elm trees were found in Ohio. They were infected with a fungus, *Ceratocystis ulmi,* previously associated with a European tree malady known as Dutch elm disease. It was known that the fungus is carried from tree to tree by elm bark beetles of the genus *Scolytus.* The origin of the disease in Ohio remained a mystery, but, in 1933, it appeared in explosive epidemics in New Jersey, New York, Connecticut, and Maryland. It was then discovered that infected elm burl logs were being imported from Europe and an embargo on such importations was put into effect. However, it was too late. In spite of costly programs to destroy infected elm trees, the disease has continued to spread. By 1946, full-scale epi-

demics were in progress in twelve states, and, by 1953, in twenty states. The entire range of the American elm has become involved, and it is now clear that the species is doomed. There are no practicable methods for control, and future generations, reading Oliver Wendell Holmes' *Autocrat of the Breakfast-Table,* may wonder what Holmes is talking about when he asks, "What makes a first-class elm?"

Wheat and Rust

In 1916 a rust epidemic destroyed almost 300 million bushels of wheat in the United States and Canada. The epidemic was ruinous to thousands of farmers, who were forced to give up farming. In 1935 the same disease destroyed 135 million bushels of wheat in the United States, primarily in the Dakotas and Minnesota. The direct losses to farmers were amplified by reduction in the quality and price of wheat occurring at the same time. The loss of the purchasing capacities of the farmers affected business in the entire wheat-growing region. This economic disaster was followed by another epidemic in 1937, when wheat was struck again by epidemics in Minnesota and the Dakotas. More recent losses were very well documented. For 1953 South Dakota suffered an 80% loss of the crop of durum wheat, and in 1954 a 75% loss. These epidemics appear in a more or less regular fashion but without much warning. One astonishing feature of all this is that urban man hardly realizes the direct cost to himself. It has been pointed out that, for every two potatoes that are brought to him in a restaurant, he pays for one he does not get, and, for every six cotton garments he buys, he pays the cost of an additional one which has been lost through diseases of cotton.

Costs and Control

Unfortunately, the costs of preventing damage by plant diseases are sometimes almost as great as the costs of the damage produced when the disease is left unchecked. The investments in machinery, chemicals, labor, and transportation add up to large sums. As a consequence, it is apparent that new approaches to control of plant diseases, particularly those caused by fungi, are urgently needed. There are virtually no methods of biological control developed for fungal plant diseases.

In those countries in which there are chronic shortages of food, the role of plant disease is quite critical, and it can be expected that it will become more critical. The fact that there are many millions of new mouths to feed every year cannot be brushed aside. The rates of human multiplication are not likely to be suddenly thrown into reverse. The study of symbiosis thus will ultimately help alleviate food problems by leading to new control measures and improvements of old control measures. We must learn to control many more diseases in a better way. This will require much more experimentation and research.

PLANT DISEASE AND HUMAN DESTINY

A Potato-Fungus Symbiosis and the Election of a President

The potato was introduced into Europe from South America in the sixteenth century and after a couple of hundred years had expanded to a major food crop. About 1830 a disease of potatoes was recognized and termed "late blight." This resulted from infection by a fungus, *Phytophthora infestans,* a symbiote long associated with wild potaotes. During the next few years the disease spread, increasing in extent and in severity, culminating in a widespread epidemic on the European continent in 1845. By this time Ireland had become heavily dependent on potatoes as a source of food and a serious famine resulted from the failure of potato crops in 1845 and 1846. Of a population of about 8 million,

more than a million died of starvation. This terrible famine, together with a somewhat backward social and political situation, led to the emigration of hundreds of thousands of Irishmen to the United States. It was, of course, also a quite decisive factor in other alterations in the social and economic policies of Ireland and subsequently contributed to the separation of Ireland from the United Kingdom. The Irish famine, then, was an important causal factor in promoting the great influx of Irishmen which occurred throughout the last half of the nineteenth century. After the Irish colonization of New York, Boston, and other cities on the eastern seaboard, other Irishmen migrated to the United States. In this migration were representatives of the Kennedy family. In the new country this family prospered and ultimately one of them was elected President of the United States. There is a probability that if a potato disease epidemic had not occurred, the Kennedys would have remained in the British Isles.

This potato famine also had an enormous stimulatory effect on the field of plant pathology and may actually represent the start of what might be called the modern development of plant pathology as an area of applied science.

How the English Became Tea Drinkers

Up until the middle of the nineteenth century, consumption of coffee in England was at least equal to that of tea. Ceylon, as well as India, Malaya, and Java, was one of the great coffee-producing countries of the world, and of course part of the British Empire. About 1867, there appeared in a coffee plantation in Ceylon a disease known as coffee rust. This involved a fungus symbiote, *Hemileia vastatrix.* This organism produced a serious disease of coffee plants and spread quite rapidly through the agency of wind, the spread also being enhanced by the large-scale growth of coffee over considerable areas. By 1871 the yield of coffee in Ceylon had dropped more than 50%, a loss of millions of dollars. By 1893, exports of coffee had dropped to less than 7% of those preceding the appearance of coffee rust. This essentially ended large-scale coffee growing in Ceylon, as well as in other East Asian countries. The Oriental Bank and the Ceylon planters were economically ruined by this catastrophe.

Following this course of events, Brazil became the main coffee-producing country of the world. Since coffee was purchased preferentially within the British Empire, the British were not anxious to shift the market to Brazil; so they changed their beverage habits. Although coffee and tea were consumed in somewhat equal amounts in the 1850's, by the twentieth century this had changed to a six-to-one ratio. This change can be attributed to the trade relations within the British Empire, and it is difficult to know whether it is continued now because of the Commonwealth economic framework or by perpetuation of habit.

HISTORY AND CAUSALITY

Some of the preceding paragraphs have ascribed historical roles of causality to some symbioses. It must be emphasized that, as history is usually written, these examples have been taken out of context. They do not detail the variety of other variables of the physical and social environment, the modifiers of infection and of disease. As will be obvious, considerably more information could be presented. Unfortunately, there would also remain much that is beyond historical recall. Even so, it may be seen that there is no simple cause and effect relationship in any case. For example, the movement of human trypanosomiasis from one part of Africa to another may not be ascribed simply to trypanosomes and their vectors. A human carrier was probably involved and an unwise hiring decision, in selecting a man to act as

guide or bearer, may have been implicated in the complex of causality. Perhaps an unwise human decision was made because an episode of relapsing malaria or an argument with his wife clouded the judgment of the employer who retained the services of a man suffering from sleeping sickness. Or, in another case, the Irish famine attributed to potato disease could only be a famine because the Irish had concentrated on potato-raising during the preceding fifty years. Thus, the prevalence of the potato itself, the prevalence of people depending on potatoes, a weak industrial economy, political unrest, and two unusually wet cool seasons were implicated as causal factors. The complications of disease phenomena in a context of historical causality thus resemble the complexities of symbioses as discussed in preceding chapters.

BIOLOGICAL CONTROL

The use of symbiotes which affect insect pests is an applied aspect of symbiology which has come into its own in the past few years. Symbiotes involved include viruses, bacteria, fungi, protozoans, and nematodes. Microbial control has mainly relied on two methods: (1) the direct introduction of a pathogenic symbiote with the aim of establishing it in an insect population and reducing it over a period, or (2) direct application of a pathogenic symbiote for rapid control, much like application of an insecticide.

Steinhaus (1955) suggested a new approach to biological control: If the environment of a pest organism can be altered to destroy its required mutualistic symbiotes (see p. 58) or to cause symbiotes to exert pathogenic effects, control of the pest might be accomplished. It may be further suggested that the introduction of pairs of symbiote species might produce pathogenic effects not produced by either symbiote when introduced alone. Virtually no experimental work along this line seems to have been done, although there is information on the synergistic action of pathogenic symbiotes of insects (Vago, 1963).

There are a few cases in which quarantine, or the exclusion of an organism, has resulted in protection from exposure to an infectious agent. Although it must be said that national quarantine legislation was enacted by European countries by 1875, the United States Congress refused to enact legislation until 1912, after much introduction of disease agents and vectors had occurred. Quarantine regulations at the state level have been of some benefit. For example, the spread of a bacterial disease, citrus canker, to the important citrus groves of the lower Rio Grande valley, California, and Arizona has been prevented by state quarantine measures, although the infection was introduced into the United States from the Orient between 1908 and 1911 and remains endemic in Alabama, Mississippi, and Louisiana.

In the use of symbiotes for long-term biological control, one of the most successful in the past twenty years has involved the use of *Bacillus popilliae* and a related species in the control of the Japanese beetle in the Eastern United States, and the use of viruses for the control of forest insects in Canada. In most cases, this type of control seems to be most successful against non-native insect pests. In some instances, more than one species may be used quite successfully against a single host. For instance, a fungus which acts against the spotted alfalfa aphid in Southern California during the winter is aided by the introduction of a parasitic wasp, *Praon,* which operates at a different season of the year. Thus, the two symbiotes are not in any sort of direct competition on a time scale.

When microbial control is used for short term elimination of insect pests, problems arise concerning the production of these agents and, as with chemical control measures, complex production methods are necessary. In addition, the methods of application are different, requiring the development of spray procedures or baiting for effective control. The residual activity of agents used in this way will also vary greatly. This latter character is of considerable importance in the case of one of the most useful bacterial symbiotes used in short term control, namely *Bacillus thuringiensis,* which has a very high residual effect. In addition to the mentioned problems, standardization of a microbial preparation becomes very important and requires the development of bioassay techniques usually utilizing selected insect hosts. Thus, short-term control methods are those involved in factory production.

Although attempts to utilize microorganisms to control insect pests has been underway for more than sixty years, during the past decade the advances and efforts in this area have markedly increased. One of the reasons for this has been the widespread appreciation of the difficulties and dangers in the use of chemical insecticides, many of which dangers do not exist with symbiotic specific pathogens. Some of the problems of microbial control of pests have been discussed by Hall (1963), and problems concerning the commercial production of symbiotic pathogens for insect pests have been discussed by Briggs (quoted in Steinhaus, 1963).

A recent additional new approach may involve the use of compounds which exert hormonal activity in insects but have negligible effects on plants or vertebrate animals. The interesting discovery of a ready plant source of such substances was made by Williams when he found that newsprint of the *New York Times, Boston Globe,* and *Wall Street Journal* contained insect juvenile hormone activity.

DYNAMIC EFFECTS OF PARASITISM

It has been repeatedly observed that the introduction of a parasitic form into a host population, having no previous historical experience with the parasite, often results in the appearance of serious disease. The terrible effects of smallpox or measles when newly introduced into human populations have been observed in American Indians, Eskimos, Hawaiians, Easter Islanders, and other isolated groups. In many cases, native populations have been so weakened by diseases introduced by European invaders that resistance to invasion was sharply reduced. When Captain Gosnold explored the New England coast in 1602, the Indians were a vigorous people. Within a few years their numbers in this region had been reduced by more than 90%, probably through the introduction and subsequent epidemic spread of smallpox. After the introduction of rinderpest virus into Africa in the 1880's, it was estimated that 80% of the cattle in the continent died from the ensuing disease.

The eventual changes occurring in a susceptible population after introduction of a "new" parasite have been described in the case of myxomatosis virus and rabbits in Australia (p. 218). Although it is not possible to obtain experimental data to prove the point, it seems probable that the smallpox and plague epidemics which swept Europe several centuries ago resulted in the selection of a human population with less susceptibility to these agents than before. As a matter of fact, the classical form of plague has almost disappeared. The discovery of cases, involving American soldiers in Viet Nam, showing the classical seventeenth-century form of the disease created a considerable stir in medical circles.

"FREEDOM" FROM DISEASE?

Man's outstanding adaptation is his capacity to exert control over his environment by mechanisms which are traditional, and thus epigenetic, rather than by mechanisms which are genetically stereotyped and hence of limited flexibility. Man does not have to wait for the accumulation and recombination of genetic mutations in order to make striking alterations in his behavior.

This capacity for response is nowhere better seen than in man's ability to bring new methods to bear in the control of undesirable symbioses involving himself or his domestic plants and animals as hosts.

It must be made clear, however, that there is virtually no probability of some sort of disease-free Utopia in which man and his associated animals and plants will be free of symbiotes and hence free of infectious disease. In preceding chapters, we have sampled a number of types of symbiosis, some of which involve man as a host, and it may be reiterated that symbiosis is almost a characteristic of the state of being alive. Being alive includes, as a primary feature, the capacity for mutability, and we are struck by the evidence presented in Chapters 9, 10, and 11 that symbiosis is not a static affair. The nature of the interactions between host and symbiote undergoes continuing change with time. Examples cited earlier in this chapter may be examined in these terms. In many cases, a disease has even disappeared without rational human intervention. For example, English sweating sickness, which struck Tudor Britain in epidemic proportions, appeared several times over a 75-year period and disappeared. It seems unlikely that the symbiote actually disappeared; its descendants are probably living among us today. It is important to emphasize that the disappearance of sweating sickness does not seem to have involved the exertion of human control.

The mysterious comings and goings of infectious disease in the short span of recorded history support the view that man's experiences with his symbiotes have been a series of unplanned adventures and will continue to be so in the future. The recent experiences of the highly modernized United States Army with *falciparum* malaria in Viet Nam suggest that our information on the mutability of these much-investigated parasites is still grossly deficient. The parasites were drug-resistant and produced a high fatality rate. The disease was brought under control with difficulty. The recently discovered possibility of an animal reservoir of malaria is further evidence that the ingenuity of nature will continue to furnish surprises. Similarly, the discovery by Reed and his co-workers that the yellow fever virus is transmitted by the mosquito *Aedes aegypti* led to mosquito control, and for a time in 1927 it was believed that yellow fever had been eradicated in the Western Hemisphere. This was swiftly followed by the disillusioning discovery that the virus persists in a variety of wild animals in tropical America, where it is transmitted by *Haemogogus,* a mosquito living in the jungle canopy. In recent years, outbreaks have occurred in Central America and Trinidad. These are specific cases in which man believed for a short time that he had indeed brough a specific infectious disease under control. Other kinds of "unplanned" complications arise when we examine the development of viruses. There is evidence that many viruses grow more rapidly and produce more dramatic cytological effects in well-nourished animals than in poorly nourished animals. Is it not a paradox that the well-fed, middleclass American may be more prone to virus-induced disease than his fellow citizens in some of the underdeveloped nations?

Burnet's suggestion that most of man's infectious diseases have appeared within the last 10,000 years must be a qualified interpretation of genetic and evolutionary history. In his relations with his symbiotes, man has differed from other kinds of hosts for a relatively short period of time. Man probably began to be less like other wild mammals when he adopted some kind of agriculture. About that time, man became "domesticated," and this may have initiated the development of disease patterns which some have regarded as characteristic of human populations. However, man certainly did not live some kind of utopian life without disease when he lived a roaming

feral life. From the examination of disease patterns in other feral mammals, we may conclude that the patterns of man's infectious diseases have undoubtedly been modified by his social history and, as indicated above, he has probably gained or lost symbiotes with the passage of time. Even in recorded history, man's patterns of disease have changed as he has lived in a more and more collectivized urban system.

"Reason" and Disease

Only with the recognition that an infectious disease was a manifestation of interaction between a host and a symbiote could man bring to bear some measure of *rational* prevention, treatment, and cure. However, the evolution of symbioses in time means that man is in the anomalous position of having to keep up with evolution in his struggle to exert control. Is this a gloomy prospect? I think not. It simply promises that human life can continue to be a series of exciting and adventurous responses to the environment rather than a sterile sameness of life in a world not worthy of examination.

Periodically, such statements as these are heard: "Parasitology, plant pathology, and bacteriology are on the way out. The conquest of infectious agents is around the corner and these fields will be obsolete." Such a statement is sheer rubbish. Methods will change; formulation of problems will change, but man's search for control of new and changing symbioses will go on indefinitely. When we carefully examine the common human infectious diseases which have been brought under some measure of control, we are struck by the fact that they are mainly the diseases of childhood. The reduction in death rates is mainly in the young. After the attainment of middle age, the probability of dying is not much different in the United States from what it was fifty years ago. The uncertainty of our control is exemplified by the occurrence of a virus disease in the astronauts of the lunar Apollo 8 mission in late 1968, which was, of course, a technological achievement of the highest order.

HAZARDS IN DISEASE CONTROL

In the search for disease control, serious side effects arising from the hasty application of new methods have frequently led to great arrays of new problems. It is fortunate, in some cases, that some suggestions for control of symbioses have not been effected, since later appreciation of the problems showed that a disaster was probably avoided by forbearance. For example, trypanosomiasis of domestic animals in Africa is a symbiosis having very serious pathogenic consequences. In contrast, many wild animals harbor the trypanosomes without the appearance of disease. After it was shown that these wild animals constituted a reservoir from which transmission of the trypanosome to domestic stock occurred, it was seriously suggested by some British workers that the large game animals of Africa should be systematically exterminated. Fortunately, this was not carried out. Leaving out of consideration the conservation of African animals for its own sake, the upset produced in the natural economy of Africa by the *planned* extermination of wild game would have had far-reaching ecological effects, some of which are undoubtedly unpredictable even today. The effects would have been much worse than the haphazard but slower extermination which is still in progress. In other instances, the hasty and broad application of a control method has actually led to serious complications. For example, the widespread use of insecticides has had undesirable side effects, some of which could be discerned but were not taken into consideration. The accumulation of certain insecticides in streams has led to the wide-scale death of species for which death was not a desired result. Birds are quite sensitive to some of these insecticides and their wide use has markedly affected some bird populations. The accumulation of some insecticides in the depot fat of certain domestic animals destined for human consumption was another such undesired effect. We are still reaping the new problems engendered by the wholesale use of insecticides although there is now slightly more temperance in their use. It remains to be determined whether the broad use of insecticides may have worse effects on human welfare than would some of the insects which they were designed to control.

THE DILEMMA OF NOW

Mention was made in Chapter 11 of the problems presented by human numbers. These have been and are being discussed by most educated persons. However, an additional remark must be made in relation to symbiology. An interesting paradox exists in that the continued lessening of epidemic disease as a control of population numbers has paralleled our development of war technology. Since we have not been capable of developing rational working mechanisms for population control, the use of war machines to this end seems almost inevitable. In addition to infectious disease, primitive man had behavioral controls on population size, including ritual sacrifice, head-hunting, cannibalism, castration, rigorous rituals for entering adulthood and marriage, and infanticide. None of these appear to be acceptable to modern man, but, with few exceptions, he has made no comparable behavioral substitutions.

The application of methods of infectious disease control has had the most dramatic effects in countries which are unprepared for large increases in population. Our neighboring country Mexico is a good example. Since 1930, at which time reliable

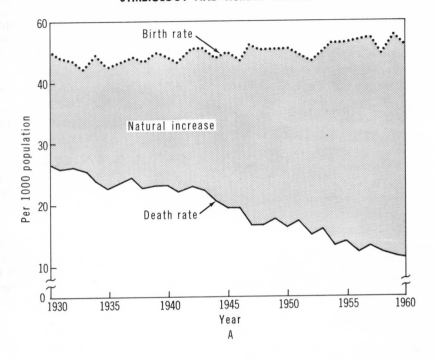

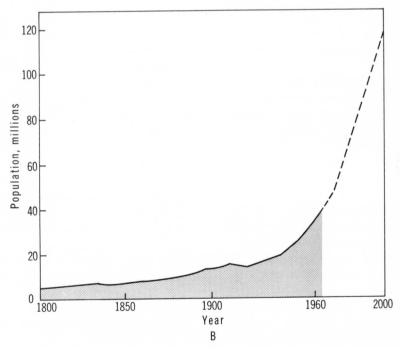

Fig. 12-1 *A.* The maintenance of high human fertility and the declining death rate in Mexico. *B.* The increase and predicted increase in the human population of Mexico. (From *Population Bulletin,* November, 1964.)

statistics became available, the birth rate in Mexico has hardly changed. It has averaged about 45 births per year per 1,000 population. During this same period the application of the new knowledge in public health, primarily in the prevention and treatment of infectious disease, spread over the world. Mexico along with many other countries, put this new knowledge to use. The mortality rate changed from 26.6 in 1930 to 10.4 in 1963. Thus, with the change in difference between these two rates, rapid population growth has ensued (Fig. 12–1). It is estimated that the Mexican population will grow from 34.9 million in 1960 to about 70 million in 1980. Can social and economic progress remain compatible with this rate of population growth? It seems doubtful.

The picture is even gloomier in countries such as Pakistan, which are less advanced than Mexico. Pakistan's population is expected to triple from its 103 million in 1965 to over 300 million in the year 2000. The reasons for this precipitate growth are similar to those described for Mexico. The birth rate in Pakistan has remained at a high level of 55 per 1,000, while the death rate has plunged from 40 to 29 between 1920 and 1965. This decrease in death rate is one of man's finest public health achievements. However, the prospects for the future are frightening. Living levels in Pakistan are already among the world's lowest, with an annual per-capita income of $80. Of the population 1% has the equivalent of a high school education; 80% cannot read.

President Ayub Khan said in 1965, "In 10 years' time human beings will eat human beings in Pakistan." When he visited the United States in 1961, he said to the people of this country, "You have the scientific knowledge, the technical know-how and the means for necessary research, and I think unless some sort of pill, some sort of drug or injection is produced which can neutralize a person *with one shot*, there will be no real answer, and I think the quicker this is realized here in the United States, the quicker we will find the answer."

Fallout from atomic weapons would accomplish the purpose, but is this the solution we choose for the problems introduced by the control of infectious disease?

CREATIVE ASPECTS OF SYMBIOSIS

We have detailed in preceding chapters many manifestations of symbiosis which are creative in character. These have been described in considerable detail in a few cases, quite inadequately described in others, and there are large numbers that are hardly described at all. The cases in which man has utilized the creative aspects of symbiosis are relatively few as compared with a number of instances in which he has developed methods for preventing or disrupting the destructive symbioses manifested as disease. Recent attempts to develop closed life systems for space travel in some cases involve symbiotic organisms, but we have only begun to investigate the power possibilities of symbiosis in this kind of system. Many other creative aspects readily suggest themselves but are essentially uninvestigated. The information on the lysogenic phages suggests the possibility of utilizing viruses to introduce genes which may be deficient in an individual. The phenomena of transduction suggest that such an idea is not at all farfetched. Attenuated viruses or bacteria, developed many years ago, which could be used as vaccines, have proved to be valuable in several cases. The so-called live polio vaccine is a case in point; however, even here we have not followed this up in as broad a fashion as would be possible. Great numbers of organisms might be developed as attenuated forms and furnish protection against disease agents. This has not been systematically explored with certain groups of parasitic agents.

A deep understanding of the mechanisms of nitrogen fixation occurring in the legume-*Rhizobium* symbiosis might yield information of enormous value in developing crops of symbiotic nitrogen-fixing organisms. One of the greatest problems of man on this planet will soon be that of obtaining enough fixed nitrogen to exist. This potential deficiency is related to one of the two most important human problems—that of malnutrition.

A mere handful of investigators have concerned themselves with the biology of lichens. Since these symbioses flourish under conditions which do not allow development of either of the component organisms, they furnish an unusual material for examining integrative processes which are highly creative in character.

The known role of symbiotes in degrading compounds such as cellulose, making available products which can be utilized by animals, would also bear broad exploration as a possible method for increasing production of animal tissue for human consumption or of making wood available as a food for human consumption. The production through photosynthesis and excretion of the carbohydrates, maltose and glycerol, by algal symbiotes offers exciting possibilities for the production of food substances. The erection of enormous hard structures in the sea, known as coral reefs, largely attributed to the joint activities of coral polyps and their symbiotes, suggests the possibility of utilizing a controlled symbiosis for the erection of undersea structures, dams, and similar installations. We need to know much more about the rates at which such activities might be carried on under controlled conditions.

Development of the creative aspects of symbiosis opens a whole world for the application of human genius to the age old problem of the control of the environment. It seems probable that there is an enormous range of yet undiscovered creative possibilities which invite investigation by creative minds.

INFECTIOUS DISEASE— SOME FUTURE PROSPECTS

With the wide recognition that various cancers of man and his domestic animals are manifestations of virus–host-cell associations, the study of oncogenic (tumor-inducing) agents is a rapidly developing area of symbiology. It is clear that understanding of these systems may hold not only answers to the problems of preventing and treating malignant tumor diseases but also new keys to the riddle of cellular differentiation and its control.

Recent developments in virology have brought to light a number of symbioses which have very broad implications in human disease problems. In 1954 Sigurdsson suggested that certain diseases of sheep which develop over a long period of time were what he termed "slow infections." Subsequently it was shown that certain "wasting" diseases are viral in character and indeed conform to Sigurdsson's ideas. As an example, visna, a central nervous system disease of sheep, appears several years after intracerebral inoculation of virus material. Several years may be required for the disease to run its course. The example in Figure 12–2 shows the course of an infection. In this case, the animal was killed after 8 years, at which time it had developed some paralysis of the hind legs. It has been pointed out that, in this type of symbiosis, several years may elapse from the time of infection to the onset of illness. Hence, a causal relationship between these two events may be difficult to realize. Some slowly developing fatal diseases of animals, and man, of unknown etiology should be reconsidered as possible virus-induced entities (Thormar and Palsson, in Pollard, 1967).

Leader (1967) has presented arguments

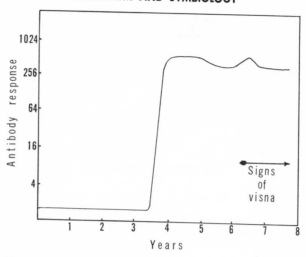

Fig. 12–2 The course of the slow virus disease visna in a sheep. The animal was inoculated with an infective brain suspension and was killed almost eight years later. (From data of Thormar and Pálsson, 1967.)

supporting the hypothesis that a number of chronic degenerative diseases of man are of virus etiology. These include multiple sclerosis, amyotrophic lateral sclerosis, kuru disease of New Guinea, rheumatoid arthritis, rheumatic fever, polyarteritis, systemic lupus, and diffuse scleroderma of man. Analogous diseases of animals, known to involve viruses, include scrapie of sheep, visnu and maedi of sheep, and Aleutian disease of mink. The medical and scientific community has shown little interest in the possibility that many of the chronic and degerative diseases of man may involve virus-host cell symbioses which undergo slow modification with time. Experimental work in this field will be difficult unless new "model" systems are developed. The slowness of the appearance of disease is in itself a discouraging prospect for the experimentalist. However, there is a distinct possibility that myocardial and circulatory diseases, chronic nephrosis, obstructive pulmonary diseases (such as emphysema), a variety of central nervous diseases, collagen diseases, and even some metabolic diseases, such as diabetes, may have their origins in symbioses involving viruses.

Although it may be premature to make a sweeping hypothesis, I cannot refrain from suggesting that aging of organisms may be a long-term manifestation of the cumulative effects of "slow" viruses as discussed above. In vertebrates, the major symptoms of aging include death of individual nerve cells, increased deposition of collagen, and modification of elastic fibers. These are symptoms which might be related to the slow growth of symbiotes which furnish increasing amounts of genetic information resulting in cell death or modification of cell function. Such an hypothesis has much to support it and would merit investigation.

It may be seen that the broad horizons of symbiology may encompass such problems as the significance of the finite life history in organisms, the evolution of new life forms, and the implications of man's relationships with other living things.

If we think of symbiology in the broadest terms as it applies to the affairs of men, certain analogies suggest themselves. For example, the transmission of information from one individual to another may be analogized with infection by a symbiote. Transmission may result in various changes in the recipient (host?). On occasion, the results may be socially pathological, while in many cases the results are beneficial. Transmission may be air-borne (verbal) or by utensils (books). The resulting "infections" may differ, depending in part on the mode of transmission. The ease with which transmission occurs may be modified by the state of susceptibility which may in turn depend on previous "infection." In some instances, a high state of resistance may be induced by previous administration of a modified form of the "agent" (vaccination?). This analogy could be pursued further and it might be profitable to apply the methods of epidemiology to it.

SUGGESTED READING

BLUM, H. F. 1963. Evolution reconsidered. University, A Princeton Magazine 17:3. (also, Amer. Sci. March, 1963).

BURNET, M. 1966. *Natural History of Infectious Disease* (3rd ed.). Cambridge University Press, London and New York.

CAREFOOT, G. L., and E. R. SPROTT. 1967. *Famine on the Wind*. Rand McNally & Co., New York.

DUBOS, R. 1961. *Mirage of Health*. Doubleday & Co. (Anchor), Garden City, N.Y.

DUBOS, R., and J. DUBOS. 1952. *The White Plague—Tuberculosis, Man and Society*. Little, Brown & Co., Boston.

FIENNES, R. 1965. *Man, Nature, and Disease*. New American Library, New York.

GOODALL, M. C. 1965.

HIRST, L. F. 1953. *The Conquest of Plague: A Study of the Evolution of Epidemiology*. Clarendon Press, Oxford.

LEADER, R. W. 1967.

LEDERBERG, J. 1966. Experimental genetics and human evolution. *Bull. Atomic Sci.*, Oct., 1966:4.

MEYER, K. F. 1948. The animal kingdom, a reservoir of human disease. *Ann. Intern. Med.* 29:326.

ORMEROD, W. E. 1961. The epidemic spread of Rhodesian sleeping sickness, 1908–1960. *Trans. Roy. Soc., Trop. Med. Hyg.* 55:525.

ROUECHÉ, B. 1965. *A Man Named Hoffman* and *Eleven Blue Men*. Berkley Publishing Corp., New York.

WHETZEL, H. H. 1928. The relation of plant pathology to human affairs. In *Mayo Foundation Lectures*. W. B. Saunders Co., Philadelphia.

ZINSSER, H. 1943. *Rats, Lice and History*. Little, Brown & Co., Boston.

Literature Cited

ACKERT, J. E., and J. H. WHITLOCK. 1940. Feeding habits of nematode parasites of vertebrates. In *Introduction to Nematology,* Sect. II, Part II (ed., J. R. CHRISTIE). M. B. Chitwood, Babylon, New York.

ADAMS, M. H. 1959. *Bacteriophages.* Interscience Publishers, New York.

AGOSIN, M., and L. ARAVENA. 1959. Studies on the metabolism of *Echinococcus granulosus.* III. Glycolysis, with special reference to hexokinases and related glycolytic enzymes. *Biochim. Biophys. Acta* 34:90.

AGOSIN, M., et al. 1957. Studies on the metabolism of *Echinococcus granulosus.* I. General chemical composition and respiratory reactions. *Exptl. Parasitol.* 6:37.

AGOSIN, M., and Y. REPETTO. 1965. Studies on the metabolism of *Echinococcus granulosus.* VIII. The pathway to succinate in *E. granulosus* scolices. *Comp. Biochem. Physiol.* 14:299.

AGOSIN, M., and Y. REPETTO. 1967. Studies on the metabolism of *Echinococcus granulosus.* IX. Protein synthesis in scolices. *Exptl. Parasitol.* 21:195.

AHMADJIAN, V. 1966. Lichens. In *Symbiosis* (ed., S. M. HENRY), Vol. 1. Academic Press, New York.

AIKAWA, M. 1966. The fine structure of the erythrocytic stages of three avian malarial parasites, *Plasmodium fallax, P. lophurae,* and *P. cathemerium. Am. J. Trop. Med. Hyg.* 15:449.

AIKAWA, M., P. K. HEPLER, C. G. HUFF, and H. SPRINZ. 1966. The feeding mechanism of avian malarial parasites. *J. Cell Biol.* 28:355.

AIKAWA, M., C. G. HUFF, and H. SPRINZ. 1966. Comparative feeding mechanisms of avian and primate malarial parasites. *Military Med.* 131:969.

AIZAWA, K. 1954. Immunological studies of the silkworm jaundice virus. I. Neutralization and absorption test of the silkworm jaundice virus. *Virus* (Osaka) 4:238.

ALLEE, W. C., A. E. EMERSON, O. PARK, T. PARK, and K. P. SCHMIDT. 1949. *Principles of Animal Ecology.* W. B. Saunders Co., Philadelphia.

ALLEN, P. J. 1953. Toxins and tissue respiration. *Phytopathol.* 43:221.

ALLEN, P. J. 1959. Physiology and biochemistry of defense. In *Plant Pathology* (eds., J. G. HORSFALL and A. E. DIMOND), Vol. 1. Academic Press, New York.

ALLEN, P. J. 1965. Metabolic aspects of spore germination in fungi. *Ann. Rev. Phytopathol.* 3:313.

ALLISON, A. C. 1957. Malaria in carriers of the sickle-cell trait and in newborn children. *Exptl. Parasitol.* 6:418.

ALLISON, A. C., and D. F. CLYDE. 1961. Malaria in African children with deficient glucose-6-phosphate dehydrogenase. *Brit. Med. J.* (May 13):1346.

ANDREEV, L. N., and M. SHAW. 1965. A note on the effect of rust infection on peroxidase isozymes in flax. *Can. J. Botan.* 43:1479.

ANFINSEN, C. B., Q. M. GEIMAN, R. W. McKEE, R. A. ORMSBEE, and E. G. BALL. 1946. Studies on malarial parasites. VIII. Factors affecting the growth of *Plasmodium knowlesi in vitro. J. Exptl. Med.* 84:607.

APARCEDO, L., M. LAYRISSE, and M. ROCHE. 1962. Further evidence for reabsorption of hemoglobin iron lost into the intestine in hookworm infected subjects. *Proc. Soc. Exptl. Biol. Med.* 110:67.

ARBER, W. 1963. Bacteriophage lysogeny. In *Symbiotic Associations.* (*Symp. Soc. Gen. Microbiol.* 13). Cambridge University Press, London and New York.

ARME, C. 1968. Effects of the plerocercoid larva of a pseudophyllidean cestode, *Ligula intestinalis,* on the pituitary gland and gonads of its host. *Biol. Bull.* 134:15.

ARME, C., and R. W. OWEN. 1967. Infections of the three-spined stickleback, *Gasterosteus aculeatus* L., with the plerocercoid larvae of

Schistocephalus solidus (Müller, 1776), with special reference to pathological effects. *Parasitology* 57:301.

ARME, C., and C. P. READ. 1968. Studies on membrane transport. II. The absorption of acetate and butyrate by *Hymenolepis diminuta* (Cestoda). *Biol. Bull.* 135:80.

ARUGA, H. 1963. Induction of virus infections. In *Insect Pathology* (ed., E. A. STEINHAUS), Vol. 1. Academic Press, New York.

BACON, G. A., T. W. BURROWS, and M. YATES. 1951. The effect of biochemical mutation on the virulence of *Bacterium typhosum*: the loss of virulence of certain mutants. *Brit. J. Exptl. Pathol.* 32:85.

BAER, J. G. 1954. Revision taxonomique et étude biologique des cestodes de la famille des Tetrabothriidae, parasites d'oiseaux de haute mer et de mammifères marins. *Mem. l'Univer. Neuchatel, Ser. 4, No. 1.* Neuchâtel, Switzerland.

BAERNSTEIN, H. D. 1963. A review of electron transport mechanisms in parasitic Protozoa. *J. Parasitol.* 49:12.

BAKER, J. R. 1963. Speculations on the evolution of the family Trypanosomatidae Doflein, 1901. *Exptl. Parasitol.* 13:219.

BAKER, J. R. 1965. The evolution of parasitic Protozoa. In *Evolution of Parasites* (ed., A. E. R. TAYLOR). Blackwell Scientific Publications, Oxford.

BALASSA, F. 1963. Genetic transformation of *Rhizobium*: A review of the work of R. Balassa. *Bacteriol. Rev.* 27:228.

BALL, G. H. 1943. Parasitism and evolution. *Am. Nat.* 77:345.

BARKSDALE, L. W. 1959. Lysogenic conversions in bacteria. *Bacteriol. Rev.* 23:202.

BEAMES, C. G., JR., and F. M. FISHER, JR. 1964. A study of the neutral lipids and phospholipids of the Acanthocephala *Macrocanthorhymchus hirudinaceus* and *Moniliformis dubius. Comp. Biochem. Physiol.* 13:401.

BEAMES, C. G., JR., B. G. HARRIS, and F. A. HOPPER, JR. 1967. The synthesis of fatty acids from acetate by intact tissue and muscle extract of *Ascaris lumbricoides suum. Comp. Biochem. Physiol.* 20:509.

BEARD, R. L. 1940. Parasitic castration of *Anasa tristis* DeG. by *Trichopoda pennipes* Fab., and its effect on reproduction. *J. Econ. Entomol.* 33:269.

BEAVER, P. B. 1937. Experimental studies on *Echinostoma revolutum* (Froelich), a fluke from birds and mammals. *Univ. Ill. Biol. Monographs.* 15:1.

BEAVER, P. C. 1956. Larva migrans. *Exptl. Parasitol.* 6:587.

BEAVER, P. C. 1966. Zoonoses, with particular reference to parasites of veterinary importance. In *Biology of Parasites* (ed., E. J. L. SOULSBY). Academic Press, New York.

BECK, S. D. 1956. The European corn borer, *Pyrausta nubilalis* (Hübn.), and its principal

host plant. *Ann. Entomol. Soc. Am.* 49:582.

BECK, S. D. 1957. The European corn borer, *Pyrausta nubilalis* (Hübn.), and its principal plant host. VI. Host plant resistance to larval establishment. *J. Insect Physiol.* 1:158.

BECKER, C. E., and Q. M. GEIMAN. 1955. Glucose dissimilation in *Entamoeba histolytica. Fed. Proc.* 14:180.

BENJAMINI, E., B. F. FEINGOLD, J. D. YOUNG, L. KARTMAN, and M. SHIMIZU. 1963. Allergy to flea bites. IV. *In vitro* collection and antigenic properties of the oral secretion of the cat flea, *Ctenocephalides felis felis* (Bouche). *Exptl. Parasitol.* 13:143.

BENNETT, T. P., and W TRAGER. 1967. Pantothenic acid metabolism during avian malaria infection: Pantothenate kinase activity in duck erythrocytes and in *Plasmodium lophurae. J. Protozool.* 14:214.

BERG, C. O. 1964. Snail control in trematode diseases: The possible value of sciomyzid larvae snail-killing Diptera. *Advan. Parasitol.* 2:259.

BERGOLD, G. H. 1963. The nature of nuclear-polyhedrosis viruses. In *Insect Pathology* (ed., E. A. STEINHAUS) 1:413. Academic Press, New York.

BERNARD, N. 1909. L'évolution dans la symbiose. *Ann. Sci. Nat. Botan.* (9) 9:1.

BERNARD, N. 1911. Sur la fonction fungicide des bulbes d'Ophrydées. *Ann. Sci. Nat. Botan.* (9) 14:221.

BERNTZEN, A. K. 1961. The *in vitro* cultivation of tapeworms. I. Growth of *H. diminuta* (Cestoda: Cyclophyllidea). *J. Parasitol.* 47:351.

BERNTZEN, A. K. 1962. *Ibid.* II. Growth and maintenance of *H. nana* (Cestoda: Cyclophyllidea). *J. Parasitol.* 48:786.

BERNTZEN, A. K. 1966. *In vitro* cultivation of parasites. *Ann. N.Y. Acad. Sci.* 139:176.

BERNTZEN, A. K., and J. F. MUELLER. 1964. *In vitro* cultivation of *Spirometra mansonoides* (Cestoda) from the procercoid to the early adult. *J. Parasitol.* 50:705.

BESCHEL, R. E. 1961. Dating rock surfaces by lichen growth and its application to glaciology and physiography (lichenometry). In *Geology of the Arctic* (ed. G. O. RAASCH). University of Toronto Press, Toronto.

BISHOP, A. 1959. Drug resistance in Protozoa. *Biol. Rev.* 34:445.

BLACKLOCK, D. B., R. M. GORDON, and J. FINE. 1930. Metazoan immunity: a report on recent investigations. *Ann. Trop. Med. Hyg.* 24:5.

BODENHEIMER, F. S. 1951. *Insects as Human Food.* Junk, The Hague.

BOÉYE, A., J. L. MELNICK, and F. RAPP. 1966. SV40-Adenovirus hybrids: Presence of two genotypes and the requirement of their complementation for viral replication. *Virology* 28:56.

BONÉ, G. J., and G. PARENT. 1963. Stearic acid, an essential growth factor for *Trypanosoma cruzi. J. Gen. Microbiol.* 31:261.

BORGSTROM, F. 1938. Experimental *Cochliomya americana* infestations. *Am. J. Trop. Med.* 18:395.

BOVARNICK, M. R., and L. SCHNEIDER. 1960a. Role of adenosine triphosphate in the hemolysis of sheep erythrocytes by typhus rickettsiae. *J. Bacteriol.* 80:344.

BOVARNICK, M. R., and SCHNEIDER, L. 1960b. The incorporation of glycine-1-C14 by typhus rickettsiae. *J. Biol. Chem.* 235:1727.

BOWMAN, I. B. R., P. T. GRANT, W. O. KERMACK, and D. OGSTON. 1961. The metabolism of *Plasmodium berghei*, the malaria parasite of rodents. *Biochem. J.* 78:472.

BOYD, M. F. 1947. A review of studies on immunity to *vivax* malaria. *J. Nat. Malaria Soc.* 6:12.

BRAGG, P. D., and R. E. REEVES. 1962. Pathways of glucose dissimilation in the Laredo strain of *Entamoeba histolytica*. *Exptl. Parasitol.* 12:393.

BRAND, T. VON. 1952. *Chemical Physiology of Endoparasitic Animals*. Academic Press, New York.

BRAND, T. VON. 1960a. Influence of oxygen on life processes. In *Nematology* (eds., J. N. SASSER and W. R. JENKINS). University of North Carolina Press, Chapel Hill, N.C.

BRAND, T. VON. 1960b. Influence of size, motility, starvation, and age on metabolic rate. In *Nematology* (eds., J. N. SASSER and W. R. JENKINS). University of North Carolina Press, Chapel Hill, N.C.

BRAND, T. VON. 1966. *Biochemistry of Parasites*. Academic Press, New York.

BRAND, T. VON, and V. S. FILES. 1947. Chemical and histological observations on the influence of *Schistosoma mansoni* infection on *Australorbis glabratus*. *J. Parasitol.* 33:476.

BRAND, T. VON, and E. M. JOHNSON. 1947. A comparative study of the effect of cyanide on the respiration of some Trypanosomidae. *J. Cellular Comp. Physiol.* 29:33.

BRAND, T. VON, P. MCMAHON, E. GIBBS, and H. HIGGINS. 1964. Aerobic and anaerobic metabolism of larval and adult *Taenia taeniaeformis*. II. Hexose leakage and absorption; tissue glucose and polysaccharides. *Exptl. Parasitol.* 15:410.

BRAND, T. VON, E. C. WEINBACH, and E. J. TOBIE. 1955. Comparative studies on the metabolism of the culture form and bloodstream form of *Trypanosoma gambiense*. *J. Cellular Comp. Physiol.* 45:421.

BRAND, T. VON, P. P. WEINSTEIN, B. MEHLMAN, and E. C. WEINBACH. 1952. Observations on the metabolism of bacteria-free larvae of *Trichinella spiralis*. *Expl. Parasitol.* 1:245.

BRAUN, A. C. 1955. A study on the mode of action of wildfire toxin. *Phytopathology* 45:659.

BRAUN, A. C. 1959. Growth is affected. In *Plant Pathology* (Eds., J. G. HORSFALL and A. E. DIMOND) 1:189. Academic Press, New York.

BRAUN, W. 1965. *Bacterial Genetics* (2d ed.). W. B. Saunders Co., Philadelphia.

BRAY, R. S. 1963. The exo-erythrocytic phase of malaria parasites. *Intern. Rev. Trop. Med.* 2:41.

BREWER, G. J., and R. D. POWELL. 1965. A study of the relationship between the content of adenosine triphosphate in human red cells and the course of falciparum malaria: A new system that may confer protection against malaria. *Proc. Natl. Acad. Sci.* 54:741.

BRIAN, P. W., et al. 1952. The phytotoxic properties of alternaric acid in relation to the etiology of plant diseases caused by *Alternaria solani* (Ell. and Mart.) Jones and Grant. *Ann. Appl. Biol.* 39:308.

BRIGGS, J. D. 1958. Humoral immunity in lepidopterous larvae. *J. Expl. Zool.* 138:155.

BROOKS, M. A., and A. G. RICHARDS. 1955. Intracellular symbiosis in cockroaches. I. Production of aposymbiotic cockroaches. *Biol. Bull.* 190:22.

BROWN, W. 1936. The physiology of host parasite relations. *Botan. Rev.* 2:236.

BUCHNER, P. 1953. *Endosymbiose der Tiere mit pflanzlichen Mikroorganismen*. Birkhauser, Basel and Stuttgart.

BUCHNER, P. 1965. *Endosymbiosis of Animals with Plant Microorganisms*. Interscience Publishers, New York.

BUCHSBAUM, R. 1937. Chick tissue cells and *Chlorella* in mixed cultures. *Physiol. Zool.* 10:373.

BUEDING, E. 1950. Carbohydrate metabolism of *Schistosoma mansoni*. *J. Gen. Physiol.* 33:475.

BUEDING, E. 1962a. Comparative aspects of carbohydrate metabolism. *Fed. Proc.* 21:1039.

BUEDING, E. 1962b. Comparative biochemistry of parasitic helminths. *Comp. Biochem. Physiol.* 4:343.

BUEDING, E., and B. CHARMS. 1952. Cytochrome c, cytochrome oxidase, and succinoxidase activities of helminths. *J. Biol. Chem.* 196:615.

BUEDING, E., E. KMETEC, C. SWARTZWELDER, S. ABADIE, and H. J. SAZ. 1961. Biochemical effects of dithiazanine on the canine whipworm, *Trichuris vulpis*. *Biochem. Pharmacol.* 5:311.

BUEDING, E., and J. A. MACKINNON. 1955a. Studies of the phosphoglucose isomerase of *Schistosoma mansoni*. *J. Biol. Chem.* 215:507.

BUEDING, E., and J. A. MACKINNON. 1955b. Hexokinases of *Schistosoma mansoni*. *J. Biol. Chem.* 215:495.

BUEDING, E., and J. M. MANSOUR. 1957. The relationship between inhibition of phosphofructokinase activity and the mode of action of trivalent organic antimonials on *Schistosoma mansoni*. *Brit. J. Pharmacol.* 12:159.

BUEDING, E., and S. A. ORRELL, JR. 1961. Sedimentation coefficient distributions of cold water-extracted glycogens of *Fasciola hepatica*. *J. Biol. Chem.* 236:2854.

BUEDING, E., H. RUPPENDER, and J. MACKINNON.

1954. Glucosamine kinase of *Schistosoma mansoni*. *Proc. Nat. Acad. Sci.* 40:773.

BUEDING, E., and H. J. SAZ. 1968. Pyruvate kinase and phosphoenolpyruvate carboxykinase activities of *Ascaris* muscle, *Hymenolepis diminuta*, and *Schistosoma mansoni*. *Comp. Biochem. Physiol.* 24:511.

BUEDING, E., and H. W. YALE. 1951. Production of alphamethylbutyric acid by bacteria-free *Ascaris lumbricoides*. *J. Biol. Chem.* 193:411.

BULL, C. G. 1915. The fate of typhoid bacilli when injected intravenously into normal rabbits. *J. Exptl. Med.* 22:475.

BURGER, O. 1903. Über das Zusammenleben von *Antholoba reticulata* Couth und *Hepatus chilensis*. *Biol. Zentr.* 23:678.

BURKHOLDER, P., and L. M. BURKHOLDER. 1960. Photosynthesis in some alcyonacean corals. *Am. J. Botan.* 47:866.

BURNET, F. M. 1959. *The Clonal Selection Theory of Acquired Immunity*. Vanderbilt University Press, Nashville, Tenn.

BURNET, F. M. 1960. *Principles of Animal Virology*. Academic Press, New York.

BURRILL, T. J. 1881. Anthrax of fruit trees; or the so-called fire blight of pear, and twig blight of apple trees. *Proc. Am. Assoc. Advan. Sci.* 29:583.

BURROWS, R. B., and W. G. LILLIS. 1964. The whipworm as a bloodsucker. *J. Parasitol.* 50:675.

BÜSING, K. H., W. DÖLL, and K. FREYTAG. 1953. Die Bakterienflora der medizinischen Blutegel. *Arch. Mikrobiol.* 19:65.

BUTEL, J. S., and F. RAPP. 1966. Replication in simian cells of defective viruses in an SV40-adenovirus "hybrid" population. *J. Bacteriol.* 91:278.

CAIRNS, J., G. S. STENT, and J. D. WATSON (eds.). 1966. *Phage and the Origins of Molecular Biology*. Cold Spring Harbor Laboratory of Quantitative Biology, Cold Spring Harbor, N.Y.

CAMPBELL, C. H. 1955. The antigenic role of the excretions and secretions of *Trichinella spiralis* in the production of immunity in mice. *J. Parasitol.* 41:483.

CAMPBELL, J. W. 1960. Nitrogen and amino acid composition of three species of anoplocephalid cestodes: *Moniezia expansa, Thysanosoma actinoides*, and *Cittotaenia perplexa*. *Exptl. Parasitol.* 9:1.

CAMERON, G. R. 1934. Inflammation in the caterpillars of Lepidoptera. *J. Pathol. Bacteriol.* 38:441.

CAMERON, T. W. M. 1964. Host specificity and evolution of helminthic parasites. *Advan. Parasitol.* 2:1.

CARPENTER, P. L. 1965. *Immunology and Serology*. W. B. Saunders Co., Philadelphia.

CHANDLER, A. C. 1937. Studies on the nature of immunity to intestinal helminths. VI. General resume and discussion. *Am. J. Hyg.* 26:309.

CHANDLER, A. C., and C. P. READ. 1961. *Introduction to Parasitology*. John Wiley & Sons, New York.

CHARNIAUX-COTTON, H. 1956. Déterminisme hormonal de la différenciation sexuelle chez les Crustacés. *Ann. Biol.* (Ser. 3), 32:371.

CHARNIAUX-COTTON, H. 1960. Sex determination. In *The Physiology of Crustacea* (Ed. T. H. WATERMAN), Vol. 1.

CHARNIAUX-COTTON, H. 1962. Androgenic gland of Crustaceans. *Gen. Comp. Endocrinol.* (Suppl.), 1:241.

CHENG, T. C., and R. W. SNYDER. 1962. Studies on host-parasite relationships between larval trematodes and their hosts. I. A review. *Trans. Am. Microscopical Soc.* 81:209.

CHESTER, K. S. 1933. The problem of acquired physiological immunity in plants. *Quart. Rev. Biol.* 8:129, 275.

CHINN, S. H. F., and R. J. LEDINGHAM. 1957. Studies on the influence of various substances on the germination of *Helminthosporium sativum* spores in soil. *Can. J. Botan.* 35:697.

CHIPMAN, P. B. 1957. The antigenic role of the excretory and secretory adult *Trichinella spiralis* in the production of immunity in mice. *J. Parasitol.* 43:593.

CHRISTIAN, J. J., and D. E. DAVIS. 1964. Endocrines, behavior, and population. *Science* 146:1550.

CHRISTIE, M. G., and W. A. G. CHARLESTON. 1965. Stimulus to exsheathing of *Nematodirus battus* infective larvae. *Exptl. Parasitol.* 17:46.

CIERESZKO, L. S. 1962. Chemistry of coelenterates. III. Occurrence of antimicrobial terpenoid compounds in the zooxanthellae of alcyonarians. *Trans. N.Y. Acad. Sci.* 92:502.

CLARK, C. H., J. M. KLING, C. H. WOODLEY, and N. SHARP. 1961. A quantitative measurement of the blood loss caused by ancylostomiasis in dogs. *Am. J. Vet. Res.* 22:370.

CLARK, C. H., G. K. KIESEL, and C. H. GOBY. 1962. Measurements of blood loss caused by *Haemonchus contortus* infection in sheep. *Am. J. Vet. Res.* 23:977.

CLAY, T. 1949. Some problems in the evolution of a group of ectoparasites. *Evolution* 3:279.

CLEGG, J. A. 1965. Secretion of lipoprotein by Mehlis' gland in *Fasciola hepatica*. *Ann. N.Y. Acad. Sci.* 118(24):969.

CLEGG, J. A., and J. D. SMYTH. 1968. Growth, development and culture methods: parasitic platyhelminthes. In *Chemical Zoology* (ed., M. FLORKIN and B. T. SCHEER) Vol. II. Academic Press, New York.

CLEVELAND, L. R. 1923. Correlation between the food and morphology of termites and the presence of intestinal Protozoa. *Am. J. Hyg.* 3:444.

CLEVELAND, L. R. 1960. Effects of insect hormones on the Protozoa of *Cryptocercus* and termites. In *Host Influences on Parasite Physiol-*

ogy (ed., L. A. STAUBER). Rutgers University Press, New Brunswick.

CLEVELAND, L. R., and A. V. GRIMSTONE. 1964. The fine structure of the flagellate *Mixotricha paradoxa* and its associated micro-organisms. *Proc. Roy. Soc.* (Series B), 159:668.

COLLIER, R. J., and A. M. PAPPENHEIMER, JR. 1964. Studies on the mode of action of diphtheria toxin. II. Effect of toxin on amino acid incorporation in cell-free systems. *J. Exptl. Med.* 120:1019.

CONWAY, P., and J. H. WHITLOCK. 1965. A study of the variables influencing artificial infections with *Haemonchus contortus*. *Cornell Vet.* 55:19.

COOK, L., P. T. GRANT, and W. O. KERMACK. 1961. Proteolytic enzymes of the erythrocytic forms of rodent and simian species of malarial plasmodia. *Exptl. Parasitol.* 11:372.

CORLISS, J. O. 1962. Faculative parasitism in Protozoa and its possible evolutionary significance. *Parasitology* 52, 10 P.

COWPERTHWAITE, J., M. M. WEBER, L. PACKER, and S. H. Hutner. 1953. Nutrition of *Herpetomonas (Strigomonas) culicidarum*. *Ann. N.Y. Acad. Sci.* 56:972.

CULBERTSON, G. G. 1961. Pathogenic *Acanthamoeba (Hartmanella)*. *Am. J. Clin. Pathol.* 35:195.

DALES, R. P. 1966. Symbiosis in marine organisms. In *Symbiosis* (ed., S. M. HENRY), Vol. 1. Academic Press, New York.

DAMIAN, R. T. 1964. Molecular mimicry: Antigen sharing by parasite and host and its consequences. *Am. Nat.* 98:129.

DANFORTH, W. F. 1967. Respiratory metabolism. In *Research in Protozoology* (ed., T. T. CHEN), 1:201. Pergamon Press, Long Island City, N.Y.

DAUGHERTY, J. W. 1952. Intermediary metabolism in helminths. I. Transaminase reactions in *Fasciola hepatica*. *Exptl. Parasitol.* 1:331.

DAUGHERTY, J. W. 1954. Synthesis of amino nitrogen from ammonia in *Hymenolepis diminuta*. *Proc. Soc. Exptl. Biol. Med.* 85:288.

DAUGHERTY, J. W., and HERRICK, C. A. 1952. Cecal coccidiosis and carbohydrate metabolism in chickens. *J. Parasitol.* 38:298.

DAVENPORT, D. 1955. Specificity and behavior in symbioses. *Quart. Rev. Biol.* 30:29.

DAVENPORT, D. 1966. The experimental analysis of behavior in symbioses. In *Symbiosis* (ed., S. M. HENRY), Vol. 1:381. Academic Press, New York.

DAVENPORT, D., and K. S. NORRIS. 1958. Observations on the symbiosis of the sea anenome *Stoichactis* and the pomacentrid fish *Amphiprion percula*. *Biol. Bull.* 115:397.

DAVENPORT, H. E. 1949. The haemoglobin of *Ascaris lumbricoides*. *Proc. Roy. Soc.* (Series B), 136:255.

DAVIS, D. E., and C. P. READ. 1958. Effect of

behavior on development of resistance in trichinosis. *Proc. Soc. Exptl. Biol. Med.* 99:269.

DAWES, B. 1960. The penetration of *Fasciola hepatica* into *Limnaea truncatula* and of *F. gigantica* into *L. auricularia*. *Trans. Roy. Soc. Trop. Med. Hyg.* 54:9.

DAWES, B. 1960. Penetration of *Fasciola gigantica Cobbold*, 1856, into snail hosts. *Nature* 185:51.

DAWES, B. 1961. On the early stages of *Fasciola hepatica* penetrating into the liver of an experimental host, the mouse. A histological picture. *J. Helminthol.* (*R. T. Leiper Suppl.*), page 41.

DAWES, B. 1963a. *Fasciola hepatica* L., a tissue feeder. *Nature* 198:1011.

DAWES, B. 1963b. The migration of juvenile forms of *Fasciola hepatica* L. through the wall of the intestines in the mouse, with some observations on food and feeding. *Parasitology* 53:109.

DAWES, B. 1963c. Hyperplasia of the bile duct in fascioliasis and its relation to the problem of nutrition in the liver fluke *Fasciola hepatica* L. *Parasitology* 53:123.

DAWES, B. 1963d. Some observations of *Fasciola hepatica* L. during feeding operations in the hepatic parenchyma of the mouse, with notes on the nature of liver damage in this host. *Parasitology* 53:135.

DAWES, B., and D. L. HUGHES. 1964. Fascioliasis: the invasive stages of *Fasciola hepatica* in mammalian hosts. *Advan. Parasitol.* 2:97.

DAY, J. H. 1935. The life-history of *Sacculina*. *Quart. J. Microbiol. Sci.* 77:549.

DE BARY, A. 1879. *Die Erscheinung der Symbiose*. Tübner, Strasbourg.

DEGIUSTI, D. L. 1963. *Rotundula hyalellae* a gregarine from the gut of *Hyalella azteca*. Its morphology, life cycle, and the relationships of moulting of the amphipod host to encystment and sexual reproduction of the gregarine. In *Progress in Protozoology* (eds., LUDVIK, LOM, and VAVRA), Academic Press, New York.

DESOWITZ, R. S. 1963. Adaptation of trypanosomes to abnormal hosts. *Ann. N.Y. Acad. Sci.* 113(1):74.

DEWEY, V. C. 1967. Lipid composition, nutrition, and metabolism. In *Chemical Zoology* (ed., G. W. KIDDER), Vol. 1. Academic Press, New York.

DIAMOND, L. S. 1961. Axenic cultivation of *Entamoeba histolytica*. *Science* 134:336.

DICKINSON, S. 1959. The behaviour of larvae of *Heterodera schachtii* on nitrocellulose membranes. *Nematologica* 4:60.

DICKINSON, S. 1960. The mechanical ability to breach the host barriers. In *Plant Pathology* (eds., J. G. HORSFALL and A. E. DIMOND), Vol. 2. Academic Press, New York and London.

DINEEN, J. K. 1963a. Immunological aspects of parasitism. *Nature* 197:268.

DINEEN, J. K. 1963b. Antigenic relationship between host and parasite. *Nature* 197:471.

DINEEN, J. K., A. D. DONALD, B. M. WAGLAND, and J. H. TURNER. 1965. The dynamics of the host-parasite relationship. II and III. *Parasitology* 55:163 and 515.

DISSANAIKE, A. S., and E. U. CANNING. 1957. The mode of emergence of the sporoplasm in microsporidia and its relation to the structure of the spore. *Parasitology* 47:92.

DIXON, K. E. 1966. The physiology of excystment of the metacercaria of *Fasciola hepatica* L. *Parasitology* 56:431.

DONALD, A. D., et al. 1964. The dynamics of the host-parasite relationship I. *Nematodirus spathiger* infection in sheep. *Parasitology* 54:527.

DORAN, D. J. 1953. Coccidiosis in the kangaroo rats of California. *Univ. Calif. Publ. Zool.* 59:38.

DORAN, D. J., and M. M. FARR. 1962. Excystation of the poultry coccidium *Eimeria acervulina*. *J. Protozool.* 9:154.

DOUGHERTY, E. C. 1951. Evolution of zoöparasitic groups in the phylum Nematoda, with special reference to host-distribution. *J. Parasitol.* 37:353.

DOUGHERTY, E. C. (Ed.). 1959. *Axenic Culture of Invertebrate Metazoa: A Goal. Ann. N.Y. Acad. Sci.* 77(2):25.

DOUTT, R. L. 1963. Pathologies caused by insect parasites. In *Insect Pathology* (ed., E. A. STEINHAUS), Vol. 1. Academic Press, New York.

DROOP, M. R. 1963. Algae and invertebrates in symbiosis. In *Symbiotic Associations.* (*Symp. Soc. Genl. Microbiol.* 13). Cambridge University Press, London and New York.

DUBOS, R. 1954. *Biochemical Determinants of Microbial Disease.* Harvard University Press, Cambridge, Mass.

DUERDEN, J. E. 1905. On the habits and reactions of crabs bearing actinians in their claws. *Proc. Zool. Soc. London* 2:494.

DULBECCO, R. 1963. Tranformation of cells in vitro by viruses. *Science* 142:932.

DURAN-REYNALS, F. 1950. The ground substance of the mesenchyme and hyaluronidase, a symposium. *Ann. N.Y. Acad. Sci.* 52:943.

EDNEY, M. 1957. Genetic analysis of the development of serum resistance in an influenza virus strain. *J. Genl. Microbiol.* 17:25.

ELLENBY, C., and A. B. GILBERT. 1957. Cardiotonic activity of the potato-root eelworm hatching factor. *Nature* 189:1105.

ENTNER, N. 1958. On the pathway of carbohydrate metabolism in *Entamoeba histolytica. J. Parasitol.* 44:638.

ENTNER, N., and H. H. ANDERSON. 1954. Lactic and succinic acid formation by *Endamoeba histolytica in vitro. Exptl. Parasitol.* 3:234.

ENTNER, N., and C. GONZALEZ. 1959. Fate of glucose in *Ascaris lumbricoides. Exptl. Parasitol.* 8:471.

ENTNER, N., L. A. EVANS, and C. GONZALEZ. 1962. Genetics of *Entamoeba histolytica*: dif-

ferences in drug sensitivity between Laredo and other strains of *Entamoeba histolytica. J. Protozool.* 9:466.

ENTNER, N., and H. MOST. 1965. Genetics of *Entamoeba:* Characterization of two new parasitic strains which grow at room temperature (and at 37° C). *J. Protozool.* 12:10.

ERASMUS, D. A., and C. Öhman. 1963. The structure and function of the adhesive organ in strigeid trematodes. *Ann. N.Y. Acad. Sci.* 113(1):7.

ERWIN, J., and K. BLOCH. 1963. Lipid metabolism of ciliated Protozoa. *J. Biol. Chem.* 238:1618.

ERWIN, J., D. HULANICKA, and K. BLOCH. 1964. Comparative aspects of unsaturated fatty acid synthesis. *Comp. Biochem. Physiol.* 12:191.

ESCH, G. W. 1964. Comparative carbohydrate metabolism of adult and larval *Multiceps serialis. J. Parasitol.* 50:72.

ESSERMAN, H. B., and P. M. SAMBELL. 1951. The uptake of radioactive phosphate by nematode parasites and by tissues of the sheep. *Australian J. Sci. Res.* B4:575.

ESSLINGER, J. H. 1958. Effects of the screw-worm on guinea pigs. *J. Parasitol.* 44:201.

EUZET, L., and A. RAIBAUT. 1960. Le développement postlarvaire de *Squalonchocotyle torpedinis* (Price, 1942) (Monogenea, Hexabothriidae). *Bull. Soc. Neuchatel. Sci. Nat.* 83:101.

FAIRBAIRN, D. 1954. The metabolism of *Heterakis gallinae.* II. Carbon dioxide fixation. *Exptl. Parasitol.* 3:52.

FAIRBAIRN, D. 1955. Embryonic and postembryonic changes in the lipids of *Ascaris lumbricoides* eggs. *Can. J. Biochem. Physiol.* 33:122.

FAIRBAIRN, D. 1957. The biochemistry of *Ascaris. Exptl. Parasitol.* 6:491.

FAIRBAIRN, D. 1958. Trehalose and glucose in helminths and other invertebrates. *Can. J. Zool.* 37:787.

FAIRBAIRN, D. 1960. The physiology and biochemistry of nematodes. In *Nematology* (eds., J. N. SASSER and W. R. JENKINS). University of North Carolina Press, Chapel Hill.

FAIRBAIRN, D., and R. F. PASSEY. 1957. Occurrence and distribution of trehalose and glycogen in the eggs and the tissues of *Ascaris lumbricoides. Exptl. Parasitol.* 6:566.

FAIRBAIRN, D., G. WERTHEIM, R. P. HARPER, and E. L. SCHILLER. 1961. Biochemistry of normal and irradiated strains of *Hymenolepis diminuta. Exptl. Parasitol.* 11:278.

FANTHAM, H. B. 1936. The evolution of parasitism among the Protozoa. *Scientia,* Milano 49:316.

FEDER, H. M. 1966. Cleaning symbiosis in the marine environment. In *Symbiosis* (ed., S. M. HENRY), Vol. 1. Academic Press, New York.

FEIST, C. F., C. P. READ, and F. M. FISHER, JR., 1965. Trehalose synthesis and hydrolysis in *Ascaris suum. J. Parasitol.* 51:76.

FELT, E. P. 1940. *Plant Galls and Gall Makers.* Comstock Publishing Associates, Ithaca, N.Y.

FENNER, F. 1959. *Myxomatosis in Australian Wild Rabbits—Evolutionary Changes in an Infectious Disease.* (The Harvey Lectures, 1957–58.) Pp. 22–55. Academic Press, New York.

FENNER, F. 1965. Conditional lethal mutants in the study of the genetics of animal viruses. In *Perspectives in Virology IV.* (ed., M. POLLARD), p. 34. Hoeber, New York.

FENNER, F., and F. N. RATCLIFFE. 1965. *Myxomatosis.* Cambridge University Press, London and New York.

FERGUSON, M. S. 1940. Excystment and sterilization of metacercariae of the avian strigeid trematode, *Posthodiplostomum minimum*, and their development into adult worms in sterile cultures. *J. Parasitol.* 26:359.

FERNANDO, M. A., and H. A. WONG. 1964. Metabolism of hookworms. II. Glucose metabolism and glycogen synthesis in adult female *Ancylostoma caninum. Exptl. Parasitol.* 15:284.

FINTER, N. (ed.). 1967. *Interferons.* Interscience Publishers, New York.

FISHER, F. M., JR. 1963. Production of host endocrine substances by parasites. *Ann. N.Y. Acad. Sci.* 113(1):63.

FISHER, F. M., JR. 1964. Synthesis of trehalose in Acanthocephala. *J. Parasitol.* 50:803.

FISHER, F. M., JR., and R. M. SANBORN. 1963. *Nosema* as a source of juvenile hormone in parasitized insects. *Biol. Bull.* 126:235.

FLAKS, J. G., J. LICHTENSTEIN, and S. S. COHEN. 1959. Virus-induced acquisition of metabolic function. II. Studies on the origin of the deoxycytidylate hydroxymethylase of bacteriophage-infected *E. coli. J. Biol. Chem.* 234:1507.

FLOR, H. H. 1956. The complementary genetic systems in flax and flax rust. *Advan. Genetics* 8:29.

FOUQUEY, C. 1961. Quoted by BRAND (1966).

FRAENKEL-CONRAT, H. 1962. *Design and Function at the Threshold of Life: The Viruses.* Academic Press, New York.

FREUDENTHAL, H. D. 1962. *Symbiodinium* gen. nov. and *Symbiodinium microadriaticum* sp. nov., a zooxanthella: Taxonomy, life cycle, and morphology. *J. Protozool.* 9:45.

FULTON, J. D., and P. T. GRANT. 1955. The preparation of a strain of *Trypanosoma rhodesiense* resistant to stilbamidine and some observations on its nature. *Exptl. Parasitol.* 4:377.

FULTON, J. D., and D. F. SPOONER. 1959. Terminal respiration in certain mammalian trypanosomes. *Exptl. Parasitol.* 8:137.

FULTON, J. D., and D. F. SPOONER. 1960. Metabolic studies on *Toxoplasma gondii. Exptl. Parasitol.* 9:293.

GAAFAR, S. M. 1966. Pathogenesis of ectoparasites. In *Biology of Parasites* (ed., E. J. L. SOULSBY). Academic Press, New York.

GAGE, J. 1966. Experiments with the behavior of the bivalves *Montacuta substriata* and *M.*

ferruginosa, 'commensals' with spatangoids. *J. Marine Biol. Assoc. U.K.* 46:71.

GARBER, E. D. 1956. A nutrition-inhibition hypothesis of pathogenicity. *Am. Nat.* 90:183.

GARBER, E. D., A. J. HACKETT, and R. FRANKLIN. 1952. The virulence of biochemical mutants of *Klebsiella pneumoniae. Proc. Natl. Acad. Sci.* 38:693.

GARBER, E. D., S. G. SHAEFFER, and M. GOLDMAN. 1956. The virulence of biochemical mutants of *Erwinia aroideae* for varieties of radish and turnip. *J. Gen. Microbiol.* 14:261.

GARNHAM, P. C. C. 1956. Microsporidia in laboratory colonies of Anopheles. *Bull. World Health Org.* 15:845.

GARNHAM, P. C. C. 1964. Factors influencing the development of Protozoa in their arthropodan hosts. In *Host-Parasite Relationships in Invertebrate Hosts* (ed., A. E. R. TAYLOR). Blackwell Scientific Publications, Oxford.

GARNHAM, P. C. C. 1967. Malaria in mammals excluding man. *Advan. Parasitol.* 5:139.

GÄUMANN, E. 1950. *Principles of Plant Infection* (transl., W. B. BRIERLY). Crosby Lockwood & Son, London.

GÄUMANN, E. 1956. Fusaric acid as a wilt toxin. *Phytopathology* 47:342.

GEMMEL, A. and F. FENNER. 1960. Genetic Studies with mammalian poxviruses. III. White (μ) mutants of rabbit pox virus. *Virology* 11:219.

GILBERT, P. W. 1944. The alga-egg relationship in *Ambystoma maculatum*, a case of symbiosis. *Ecology* 25:366.

GILL, J. W., and H. J. VOGEL. 1963. A bacterial endosymbiote in *Crithidia oncopelti*: Biochemical & morphological aspects. *J. Protozool.* 10:148.

GINGER, C. D., and D. FAIRBAIRN. 1966a. Lipid metabolism in helminth parasites. I. The lipids of *Hymenolepis diminuta* (Cestoda). *J. Parasitol.* 52:1086.

GINGER, C. D., and D. FAIRBAIRN. 1966b. Lipid metabolism in helminth parasites. II. The major origins of the lipids of *Hymenolepis diminuta* (Cestoda). *J. Parasitol.* 52:1097.

GLOCKLIN, V. C., and D. FAIRBAIRN. 1952. The metabolism of *Heterakis gallinae.* I. Aerobic and anaerobic respiration: Carbohydrate-sparing action of carbon dioxide. *J. Cell Comp. Physiol.* 39:341.

GODFREY, D. G. 1957. Anti-parasitic action of dietary cod liver oil upon *Plasmodium berghei* and its reversal by vitamin E. *Exptl. Parasitol.* 6:555.

GODFREY, D. G. 1958. Influence of dietary cod liver oil upon *Trypanosoma congolense, T. cruzi, T. vivax,* and *T. brucei. Exptl. Parasitol.* 7:255.

GOLDBERG, E. 1957. Studies on the intermediary metabolism of *Trichinella spiralis. Exptl. Parasitol.* 6:367.

GOLDMAN, M., N. N. GLEASON, and R. K. CARVER. 1962. Antigenic analysis of *Entamoeba histolytica* by means of fluorescent antibody. II. *E.*

histolytica and *E. hartmanni*. *Exptl. Parasitol.* 10:366.

GOMPERTZ, S. M., and W. M. WATKINS. 1963. UDP-galactose 4-epimerase, UDP-N-acetylglucosamine 4-epimerase, UDP-glucose pyrophosphorylase and UDP-galactose pyrophosphorylase in extracts of *Trichomonas foetus*. *Biochem. J.* 88:6P.

GOODALL, M. C. 1965. *Science and the Politician.* Schenkman Publishing Co., Cambridge, Mass.

GORDON, H. T. 1959. Minimal nutritional requirements of the German roach, *Blatella germanica* L. *Ann. N.Y. Acad. Sci.* 77:290.

GOREAU, T. F., and GOREAU, N. I. 1960. Distribution of labelled carbon in reef building corals with and without zooxanthellae. *Science* 131:668.

GRANT, P. T., and J. R. SARGENT. 1961. L-α-glycerophosphate dehydrogenase, a component of an oxidase system in *Trypanosoma rhodesiense*. *Biochem. J.* 81:206.

GRANT, P. T., J. R. SARGENT, and J. F. RYLEY. 1961. Respiratory systems in the Trypanosomidae. *Biochem. J.* 81:200.

GRAY, H. E., and G. FRAENKEL. 1954. The carbohydrate components of honeydew. *Physiol. Zool.* 27:56.

GREENWOOD, M., A. B. HILL, W. W. C. TOPLEY, and J. WILSON. 1936. *Experimental Epidemiology.* Med. Res. Council Special Reports Series 209, London.

GRIFFEN, A. M., and W. G. McCARTEN. 1949. Sterols and fatty acids in the nutrition of entozoic amoebae in cultures. *Proc. Soc. Exptl. Biol. Med.* 72:645.

GRIFFITH, F. 1928. The significance of pneumococcal types. *Jour. Hyg.* 27:113.

GROVES, R. E. 1945. An ecological study of *Phyllodistomum solidum* Rankin, 1937 (Trematoda: Gorgoderidae). *Trans. Am. Microscop. Soc.* 64:112.

GUDGER, E. W. 1950. Fishes that live as inquilines (lodgers) in sponges. *Zoologica* 35:121.

GUTIERREZ, J., P. P. WILLIAMS, R. E. DAVIS, and E. J. WARWICK. 1962. Lipid metabolism of rumen ciliates and bacteria. I. Uptake of fatty acids by *Isotricha prostoma* and *Entodinium simplex*. *Appl. Microbiol.* 10:548.

GUTTMAN, H. N. 1963. Experimental glimpses at the lower Trypanosomatidae. *Exptl. Parasitol.* 14:129.

GUTTMAN, H. N. 1966. First defined media for *Leptomonas* spp. from insects. *J. Protozool.* 13:390.

GUTTMAN, H. N., and F. G. WALLACE. 1964. Nutrition and physiology of the Trypanosomatidae. In *Biochemistry and Physiology of the Protozoa* (ed., S. H. HUTNER), Vol. 3. Academic Press, New York.

HACK, M. H., R. G. YAEGER, and T. D. McCAFFERY. 1962. Comparative lipid biochemistry. II. Lipids of plant and animal flagellates, a non-motile alga, an ameba and a ciliate. *Comp. Biochem. Physiol.* 6:247.

HACKER, C. 1969. Ph.D. dissertation, Rice University, Houston, Texas.

HALAWANI, A. E., A. HAFEZ, J. NEWSOME, and S. G. COWPER. 1949. Miracil D: Effect on *B. mansoni* in vitro and in the treatment of urinary bilharziasis. *J. Roy. Egypt. Med. Assoc.* 32:29.

HALEVY, S. 1963. Lipid composition and metabolism of *Trichomonas foetus*. *Proc. Soc. Exptl. Biol. Med.* 113:47.

HALL, W. T., and G. CLAUS. 1963. Ultrastructural studies on the blue-green symbiont in *Cyanophora paradoxa* Korschikoff. *J. Cell Biol.* 19:551.

HARLOW, D. R., and W. MERTZ. 1967. Insulin-like activity from the sparganum of *Spirometra mansonoides*. *J. Parasitol.* 53:449.

HARRINGTON, G. W. 1965. The lipid content of *Hymenolepis diminuta* and *Hymenolepis citelli*. *Exptl. Parasitol.* 17:287.

HARVEY, E. N. 1952. *Bioluminescence.* Academic Press, New York.

HAWKING, F. 1954. Milk, *p*-aminobenzoate and malaria of rats and monkeys. *Brit. Med. J.* 1954:425.

HAYES, W. 1964. *The Genetics of Bacteria and Their Viruses.* John Wiley & Sons, New York.

HAYES, J. E., F. E. HAHN, Z. A. COHN, E. B. JACKSON, and J. E. SMADEL. 1957. Metabolic studies of rickettsiae. IV. Terminal respiratory enzymes in *Rickettsia mooseri*. *Biochim. Biophys. Acta* 26:570.

HENRY, S. M. 1962. The significance of microorganisms in the nutrition of insects. *Trans. N.Y. Acad. Sci.* II, 24:676.

HENRY, S. M. (ed.). 1966–1967. *Symbiosis* (2 vols.). Academic Press, New York.

HENRY, S. M., and R. J. BLOCK. 1960. The sulfur metabolism of insects. IV. The conversion of inorganic sulfate to organic sulfur compounds. The role of intracellular symbionts. *Contrib. Boyce Thompson Inst.* 20:317.

HENRY, S. M., and T. W. COOK. 1964. Amino acid supplementation by symbiontic bacteria in the cockroach. *Contrib. Boyce Thompson Inst.* 22:507.

HERTIG, M., W. H. TALIAFERRO, and B. SCHWARTZ. 1937. Report of the Committee on Terminology. *J. Parasitol.* 23, 325.

HIRST, G. K. 1962. Genetic recombination with Newcastle disease virus, polioviruses and influenza. *Cold Spring Harbor Symp. Quant. Biol.* 27:303.

HOARE, C. A. 1957. The classification of trypanosomes of veterinary and medical importance. *Vet. Rev. Annotations* 3:1.

HOARE, C. A. 1967. Evolutionary trends in mammalian trypanosomes. *Advan. Parasitol.* 5:47.

HOARE, C. A., and F. G. WALLACE. 1966. Developmental stages of trypanosomatid flagellates: a new terminology. *Nature* 212:1385.

HOBSON, A. D. 1948. The physiology and cultivation in artificial media of nematodes parasitic in the alimentary tract of animals. *Parasitology* 38:183.

HOEPPLI, R. 1954. The knowledge of parasites and parasitic infections from ancient times to the 17th century. *Exptl. Parasitol.* 5:398.

HOEPPLI, R. 1959. *Parasites and Parasitic Infections in Early Medicine and Science.* University of Malaya Press, Singapore.

HOLMES, J. C. 1961. Effects of concurrent infections on *Hymenolepis diminuta* (Cestoda) and *Moniliformis dubius* (Acanthocephala). I. General effects and comparison with crowding. *J. Parasitol.* 47:209.

HONIGBERG, B. M. 1967. Chemistry of parasitism among some Protozoa. In *Chemical Zoology* (eds., M. FLORKIN and B. T. SCHEER), 1:695. Academic Press, New York.

HONIGBERG, B. M. and C. P. READ. 1960. Virulence transformation of a trichomonad protozoan. *Science* 131:352.

HOPKINS, C. A. 1967. The *in vitro* cultivation of cestodes with particular reference to *Hymenolepis nana.* In *Problems of In Vitro Culture* (ed., A. E. R. TAYLOR). Blackwell Scientific Publications, Oxford and Edinburgh.

HOPKINS, G. H. E. 1957. Host-associations of Siphonaptera. In *First Symposium on Host Specificity Among Parasites of Vertebrates*, p. 64. Inst. Zool., University of Neuchâtel.

HOTCHKISS, R. D. 1951. Transfer of penicillin resistance in pneumococci by the desoxyribonucleate derived from resistant cultures. *Cold Spring Harbor Symp. Quant. Biol.* 16:457.

HOUSE, H. L. 1958a. Nutritional requirements of insects associated with animal parasitism. *Exptl. Parasitol.* 7:555.

HOUSE, H. L. 1958b. The nutrition of insects with particular reference to entomophagous parasites. *Proc. Tenth Intern. Congr. Entomol.* 2:139.

HOUSE, H. L. 1959. Nutrition of the parasitoid *Pseudosarcophaga affinis* (Fall.) and of other insects. In Axenic culture of invertebrate Metazoa: A goal. *Ann. N.Y. Acad. Sci.* 77:394.

HSÜ, H. F. 1938a. Studies on the food and the digestive system of certain parasites. I. On the food of the dog hookworm, *Ancylostoma caninum. Bull. Fan Memorial Inst. (Zool. Series)* 8:121.

HSÜ, H. F., and S. Y. L. HSÜ. 1958. On the size and shape of the eggs of the geographic strains of *Schistosoma japonicum. Am. J. Trop. Med. Hyg.* 7:125.

HUFF, C. G. 1931. A proposed classification of disease transmission by arthropods. *Science* 74:456.

HUFF, C. G. 1938. Studies on the evolution of some disease-forming organisms. *Quart. Rev. Biol.* 13:196.

HUFF, C. G. 1941. Factors influencing infection of *Anopheles* with malarial parasites. In *A Symposium on Human Malaria. AAAS Publ.* 15:108.

HUFF, C. G. 1956. Parasitism and parasitology. *J. Parasitol.* 42:1.

HUFF, C. G. 1958. Host influences on some haemosporidian parasites. *Rice Inst. Pam.* 45(1):55.

HUFF, C. G. 1963. Experimental research on avian malaria. In *Advances in Parasitology* (ed., B. DAWES). Vol. 1, p. 1. Academic Press, New York.

HUFF, C. G. 1965. Susceptibility of mosquitoes to avian malaria. *Exptl. Parasitol.* 16:107.

HUFF, C. G., A. C. PIPKIN, A. B. WEATHERSBY, and D. V. JENSEN. 1960. The morphology and behavior of living exocrythrocytic stages of *Plasmodium gallinaceum* and *P. fallex* and Thai host cells. *J. Biophys. Biochem. Cytol.* 7:93.

HUGHES, T. E. 1940. The effects on the fat and starch metabolism of *Gebia* by the parasite *Gyge branchiolis. J. Exptl. Biol.* 17:331.

HUNGATE, R. E. 1943. Quantitative analyses on the cellulose fermentation by termite Protozoa. *Ann. Entomol. Soc. Amer.* 36:730.

HUNGATE, R. E. 1955. Mutualistic intestinal Protozoa. In Biochemistry and Physiology of Protozoa (eds., S. H. HUTNER and A. LWOFF) 2:159. Academic Press, New York.

HUNGATE, R. E. 1966. *The Rumen and Its Microbes.* Academic Press, New York.

HUNTER, F. R. 1960. Aerobic metabolism of *Crithidia fasciculata. Exptl. Parasitol.* 9:271.

HUNTER, G. W., C. J. WEINMANN, and R. G. HOFFMANN. 1961. Studies on schistosomiasis. XVII. Non-reciprocal acquired resistance between *Schistosoma mansoni* and *Schistosomatium douthitti* in mice. *Exptl. Parasitol.* 11:133.

HUTNER, S. H., H. BAKER, S. AARONSON, H. A. NATHAN, E. RODRIGUEZ, S. LOCKWOOD, M. SANDERS, R. A. PETERSON. 1957. Growing *Ochromonas malhamensis* above 35° C. *J. Protozool.* 4:259.

INGLIS, W. G. 1965. Patterns of evolution in parasitic nematodes. In *Evolution of Parasites* (ed., A. E. R. TAYLOR), p. 79. Blackwell Scientific Publications, Oxford.

INOKI, S. and A. MATSUSHIRO. 1960. Transformation of drug-resistance in *Trypanosoma. Biken's J.* 3:101.

JACKSON, A. R. B. 1962. Excystation of *Eimeria arloingi* (Marotel, 1905): stimuli from the host sheep. *Nature* 194:847.

JACKSON, G. J. 1962. The parasitic nematode, *Neoplectana glaseri*, in axenic culture. II. Initial results with defined media. *Exptl. Parasitol.* 12:25.

JACKSON, G. J., and N. R. STOLL. 1964. Axenic culture studies of *Entamoeba* species. *Amer. J. Trop. Med. Hyg.* 13:520.

JACOBSEN, N. S., and D. FAIRBAIRN. 1967. Lipid metabolism in helminth parasites. III. Biosynthesis and interconversion of fatty acids by *Hymenolepis diminuta* (Cestoda). *J. Parasitol.* 53:355.

JENNINGS, J. B. 1968. Digestion in flatworms. In *Chemical Zoology* (eds., M. FLORKIN and B.

SCHEER), Vol. 2. Academic Press, New York.

JENNINGS, F. W., W. MULLIGAN, and G. M. URQUHART. 1956. Radioisotope studies on the anaemia produced by infection with *Fasciola hepatica. Exptl. Parasitol.* 5:458.

JERNE, N. K. 1955. The natural-selection theory of antibody formation. *Proc. Natl. Acad. Sci.* 41:849.

JEZYK, P. F., and D. FAIRBAIRN. 1967a. Ascarosides and ascaroside esters in *Ascaris lumbricoides* (Nematoda). *Comp. Biochem. Physiol.* 23:691.

JEZYK, P. F., and D. FAIRBAIRN. 1967b. Metabolism of ascarosides in the ovaries of *Ascaris lumbricoides* (Nematoda). *Comp. Biochem. Physiol.* 23:707.

JOHNSON, T. 1960. Genetics of pathogenicity. In *Plant Pathology* (eds., J. G. HORSFALL and A. E. DIMOND). Academic Press, New York.

JOKLIK, W. K. 1966. The poxviruses. *Bacterial Rev.* 30:33.

JONGH, P. DE. 1938. On the symbiosis of *Ardisia crispa* (Thunb.). *Verhandel. Koninkl. Ned. Akad. Wetenschap., Afdel. Natuurk.,* Sect. II; Vol. 37, No. 6.

JOSEPHINE, M. A. 1958. Experimental studies on *Entamoeba histolytica* in kittens. *Am. J. Trop. Med. Hyg.* 7:158.

JUNG, R. C. and D. B. JELLIFFE. 1952. The clinical picture and treatment of whipworm infection. *West African Med. J.* 1:11.

KABAT, E. A., and M. M. MAYER. 1962. *Experimental Immunochemistry.* 2nd Ed. Chas. C Thomas, Springfield, Ill.

KAGAN, I. G. 1958. Contributions to the immunology and serology of schistosomiasis. *Rice Inst. Pam.* 45(1):151.

KARAKASHIAN, S. J. 1963. Growth of *Paramecium bursaria* as influenced by the presence of algal symbionts. *Physiol. Zool.* 36:52.

KARAKASHIAN, S. J., and R. W. SIEGEL, 1965. A genetic approach to endocellular symbiosis. *Exptl. Parasitol.* 17:103.

KARAKASHIAN, S. J., M. W. KARAKASHIAN, and M. A. RUDZINSKA. 1968. Electron microscopic observations on the symbiosis of *Paramecium bursaria* and its intracellular algae. *J. Protozool.* 15:113.

KARTMAN, L. 1953. Factors influencing infection of the mosquito with *Dirofilaria immitis* (Leidy, 1856). *Exptl. Parasitol.* 2:27.

KASSANIS, B. 1963. Interaction of viruses in plants. *Advances Virus Res.* 10:219.

KASSANIS, B., and I. MACFARLANE. 1965. Interaction of virus strain, fungus isolate, and host species in the transmission of tobacco necrosis virus. *Virology* 26:603.

KATES, M., A. C. ALLISON, D. A. J. TYRELL, and A. T. JAMES. 1962. Origin of lipids of influenza virus. *Cold Spring Harbor Symp. Quant. Biol.* 27:293.

KEARN, G. C. 1967. Experiments on host-findings and host-specificity in the monogenean skin parasite *Entobdella soleae. Parasitology* 57:585.

KEEBLE, F. 1908. The yellow-brown cells of *Convoluta paradoxa. Quart. J. Microscop. Sci.* 52:431.

KEEBLE, F. 1910. *Plant-Animals. A Study in Symbiosis.* Cambridge University Press, London.

KEEBLE, F., and F. W. GAMBLE. 1907. The origin and nature of the green cells of *Convoluta roscoffensis. Quart. J. Microscop. Sci.* 51:167.

KEITT, G. W. 1959. History of Plant Pathology. In *Plant Pathology* (eds., J. G. HORSFALL and A. E. DIAMOND). Academic Press, New York.

KEITT, G. W., and M. H. LANGFORD. 1941. *Venturia inaequalis* (Cke.) Wint. I. A groundwork for genetic studies. *Am. J. Botan.* 28:805.

KEITT, G. W., M. H. LANGFORD, and J. R. SHAY. 1943. *Venturia inaequalis* (Cke). Wint. II. Genetic studies on pathogenicity and certain mutant characters. *Am. J. Botan.* 30:4091.

KEITT, G. W., C. C. LEBEN, and J. R. SHAY. 1948. Ibid. IV. Further studies on the inheritance of pathogenicity. *Am. J. Botan.* 35:334.

KENDALL, S. B. 1964. Some factors influencing the development and behaviour of trematodes in their molluscan hosts. In *Host-Parasite Relationships in Invertebrate Hosts* (ed., A. E. R. TAYLOR). Blackwell Scientific Publications, Oxford.

KEPPIE, J. 1964. Host and tissue specificity. In *Microbial Behaviour 'In Vivo' and 'In Vitro'* (eds. H. SMITH and J. TAYLOR). (14th *Symp. Soc. Genl. Microbiol.*) Cambridge University Press, London.

KERR, A. 1956. Some interactions between plant roots and pathogenic soil fungi. *Australian. J. Biol. Sci.* 9:45.

KERR, A., and N. T. FLENTJE. 1957. Host infection in *Pellicularia filamentosa* controlled by chemical stimuli. *Nature* 179:204.

KIMURA, R., et al. 1955. The uptake of radioactive phosphorus into phosphorus compounds in the brains of virus-infected mice. *Experientia* 11:160.

KIRBY, H., JR. 1941. Relationships between certain Protozoa and other animals. In *Protozoa in Biological Research* (ed., G. N. CALKINS and F. M. SUMMERS). Columbia University Press, New York.

KLEIN, D. T., and R. M. KLEIN. 1956. Quantitative aspects of transformation of virulence in *Agrobacterium tumefaciens. J. Bacteriol.* 72:308.

KLIENEBERGER-NOBEL, E. 1964. *Pleuropneumonialike Organisms (PPLO): Mycoplasmataceae.* Academic Press, London.

KLINE, D. M., D. M. BOONE, and G. W. KEITT. 1957. *Venturia inaequalis* (Cke.) Wint. XIV. Nutritional control of pathogenicity of certain induced biochemical mutants. *Am. J. Botan.* 44:797.

KLUYVER, A. J. and C. B. VAN NIEL. 1956. *The Microbe's Contribution to Biology.* Harvard University Press, Cambridge, Mass.

KMETEC, E., and E. BUEDING. 1965. Production of succinate by the canine whipworm *Trichuris vulpis. Comp. Biochem. Physiol.* 15:271.

KOCH, A. 1960. Intracellular symbiosis in insects. *Ann. Rev. Microbiol.* 14:121.

KORN, E. D. 1964. Biosynthesis of unsaturated fatty acids in *Acanthamoeba* sp. *J. Biol. Chem.* 239:396.

KORN, E. D., and C. L. GREENBLATT. 1963. Synthesis of α-linolenic acid by *Leishmania enrietti*. *Science* 142:1301.

KORN, E. D., C. L. GREENBLATT, and A. M. LEES. 1965. Synthesis of unsaturated fatty acids in the slime mold *Physarum polycephalum* and the zooflagellates *Leishmania tarentolae*, *Trypanosoma lewisi*, and *Crithidia* sp.: A comparative study. *Lipid Res.* 6:43.

KRASSNER, S. M. 1966. Cytochromes, lactic dehydrogenase and transformation in *Leishmania*. *J. Protozool.* 13:286.

KRUSBERG, L. R. 1960. Hydrolytic and respiratory enzymes of species of *Ditylenchus* and *Pratylenchus*. *Phytopathology* 50:9.

KRETSCHMAR, W. 1965. The effect of stress and diet on resistance to *Plasmodium berghei* and malaria immunity in the mouse. *Ann. Soc. Belge Med. Trop.* 45:325.

KROON, A. M. 1965. Protein synthesis in mitochondria. III. On the effects of inhibitors on the incorporation of amino acids into protein by intact mitochondria and digitonin fractions. *Biochim. Biophys. Acta* 108:275.

KUN, E., J. L. BRADIN, and J. M. DECHARY. 1956. Correlation between CO_2 and H_2S production by *Endamoeba histolytica*. *Biochim. Biophys. Acta* 19:153.

KUNKEL, L. O. 1918. Tissue invasion of *Plasmodiophora brassicae*. *J. Agr. Res.* 14:543.

LANG, N. J., and P. M. M. RAE. 1967. Structures in a blue-green alga resembling prolamellae bodies. *Protoplasma* 64:67.

LANGE, R. T. 1966. Bacterial symbiosis with plants. In *Symbiosis* (ed., S. M. HENRY), Vol. I. Academic Press, New York.

LARSON, R. H. 1934. Wound infection and tissue invasion by *Plasmidiophora brassicae*. *J. Agr. Res.* 49:607.

LAURIE, J. S. 1957. The in vitro fermentation of carbohydrate by two species of cestodes and one species of Acanthocephala. *Exptl. Parasitol.* 6:245.

LAURIE, J. S. 1959. Aerobic metabolism of *Moniliformis dubius* (Acanthocephala) *Exptl. Parasitol.* 8:188.

LAURIE, J. S. 1961. Carbohydrate absorption in cestodes from elasmobranch fishes. *Comp. Biochem. Physiol.* 4:63.

LAYRISSE, M., A. PAZ, N. BLUMENFELD, M. ROCHE. 1961. Hookworm anemia: Iron metabolism and erythrokinetics. *Blood* 18:61.

LEADER, R. W. 1967. Speculations on viral etiology of chronic degenerative diseases. In *Perspectives in Virology V.* (ed., M. Pollard), p. 309. Academic Press, New York.

LEAKE, D. V. 1939. Preliminary note on the production of motile cells in *Basicladia*. *Proc. Okla. Acad. Sci.* 19:109.

LEBEAU, J. B., and J. G. DICKSON. 1953. Preliminary report on the production of hydrogen cyanide by a snow-mold pathogen. *Phytopathology* 43, 581.

LEE, D. L. 1962. The distribution of esterase enzymes in *Ascaris lumbricoides*. *Parasitology* 52:241.

LEE, D. L. 1965. *The Physiology of Nematodes*. Oliver and Boyd, Edinburgh and London.

LEE, D. L., and M. H. SMITH. 1965. Hemoglobins of parasitic animals. *Exptl. Parasitol.* 16:392.

LEES, A. I. 1948. The sensory physiology of the sheep tick, *Ixodes ricinus* L. *J. Exptl. Biol.* 25:145.

LEDERBERG, J. 1952. Cell genetics and hereditary symbiosis. *Physiol. Rev.* 32:403.

LEDINKO, N. 1963. Genetic recombination with poliovirus type I. Studies of crosses between a normal horse serum resistant mutant and several guanidine resistant mutants of the same strain. *Virology* 20:107.

LELAND, S. E. 1963. Studies on the in vitro growth of parasitic nematodes. I. Complete or partial development of some gastro-intestinal nematodes of sheep and cattle. *J. Parasitol.* 49:600.

LEMMA, A., and E. L. SCHILLER. 1964. Extracellular cultivation of the leishmanial bodies of species belonging to the protozoan genus *Leishmania*. *Exptl. Parasitol.* 15:503.

LENHOFF, H. M., and K. F. ZIMMERMAN. 1959. Biochemical studies of symbiosis in *Chlorohydra viridissima*. *Anat. Record.* 134:599.

LESSER, E. 1953. The effects of some hormones and related compounds on the bacteria-free culture of *Entamoeba invadens* and free-living amoebae. *Can. J. Zool.* 31:511.

LEVY, H. B., and S. BARON. 1957. The effect of animal viruses on host cell metabolism. *J. Infectious Diseases* 100:109.

LEWERT, R. M. 1958. Invasiveness of helminth larvae. *Rice Inst. Pamph.* 45(1):97.

LEWIS, R. W. 1953. An outline of the balance hypothesis of parasitism. *Am. Nat.* 87:273.

L'HÉRITIER, P. 1958. The hereditary virus of *Drosophilia*. *Advan. Virus Res.* 5:195.

LINCOLN, R. E. 1940. Bacterial wilt resistance and genetic host-parasite interactions in maize. *J. Agr. Res.* 60:217.

LINFORD, M. B. 1937. The feeding of some hollow-stylet nematodes. *Proc. Helminthol. Soc. Wash.* 4:41.

LIPKE, H., and G. FRAENKEL. 1956. Insect Nutrition. *Ann. Rev. Entomol.* 1:17.

LLEWELLYN, J. 1965. The evolution of parasitic Platyhelminthes. In *Evolution of Parasites* (ed., A. E. R. TAYLOR), p. 47., Blackwell, Oxford.

LUND, P. G., and M. S. SHORB. 1962. Steroid requirements of trichomonads. *J. Protozool.* 9:151.

LUND, E. E., E. E. WEHR, and D. J. ELLIS. 1966. Earthworm transmission of *Heterakis* and *Histomonas* to turkeys and chickens. *J. Parasitol.* 52:899.

LURIA, S. E., and J. E. DARNELL, JR.. 1967. *Gen-*

eral Virology. John Wiley & Sons, New York.

LWOFF, A. 1944. *L'Évolution Physiologique: Études des Pertes de Fonctions chez les Micro-organismes.* Herman et Cie., Paris.

LWOFF, A. 1962. *Biological Order.* M.I.T. Press, Cambridge, Mass.

LWOFF, M. 1951. The nutrition of parasitic flagellates (Trypanosomidae, Trichomonadinae). In *Biochemistry and Physiology of Protozoa* (ed., A. LWOFF), Vol. 1. Academic Press, New York.

McCONNACHIE, E. W. 1960. Experiments on the encystation of *Opalina* in *Rana temporaria. Parasitology* 50:171.

McCUE, J. F., and R. E. THORSON. 1964. Behavior of parasitic stages of helminths in a thermal gradient. *J. Parasitol.* 50:67.

MacDONALD, W. W. 1962. The genetic basis of susceptibility to infection with semi-periodic *Brugia malayai* in *Aedes aegypti. Ann. Trop. Med. Parasitol.* 56:373.

MacDONALD, W. W., and C. P. RAMACHANDRAN. 1965. The influence of the gene f^m (filarial susceptibility, *Brugia malayi*) on the susceptibility of *Aedes aegypti* to seven strains of *Brugia, Wuchereria* and *Dirofilaria. Ann. Trop. Med. Parasitol.* 59:64-73.

MacINNIS, A. J. 1965. Responses of *Schistosoma mansoni* miracidia to chemical attractants. *J. Parasitol.* 51:731.

MacINNIS, A. J., F. M. FISHER, and C. P. READ. 1965. Membrane transport of purines and pyrimidines in a cestode. *J. Parasitol.* 51:260.

McKEE, R. W. 1951. Biochemistry of *Plasmodium* and the influence of antimalarials. In *Biochemistry and Physiology of Protozoa* (ed., A. LWOFF), Vol. 1. Academic Press, New York.

McLAUGHLIN, J. J. A., and P. A. ZAHL. 1959. III. Axenic zooxanthellae from various invertebrate hosts. *Ann. N.Y. Acad. Sci.* 77:55.

McLAUGHLIN, J. J. A., and P. A. ZAHL. 1966. Endozoic algae. In *Symbiosis* (ed., S. M. HENRY), Vol. 1. Academic Press, New York.

MacMILLAN, J., and P. J. SUTER. 1958. The occurrence of gibberellin A in higher plants and isolation from the seed of the runner bean (*Phaseolus multiflorus*). *Naturwissenschaften* 45:46.

MADSEN, H., and J. H. WHITLOCK. 1958. The inheritance of resistance to trichostrongylidosis in sheep. III. Preliminary studies using a gastric pouch. *Cornell Vet.* 48:145.

MAEGRAITH, B. 1958. Schistosomiasis in China. *Lancet,* January 25, 1958:208.

MAKOWER, M., and E. A. BEVAN. 1963. The inheritance of a killer character in yeast (*Saccharomyces cerevisiae*). *Proc. Eleventh Intern. Congr. Genet.* 1:202.

MANSOUR, T. E. 1969. Studies on carbohydrate metabolism of the liver fluke, *Fasciola hepatica. Biochim. Biophys. Acta* 34:456.

MANSOUR, T. E. 1967. Effect of hormones on carbohydrate metabolism of invertebrates. *Fed. Proc.* 26:1179.

MANSOUR, T. E. and E. BUEDING. 1953. Kinetics of lactic dehydrogenases of *Schistosoma mansoni* and of rabbit muscle. *Brit. J. Pharmacol. Chemotherapy* 8:431.

MANSOUR, T. E. and E. BUEDING. 1954. The actions of antimonials on glycolytic enzymes of *Schistosoma mansoni. Brit. J. Pharmacol. Chemotherapy* 9:459.

MANSOUR, T. E., E. BUEDING, and A. B. STAVITSKY. 1954. The effect of antiserum on the activities of lactic dehydrogenase of mammalian muscle and of *Schistosoma mansoni. Brit. J. Pharmacol. Chemotherapy* 9:182.

MANTER, H. W. 1955. The zoogeography of trematodes of marine fishes. *Exptl. Parasitol.* 4:62.

MANTER, H. W. 1966. Parasites of fishes as biological indicators of recent and ancient conditions. In *Host-Parasite Relationships* (ed., J. E. McCAULEY). Oregon State University Press, Corvallis, Ore.

MARAMOROSCH, K. 1960. Friendly viruses. *Sci. Am.* 203(2):138.

MARAMOROSCH, K. 1963. Harmful and beneficial effects of plant viruses in insects. *Ann. Rev. Microbiol.* 17:495.

MARMUR, J., S. FALKOW, and M. MANDEL. 1963. New approaches to bacterial taxonomy. *Ann. Rev. Microbiol.* 17:329.

MARTIN, C. J., and I. CLUNIES-ROSS. 1934. A minimal computation of the amount of blood removed daily by *Haemonchus contortus. J. Helminthol.* 12:137.

MARTIN, J. T., R. F. BATT, and R. T. BURCHILL. 1957. Defense mechanisms of plants against fungi. *Nature* 180:796.

MASSEY, V., and W. P. ROGERS. 1950. The intermediary metabolism of nematode parasites. I. The general reactions of the tricarboxylic acid cycle. *Australian J. Sci. Res.,* B, 3:251.

MASSEY, V., and W. P. ROGERS. 1951. Conditions affecting the action of fluoroacetate on the metabolism of nematode parasites and vertebrate animals. *Australian J. Sci. Res.,* B, 4:561.

MAYR, E. 1957. Evolutionary aspects of host specificity among parasites of vertebrates. In *First Symposium on Host Specificity among Parasites of Vertebrates.* University of Neuchâtel, Switzerland.

MEDAWAR, P. B. 1960. *The Future of Man.* Methuen & Co., London.

MELIN, E. 1963. Some effects of forest tree roots on mycorrhizal Basidiomycetes. In *Symbiotic Associations* (eds., P. S. NUTMAN and B. MOSSE). Cambridge University Press, London and New York.

MELLANBY, K., C. G. JOHNSON, W. C. BARTLEY, and P. BROWN. 1942. Experiments on the survival and behavior of the itch mite *Sarcoptes scabiei* DeG. var. *hominis. Bull. Entomol. Res.* 33:267.

MERCADO, T. I., and T. VON BRAND. 1967. Histochemical localization of glycogen-synthesizing enzymes during parasitic infections. *Exptl. Parasitol.* 21:325.

MESELSON, M. 1967. The molecular basis of genetic recombination. In *Heritage from Mendel* (ed., R. A. BRINK), p. 81. University of Wisconsin Press, Madison.

METALNIKOV, S., and V. CHORINE. 1930. Étude sur l'immunité naturelle et acquise des *Pyrausta nubilalis. Ann. inst. Pasteur* 44:273.

METCHNIKOFF, E. 1905. *Immunity in Infective Diseases* (Transl., F. G. BINNIE). Cambridge University Press, London and New York.

MEYER, H., and G. G. HOLZ, JR. 1966. Biosynthesis of lipids by kinetoplastid flagellates. *J. Biol. Chem.* 241:5000.

MIRETSKI, O. Y. 1951. Experiment on controlling the processes of vital activity of the helminth by influencing the condition of the host. *Dokl. Ob. Soft. Akad. Nauk SSSR* 78:613.

MICHAJLOW, W. 1951. Stadialnosc rozwoju niektorych tasiemcow (Cestoda). *Ann. Univ. Mariae Curie-Sklowdowska* 6:77.

MICKS, D. W. 1949. Investigations on the mosquito transmission of *Plasmodium elongatum* Huff, 1930. *J. Natl. Malaria Soc.* 8:206.

MICKS, D. W., and M. J. FERGUSON. 1961. Microorganisms associated with mosquitoes. III. Effect of reduction in the microbial flora of *Culex fatigans* Weidemann on the susceptibility to *Plasmodium relictum* Grassi and Feletti. *J. Insect. Pathol.* 3:244.

MILLEMANN, R. E. 1955. Studies on the life-history and biology of *Oochoristica deserti* n. sp. (Cestoda: Linstowiidae) from desert rodents. *J. Parasitol.* 41:424.

MILLEMANN, R. E. and J. C. THONARD. 1959. Protease activity in schistosome cercariae. *Exptl. Parasitol.* 8:129-136.

MOEHRING, T. J., J. M. MOEHRING, R. J. KUCHLER, and M. SOLOTOROVSKY. 1967. The response of cultured mammalian cells to diphtheria toxin. I. Amino acid transport, accumulation, and incorporation in normal and intoxicated cells. *J. Exptl. Med.* 126:407.

MOFTY, M. M. EL, and J. D. SMYTH. 1959. Endocrine control of sexual reproduction in *Opalina ranarum* parasitic in *Rana temporaria. Nature* 186:559.

MOFTY, M. M. EL, and J. D. SMYTH. 1964. Endocrine control of encystation in *Opalina ranarum* parasitic in *Rana temporaria. Exptl. Parasitol.* 15:185.

MOREAU, R. E. 1933. The food of the red-billed oxpecker, *Buphagus erythrorhynchus* (Stanley). *Bull. Entomol. Res.* 24:325.

MORSE, M. L. 1959. Transduction by staphylococcal bacteriophage. *Proc. Natl. Acad. Sci.* 45:722.

MORSE, M. L., E. M. LEDERBERG, and J. LEDERBERG. 1956. Transduction in *Escherichia coli* K$_{12}$. *Genetics* 41:142.

MOSER, J. C. 1964. Inquiline roach responds to trail-marking substance of leaf-cutting ants. *Science* 143:1048.

MOSER, J. C., and M. S. BLUM. 1963. Trail marking substance of the Texas leaf-cutting ant: Source and potency. *Science* 140:1228.

MOSSE, B. 1963. Vesicular-arbuscular mycorrhiza: An extreme form of fungal adaptation. In *Symbiotic Associations* (eds., P. S. NUTMAN and B. MOSSE). Cambridge University Press, London and New York.

MOULDER, J. W. 1962. *The Biochemistry of Intracellular Parasitism.* University of Chicago Press, Chicago.

MOULDER, J. W. 1964. *The Psittacosis Group as Bacteria.* John Wiley & Sons, New York.

MOULDER, J. W., and E. A. EVANS, JR. 1946. The biochemistry of the malaria parasite. VI. Studies on the nitrogen metabolism of the malaria parasite. *J. Biol. Chem.* 164:145.

MUELLER, J. A. 1963. Separation of kappa particles with infective activity from those with killing activity and identification of the infective particles in *Paramecium aurelia. Exptl. Cell Res.* 30:492.

MUELLER, J. F. 1959. The laboratory propagation of *Spirometra mansonoides* (Mueller, 1935) as an experimental tool. III. In vitro cultivation of the plerocercoid larva in a cell-free medium. *J. Parasitol.* 45:561.

MUELLER, J. F. 1963. Parasite-induced weight gains in mice. *Ann. N.Y. Acad. Sci.* 113(1):217.

MUELLER, J. F. 1965. Further studies on parasitic obesity in mice, deer mice, and hamsters. *J. Parasitol.* 51:523.

MUELLER, K. O. 1950. Affinity and reactivity of Angiosperms to *Phytophthora infestans. Nature* 166:392.

MUELLER, K. O. 1953. The nature of resistance of the potato plant to blight-*Phytophthora infestans. J. Natl. Inst. Agr. Botan.* 6:346.

MUELLER, K. O. 1956. Einige einfache Versuche zum Nachweis von Phytoalexinen. *Phytopathol. Zeit.* 27:237.

MUELLER, K. O. 1959. Hypersensitivity. In *Plant Pathology* (eds., J. G. HORSFALL and A. E. DIMOND), Vol. 1. Academic Press, New York.

MUSCATINE, L. 1965. Symbiosis of hydra and algae. III. Extracellular product of the algae. *Comp. Biochem. Physiol.* 16:77.

MUSCATINE, L. 1967. Glycerol excretion by symbiotic algae from corals and *Tridacna* and its control by the host. *Science* 156:516.

MUSCATINE, L., S. J. KARAKASHIAN, and M. W. KARAKASHIAN. 1967. Soluble extracellular products of algae symbiotic with a ciliate, a sponge, and a mutant hydra. *Comp. Biochem. Physiol.* 20:1.

MUSCATINE, L., and H. M. LENHOFF. 1963. Symbiosis: On the role of algae symbiotic with hydra. *Science* 142:956.

MUSCATINE, L., and H. M. LENHOFF. 1965. Symbiosis of hydra and algae. II. Effects of limited food and starvation on growth of symbiotic and aposymbiotic hydra. *Biol. Bull.* 129:316.

NEWTON, B. A. 1956. A synthetic growth medium for the trypanosomid flagellate, *Strigomonas* (*Herpetomonas*) *oncopelti*. *Nature* 177:279.

NEWTON, W. L. 1952. The comparative tissue reaction of two strains of *Australorbis glabratus* to infection with *Schistosoma mansoni*. *J. Parasitol*. 38:362.

NEWTON, W. L. 1953. The inheritance of susceptibility to infection with *Schistosoma mansoni* in *Australorbis glabratus*. *Exptl. Parasitol*. 2:242.

NIGRELLI, R. F. 1937. Further studies on the susceptibility and acquired immunity of marine fishes to *Epibdella melleni*. *Zoologica* 22:185.

NISHI, M. 1933. Ancylostomiasis ni miru kinketsu no seiin ni kansuru jikkenteki kenkyu. *J. Med. Assoc. Formosa* 32:677.

NOBLE, E. R., and G. A. NOBLE. 1964. *Parasitology: The Biology of Animal Parasites* (2nd ed.). Lea & Febiger, Philadelphia.

NÜESCH, J. 1963. Defence reactions in orchid bulbs. In *Symbiotic Associations* (*Symp. Soc. Genl. Microbiol*. 13). Cambridge University Press, London and New York.

NUTMAN, P. S. 1963. Factors influencing the balance of mutual advantage in legume symbiosis. In *Symbiotic Associations* (*Symp. Soc. Genl. Microbiol*. 13) (eds., P. S. NUTMAN and B. MOSSE). Cambridge University Press, London and New York.

NYBERG, P. A., D. H. BAUER, and S. E. KNAPP. 1968. Carbon dioxide as the initial stimulus for excystation of *Eimeria tenella* oocysts. *J. Protozool*. 15:144.

NYBERG, W. 1958. The uptake and distribution of Co^{60}-labeled vitamin B_{12} by the fish tapeworm, *Diphyllobothrium latum*. *Exptl. Parasitol*. 7:178.

NYBERG, W. 1963. The effect of changes in nutrition on the host-parasite relationship. *Diphyllobothrium latum* and human nutrition, with particular reference to vitamin B_{12} deficiency. *Proc. Nutr. Soc., London* 22:8.

ODUM, E. P. 1959. *Fundamentals of Ecology* (2nd ed.). W. B. Saunders, Philadelphia.

ODUM, H. T., and ODUM, E. P. 1955. Trophic structure and productivity of a windward coral reef community on Eniwetok Atoll. *Ecol. Monographs* 25:291.

OSCHMAN, J. L. 1966. Development of the symbiosis of *Convoluta roscoffensis* Graff and *Platymonas* sp. *J. Phycol*. 2:105.

OSCHMAN, J. L. 1967. Structure and reproduction of the algal symbionts of *Hydra viridis*. *J. Phycol*. 3:221.

OKAZAKI, T., R. W. BRIEHL, J. B. WITTENBERG, and B. A. WITTENBERG. 1965a. The hemoglobin of *Ascaris* perienteric fluid. II. Molecular weight and subunits. *Biochim. Biophys. Acta* 111:496.

OKAZAKI, T., and J. B. WITTENBERG. 1965b. The hemoglobin of *Ascaris* perienteric fluid. III. Equilibria with oxygen and carbon monoxide. *Biochim. Biophys. Acta* 111:503.

PANT, N. C., and G. FRAENKEL. 1954. Studies on the symbiotic yeasts of two insect species, *Lasioderma serricorne* F. and *Stegobium paniceum* L. *Biol. Bull*. 107:420.

PARKE, M., and I. MANTON. 1967. The specific identity of the algal symbiont in *Convoluta roscoffensis*. *J. Marine. Biol. Assoc. U.K.* 47:445.

PARK, T. 1948. Experimental studies of interspecies competition. I. Competition between populations of the flour beetles *Tribolium confusum* Duval and *Tribolium castaneum* Herbst. *Ecol. Monographs* 18:265.

PAUL, J. R. 1958. *Clinical Epidemiology*. University of Chicago Press, Chicago.

PEARSON, I. G. 1963. Use of the chromium radioisotope ^{51}Cr to estimate blood loss through ingestion by *Fasciola hepatica*. *Exptl. Parasitol*. 13:186.

PECK, S. S., W. H. WRIGHT, and J. Q. GANT. 1943. Cutaneous reactions due to the body louse (*Pediculus humanus*). *J. Am. Med. Assoc*. 123:821.

PFEFFERKORN, E. R., and R. L. CLIFFORD. 1964. The origin of the protein of Sindbis virus. *Virology* 23:217.

PHIFER, K. O. 1960a. Permeation and membrane transport in animal parasites: The absorption of glucose by *Hymenolepis diminuta*. *J. Parasitol*. 46:51.

PHIFER, K. O. 1960b. Permeation and membrane transport in animal parasites: Further observations on the uptake of glucose by *Hymenolepis diminuta*. *J. Parasitol* 46:137.

PHIFER, K. O. 1960c. Permeation and membrane transport in animal parasites: On the mechanism of glucose uptake by *Hymenolepis diminuta*. *J. Parasitol*. 46:145.

PIMENTEL, D., R. AL-HAFIDH, E. H. FEINBERG, J. L. MADDEN, W. P. NAGEL, N. J. PARKER, and F. A. STREAMS. 1962 Self-regulation in natural communities *Cornell Plantations* 17:51.

PITELKA, D. R. 1963. *Electron-Microscopic Structure of Protozoa*. Macmillan Co., New York.

PIZZI, T., and W. H. TALIAFERRO. 1960. A comparative study of protein and nucleic acid synthesis in different species of trypanosomes. *J. Infectious Diseases* 107:100.

PLUMB, G. H. 1953. The formation and development of the Norway spruce gall caused by *Adelges abietis* L. *Conn. Agr. Expt. Sta. Bull*. 566:1.

POLLAK, J. K. 1957. The metabolism of *Ascaris lumbricoides* ovaries. III. The synthesis of alanine from pyruvate and ammonia. *Australian J. Biol. Sci*. 10:465.

POLLAK, J. K., and D. FAIRBAIRN. 1955. The metabolism of *Ascaris lumbricoides* ovaries. II. Amino acid metabolism. *Can. J. Biochem. Physiol*. 33:307.

POLLARD, M. (ed.). 1967. *Perspectives in Virology V*. Academic Press, New York.

PREER, J. R., JR., L. A. HUFNAGEL, and L. B. PREER. 1966 Structure and behavior of R bodies from killer paramecia. *J. Ultrastructure Res.* 15:131.

PRESCOTT, L. M., and J. W. CAMPBELL. 1965. Phosphoenolpyruvate carboxylase activity and glycogenesis in the flatworm *Hymenolepis diminuta*. *Comp. Biochem. Physiol.* 14:491.

PRÉVOST, B. 1807. Mémoire sur la cause immédiate de la carie ou charbon des blés, et de plusieurs autres maladies des plantes, et sur les préservatifs de la carie. Bernard, Paris. (English translation by G. W. KEITT in Phytopathol. Classics No. 6, 1939.)

PUCK, T. T., and H. H. LEE. 1955. Mechanisms of cell wall penetration of viruses. II. Demonstration of cyclic permeability change accompanying virus infection of *Escherichia coli* B cells. *J. Exptl. Med.* 101:151.

RACKER, E. 1954. Metabolism of infected cells. In *Cellular Metabolism and Infections*. (Ed., E. RACKER). Academic Press, New York.

RAILLIET, A. 1890. Une expérience propre à établir le mode d'alimentation du distome hépatique. *Bull. Soc. Zool. France* 15:88.

RAPP, F., and J. L. MELNICK. 1966. Papovirus SV40, adenovirus and their hybrids: Transformation, complementation and transcapsidation. *Prog. Med. Virol.* 8:349.

RATCLIFFE, L. H., H. M. TAYLOR, J. H. WHITLOCK, and W. R. LYNN. 1969. Systems analysis of a host-parasite interaction *Parasitol.* 59:649-661.

RATHBONE, L. 1955. Oxidative metabolism in *Ascaris lumbricoides* from the pig. *Biochem. J.* 61:574.

READ, C. P. 1950. The vertebrate small intestine as an environment for parasitic helminths. *Rice Inst. Pamphl.* 37(2):1.

READ, C. P. 1955. Intestinal physiology and the host-parasite relationship. In *Some Physiological Aspects and Consequences of Parasitism*. Rutgers University Press, New Brunswick, N.J.

READ, C. P. 1956. Carbohydrate metabolism of *Hymenolepis diminuta*. *Exptl. Parasitol.* 5:325.

READ, C. P. 1957. Comparative studies on the physiology of trichomonad Protozoa. *J. Parasitol.* 43:385.

READ, C. P. 1958. Status of behavioral and physiological "resistance." *Rice Institute Pamp.* 45(1):36.

READ, C. P. 1959. The role of carbohydrate in the biology of cestodes. VIII. Some conclusions and hypotheses. *Exptl. Parasitol.* 8:365.

READ, C. P. 1961. Carbohydrate metabolism of worms. In *Comparative Physiology of Carbohydrate Metabolism in Heterothermic Animals* (ed., A. W. MARTIN), University of Washington Press, Seattle.

READ, C. P. 1961. Competitions between sugars in their absorption by tapeworms. *J. Parasitol.* 47:1015.

READ, C. P. 1966. Nutrition of intestinal helminths. In *Biology of Parasites* (ed., E. J. L. SOULSBY). Academic Press, New York.

READ, C. P. 1968. Intermediary metabolism of

flatworms. In *Chemical Zoology* (ed., B. SCHEER and M. FLORKIN), Vol. 2. Academic Press, New York.

READ, C. P., and A. H. ROTHMAN. 1957. The role of carbohydrates in the biology of cestodes. II. The effect of starvation on glycogenesis and glucose consumption in *Hymenolepis*. *Exptl. Parasitol.* 6:280.

READ, C. P. and A. H. ROTHMAN. 1958. The carbohydrate requirement of *Moniliformis* (Acanthocephala). *Exptl. Parasitol.* 7:191.

READ, C. P., A. H. ROTHMAN, and J. E. SIMMONS, JR. 1963. Studies on membrane transport, with special reference to parasite-host integration. *Ann. N.Y. Acad. Sci.* 113:154.

READ, C. P., and J. E. SIMMONS, JR. 1963. The biochemistry and physiology of tapeworms. *Physiol. Rev.* 43:263.

REICHMAN, M. E. 1964. The satellite tobacco necrosis virus: A single protein and its genetic code. *Proc. Natl. Acad. Sci.* 52:1009.

REID, W. M. 1945a. The relationship between glycogen depletion in the nematode *Ascaridia galli* (Schrank) and elimination of the parasite by the host. *Am. J. Hyg.* 41:150.

REID, W. M. 1945b. Comparison between *in vitro* and *in vivo* glycogen utilization in the fowl nematode *Ascaridia galli*. *J. Parasitol.* 31:406.

REID, W. M. 1967. Etiology and dissemination of the blackhead disease syndrome in turkeys and chickens. *Exptl. Parasitol.* 21:249.

REINHARD, E. G. 1956. Parasitic castration of Crustacea. *Exptl. Parasitol.* 5:79.

RHOADES, H. L., and M. B. LINFORD. 1959. Molting of preadult nematodes of the genus *Paratylenchus* stimulated by root diffusates. *Science* 130:1476.

RICHARDS, A. G., and M. A. BROOKS. 1959. Internal symbiosis in insects. *Ann. Rev. Entomol.* 3:37.

ROBERTS, L. S., and D. FAIRBAIRN. 1965. Metabolic studies on adult *Nippostrongylus brasiliensis* (Nematoda: Trichostrogyloidea). *J. Parasitol.* 51:129.

ROBINSON, E. J. 1961. Survival of *Trichinella* in stressed hosts. *J. Parasitol.* 47:16.

ROBINSON, D. L. H. 1956. A routine method for the maintenance of *Schistosoma mansoni in vitro*. *J. Helminthol.* 29:193.

ROCHE, M., and C. MARTINEZ-TORRES. 1960. A method for *in vitro* study of hookworm activity. *Exptl. Parasitol.* 9:250.

ROCHE, M., and M. E. PEREZ-GIMENÉZ. 1959. Intestinal loss and reabsorption of iron in hookworm infection. *J. Lab. Clin. Med.* 54:49.

ROCHE, M., M. E. PEREZ-GIMENÉZ, M. LAYRISSE, and E. DIPRISCO. 1957. Study of urinary and fecal excretion of radioactive chromium Cr^{51} in man. Its use in the measurement of intestinal blood loss associated with hookworm infection. *J. Clin. Invest.* 36:1183.

ROGERS, W. P. 1940a. Haematological studies on

the gut contents of certain nematode and trematode parasites. *J. Helminthol.* 18:53.

ROGERS, W. P. 1940b. The occurrence of zinc and other metals in the intestine of *Strongylus* spp. *J. Helminthol.* 18:103.

ROGERS, W. P. 1941. Digestion in parasitic nematodes. The digestion of proteins. *J. Helminthol.* 19:47.

ROGERS, W. P. 1949. On the relative importance of aerobic metabolism in small nematode parasites of the alimentary tract. I and II. *Australian J. Sci. Res.* (B)2:157, 166.

ROGERS, W. P. 1958. The physiology of the hatching of eggs of *Ascaris lumbricoides*. *Nature* 181:1410.

ROGERS, W. P. 1960. The physiology of infective processes of nematode parasites; the stimulus from the animal host. *Proc. Roy. Soc.* (B)152:367.

ROGERS, W. P. 1962. *The Nature of Parasitism*. Academic Press, New York.

ROGERS, W. P. 1963. Physiology of infection with nematodes: Some effects of the host stimulus on infective stages. *Ann. N.Y. Acad. Sci.* 113:298.

ROGERS, W. P. 1965. The role of leucine aminopeptidase in the moulting of nematode parasites. *Comp. Biochem. Physiol.* 14:311.

ROGERS, W. P. 1966a. Reversible inhibition of a receptor governing infection with some nematodes. *Exptl. Parasitol.* 19:15.

ROGERS, W. P. 1966b. Exsheathment and hatching mechanisms in helminths. In *Biology of Parasites* (ed., E. J. L. SOULSBY). Academic Press, New York.

ROGERS, W. P. 1966c. The reversible inhibition of exsheathment in some parasitic nematodes. *Comp. Biochem. Physiol.* 17:1103.

ROGERS, W. P., and M. LAZARUS. 1949. The uptake of radioactive phosphorus from host tissues and fluids by nematode parasites. *Parasitology* 39:245.

ROGERS, W. P., and R. I. SOMMERVILLE. 1963. The infective stage of nematode parasites and its significance in parasitism. *Advan. Parasitol.* 1:109.

ROHRBACHER, G. H. 1957. Observations on the survival *in vitro* of bacteria-free adult common liver flukes, *Fasciola hepatica* Linn., 1758. *J. Parasitol.* 43:9.

ROLLO, I. M. 1955. The mode of action of sulphonamides, proguanil and pyrimethamine on *Plasmodium gallinaceum*. *Brit. J. Pharmacol. Chemotherap.* 10:208.

ROSATO, R. R., and J. A. CAMERON. 1964. The bacteriophage receptor sites of *Staphylococcus aureus*. *Biochim. Biophys. Acta* 83:113.

ROSS, D. M. 1960. The association between the hermit crab *Eupagurus bernhardus* (L.) and the sea anemone *Calliactis parasitica* (Couch). *Proc. Zool. Soc., London.* 134:43.

ROSS, D. M., and SUTTON, L. 1961. The association between the hermit crab *Dardanus arrosor*

(Herbst) and the sea anemone *Calliactis parasitica* (Couch). *Proc. Roy. Soc.* (Series B) 155:282–291.

ROTHMAN, A. H. 1958. The role of bile salts in the biology of tapeworms. I. Effects of bile salts on the metabolism of *Hymenolepis diminuta* and *Oochoristica symmetrica*. *Exptl. Parasitol.* 7:328-337.

ROTHMAN, A. H. 1959. Ibid. II. Further observations on the effects of bile salts on metabolism. *J. Parasitol.* 45:379.

ROTHMAN, A. H., and F. M. FISHER. 1964. Permeation of amino acids in *Moniliformis* and *Macracanthorhynchus* (Acanthocephala). *J. Parasitol.* 50:410.

ROTHSCHILD, M., and B. FORD. 1966. Hormones of the vertebrate host controlling ovarian regression and copulation of the rabbit flea. *Nature* 211:261.

ROWE, W. P. 1967. Some interactions of defective animal viruses. In *Perspectives in Virology* (ed., M. POLLARD), Vol. 5, p. 123. Academic Press, New York.

RUBIN, H. 1964. A defective cancer virus. *Sci. Am.*, June, 1964:46.

RUBIN, H. 1964. Virus defectiveness and cell transformation in Rous sarcoma. *J. Cell. Comp. Physiol.* 64 (Suppl. 1):173.

RUDZINSKA, M. A., P. A. D'ALESANDRO, and W. TRAGER. 1964. The fine structure of *Leishmania donovani* and the role of the kinetoplast in the leishmania-leptomonad transformation. *J. Protozool.* 11:166.

RUDZINSKA, M. A., and W. TRAGER. 1957. Intracellular phagotrophy by malaria parasites: An electron microscope study of *Plasmodium lophurae*. *J. Protozool.* 4:190.

RUDZINSKA, M. A., and W. TRAGER. 1959. Phagotrophy and two new structures in the malaria parasite *Plasmodium berghei*. *J. Biophys. Biochem. Cytol.* 6:103.

RUDZINSKA, M. A., and W. TRAGER. 1962. Intracellular phagotrophy in *Babesia rodhaini* as revealed by electron microscopy. *J. Protozool.* 9:279.

RUDZINSKA, M. A., W. TRAGER, and R. S. BRAY. 1965. Pinocytotic uptake and the digestion of hemoglobin in malaria parasites. *J. Protozool.* 12:563.

RYLEY, J. F. 1955. Studies on the metabolism of the Protozoa. 4. Metabolism of the parasitic flagellate *Strigomonas oncopelti*. *Biochem. J.* 59:353.

RYLEY, J. F. 1967. Carbohydrates and respiration. In *Chemical Zoology* (ed., G. W. KIDDER), Vol. 1. Academic Press, New York.

SADASIVAN, T. S., and C. V. SUBRAMANIAN. 1960. Interaction of pathogen, soil, other microorganisms in the soil, and the host. In *Plant Pathology* (eds., J. G. HORSFALL and A. E. DIMOND), Vol. 2, Academic Press, New York.

SAGEN, L. 1967. On the origin of mitosing cells. *J. Theoret. Biol.* 14:225.

SAKAGUCHI, B., and D. F. POULSON. 1963. Interspecific transfer of the 'sex-ratio' condition from *Drosphila willistoni* to *D. melanogaster*. *Genetics* 48:841.

SALT, G. 1960a. Experimental studies in insect parasitism, XI. The haemocytic reaction of a caterpillar under varied conditions. *Proc. Roy. Soc.* (Series B) 151:446.

SALT, G. 1960b. Surface of a parasite and the haemocytic reaction of its host. *Nature* 188:162.

SALT, G. 1961. The haemocytic reaction of insects to foreign bodies. In *The Cell and Organism*. Cambridge University Press, New York.

SALT, G. 1963. The defence reactions of insects to metazoan parasites. *Parasitology* 53:527.

SARGENT, M. S., and AUSTIN, T. S. 1954. Biologic economy of coral reefs. *U.S. Geol. Surv. Profess. Papers* 260–E:293.

SASTRY, A. N., and R. W. MENZEL. 1962. Influence of hosts on the behavior of the commensal crab *Pinnotheres maculatus* Say. *Biol. Bull.* 123:388.

SAYRE, F. W., E. L. HANSEN, and E. A. YARWOOD. 1963. Biochemical aspects of the nutrition of *Caenorhabditis briggsae*. *Exptl. Parasitol.* 13:98.

SAZ, H. J., and E. BUEDING. 1966. Relationships between anthelmintic effects and biochemical and physiological mechanisms. *Pharmacol. Rev.* 18:871.

SAZ, H. J., and O. L. LESCURE. 1966. Interrelationships between the carbohydrate and lipid metabolism of *Ascaris lumbricoides* egg and adult stages. *Comp. Biochem. Physiol.* 18:845.

SAZ, H. J., and A. VIDRINE. 1959. The mechanism of formation of succinate and propionate by *Ascaris lumbricoides* muscle. *J. Biol. Chem.* 234:2001.

SAZ, H. J., A. VIDRINE, JR., and J. A. HUBBARD. 1958. The formation of alpha-acetolactic acid and acetylmethyl-carbinol by *Ascaris lumbricoides*. *Exptl. Parasitol.* 7:477.

SAZ, H. J., and A. WEIL. 1960. The mechanism of the formation of α-methylbutyrate from carbohydrate by *Ascaris lumbricoides* muscle. *J. Biol. Chem.* 235:914.

SCHAD, G. A. 1963. Niche diversification in a parasitic species flock. *Nature* 198:404.

SCHAD, G. A. 1966. Immunity, competition, and natural regulation of helminth populations. *Am. Naturalist* 100:359.

SCHEIBEL, L. W., and H. J. SAZ. 1966. The pathway for anaerobic carbohydrate dissimilation in *Hymenolepis diminuta*. *Comp. Biochem. Physiol.* 18:151.

SCHEIBEL, L. W., H. J. SAZ, and E. BUEDING. 1968. The anaerobic incorporation of ^{32}P into adenosine triphosphate by *Hymenolepis diminuta*. *J. Biol. Chem.* 243:2229.

SCHILLER, E. L. 1959. Experimental studies on morphological variation in the cestode genus *Hymenolepis*. IV. Influence of the host on variation in *H. nana*. *Exptl. Parasitol.* 8:581.

SCHILLER, E. L. 1965. A simplified method for the *in vitro* cultivation of the rat tapeworm *H. diminuta*. *J. Parasitol.* 51:516.

SCHNEIDER, F. 1951. Einige physiologische Beziehungen zwischen Syrphiden-larven und ihren Parasiten. *Z. Angew. Entomol.* 33:150.

SCHNEIDER, H. A. 1956. Nutritional and genetic factors in the natural resistance of mice to *Salmonella* infections. *Ann. N.Y. Acad. Sci.* 66:337.

SCRIMSHAW, N. W., C. E. TAYLOR, and J. E. GORDON. 1959. Interactions of nutrition and infection. *Am. J. Med. Sci.* 237:367.

SELYE, H. 1950. *Stress*. Acta, Inc., Montreal.

SEMPIO, C. 1950. Metabolic resistance to plant disease. *Phytopathology* 40:799.

SENFT, A. W. 1965. Recent developments in the understanding of amino acid and protein metabolism by *Schistosoma mansoni in vitro*. *Ann. Trop. Med. Parasitol.* 59:164.

SHAFFER, J. G., and V. IRALU. 1963. The selective ability of strains of *Entamoeba histolytica* to hemolyze red cells. *Am. J. Trop. Med. Hyg.* 12, 315.

SHAW, M. 1963. The physiology and host-parasite relations of the rusts. *Ann. Rev. Phytopathol.* 1:259.

SHAW, M. 1967. Cell biological aspects of host-parasite relations of obligate fungal parasites. *Can. J. Botan.* 45:1205.

SHEPARD, C. C. 1955. Phagocytosis by Hela cells and their susceptibility to infection by human tubercle bacilli. *Proc. Soc. Exptl. Biol. Med.* 90:392.

SHEPPE, W. A., and J. R. ADAMS. 1957. The pathogenic effect of *Trypanosoma duttoni* on hosts under stress conditions. *J. Parasitol.* 43:55.

SHERMAN, I. W., and G. J. JACKSON. 1963. Zymograms of the parasitic nematodes, *Neoaplectana glaseri* and *N. carpocapsae*, grown axenically. *J. Parasitol.* 49:392.

SHERMAN, I. W., J. B. MUDD, and W. TRAGER. 1965. Chloroquine resistance and the nature of malarial pigment. *Nature* 208:691.

SHERMAN, I. W., and I. P. TING. 1966. Carbon dioxide fixation in malaria (*Plasmodium lophurae*). *Nature* 212:1387.

SHOPE, R. E. 1940–42. The swine lungworm as a reservoir and intermediate host for swine influenza virus. I–IV. *J. Exptl. Med.* 74:41–68; 77:111–126; 127–138.

SHORB, M. S. 1964. The physiology of trichomonads. In *Biochemistry and Physiology of Protozoa* (ed. S. H. HUTNER). Vol. 3, p. 384. Academic Press, New York.

SHORB, M. S., and P. G. LUND. 1959. Requirement of trichomonads for unidentified growth factors, saturated and unsaturated fatty acids. *J. Protozool.* 6:122.

SIEGEL, R. W. 1960. Hereditary endo-symbiosis in *Paramoecium bursaria*. *Exptl. Cell. Res.* 19:239.

SIEGEL, R. W., and K. HECKMANN. 1966. Inheritance of autogamy and the killer trait in *Euplotes minuta*. *J. Protozool.* 13:34.

SILVERMAN, P. H. 1965. *In vitro* cultivation procedures for parasitic helminths. *Advan. Parasitol.* 3:159. Academic Press, New York.

SILVERMAN, P. H., and R. B. MANEELY. 1955. Studies on the biology of some tapeworms of the genus *Taenia*. III. The role of the secreting gland of the hexacanth embryo in the penetration of the intestinal mucosa of the intermediate host, and some of its histochemical reactions. *Ann. Trop. Med. Parasitol.* 49:326.

SILVERMAN, P. H., and K. R. PODGER. 1964. *In vitro* exsheathment of some nematode infective larvae. *Exptl. Parasitol.* 15:314.

SIMMONS, J. E., JR. 1961. Urease activity in trypanorhynch cestodes. *Biol. Bull.* 121:535.

SIMMONS, J. E., JR., C. P. READ, and A. H. ROTHMAN. 1960. Permeation and membrane transport in animal parasites: Permeation of urea into cestodes from elasmobranchs. *J. Parasitol.* 46:43.

SINCLAIR, K. B. 1964. Studies on the anemia of ovine fascioliasis. *Brit. Vet. J.* 120:212.

SISSAKIAN, N. M., I. I. FILIPPOVICH, E. N. SVETAILO, and K. A. ALIYER. 1965. On the protein-synthesizing system of chloroplasts. *Biochim. Biophys. Acta* 95:474.

SMITH, H., and J. TAYLOR (ed.). 1964. Microbial Behavior 'In Vivo' and 'In Vitro.' (*Symp. Soc. Genl. Microbiol* 14.) Cambridge University Press, London and New York.

SONNEBORN, T. M. 1949. Beyond the gene. *Am. Sci.* 37:33.

SONNEBORN, T. M. 1951. Beyond the gene—two years later. In *Science in Progress* (ed., G. A. BAITSELL). Yale University Press, New Haven, Conn.

SONNEBORN, T. M. 1959. Kappa and related particles in *Paramecium*. *Advan. Virus Res.* 6:229.

SLOBODKIN, L. B. 1961. *Growth and Regulation of Animal Populations.* Holt, Rinehart & Winston, New York.

SLOBODKIN, L. B. 1964. Experimental populations of Hydrida. *J. Ecol. (Suppl.)* 52:131.

SMITH, D. C. 1963. Experimental studies of lichen physiology. In *Symbiotic Associations* (eds., P. S. NUTMAN and B. MOSSE). Cambridge University Press, London and New York.

SMITH, G. 1913. Studies in the experimental analysis of sex. *Quart. J. Microsc. Sci.* 59:267.

SMITH, G. W. 1906. Rhizocephala. *Fauna Flora Golf. Neapel* 29:1.

SMITH, H. 1960. Studies on organisms grown *in vivo* to reveal the bases of microbial pathogenicity. *Ann. N.Y. Acad. Sci.* 88:1213.

SMITH, H., and J. KEPPIE. 1955. Studies on the chemical basis of the pathogenicity of *Bacillus anthracis* using organisms grown *in vivo*. In *Mechanisms of Microbial Pathogenicity* (eds., J. W. HOWIE and A. J. O'HEA), p. 126. Cambridge University Press, London.

SMITH, K. M. 1959. The insect viruses. In *The Viruses* (eds., F. M. BURNET and W. M. STANLEY) 3:369. Academic Press, New York.

SMITH-SONNEBORN, J. E., and W. J. VAN WAGTEN-

DONK. 1964. Purification and chemical characterization of kappa of stock 51, *Paramecium aurelia*. *Exptl. Cellular Res.* 33:50.

SMYTH, J. D. 1949. Studies on tapeworm physiology IV. Further observations on the development of *Ligula intestinalis*, in vitro. *J. Exptl. Biol.* 26:1.

SMYTH, J. D. 1959. Maturation of larval pseudophyllidean cestodes and strigeid trematodes under axenic conditions; the significance of nutritional levels in platyhelminth development. *Ann. N.Y. Acad. Sci.* 77:102.

SMYTH, J. D. 1961. Lysis of *Echinococcus granulosus* by surface-active agents in bile and the role of this phenomenon in determining host specificity in helminths. *Proc. Roy. Soc.* (Series B) 156:553.

SMYTH, J. D. 1967. Studies on tapeworm physiology XI. *In vitro* cultivation of *Echinococcus granulosus* from the protoscolex to the strobilate stage. *Parasitology* 57:111.

SMYTH, J. D., and J. A. CLEGG. 1959. Egg-shell formation in trematodes and cestodes. *Exptl. Parasitol.* 8:286.

SMYTH, J. D., and G. A. D. HASLEWOOD. 1963. The biochemistry of bile as a factor in determining host specificity in intestinal parasites, with particular reference to *Echinococcus granulosus*. *Ann. N.Y. Acad. Sci.* 113(1):234.

SNOW, J. 1855. *On the Mode of Communication of Cholera.* J. and A. Churchill, London.

SOLDO, A. T. 1963. Axenic culture of *Paramecium* —some observations on the growth behavior and nutritional requirements of a particle-bearing strain of *P. aurelia* 299 lambda. *Ann. N.Y. Acad. Sci.* 108:380.

SOMMER, F. 1880. Die Anatomie des Leberegels *Distomum hepaticum* L. *Z. Wiss. Zool.* 34:539.

SOMMERVILLE, R. I. 1957. The exsheathing mechanism of nematode infective larvae. *Exptl. Parasitol.* 6:18.

SOULSBY, E. J. L., R. I. SOMMERVILLE, and D. F. STEWART. 1959. Antigenic stimulus of exsheathing fluid in self-cure of sheep infected with *Haemonchus contortus*. *Nature*, 183:553.

SPECK, J. F., J. W. MOULDER, and E. A. EVANS, JR. 1946. The biochemistry of the malarial parasite. V. Mechanism of pyruvate oxidation in the malaria parasite. *J. Biol. Chem.* 164:119.

SPOONER, G. N. 1957. In *Plymouth Marine Fauna* (3rd ed.), p. 112.

SPRENT, J. F. A. 1962. The evolution of the Ascaridoidea. *J. Parasitol.* 48:818.

STABLER, R. M., and T. T. CHEN. 1936. Observations on an *Endamoeba* parasitizing opalinid ciliates. *Biol. Bull.* 70:56.

STAKMAN, E. C., and C. M. CHRISTENSEN. 1946. Aerobiology in relation to plant disease. *Bot. Rev.* 12:205.

STANIER, R. Y., and C. B. VAN NIEL. 1941. The main outlines of bacterial classification. *J. Bacteriol.* 42:437.

STAPLES, R. C., and M. A. STAHMANN. 1964.

Changes in proteins and several enzymes in susceptible bean leaves after infection by the bean rust fungus. *Phytopathology* 54:760.

STAUBER, L. A. 1958. Host resistance to the Khartoum strain of *Leishmania donovani*. *Rice Inst. Pam.* 45:80.

STEINERT, M. 1958. Action morphogenetique de l'urée sur le trypanosome. *Exptl. Cell Res.* 15:431.

STEINERT, M. 1958. Études sur le déterminisme de la morphogenèse d'un trypanosome. *Exptl. Cell Res.* 15:560.

STEINERT, M., and G. J. BONNÉ. 1956. Induced change from culture form to bloodstream form in *Trypanosoma mega*. *Nature* 178:362.

STEINERT, M., and G. STEINERT. 1960. Inhibition de la synthèse de l'acide désoxyribonucléique de Trypanosoma méga par l'urée à faible concentration. *Exptl. Cell Res.* 19:421.

STEINHAUS, E. A. 1955. Observations on the symbiotes of certain Coccidae. *Hilgardia* 24:185.

STEINHAUS, E. (ed.). 1963. *Insect Pathology*. Academic Press, New York.

STEINMAN, H. G., V. L. OYAMA, and H. O. SCHULZE. 1954. Cocarboxylase, citrovorum factor, and coenzyme A as essential growth factors for non-pathogenic treponeme. *Fed. Proc.* 13:512.

STENT, G. S. 1963. *Molecular Biology of Bacterial Viruses*. W. H. Freeman, San Francisco and London.

STEPHENS, J. M. 1959. Immune responses of some insects to some bacterial antigens. *Can. J. Microbiol.* 5:203.

STEPHENS, J. M. 1962. Bactericidal activity of the blood of actively immunized wax moth larvae. *Can. J. Microbiol.* 8:491.

STEPHENSON, W. 1947. Physiological and histochemical observations on the adult liver fluke, *Fasciola hepatica* L. *Parasitology* 38:123.

STEWART, D. F. 1950–53. Studies on resistance of sheep to infestation with *Haemonchus contortus* and *Trichostrongylus* spp. and on the immunological reactions of sheep exposed to infestation. I–V. *Australian J. Agric. Res.* 1:285–300, 301–321, 413–426, 427–439; 4:100–117.

STEWART, D. F. 1955. "Self-cure" in nematode infestations of sheep. *Nature* 176:1273.

STIREWALT, M. A. 1966. Skin penetration mechanisms of helminths. In *Biology of Parasites* (ed., E. J. L. SOULSBY). Academic Press, New York.

STITT, C., P. J. CHARLEY, E. M. BUTT, and P. SALTMAN. 1962. Rapid induction of iron deposition in spleen and liver with an iron-fructose chelate. *Proc. Soc. Exptl. Biol. Med.* 110:70.

STODOLA, F. H. 1958. *Chemical Transformations by Microorganisms*. John Wiley & Sons, New York.

STOLL, N. 1947. This wormy world. *J. Parasitol.* 33:1.

STOLL, N. R. 1957. Axenic serial culture in cell-free medium of *Entamoeba invadens*, a pathogenic amoeba of snakes. *Science* 126:1236.

STOLL, N. R. 1959. Conditions favoring the axenic culture of *Neoaplectana glaseri*, a nematode parasite of certain insect grubs. *Ann. N.Y. Acad. Sci.* 77(2):126.

TALIAFERRO, W. H., and H. W. MULLIGAN. 1937. The histopathology of malaria with special reference to the function and origin of the macrophages in defence. *Indian Med. Res. Mem.* 29:1.

TALIAFERRO, W. H., and L. G. TALIAFERRO. 1922. The resistance of different hosts to experimental trypanosome infections, with special reference to a new method of measuring this resistance. *Am. J. Hyg.* 2:264.

TAYLOR, F. H., and R. E. MURRAY. 1946. *Spiders, Ticks and Mites*. Serv. Publ. No. 6 (School of Public Health and Tropical Medicine). Australasian Medical Publications, Glebe, N.S.W., Australia.

TAYLOR, A., and J. H. WHITLOCK. 1960. The exsheathing stimulus for infective larvae of *Haemonchus contortus*. *Cornell Vet.* 50:339.

TEAKLE, D. S. 1962. Transmission of tobacco necrosis virus by a fungus, *Olpidium brassicae*. *Virology* 18:224.

TEAKLE, D. S., and A. H. GOLD. 1963. Further studies of *Olpidium* as a vector of tobacco necrosis virus. *Virology* 19:310.

TERZIAN, L. A., and N. STAHLER. 1960. Some inorganic acids, bases and salts as determinants of innate immunity in the mosquito. *J. Infectious Diseases* 106:45.

TERZIAN, L. A., N. STAHLER, and F. IRREVERRE. 1956. The effects of ageing and the modifications of these effects, on the immunity of mosquitoes to malarial infection. *J. Immunol.* 76:308.

THOMPSON, A. D. 1961. Interactions between plant viruses. I. Appearance of new strains after mixed infections with potato virus X strains. *Virology* 13:507.

THOMPSON, M. J., E. MOSETTIG, and T. VON BRAND. 1960. Unsaponifiable lipids of *Taenia taeniaeformis* and *Moniezia* sp. *Exptl. Parasitol.* 9:127.

THORPE, W. H. 1939. Further studies in preimaginal olfactory conditioning in insects. *Proc. Roy. Soc.* (Series B) 127:424.

THORSELL, W., and N. BJÖRKMAN. 1965. Morphological and biochemical studies on absorption and secretion in the alimentary tract of *Fasciola hepatica* L. *J. Parasitol.* 51:217.

THORSON, R. E. 1953. Studies on the mechanism of immunity in the rat to the nematode, *Nippostrongylus muris*. *Am. J. Hyg.* 58:1.

THORSON, R. E. 1956a. Proteolytic activity in extracts of the esophagus of adults of *Ancylostoma caninum* and the effect of immune serum on this activity. *J. Parasitol.* 42:21.

THORSON, R. E. 1956b. The stimulation of acquired immunity in dogs by injections of extracts of the esophagus of adult hookworms. *J. Parasitol.* 42:501.

TILLET, M. 1755. Dissertation on the cause of the corruption and smutting of the kernels of wheat in the head (transl., H. B. HUMPHREY). In Phytopathol. Classics No. 5, 1937. American Phytopathological Society, Ithaca, New York.

TIMMS, A. R., and E. BUEDING. 1959. Studies of a proteolytic enzyme from *Schistosoma mansoni*. *Brit. J. Pharmacol. Chemotherapy* 14:68.

TING, I. P., and I. W. SHERMAN. 1966. Carbon dioxide fixation in malaria. I. Kinetic studies in *Plasmodium lophurae*. *Comp. Biochem. Physiol.* 19:855.

TOPLEY, W. W. C. 1942. The biology of epidemics. *Proc. Roy. Soc.* (Series B) 130:337.

TRACEY, M. V. 1958. Cellulase and chitinase in plant nematodes. *Nematologica* 3:179.

TRAGER, W. 1932. A cellulase from the symbiotic intestinal flagellates of termites and the roach, *Cryptocercus punctulatus*. *Biochem. J.* 26:1762.

TRAGER, W. 1937. The hatching of spores of *Nosema bombycis* Nageli and the partial development of the organism in tissue cultures. *J. Parasitol.* 23:226.

TRAGER, W. 1941. Studies on conditions affecting the survival *in vitro* of a malarial parasite (*Plasmodium lophurae*). *J. Exptl. Med.* 74:441.

TRAGER, W. 1942. A strain of the mosquito *Aedes aegypti* selected for susceptibility to the avian malaria parasite *Plasmodium lophurae*. *J. Parasitol.* 28:457.

TRAGER, W. 1943. Further studies on the survival and development *in vitro* of a malarial parasite. *J. Exptl. Med.* 77:411.

TRAGER, W. 1956. The intracellular position of malarial parasites. *Trans. Roy. Soc. Trop. Med. Hyg.* 50:419.

TRAGER, W. 1957. Nutrition of a hemoflagellate (*Leishmania tarentolae*) having an interchangeable requirement for choline or pyridoxal. *J. Protozool.* 4:269.

TRAGER, W. 1959. Tsetse-fly tissue cultures and the development of trypanosomes to the infective stage. *Ann. Trop. Med. Parasitol.* 53:473.

TRAGER, W. 1960. Intracellular parasitism and symbiosis. In *The Cell* (eds., J. BRACHET and E. A. MIRSKY) 4:151. Academic Press, New York.

TRAGER, W. 1964. Cultivation and physiology of erythrocytic stages of malaria. *Am. J. Trop. Med. Hyg.* 13:162.

TRAGER, W. 1967. Adenosine triphosphate and the pyruvic and phosphoglyceric kinases of the malaria parasite *Plasmodium lophurae*. *J. Protozool.* 14:110.

TRAGER, W., R. KLATT, and S. SMITH. 1967. Loss of chloraquine resistance on transfer of *Plasmodium berghei* from mouse to hamster. *J. Parasitol.* 53:1111.

TRAGER, W., M. A. RUDZINSKA, and P. C. BRADBURY. 1966. The fine structure of *Plasmodium falciparum* and its host erythrocytes in natural malarial infections in man. *Bull. World Health Org.* 35:883.

TREMBLY, H. L., and J. GREENBERG. 1954. Further studies on the hybridization of strains of *Plasmodium gallinaceum*. *J. Parasitol.* 40:475-479.

URITANI, I. 1963. The biochemical basis of disease resistance induced by infection. In *Perspectives of Biochemical Plant Pathology* (ed., S. RICH). *Conn. Agr. Expt. Sta. Bull.* 663:4.

URITANI, I., and AKAZAWA, T. 1959. Alteration of the respiratory pattern in infected plants. In *Plant Pathology* (eds., J. G. HORSFALL and A. E. DIMOND), Vol. 1. Academic Press, New York.

UTIDA, S. 1953. Interspecific competition between two species of bean weevil. *Ecology* 22:139.

VAGO, C. 1963. Predispositions and interrelations in insect diseases. In *Insect Pathology* (ed., E. A. STEINHAUS), Vol. 1. Academic Press, New York.

VAN DE VIJVER, G. 1964. Métabolisme respiratoire de la larve de *Gastrophilus intestinalis*. *Exptl. Parasitol.* 15:97.

VAN HEYNINGEN, W. E. 1955. The role of toxins in pathology. In: *Mechanisms of Microbial Pathogenicity* (eds., J. W. HOWIE and A. J. O'HEA), p. 17. Cambridge University Press, London.

VAN WAGTENDONK, W. J., A. D. CLARK, and G. A. GODOY. 1963. The biological status of lambda and related particles. *Proc. Natl. Acad. Sci.* 50:835.

VICKERMAN, K. 1965. Polymorphism and mitochondrial activity in sleeping sickness trypanosomes. *Nature* 208:762.

VISHNIAC, H. S., and F. J. NIELSEN. 1956. Biological conversion of cholestenone-4-C^{14} to an unsaturated 3β-OH sterol. *Fed. Proc.* 15:620.

VOGE, M., and J. A. TURNER. 1956. Effect of temperature on larval development of the cestode, *Hymenolepis diminuta*. *Exptl. Parasitol.* 5:580.

WALKER, J. C. 1957. *Plant Pathology*. McGraw-Hill Book Co., New York.

WALLACE, F. G. 1966. The trypanosomatid parasites of insects and arachinds. *Exptl. Parasitol.* 18:124.

WALLACE, W. R. 1966. Fatty acid composition of lipid classes in *Plasmodium lophurae* and *Plasmodium berghei*. *Am. J. Trop. Med. Hyg.* 15:811.

WARD, R. A. 1963. Genetic aspects of the susceptibility of mosquitoes to malarial infection. *Exptl. Parasitol* 13:328.

WARREN, L. G., and T. BORSOS. 1959. Studies on immune factors occurring in sera of chickens against the crithidia stage of *Trypanosoma cruzi*. *J. Immunol.* 82:585.

WARREN, L. G., and A. GUEVARA. 1962. Nematode metabolism with special reference to *Ancylostoma caninum*. *Rev. Biol. Trop., Univ. Costa Rica* 10:49.

WEATHERSBY, A. B. 1963. Quoted by GARNHAM, 1964.

WEBER, N. A. 1957. Fungus-growing ants and their fungi: *Cyphomyrmex costatus*. *Ecology* 38:489.

WEBSTER, L. T. 1946. Experimental epidemiology. *Medicine* 25:77.

WEINLAND, E., and T. VON BRAND. 1926. Beobachtungen an *Fasciola hepatica* (Stoffwechsel und Lebenweise). *Z. vergleich. Physiol.* 4:212.

WEINMANN, C. J., and A. H. ROTHMAN. 1967. Effects of stress upon acquired immunity to the dwarf tapeworm, *Hymenolepis nana*. *Exptl. Parasitol.* 21:61.

WEINSTEIN, P. P. 1966. The *in vitro* cultivation of helminths with reference to morphogenesis. In *Biology of Parasites* (ed. E. J. L. SOULSBY). Academic Press, New York.

WEINSTEIN, P. P., and M. F. JONES. 1959. Development *in vitro* of some parasitic nematodes of vertebrates. *Ann. N.Y. Acad. Sci.* 77:137.

WEITZ, B. 1960. Feeding habits of bloodsucking arthropods. *Exptl. Parasitol.* 9:63.

WELLS, H. S. 1931. Observations on the blood sucking activities of the hookworm *Ancylostoma caninum*. *J. Parasitol.* 17:167.

WELSH, J. H. 1931. Specific influence of the host on the light responses of parasitic water mites. *Biol. Bull.* 61:497.

WELSH, M. F. 1936. Oxygen production by zooxanthellae in a Bermudan turbellarian. *Biol. Bull.* 70:282.

WELTER, C. J. 1960. The effect of various stresses upon histomoniasis in chickens and turkeys. *Poultry Sci.* 39:361.

WENYON, C. M. 1926. *Protozoology*, Vols. 1 and 2. Bailliere, Tindall & Cox, London.

WERTHEIM, G., R. ZELEDON, and C. P. READ. 1960. Transaminases of tapeworms. *J. Parasitol.* 46:497.

WHEELER, W. M. 1901. An extraordinary antguest. *Am. Nat.* 35:1007.

WHITLOCK, J. H. 1962. Bionics and experimental epidemiology. *Biol. Prototypes Syn. Systems* 1:39.

WHO EXPERT COMMITTEE. 1965. Nutrition and infection. WHO Technical Report Series, No. 314. Geneva.

WIJERS, D. J. B. 1958. Factors that may influence the infection rate of *Glossina palpalis* with *Trypanosoma gambiense*. I. The age of the fly at the time of the infective feed. *Ann. Trop. Med. Parasitol.* 52:385.

WILLETT, K. C. 1966. Development of the peritrophic membrane in *Glossina* (tsetse flies) and its relation to infection with trypanosomes. *Exptl. Parasitol.* 18:390.

WILLIAMS, C. M. 1961. The juvenile hormone. II. Its role in the endocrine control of molting, pupation, and adult development in the Cecropia silkworm. *Biol. Bull.* 121:572.

WILLIAMS, P. P., J. GUTIERREZ, and R. E. DAVIS.

1963. Lipid metabolism of rumen ciliates and bacteria. *Appl. Microbiol.* 11:260.

WILSON, G. S. and A. A. MILES. 1957. *Principles of Bacteriology and Immunity*. Williams and Wilkins, Baltimore, Md.

WILSON, P. A. G. 1958. The effect of weak electrolyte solutions on the hatching rate of the eggs of *Trichostrongylus retortaeformis* (Zeder) and its interpretation in terms of a proposed hatching mechanism of strongyloid eggs. *J. Exptl. Biol.* 35:584.

WILSON, P. A. G., and D. FAIRBAIRN. 1961. Biochemistry of sporulation in oocysts of *Eimeria acervulina*. *J. Protozool.* 8:410.

WITTENBERG, B. A., T. OKAZAKI, and J. B. WITTENBERG. 1965. The hemoglobin of *Ascaris* perienteric fluid. I. Purification and spectra. *Biochim. Biophys. Acta* 111:485.

WOOD, R. K. S. 1960. Chemical ability to breach the host barrier. In *Plant Pathology* (eds., J. G. HORSFALL and A. E. DIMOND). Academic Press, New York.

WOOD, W. B., JR. 1953. Studies on the cellular immunology of acute bacterial infections. *Harvey Lectures* 47:72.

WOOD, W. B. 1960. Phagocytosis with particular reference to encapsulated bacteria. *Bacteriol. Rev.* 24:41.

WÜLKER, W. 1964. Parasite-induced changes of internal and external sex characters in insects. *Exptl. Parasitol.* 15:561.

YARWOOD, C. E. 1959. Predisposition. In *Plant Pathology* (eds., J. G. HORSFALL and A. E. DIMOND). Academic Press, New York.

YOKAGAWA, M. 1965. *Paragonimus* and paragomimiasis. *Advan. Parasitol.* 3:99.

YOKAGAWA, S., W. W. CORT, and M. YOKAGAWA. 1960. Pargonimus and paragonimiasis. *Exptl. Parasitol.* 10:81-137; 139-205.

YONGE, C. M. 1936. Mode of life, feeding, digestion and symbiosis with zooxanthellae in the Tridacnidae. *Rept. Gt. Barrier Reef Expedition* 1:283.

YONGE, C. M. 1944. Experimental analysis of the association between invertebrates and unicellular algae. *Biol. Rev.* 19:68.

YONGE, C. M. 1957. Symbiosis. In Treatise on marine ecology and paleoecology. *Geol. Soc. Am. Mem.* 67:429.

YOUNG, J. D., E. BENJAMINI, B. F. FEINGOLD, and H. NOLLER. 1963. Allergy to flea bites. V. Preliminary results of fractionation, characterization, and assay for allergenic activity of material derived from the oral secretion of the cat flea, *Ctenocephalides felis felis*. *Exptl. Parasitol.* 13:155.

ZAHL, P. A., and J. J. A. McLAUGHLIN. 1959. Studies in marine biology. IV. On the role of algal cells in the tissues of marine invertebrates. *J. Protozool.* 6:344.

ZAMENHOF, S., and H. H. EICHORN. 1967. Study of microbial evolution through loss of biosynthetic functions: Establishment of "defective" mutants. *Nature* 216:456.

ZELEDON, R. 1960. Comparative physiological studies on four species of hemoflagellates in culture. V. Transaminases. *Rev. Brasil. Biol.* 20:409.

ZELLE, M. R. 1942. Genetic constitutions of host and pathogen in mouse typhoid. *J. Infect. Dis.* 71:131.

ZINDER, N. D., and J. LEDERBERG. 1952. Genetic exchange in *Salmonella. J. Bacteriol.* 64:679.

Index

309